Shaping Nations

The Centre on Governance Series

Governance is about guiding: it is the process whereby an organization steers itself. Studying governance means probing the distribution of rights, obligations, and power that underpins organizations and social systems; understanding how they co-ordinate their parallel activities and maintain their coherence; exploring the sources of dysfunction and lacklustre performance; and suggesting ways to redesign organisations whose governance is in need of repair. Governance also has to do with the complex ways in which the private, public, and civic sectors co-ordinate their activities, with the manner in which citizens produce governance through their active participation in a democratic society, and with the instruments and processes required to ensure good and effective stewardship.

This series welcomes a range of contributions – from conceptual and theoretical reflections, ethnographic and case studies, and proceedings of conferences and symposia to works of a very practical nature – that deal with particular problems or nexus of issues on the governance front.

Centre on Governance http://www.governance.uottawa.ca

Governance Series

Shaping Nations: Constitutionalism and Society in Australia and Canada

Edited by
Linda Cardinal and
David Headon

University of Ottawa Press

National Library of Canada Cataloguing in Publication Data

Main entry under title:
Shaping nations: constitutionalism and society in Australia and Canada

(Governance series)
Includes bibliographical references.
ISBN 0-7766-3020-2 (bound) ISBN 0-7766-0533-X (pbk.)

1. Australia—Politics and government—Congresses.
2. Canada—Politics and government—Congresses.
3. Constitutional history—Australia—Congresses. 4. Constitutional history—Canada—Congresses. 5. Federal government—Canada—Congresses. 6. Federal government—Australia—Congresses.
I. Cardinal, Linda, 1959- II. Headon, David John, 1950-
III. Series: Governance series (Ottawa, Ont.)

KE4226.S53 2002 320.994 C2001-904038-5

University of Ottawa Press gratefully acknowledges the support extended to its publishing program by the Canada Council, the Department of Canadian Heritage, and the University of Ottawa.

Cover Design: John Beadle; Cover Concept: Robert Dolbec

ISBN 0-7766-3020-2 (bound)
ISBN 0-7766-0533-X (pbk.)

542 King Edward, Ottawa (Ont.), Canada K1N 6N5
press@uottawa.ca http://www.uopress.uottawa.ca

Printed and bound in Canada

Shaping Nations: Constitutionalism and Society in Australia and Canada

Edited by Linda Cardinal and David Headon

Table of Contents

Contributors

(in alphabetical order)

Jeff Brownrigg is Director of "The People's Voice" project of the National Council for Centenary of Federation. He holds a position as Head of Academic Outreach and Research at Screen Sound Australia, formerly the National Film and Sound Archive. With David Headon he edited *The People's Conventions: Corowa* (1893) and Bathurst (1896), recently published by the Australian Senate. His account of the life and career of Amy Castles is due for publication in late 2001. He is currently preparing a biography of Roger Garran which has the working title *Federation's Prodigy.*

Linda Cardinal is Professor of Political Science at the University of Ottawa. She has published widely on linguistic minorities as well as on identity and citizenship issues in Canada. She also has a special interest in Canadian and Quebec political theory. She is author of *L'engagement de la pensée* (1997), *Chroniques d'une vie politique mouvementée. L'Ontario francophone de 1986 à 1996* (2001) and has co-edited *La démocratie à l'épreuve de la gouvernance* (with C. Andrew, 2001). She is the Editor of *Politique et Sociétés*, the journal of the Québec association of political science.

David Headon is Cultural Adviser to the National Capital Authority and Director of the Centre for Australian Cultural Studies (Canberra). He teaches in the School of English, University of New South Wales (Australian Defence Force Academy). His publications include: *Crown or Country - The Traditions of Australian Republicanism* (1994), *The Abundant Culture – Meaning and Significance in Everyday Australia* (1995), *Our First Republicans: Selected Writings of John Dunmore Lang, Charles Harpur and Daniel Henry Deniehy 1840–60* (1998) and Makers of Miracles, the Cast of the Federation Story (2000).

Helen Irving is currently Director of the 1901 Centre at the University of Technology (Sydney) and a Senior Lecturer in the Faculty of Humanities and Social Sciences at the same University. In July 2001, she joined the Faculty of Law at the University of Sydney as a Senior Lecturer in constitutional law. She is author of *To Constitute a Nation* (1997). Editor of *A Woman's Constitution?* (1996) and *The Centenary Companion to Australian Federation* (1999) and co-editor of *No Ordinary Act: Essays on Federation and the Constitution by J. A. La Nauze* (2001).

Jeffrey Keshen is an Associate Professor of History at the University of Ottawa. He is the author of *Propaganda and Censorship during Canada's Great War* and the editor of several other works including *Age of Contention: Canadian Social History, 1900-1945, Material Memory: Documents in Post-Confederation Canadian History* and *Social Welfare in Canada: Historical Readings*. His current research involves morality and the family in World War II Canada.

Patrick Keyzer is Senior Lecturer and Director of Research at the Faculty of Law, University of Technology (Sydney) and was formerly Executive Associate to the Chief Justice of Australia. His principal research interest and professional practice is Federal constitutional law. He is also author of a textbook on Constitutional Law and co-author of the Constitutional Law title of *Halsbury's Laws of Australia*. His most recent book is *Comparative Notes On Intellectual Property Law and Practice in Thailand.*

Judith McCann was born in New Zealand, educated in Canada and launched her professional career in film in 1980 with the Canadian Film Development Corporation (now Telefilm Canada) where she held the position of Deputy Director from 1985 to 1988. In 1989 she returned to New Zealand as Executive Director of the New Zealand Film Commission, guiding its investment in films from Jane Campion's *Angel At My Table* to the box office success *Once Were Warriors*.Recruited to Australia in 1994 as CEO of the South Australian Film Corporation, she was responsible for its investment in over 30 films and television productions including the acclaimed international hit *Shine*. She recently returned to Canada and is working in Ottawa as a film and television consultant.

Mark McKenna is a Research Fellow in the Political Science Program of the Research School of Social Sciences at the Australian National University (Canberra). He is the author of *The Captive Republic: A History of Republicanism in Australia 1788-1996* (1996). He is currently writing a book on the politics of Australian history entitled *Looking for Blackfella's Point: Politics and History in Australia 1788-2000.*

Errol P. Mendes is Professor of Law at the University of Ottawa. He has taught, researched, consulted and published extensively in the area of International Business Law and Ethics, Constitutional Law and Human Rights law. He is Editor-in-Chief of *The National Journal of Constitutional Law.* He also has extensive experience as a Human Rights Adjudicator under the Ontario Human Rights Code. He is currently Director of the Human Rights Research and Education Centre at the University of Ottawa. He is a member of the Canadian Bar Association and has been a volunteer advisor to the ethnocultural organizations on matters relating to human rights and constitutional law.

Desmond Morton is a graduate of the Collège Militaire Royal de St-Jean, the Royal Military College of Kingston, Oxford University and the London School of Economics. After twelve years in the Canadian army and four in politics, he has taught history at the universities of Ottawa, Toronto, Western and Michigan State before coming to McGill in 1994 as Professor of History and Director of the McGill Institute for the Study of Canada. He has written 36 books on Canadian political, military and industrial relations history. He was appointed a fellow of the Royal Society of Canada in 1985 and was named an Officer in the Order of Canada in 1996.

Kim Richard Nossal is Professor of Political Science and Head of the Department at Queen's University (Kingston, Ontario). He is the author of a number of works, including *Rain Dancing: Sanctions in Canadian and Australian Foreign Policy* (1994); *Relocating Middle Powers: Australia and Canada in a Changing World Order* (with Andrew F. Cooper and Richard A. Higgott, 1993).

Gilles Paquet is the Director of the Centre on Governance at the University of Ottawa. He studied philosophy, social sciences and economics at Laval, Queen's (Canada) and at the University of California where he was a Postdoctoral Fellow in Economics. He was Dean of the Faculty of Graduate Studies and Research at Carleton in the1970s and Dean of the Faculty of Administration at the University of Ottawa in the 1980s. He is a Fellow of the Royal Society of Canada and of the Royal Society of Arts of London and was named a Member of the Order of Canada in 1992. He has been active in broadcasting and has written a number of books and many papers in various journals on Canadian economic history, public policy and governance issues.

Galen Roger Perras, now an Assistant Professor of History at Bishop's University, is a former strategic analyst for the Canadian Department of National Defence and has taught at the University of Calgary and the University of Alberta. He has written extensively about American, Canadian and Australian history, and his first book, *Franklin Roosevelt and the Origins of the Canadian-American Security Alliance, 1933-1945: Necessary But Not Necessary Enough,* was published by Praeger Books in 1998.

W. Wesley Pue is Nemetz Professor of Legal History at the University of British Columbia. He served as Distinguished Visiting Professor in history, law and British studies at the University of Adelaide during 1999 and is currently engaged in research on the history of legal professionalism and lawyers, colonialism and state formation. His most recent book, *Pepper in Our Eyes: The APEC Affair* (UBC Press, 2000), deals with legal and constitutional issues relating to political direction of the police in Canada.

Angelika Sauer received her Ph.D. in Canadian History from the University of Waterloo. From 1994 to 2000 she taught Canadian immigration and ethnic history at the University of Winnipeg. Currently she is working in the Department of History at Texas Lutheran University near San Antonio (Texas). She has published several articles on comparative aspects of Canadian and Australian immigration history.

David E. Smith is a Professor of Political Studies at the University of Saskatchewan. He is the author of *Prairie Liberalism: The Liberal Party in Saskatchewan, 1905-71; Regional Decline of a National Party: Liberals on the Prairies*; (with Norman Ward and James G. Gardiner) : *Relentless Liberal; The Invisible Crown: The First Principle of Canadian Government*; and editor of *Building a Province: A History of Saskatchewan in Documents*, as well as co-editor of *After Meech Lake: Lessons for the Future; Drawing Boundaries: Courts, Legislatures and Electoral Values, and Citizenship, Diversity and Pluralism; The Republican Option in Canada, Past and Present.* He was elected Fellow of the Royal Society of Canada in 1981. In 1994-95 he was President of the Canadian Political Science Association. His current research interest is bicameralism in Canada and abroad.

John Williams is a Senior Lecturer in Law at the University of Adelaide (Australia). He has degrees from the University of New South Wales, the University of Tasmania and the Australian National University. His main areas of research are constitutional law, human rights and Australian legal history. He is co-editor of two journals. *The New Federalist* and *The Australian Journal of Legal History*. His most recent publications include *Makers of Miracles: The Cast of the Federal Story* (2000, MUP) and *Manning Clark's Ideal of De Tocqueville* (with Dymphna Clark and David Headon, 2000).

Greg Wood was the Australian High Commissioner to Canada from 1997 to 2001. He was Deputy Secretary in the Australian Department of the Prime Minister and Cabinet from 1994 to 1997. He was responsible for advising the Prime Minister on foreign and trade policy, defence, security and intelligence, environment, forests and resources issues. Other areas in the Prime Minister and Cabinet for which he held responsibility included structure of Australian Government, constitutional and legal issues, indigenous affairs and multicultural affairs. Mr. Wood has also held numerous senior positions in the Department of Foreign Affairs and Trade and the Department of Trade in Australia and overseas.

Foreword

GREG WOOD, Australian High Commissioner to Canada

I found as I work as Australia's representative in Ottawa that Australian history works with me. This was brought home to me in my initial meetings with some of the highest in the land. On two separate occasions I found myself being cross-questioned, not only about Australia's excellent economic performance and foreign policy, but about Western Australia's attempt in 1933-34 to secede from the Australian Commonwealth.

Very few Australians, indeed very few West Australians for that matter, would have the slightest inkling that Western Australia ever endeavoured to separate. But it did. I was being quizzed, in depth, about the causes of the Western Australian move, how Western Australia sought to secede and why and how the attempt faltered. I was also asked whether it could happen again. Most of it I got right; some of the questions I took on notice. I said 'no' to the last-mentioned query. In the course of the discussion it became obvious that my hosts knew much more about that aspect of our history than did 999 out of 1,000 Australians. Anyone with an iota of awareness of Canada can guess the reason for their interest.

In fact, I find myself routinely quizzed about Australian constitutional issues, about the workings of our Federation and about the generality and the minutiae of Australian public policy, both domestic and foreign. Interest in Australian constitutional issues has been particularly intense in recent years as we Australians debated, then voted on, the Republic. The issue has featured conspicuously in the Canadian media. In the main, that coverage was extremely perceptive. A number of the major Canadian news organizations sent representatives to Australia for the November 6, 1999 vote and, generally, read the situation very accurately.

Canadians were certainly interested in whether Australia would retain the constitutionally separate, but physically identical, head of state that we share. From my personal polling, Canadians, unlike Australians, were pretty evenly divided on the merits of that idea. But in addition, Canadians were interested in whether the referendum question was "clear" in its expression. Again, the subtext concerned Quebec, and the Canadian Supreme Court's stipulation that any future referendum question needs to be "clear". Right now, there is a very interesting debate in the Canadian body politic as to whether or not Ottawa should legislate to ensure both a clear question and a clear majority, in the event of a future Quebec referendum. Similarly, there was interest in the mechanism by which referendums are decided in Australia, the so-called double majority concept. So constitutional practice in Australia has resonance in Canada. It's not an arcane issue.

Australia and Canada transact a great deal more than goods and services. We vigorously transact values, ideas, policy perspectives, designs for government programs (both domestic and international), practical experience, techniques of governance and people, for that matter... as well as goods and services.

You get a sense of that from some of the questions asked, and some of the comparisons drawn, in the debates in the Canadian Parliament in recent years. For example, of constitutional interest is the fact that some Canadian parliamentarians advocated that Canada adopt compulsory voting, as in Australia. Others referred to our recently adopted practices with respect to consultation with the states on treaties. Another issue discussed was our Section 128 referendum procedure and the nature of the majorities required. There was reference made to Western Australia's 1933 vote to secede from the Australian Commonwealth. Also mentioned were differences in the Canadian and Australian constitutions' treatment of the Supreme Court/High Court, Australia's statutory disallowance procedures in relation to regulation making.

Over the same period Australia's policies on people smuggling immigration laws, refugee rights, boat arrivees, and the absence of a charter of rights in Australia were a source of comment, as were law enforcement co-operation; Australia's policy on airline ownership; the profitability and competitive framework of our airlines; and respective approaches to administering transport safety, defence policy, East Timor, trade, agriculture, genetically modified material, aboriginal affairs, education, health care and film financing.

This may lead you to wrongly conclude that Canadians spend all their time comparing themselves to us. (In fact, they spend most of their time comparing themselves to the Americans). But it's hard to claim that we're not newsworthy as far as Canada is concerned.

The trade applies equally in the opposite direction. In just a two-month period in 1999 numerous Australians visited Canada primarily to learn from Canadian experience. There was an all-party parliamentary delegation led by the President of the Australian Senate, whose particular areas of interest included indigenous affairs, environmental regulation and parliamentary practice. Another visitor was the Defence Minister, in Canada to thank the country for its much appreciated contribution to the U.N. mandated peacekeeping force in East Timor. Some fifteen senior state government officials, academics and lawyers participated in the International Conference on Federalism, which the Canadian government, albeit by proxy, organized at Mont Tremblant. (President Clinton gave a speech there that was quite profound in its analysis and implications though it attracted scant attention outside of Canada.) Yet another visitor was former leader of the Queensland Parliament Rob Borbidge with a broad agenda around representative government. Our Agriculture Minister, Warren Truss, came to pursue common interests and bilateral concerns. On it goes.

An effect of close similarity is that one becomes acutely conscious of small differences. Constitutions may shape nations but circumstances shape constitutions and, just as importantly, shape the interpretation of constitutions. By this means both the Australian and Canadian constitutions have "inverted" in the sense that the intended presumption around the balance of federal/state powers has reversed in each case.

I don't want to get going on an analysis of Australia versus Canada. Most foreign relations start roughly at the point: "I don't understand you, you don't understand me; what else do we have in common?" With Australia and Canada, the starting point is very different.

The main difference to me is that Australia feels, rightly or wrongly, that it cannot assume a benign external environment. Canada, rightly or wrongly, believes it can, or if it can't, that it can't do much about it over and beyond what the United States would do anyway. Hence we focus on national security, whereas Canada emphasizes human security.

Equally, Australia does presume on durable internal cohesion notwithstanding Western Australia and 1933. Canada can't, or at least Canada doesn't. All Canadian policies are weighed with an eye to national unity.

I hope I have stirred things up at least a little, and I hope you enjoy the following papers as much as I did listening to them.

Introduction

LINDA CARDINAL and DAVID HEADON

As early as 1852, Australia's then most celebrated republican, the Reverend John Dunmore Lang, stated in his classic work *Freedom and Independence for the Golden Lands of Australia* that "Remote as [Australia and Canada] are from each other, there is a secret sympathy between these two countries". This connection, this simpatico relationship, would continue for several decades after Lang's perceptive observation upto the 1890s and Federation in 1901. During the latter period other countries such as the United States of America, Germany and Switzerland also figured in this trans-Pacific debate, helping to shape a mature response to the central issue of federalism versus state (provincial) rights.

One hundred years later, there is reinvigorated interest in Australia's constitutional debate concerning the issue of becoming a republic. Questions concerning nationhood and national identity, it seems, continue to preoccupy both Australia and Canada. Lang's "secret sympathy" is probably more accurate now than ever before.

It was in response to this renewed sense of shared political and social ground that scholars from both Australia and Canada gathered at a conference, "Shaping Nations", hosted by the Institute of Canadian Studies at the University of Ottawa in December 1999. The conference grew out of a fortuitous connection between the Australian High Commission in Ottawa, the Institute and the Centre for Australian Cultural Studies (Canberra) and the energy and enthusiasm of the organizing committee at the Institute. The contributing scholars at the conference built generously on this enthusiasm, producing a collective narrative that will enlighten readers of this volume about the drama, pragmatism and vision of nineteenth century debate, and at the same time canvas the challenges presented by recent constitutional history in both countries.

This book is divided into five parts. In part 1, John Williams and Helen Irving discuss the almost unavoidable reference to the Canadian Constitution in the debates leading to Australian federation. Williams and Errol P. Mendes also look at contemporary constitutionalism and suggest that the two countries are still influencing each other's understanding of rights issues and federalism. In part 2, Jeff Brownrigg, W. Wesley Pue and Angelika Sauer show that creating a new country cannot be done in a cultural void. Both Australia and Canada needed a cultural and legal ethos in order to forge their new nations. Thus, while new immigrants were welcome, and came from all over Europe, they would have to espouse the cause of Britishness. As Sauer discusses in her chapter, there is a framework of imperial-national thinking that 'centres around a narrative of colonial progress.' For Sauer, Canada was the most commonly cited colonial prototype and British officials hoped the Australian colonies would emulate their Canadian sister.

In part 3, authors Galen Roger Perras, Kim Richard Nossal, Desmond Morton and Jeffrey Keshen show how the ties between Australia and Canada go beyond matters of the constitution into issues of diplomatic relations and war. For both countries, the two world wars had important consequences for their patterns of governance and for their relationship with Britain. Part 4 addresses more contemporary issues in Australian politics principally, the defeated referendum in November 1998, when Australians chose to remain a constitutional monarchy in controversial circumstances. Mark McKenna and David Headon both scrutinize and analyze the complexities of that debate. David E. Smith then asks why there is no such movement in Canada. In part 5, authors Patrick Keyzer, Gilles Paquet, Judith McCann and Greg Wood look at the patterns of governance in Australia and Canada as they apply to law, public policy and film industries.

Collectively, these contributions will be of particular interest to students of Australian and Canadian politics. The volume is published at a particularly intense cultural moment for both countries and we hope it will serve as a catalyst for a series of collaborations that explore the dimensions of Lang's "secret sympathy" well into the 21st century.

This book was made possible through the efforts and support of our partners: the Australian High Commission in Canada, the Australian and New Zealand Association of Canadian Studies, the Centre for the Study of Governance and the Institute of Canadian Studies at the University of Ottawa. Our special thanks to Chad Gaffield at the Institute of Canadian Studies for supporting this project from its inception.

PART I

Constitutionalism

1

"The Blizzard and Oz": Canadian Influences on the Australian Constitution Then and Now[1]

JOHN WILLIAMS

Introduction

With typical rhetorical flourish Lord Denning noted that it was "bluebell time in Kent" before he addressed himself to the quantum of damages occasioned by a nervous shock.[2] The time of the season, as the title of this chapter suggests, may be one other reason why Canadians and Australians are drawn to investigate our respective approaches to public policies. As the northern winter descends, Australia, reclining in summer, must appear to be an inviting research topic.

This chapter investigates the points of convergence and divergence between Canadian and Australian constitutional law. There is something both appropriate and absurd about the comparison of Australia's and Canada's constitutional and political history. Clearly we share the historical link of English common law, a federal system of government and a desire to be more than just "A New Britannia in Another World!"[3] Yet it is the divergence from this common heritage, as the very different environments took hold of the transplanted specimen, that is the critical factor.[4] It is, as Manning Clark often noted when discussing Australia, the "spirit of place" that is perhaps the deceptive agent in this mix.[5] This "spirit" can be seen in the law as well as in the way in which our respective cultures portray themselves. There is something quintessentially Australian about the Heidelberg School of Australian landscape. So too, The Group of Seven is one expression of a Canadian understanding of itself.

In the Beginning

The drafting of the Australian Constitution was more a process than an event. The decade of the 1890s is marked by various conventions and conferences that debated and refined the draft Constitution. Running parallel with, and critical to, this process was information gathering and discussion by the various Federation Leagues and Associations. This process was Australia's first sustained attempt at comparative constitutional research. Once a federal system was determined to be the basis for the union of the colonies, the Canadian, American, German and Swiss constitutions were obvious starting points. Richard Chaffey Baker, for instance, in his *Manual* for the delegates to the 1891 Sydney Convention, drew upon the federal constitutions of America, Canada, Switzerland and South Africa.[6]

The question of the use of Canadian precedents raised itself on the first day of the 1890 Melbourne Conference. It was not, however, the "watertight" compartments of the federal structure,[7] but the leakage of the proceedings into the pages of the press and public that concerned the delegates. As Thomas Playford, the South Australian delegate, noted:

> Without disapproving of the admission of the Press, we have no precedent for it in Conferences, either in the Colonies or in America. The Americans never admitted the Press when they made their Constitution; the Canadians at Quebec did not admit the Press; and you cannot point out, I believe, one single precedent for admitting the Press to deliberations of this sort.[8]

While the issues were resolved with the admission of both the Press and the public, a point that underscores the democratic nature of the convention process, it was by no means the only use of Canadian precedents.[9]

At the 1890 Melbourne Conference the *British North America Act*, was on the agenda. Sir Samuel Griffith, the future Chief Justice of the High Court, spoke in glowing terms of that federation:

> I would like to trespass on the time of members of the Conference for a few moments for the purpose of mentioning some of the subjects which are enumerated in that great Act of British North America. I have before me a list of the subjects which are the exclusive business of the general legislature. These subjects include the following:-Public Debt and Property, Regulation of Trade and Commerce, Raising of Money by Taxation, Borrowing of Money on Public Credit, Postal Services, Census and Statistics, Militia, Military and Naval Forces, Defence, Beacons, Lighthouses, Navigation and Shipping, Quarantine, Ferries between Provinces, Currency and Coinage, Banking and Paper Money, Weights and Measures, Bills of Exchange and Promissory Notes, Interest, Bankruptcy and Insolvency, Patents, Copyrights, Naturalization and Alienage, Marriage and Divorce, and Criminal Law.[10]

Griffith's attraction to the *British North America Act* had been demonstrated a few months before in the mire that was Queensland politics at the time. In April 1890, Griffith, supporting McIlwraith, overthrew the Morehead ministry to become Queensland premier for the second time. The persistent claims for northern separation were an issue that was to be confronted in the early days of his administration. This time it was through a motion, by Macrossan, for the separation of North Queensland from the rest of the colony. In defeating the motion Griffith displayed deft political skills by placating both British investors and territorial separationists. He achieved this by proposing in November 1890 the division of Queensland into three provincial legislatures.[11]

Griffith structured his proposed division of Queensland along federal lines. There was to be both a parliament representing the United Provinces as well as local parliaments. In general terms, the United Provinces were to consist of two Houses, one chosen by Legislatures of the Provinces, the other by the "European" people of the three provinces. In each province there was to be a bicameral parliament.

In assessing Griffith's model, the influence of the *British North America Act* in its final form is clear. As with the Canadian Constitution, Griffith chose to express the powers of both the United Provinces and the provincial administrations. In doing so, he avoided the American Constitution which ascribed limited legislative powers to the Congress with the residue being with the states.

In many places in Griffith's Queensland Constitution the outcome reflected a direct copy of powers and phrases from the Canadian Constitution. This could have only been achieved by close study. For instance, "currency and coinage", "census and statistics", and "weights and measures" and others are direct transcriptions from the Canadian Constitution. Other powers are expressed in similar terms with minor variations. For example, "postal service" in the Canadian Constitution becomes "postal service and telegraphs" in Griffith's draft Queensland Constitution.[12] The powers of the provinces in Griffith's draft again followed the Canadian constitutional model. For example, the draft Queensland Constitution included such powers as "property and civil rights" and "the imposition of punishment and fines".

The influence of the Canadian Constitution reflected early constitutional research by the framers. The link to the Crown and the requirement to protect local sentiment from the incursion of federal power would have immediately suggested the Canadian model. Yet the Canadian model was not without its detractors. Inglis Clark, the Attorney General of Tasmania, took a contrary position to Griffith's. He plumped for the American Constitution over the Canadian. As he stated:

> The question of the Canadian Constitution has been several times mentioned in the course of our proceedings, and its difference from that of the United States has been somewhat touched upon. On this point I would say that I think it would be well were each of us to state more or less precisely what kind of confederation we would individually advocate, and also what kind of confederation each colony represented by us would respectively be satisfied with. For my part I would prefer the lines of the American Union to those of the Dominion of Canada. In fact, I regard the Dominion of Canada as an instance of amalgamation rather than of federation, and I am convinced that the different Australian Colonies do not want absolute amalgamation. What they want is federation in the true sense of the word.
>
> The *British North America Act*, under which the Dominion of Canada was established, not only goes on the principle of defining the powers of the local Legislatures, as well as the powers of the Central Legislature, but also says that everything not included in the jurisdiction of the former is included in the jurisdiction of the latter, and it enables the Central Executive to veto the Acts of the local Legislatures. Well, I believe that, in the

> course of time, those who live to see the outcome will find the local Legislatures of the Dominion reduced to the level of the position of large municipalities, and that Canada will have ceased to be, strictly speaking, a federation at all.[13]

While there was some jockeying over the appropriate constitutional template, it is clear that both the Canadian and the American examples would be critical to the process of constitutional drafting. This point was made by Dr. Cockburn, the South Australian delegate, while generally supporting Inglis Clark's position[14]:

> Much of the work done by Inglis Clark and his draft Constitution expresses the close link between the 'machinery provisions' of the *British North America Act* and the substantive features of the American Constitution.[15]

While the Canadian Constitution provided the 'continuity of existing forms appropriate to the continuance of the colonies as dependencies of the British Empire',[16] Inglis Clark and others were adamant that it was to the United States of America, and not Canada, that Australia should look.

Ultimately the Canadian Constitution was not to be the model by which the framers were to forge the Australian Constitution. The reason for this can be explained at a number of levels. In terms of constitutional reassurance, the Canadian approach had its supporters. It achieved what Playford from South Australia expressed in 1891 were the concerns of the smaller colonies. There was a need, "to most strictly define and limit the powers of the central government, and leave all other powers not so defined to the local legislatures".[17] Yet the Canadian Constitution, as portrayed by experts like Inglis Clark, was an "amalgamation", whereas the American Constitution offered the greatest chance to meet the concerns that Playford and others expressed. "It would", as Leslie Zines has noted, "have been quite unthinkable for the Australian delegates to have contemplated giving the Australian government the power to disallow State legislation or to appoint State Governors".[18]

The *Engineers* Case

The choice of the American Constitution, with its decentralized federal structure, over the Canadian one was vindicated by the early High Court. Drawn from those with intimate knowledge of the drafting and principles behind the Constitution the original three members of the High

Court set about interpreting the document to give effect to that intention. The twin jurisprudential features of this period were the formulation of the doctrine of "reserve powers" and the "implied doctrine of immunity of instrumentalities". The "reserve powers" doctrine was founded on a view that the states were to be protected from the Commonwealth and that states were to have exclusive power with respect to domestic affairs. The theory behind the "implied immunity" doctrine, which was reciprocal, was to see the states and the Commonwealth as sovereign polities and within their spheres. As such, they were to be free to act without burdens or interference.[19]

Ultimately, these two approaches came under strain as different visions of the Constitution were added to the High Court. This coincided with the development of the nation and meant that such artificial restrictions on the Commonwealth became outmoded. These approaches were finally 'exploded' by the High Court in 1920 in the seminal case the *Amalgamated Society of Engineers v. Adelaide Steamship Co Ltd.*[20]

The effect of the Engineers case has been profound on Australian jurisprudence. While the case has been criticized for its lack of clarity, it rejected the limitations on the reach of the Commonwealth's legislative powers in respect of the states.[21] In terms of jurisprudential approaches, the case refocused Australian law away from the American Constitution back to the British. As R.T.E. Latham critically concluded, the case

> cut off Australian constitutional law from American precedents, a copious source of thoroughly relevant learning in favour of the crabbed English rules of statutory interpretation, which are, as we have seen, particularly unsuited to the interpretation of a rigid constitution.[22]

The turning to "crabbed English rules of statutory interpretation'"did not in itself bring the Canadian and Australian constitutions closer together. While in theory the Privy Council remained at the apex of both legal systems, the Australians had already shown an unwillingness to seek review at the feet of the Empire. During the Constitutional Conventions in the 1890s the issue of the right of appeal from the High Court or state courts to the Privy Council had been hotly debated. This debate continued as the delegates left for England in 1900 to shepherd the Constitutional Bill through the Imperial Parliament.[23] Ultimately, there was a compromise (after much pressure from British investors and some members of the Australian judiciary) with a limit on appeal on constitutional matters to the Privy Council unless certified by the High Court.[24]

The High Court was established in 1903 and immediately demonstrated a reluctance to give certification for appeal against its decision[25] and rejected Privy Council decisions when they were inconsistent with their views on the Constitution.[26] The winding back of the influence of the Privy Council on Australia was achieved with the passage of certain acts limiting appeals from the Australian judiciary.[27] Notwithstanding the severing of this link, the comparative nature of Australian and Canadian constitutional law remains.

Federalism

The Australian Constitution looks, as the framers intended, to be the essence of a decentralized federal state. Yet constitutions are what their respective final courts of adjudication say that they are. As was demonstrated by the *Engineers* case, Australia's High Court has been fundamental in shaping the Constitution. The High Court has not, in the constitutional arena, given an overwhelming degree of notice to the Canadian Constitution.[28] What consideration there has been has usually highlighted the divergence in approach. For instance, the High Court's consideration of the *British North America Act* and its regulative approach to "trade and commerce" and "property and civil rights" was considered in *Huddart Parker & Co Pty Ltd v. Commonwealth.*[29] In that case Justice Evatt made what is one of the better comments on the distinctions between the two constitutions. For Justice Evatt the differences between the two documents were profound and 'little assistance' could be drawn from the Canadian Constitution. As he states, the task of interpretation is

> essentially different under the Australian Constitution. The question is still one of construction ... but it is construction of the express powers conferred upon the central Parliament. No doubt the powers of the States are very important, but their existence does not control or predetermine those duly granted to the Commonwealth. The legislative powers of the States are only exclusive in respect of matters not covered by the specific enumeration of Commonwealth powers. It is the grant to the Commonwealth which must first be ascertained. Whatever self-governing powers belong exclusively to the States.[30]

This factor was highlighted as the reason to discount the use of the Canadian precedent in the area of trade and commerce.

In 1982, Justice Stephen in *Actors and Announcers Equity Association v. Fontana Films Pty. Ltd*[31] made similar observations. He stated that:

> The pattern of distribution of legislative power in Australia is not based on a concept of mutual exclusiveness. It differs from that found in Canada's *British North America Act* of 1867, with its two lists of mutually exclusive matters, granted, by ss. 91 and 92, to the Canadian and provincial legislatures respectively.[32]

For Justice Stephen the concurrence of Australian federalism was a justification for not following the Canadian approach. The lack of freedom offered by non-exclusive grants of powers has allowed the Australian High Court to develop the notion of dual characterization. That is, legislative action may be characterized as having one or more purposes, yet only one of these purposes needs to be with the power of the Commonwealth Constitution.

From the above, a picture emerges of an Australian Court that has diverged substantially from the approach taken from the Canadian Court. Federalism provides an ongoing example of this trajectory.

In his classic work *Constitutional Law of Canada*, Peter W. Hogg projects Canadian constitutional law in terms of a swinging pendulum.[33] The balance between federal and provincial power has moved back and forth since the Depression. The movement toward the centre after the Depression and the First World War emphasized the development of a national economy. The retention of this position after the mid-1950s is explained by a number of factors. These include the growth in federal power; postwar reconstruction; humanitarian and egalitarian ideals (especially those relating to Canadian citizenship and services); a single taxing authority and the political and economic advantages of not having to administer a collection system. Pulling in the opposite direction to these centralizing forces are factors that include the autonomous sentiment in Quebec and, after 1962, the provinces' own taxation collection.

In Australia the movement has not been so balanced. In reality, the movement has been towards the centre and despite the various rounds of "new federalism"[34] the states are, as Alfred Deakin predicted, "financially bound to the chariot wheels of the central Government".[35] Why is this so? There are a number of explanations for this outcome.

First, after the *Engineers* case in 1920 rejected the implications based on a particular view of federalism, the limits on the full extent of the Commonwealth's powers were removed. Without these artificial implications the legislative capacity of the states was open to the encroachment of the Commonwealth.

Second, as with Canada, the Commonwealth took over control of taxation during the Second World War. This was achieved under the so-called uniform taxation scheme. The Commonwealth used a raft of constitutional powers to support the legislation by which the Commonwealth imposed income taxation at a level high enough to equal the amount raised previously by the states and the Commonwealth. The states were then offered grants equal to that of their previous taxation on the condition that they levied no income tax. Despite constitutional challenges, the states have been unsuccessful in re-entering the field of income taxation.[36]

Associated with the uniform taxation scheme was the use by the Commonwealth of section 96 of the Constitution.[37] This power enables the Commonwealth to "grant financial assistance to any State on such terms and conditions as the Parliament thinks fit." While the Commonwealth cannot require a state to take a grant on particular terms and conditions, the relative financial weakness has meant that the Commonwealth has been able to "buy" itself into areas where it lacks express constitutional power. For instance, the use of tied grants has given the Commonwealth power to shape health, education and public housing policy in Australia.

There is one further element that has been highlighted in recent times to underscore the increasing dominance of the Commonwealth in the Australian federation. Indeed, it has been described as making a "mockery" of the federation.[38] The Constitution gives the Commonwealth Parliament power (section 51(xxix)) with respect to "external affairs". At the time of federation the ambit of "external affairs" outside the policy of the Empire would have been limited. As Quick and Garran noted:

> There is nothing in it indicative of an intention of the Imperial Parliament to divest itself absolutely of all authority over the external affairs of Australia and to commit them exclusively to the Parliament of the Commonwealth.[39]

In this sense the attitude of the framers of the Australian Constitution was not markedly different from the sentiments contained in section 132 of the *British North America Act*. The external affairs power has enabled the Commonwealth to legislate for those things physically external to Australia[40] as well as in terms of Australia's international obligations. In a series of cases in the 1980s, the High Court was asked to adjudicate on the Commonwealth legislation purporting to implement Australia's treaty obligations into domestic law. Such issues as racial discrimination,[41] the protection of world heritage areas[42] and international labour standards[43] have been the means by which the Commonwealth has expanded into areas traditionally within the purview of the states.

Some members of the High Court, at the time that these constitutional questions were being put, looked for limitations on the Commonwealth's power to implement these obligations. As Chief Justice Gibbs noted in Koowarta v. *Bjelke-Petersen*:

> [I]f s. 51(xxix) empowers the Parliament to legislate to give effect to every international agreement which the executive may choose to make, the Commonwealth would be able to acquire unlimited legislative power. The distribution of powers made by the Constitution could in time be completely obliterated; there would be no field of power which the Commonwealth could not invade, and the federal balance achieved by the Constitution could be entirely destroyed.[44]

Notwithstanding these concerns, the High Court has reaffirmed on a number of occasions the ability of the Commonwealth Parliament to implement into domestic law its international obligations.

Excise and State Finances

While the High Court and the political community have been reluctant to follow Canadian precedent in relationship to the Australian Constitution, there are a number of areas where the lessons of Canada have been predicant.

The issue of fiscal federalism has remained since federation an "unholy scramble".[45] In this area the Canadian constitutional arrangements have been more influential on Australian constitutional development than it would generally be appreciated. In 1887 the Privy Council upheld a provincial law that imposed a tax on the banks.[46] In holding that the Act was within section 92 of the *British North America Act*, their Lordships expressed a view on the nature of taxation. In his speech, Lord Hobhouse drew heavily on the work of John Stuart Mill. For Mill there was a distinction to be drawn between direct and indirect taxes. As he said:

> Taxes are either direct or indirect. A direct tax is one which is demanding from the very persons who it is intended or desired

> should pay it. Indirect taxes are those which are demanded from one person in the expectation or intention that he shall indemnify himself at the expense of another: such as the excise or customs.
>
> The producer or importer of a commodity is called upon to pay a tax on it, not with the intention to levy a peculiar contribution upon him, but to tax through him the consumers of the commodity, from whom it is supposed that he will recover the amount by means of an advance price.[47]

Their Lordships' adoption of the approach of this "eminent writer" influenced the Australian High Court in 1904 in *Peterswald v. Bartley*.[48] While the Court has dramatically limited the definition of "excise" within section 90, the indirect/direct distinction has been a continuing theme in the jurisprudence. The importance of the definition of "excise" has been the ability of the states to raise taxes through the use of licence fees (that do not of themselves constitute an excise duty). The history of the section demonstrates an increasing expansion of the definition of "excise" with a number of anomalous categories of exception. These categories include "licence fees" designed to use backdating devices on alcohol, tobacco and petrol.[49]

From the 1980s onward, the High Court entertained challenges on the basis that these levies where in fact excises (as a tax on a good) and should be ruled unconstitutional. On a number of occasions, members of the High Court sought either to return the definition of excise to a narrower one or to limit the application of the general principle. This latter approach was based on the special nature of the product or the fiscal arrangements that the states had made on the basis of past High Court decisions[50] – in other words, a pragmatic approach to the interpretation of the section.

By 1997 the situation was again in the High Court in a case called *Ha v. New South Wales*.[51] In this case a majority of the High Court resisted calls by the states to roll back the definition of an excise, the effect of which would have been to give the states an expanded taxation base. Instead, the High Court eliminated the anomalies of petrol, tobacco and alcohol. The effect was to remove from the states AUS$5.5 billion. The decision was described as an "administrative nightmare" by the then Queensland Treasurer Joan Sheldon[52] and incredibly by one commentator as a "Marxist approach to tax reform".[53]

The states' response to the pressure on their taxation bases was to look for other sources of revenue. Historically, the state governments had restructured their revenue base by a combination of generous Commonwealth grants during the 1970s and state governments eroding their major tax base by concessions with respect to land and payroll tax, and the abolition of estate and gift duties.[54] With the financial cutbacks of the Hawke and Keating governments and the pressure on the states' indirect taxation base (including excise fees) the states turned to gambling as a lucrative source of revenue. Thus Australia entered a period of the introduction of casinos and the expansion of gambling-machines into new venues. The roll-out of gambling productions coincided with the High Court's tightening of the definition of excise.[55] Gambling, as a tax on a service, is not caught by the constitutional restrictions of section 90.

In a recent report, the Productivity Commission investigated the incidents and events relating to gambling in Australia. The Commission made a number of findings in its Final Report.[56] In particular, the Commission found that around 290,000 Australians (2.1 percent of the adult population) are "problem gamblers". These problem gamblers comprise 15 percent of regular (non-lottery) gamblers and lose on average nearly $12,000 per year, compared with $625 for other gamblers. Perhaps of greater concern was the finding relating to the emotional damage faced by problem gamblers:

> – one in four gamblers reported divorce or separation as a result of gambling;
>
> – one in ten said they have contemplated suicide due to gambling; and
>
> – nearly half those in counselling reported losing time from work or study due to gambling in the past year.

The Commission found that the prevalence of problem gambling was directly related to the degree of accessibility of gambling, particular gambling machines:

> The States derive about 12% of their tax revenue from gambling taxes. This figure in the case of some States, such as Victoria, represents a dramatic change in the attitude of the government to its role with respect of gambling.[57]

It is not possible, nor should it be attempted, to link the Canadian jurisprudence in the 1880s to the current fiscal situation of the Australian states. Yet there is a direct line of case law between the two. The more substantive point however, is the divergence in the economic position of the sub-national polities in the two federal systems. The Australian States have become emerged in the Commonwealth's position more than the framers could have dreamed.

Rights Talk

"Rights talk" is now an international language. Taking rights seriously is now a standard that is applied to national and international organizations. Australia, like Canada, prides itself on its adherence to, and promulgation of, international human rights standards.

Since the 1980s, Australia has witnessed both formal and jurisprudential moves toward a greater entrenchment of rights in Australian constitutional law.[58] For instance, the 1988 Constitutional Commission was established to investigate and report on the Australian Constitution including how "democratic rights are guaranteed".[59] In its Final Report the Commission argued that a new chapter should be added to the Constitution dealing with "Rights and Freedoms". These rights include the freedoms of conscience and movement; equity rights; search and seizure; the liberty of the person; the rights of the arrested and charged; and a prohibition of cruel and inhuman punishment.

In terms of the limits on these rights the Commission recommended that:

> The rights and freedoms guaranteed by this Chapter may be subject only to such reasonable limits prescribed by law as can be demonstrably justified in a free and democratic society.[60]

The Commission divided on the ability of the Parliaments to "opt-out" from the operation of the Charter. The majority (Sir Maurice Byers, Sir Rupert Hamer and Mr. Whitlam) took the view that it was inconsistent with the "whole process of entrenching rights." The minority (Professors Campbell and Zines) expressed the view that in many cases there will be various possible answers to constitutional questions and "in such circumstances, the judgment of an unelected judiciary should not necessarily be preferred to that of a democratically elected Parliament."[61] They recommended the adoption of a section modelled on section 33 of the Canadian Charter of Rights and Freedoms, the so-called "notwithstanding" section.

Ultimately, these recommendations were not put to the Australian people. However, the influence of the Canadian Constitution is evident in the approach adopted by the Commission. The debate as to the future of formal constitutional change to entrench a bill or charter of rights will inevitably involve a close consideration of the events and approaches of the Canadian Charter of Rights and Freedoms.

In terms of constitutional interpretation, the 1990s witnessed the awakening of a rights consciousness among the High Court. The High Court in a number of cases raised the concept of an implied bill of rights.[62] In particular, in the area of political communication deriving from representative government, the Court demonstrated a willingness to hold Commonwealth legislation invalid.[63] In many ways the implications founded on representative government are reminiscent of the 'implied bill of rights' detected in Canada in the *Alberta Press* case.[64] As Chief Justice Mason noted in *ACTV*:

> Freedom of communication in the sense just discussed is so indispensable to the efficacy of the system of representative government for which the Constitution makes provision that it is necessarily implied in the making of that provision. Much the same view was taken in Canada under the *British North America Act* 1867 (Imp) (30 and 31 Vict. c.3) which contained no express guarantee of freedom of speech or freedom of communication.[65]

Citing *Switzman v. Elbling,*[66] *Re Ontario Public Service Employees' Union and Attorney-General (Ontario)*[67] and *Retail, Wholesale and Department Store Union, Local 580 v. Dolphin Delivery Ltd,*[68] Chief Justice Mason said:

> It seems that the Supreme Court of Canada has ascertained from the structure of the Constitution granted by the *British North America Act* and its preamble an implied freedom of speech and expression which may be more extensive as to subject matter than the implied freedom I have identified so far from my analysis of the Australian Constitution. Whether freedom of communication in relation to public affairs and political discussion is substantially different from an unlimited freedom of communication and, if so, what is the extent of the difference, are questions which were not debated and do not call for decision. What is presently significant is that the implied freedom of speech and expression in Canada is founded on the view that it is indispensable to the efficacious working of Canadian representative parliamentary democracy.[69]

In terms of the limitation of this right, the approach taken by the High Court demonstrates some similarity to the Supreme Court's approach in *Oakes*.[70] In *Oakes*, the Supreme Court adopted a two-step test to determine the validity of the challenged legislation. First, the objective of the legislation must be of sufficient importance to warrant overriding a constitutionally protected right or freedom.[71] Second, the means chosen must be reasonable and demonstrably justified. This involves "a form of proportionality test".[72]

The High Court has approached the balancing of political communication rights in similar terms. It is well acknowledged in case law that the freedom or right to political communication is not absolute. The use of a proportionality test, or a discussion of whether the restriction is appropriate and adapted to a legitimate end, has become a routine element in determining the validity of the impugn legislation.

Constitutional Change

In his seminal work *Constitutional Odyssey*, Peter H. Russell posed the question "Can Canadians become a sovereign people?". In formulating this question he compares the position of Canada with that of Australia. He states: In Australia there was never any doubt that the legitimacy of the Constitution depended on popular consent. The events of November 1999 have simultaneously endorsed and challenged this view.

The decision by the Australian electorate to reject the republican model proposed to it in 1999 must be seen in the context of difficult constitutional reform. As Geoffrey Sawer noted in 1967:

> Radical amendment of the Constitution under S. 128 now appears unlikely for an indefinite time... Only a defence peril or economic catastrophe of great proportions is likely to change this constitutional system, and one would not wish for such events. Constitutionally speaking, Australia is the frozen continent.

Australians have endorsed only eight amendments to the Constitution from 44 attempts. Explanations for this unwillingness have been many, though in general it has been an inability to secure bipartisan support for the change. Notwithstanding the difficulty of section 128 with its double majorities, constitutional reform has not floundered because of this substantial threshold. Rather, the people have generally voted against the attempt to transfer power from the states to the centre.

While Australians have been willing to constitute themselves as a sovereign people in terms of their ability to determine the future of the Constitution, their decisions are less adamant. To vote against the republic is, in one sense, a vote for the status of subject and dependence to the British Crown. Is this the action of a sovereign people?

Canada, like Australia, has embarked on constitutional reform. Unlike Australia, Canada has chosen mega constitutional reform. When Canada sets down another round of constitutional reform, it will dwarf all other issues in public life. The various constitutional encounters in Canada have led to a form of constitutional exhaustion. Indeed, the feeling that any change, no matter how minor, will quickly spiral into yet another round of mega constitutional reform has checked enthusiasm for the issue. The republican referendum in Australia has underlined the difficulty for further constitutional reform. It is arguable that the Australian Constitution needs some attention. However, even modest constitutional change must appear doubtful given the events of November 1999. It may well be that in constitutional terms Australia and Canada now share a common Ice Age.

Conclusion

Australians and Canadians remain drawn to each other for many reasons. As a result, the points of convergence and divergence have become apparent. Richard Cullen has noted that the divergence in the two constitutions speaks more than anything else, of entrenched, geographically dispersed, social, economic, cultural and political divisions in Canada *and the relative lack thereof* in the case of Australia. Notwithstanding this, there is a common heritage, as well as a willingness on the part of both countries to be more than the sum of their pasts. Canada will remain a frequent constitutional port of call for Australia as we struggle to face issues that confront all liberal democracies.

Notes

1. The author would like to express his gratitude to Lawrence Hanson and Peter Berry for their endless assistance in things Canadian.

2. *Hinz v. Berry,* [1970] 1 ALL ER 1074 at 1075.

3. W.C. Wentworth, *Australasia,* (1823).

4. Others have written on the obvious comparisons: Christopher D. Gilbert, *Australian and Canadian Federalism, 1867-1984* (Melbourne: Melbourne University Press, 1986); Richard Cullen, "Canada and Australia: A Federal Parting of the Ways", *Federal Law Review,* 18 (1989).

5. Manning Clark, *A Discovery of Australia* (Sydney: ABC Books, 1976), 14.

6. Richard Chaffey Baker, *A Manual of Reference to Authorities for the Use of the Members of the National Australasian Convention* (Adelaide: W.K. Thomas & Co., 1891).

7. *Attorney-General (Canada) v. Attorney-General (Ontario)* [1937] Appeal Cases 326 at 355.

8. *Official Debates of the Australasian Conference, Melbourne, 1890 ("Melbourne Debates")* (Melbourne: Government Printer, 1890), vii.

9. Helen Irving, *To Constitute a Nation: A Cultural History of Australia's Constitution* (Melbourne: Cambridge University Press, 1997 and 1999), 62-63.

10. Ibid., 11.

11. See G.C. Bolton, "Samuel Griffith: The Great Provincial", *Royal Historical Society of Queensland Journal,* vol 14, (1991): 355, and R. Joyce, *Samuel Walker Griffith* (St. Lucia: Queensland University Press, 1984), 172.

12. John M. Williams, "Samuel Griffith and the Australian Constitution: Shaking Hands with the New Chief Justice", *The New Federalist,* (1999): 37.

13. *Melbourne Debates,* 105-106.

14. Ibid., 134.

15. F.M. Neasey, "Andrew Inglis Clark Senior and Australian Federation", *Australian Journal of Politics and History*, (1969), 15: 8.

16. Ibid.

17. *Official Record of Debates of the Australasian Federal Convention, Sydney, 1891 ("Sydney Debates")* (Sydney: Government Printer, 1891), 328.

18. Leslie Zines, *Constitutional Change in the Commonwealth* (Cambridge: Cambridge University Press, 1991), 78-79.

19. For an account of this period of the High Court, see Leslie Zines, *The High Court and the Constitution* (Sydney: Butterworths, 1997), chap. 1.

20. (1920), 29 CLR 129.

21. A point later clarified in *Melbourne Corporation v. Commonwealth* (1947), 74 CLR 31.

22. R.T.E. Latham, "The Law and the Commonwealth", *Survey of British Commonwealth Affairs*, ed. W.K. Hancock, vol. 1 (London: Oxford University Press, 1937), 564.

23. J.A. La Nauze, *The Making of the Australian Constitution* (Melbourne: Melbourne University Press, 1972).

24. Section 74 of the Commonwealth Constitution.

25. The Court has only once certified an appeal in *Attorney-General (Commonwealth) v. Colonial Sugar Refining Co Ltd* (1913), 37 CLR 644 (PC).

26. *Baxter v. Commissioners of Taxation (NSW)* (1907), 4 CLR 1087.

27. *Privy Council (Limitation of Appeals) Act* (Commonwealth), 1968; *Privy Council (Appeals from the High Court)* (Commonwealth), 1975; and *Australia Act* (Commonwealth), 1986.

28. For a detailed account of the citations, see Patrick Keyzer, chapter 14.

29. (1931), 44 CLR 492.

30. Ibid., 527.

31. (1982), 150 CLR 169.

32. Ibid., 191.

33. Peter W. Hogg, *Constitutional Law of Canada* (Toronto: Carswell, 1985), 127-131.

34. For an account of the endless rounds of "new federalism" see Brian Galligan, *A Federal Republic* (Melbourne: Cambridge University Press, 1995), 203-213.

35. Alfred Deakin, *Federated Australia: Selections from Letters to the Morning Post, 1900-1910* (Melbourne: Melbourne University Press, 1968), 97.

36. *South Australia v. The Commonwealth (First Uniform Tax Case)* (1942), 65 CLR 373, and *Victoria v Commonwealth (Second Uniform Tax Case)* (1957), 99 CLR 575.

37. *Victoria v. Commonwealth (Federal Roads Case)* (1920), 38 CLR 399.

38. Sir Harry Gibbs, "The Decline of Federalism?", *University of Queensland Law Journal* 18, (1994): 5.

39. J. Quick and R.R. Garran, *The Annotated Constitution of the Australian Commonwealth* (Sydney: Angus and Robertson, 1901), 631.

40. *Polyukhovich v. Commonwealth* (1991), 172 CLR 501.

41. *Koowarta v. Bjelke-Petersen* (1982), 153 CLR 168.

42. *Commonwealth v. Tasmania* (1983), 158 CLR 1.

43. *Victoria v. Commonwealth* (1996), 187 CLR 416.

44. (1982), 153 CLR 168, 198.

45. See Cheryl Saunders, "Fiscal Federalism: A General and Unholy Scramble", *Australian Federation*, ed. Greg Craven (Melbourne: Melbourne University Press, 1992), 101.

46. *Bank of Toronto v. Lambe* (1887), 12 App Cas 575.

47. Ibid, 583.

48. (1904), 1 CLR 497, 512.

49. *Dennis Hotels Pty Ltd v. Victoria* (1960), 104 CLR 529; *Dickenson's Arcade Pty Ltd v. Tasmania* (1974), 130 CLR 177; and *H C Sleigh Ltd v. South Australia* (1977), 136 CLR 475.

50. *Philip Morris Ltd v. Commissioner of Business Franchises (Vic)* (1989), 167 CLR 399, 438.

51. (1997), 189 CLR 465.

52. *The Australian* (August 6, 1997): 2.

53. A. Mitchell, "Marxist Approach to Reform Courts Disaster", *The Australian Financial Review*, (August 6, 1997): 5.

54. J. Smith, *Gambling Taxation in Australia* (Sydney: Austarlian Tax Research Foundation, 1998), 25.

55. See John M. Williams, "'Come in Spinner': Section 90 of the Constitution and the Future of State Government Finances", *Sydney Law Review*, 21, no. 4 (1999): 627.

56. Productivity Commission, *Australia's Gambling Industries*, Report No. 10 (Canberra: Ausinfo, 1999), 2-4.

57. Ibid., vol. 2, 19.7.

58. H. Charlesworth, "The Australian Reluctance About Rights", Toward an Australian Bill of Rights, ed. P. Alston (Canberra: Centre for International and Public Law, 1994).

59. *Final Report of the Constitutional Commission* (Australian Government Printer, Canberra, 1988).

60. Ibid., 39.

61. Ibid., 43.

62. Leslie Zines, "A Judicially Created Bill of Rights?", *Sydney Law Review*, 16 (1994): 166-184.

63. *Australian Capital Television Pty Ltd v. The Commonwealth* (1992), 177 CLR 106. A companion case was *Nationwide News Pty Ltd v. Wills* (1992), 177 CLR 1.

64. *Reference Re Alberta Statutes*, [1938] SCR 100. See Dale Gibson, "Constitutional Amendment and the Implied Bill of Rights", *McGill Law Journal*, 12, no. 4 (1967): 495-501.

65. *Australian Capital Television Pty Ltd v. The Commonwealth* (1992), 177 CLR 106, 140.

66. [1957] S.C.R. 285.

67. [1987] 2 S.C.R. 2.

68. [1986] 2 SCR 573.

69. *Australian Capital Television Pty Ltd v. The Commonwealth* (1992), 177 CLR 106, 141.

70. *R. v. Oakes* [1986] 1 S.C.R. 103.

71. Ibid., 138.

72. Ibid., at 139 (footnote omitted). For a discussion of the *Oakes* test and section 1, see Janet L. Hiebert, *Limiting Rights: The Dilemma of Judicial Review* (Montreal: McGill-Queen's University Press, 1996).

2

Sister Colonies with Separate Constitutions: Why Australians Federationists Rejected the Canadian Constitution

HELEN IRVING

In the sequence of events in the last decade of the 19th century that led – inexorably now, it seems – to the federation of Australia's colonies in 1901, one Canadian plays a small part. In early 1889, George Parkin, representing the Canadian branch of the Imperial Federation League, toured the colonies, bringing the gospel of British supremacy and imperial unity. The goal of the imperial federationists (who achieved only a short-lived and small following) was a federated Empire, with a central parliament in London, and member parliaments in each of the self-governing colonies. Parkin thought that Canada, having federated some 20 years earlier, had gone a good distance in preparing itself for this greater federal union, and he extolled the progress made in his own country in replacing provincialism with national feeling. He hinted that the Australians might take note of his country's example. In the Australian context, this was a mistake. At the best of times, Australians were inordinately sensitive to suggestions that things were done better anywhere else. In the 1880s, this cultural reflex was especially strong, as emerging nationalism and growing resentment against Britain's colonial policy fed each other. Sensitivity over the failure to bring about the long-sought union of the Australasian colonies was at its height.

Parkin's lectures, commented the *Bulletin* (that great journal of Australian nationalism, founded nine years earlier) were concerned only with the all round majesty of everything British, the surpassing smartness of the Canadians, and the phenomenal acuteness of Mr. Parkin himself. Parkin, it was reported, described his audience as British, provoking the cries of No, it's Australian.[1] Even worse, he asserted that the inhabitants of a cold country, like Canada, are stronger and more vigorous than men of a warm climate like our own.[2] The press was outraged. Parkin's talks were a failure. Imperial Federation, said the *Bulletin*, was an unsaleable drug in the Australian market.[3]

But Parkin's tour did have another effect. Around the time of the Canadian's arrival in Sydney, Sir Henry Parkes, that grand, inflated, many-times Premier of New South Wales, was in conversation with the Governor of his colony, Lord Carrington, after the weekly Executive Council meeting. The topic of Parkin came up. Acutely aware that Canada had achieved in 1867 what he, Parkes, had first proposed for the Australian colonies at an intercolonial postal conference in that same year, the Premier was led to make a now famous boast. Canada had federated and he, Henry Parkes, could confederate these colonies within twelve months. Carrington replied: Then, why don't you?[4]

Parkes wrote immediately to the Victorian Premier, Duncan Gillies, proposing that they and other leading men should meet together in a Parliamentary Convention of Australasia. A period of intense negotiations followed, resulting in the Australasian Federation Conference in Melbourne in February 1890, less than nine months after Parkin's visit. This Conference concluded with a commitment to a further meeting where a federal Constitution for the colonies of Australasia should be written. The Australasian Federal Convention met in Sydney one year later and concluded with a full draft Constitution Bill. That Bill ultimately served as the basis for redrafting a new and (with a couple of subsequent amendments) final Constitution at the second Federal Convention six years later. The new Constitution Bill passed successfully through a series of colonial referendums in 1899 and was transformed into an Act by the Imperial Parliament the following year. The Indissoluble Federal Commonwealth of Australia was inaugurated on January 1, 1901.

The boasts of a Canadian set the ball rolling in 1889. But the example of Canada served another purpose for the framers of Australia's Constitution. This was established early in the proceedings of the 1890 Conference. Australia's Constitution-making began with an exploration of the range of existing federal constitutions: those of the United States,

Switzerland, Canada and Germany. All had some attractive features. But one alone was a federation under the Crown. It was the very thing the Australians wanted to achieve. In this most fundamental respect, Canada's Constitution should have served as a model, if not a template. Some leading men at the beginning assumed that it would. In one of his preliminary communications with the Victorian Premier, Henry Parkes had written that the scheme of Federal Government he had in mind would necessarily follow close upon the type of the Dominion Government of Canada.[5] At the Conference in Melbourne, he began by moving the resolution: That ... the best interests and the present and future prosperity of the Australasian Colonies will be promoted by an early union under the Crown ... on principles just to the several Colonies.[6] With the exception of the command to be early, these were the very words of the first resolution of the 1864 Quebec Convention, adapted to the local setting. Parkes, who had visited the United States in the early 1880s, and returned full of admiration for the American way of doing things, still took his first lead from the Canadian example.

At the Conference, Sir Samuel Griffith (later first Chief Justice of the High Court) immediately followed Parkes, speaking at some length about the British North America Act. He enumerated its federal powers, as if taking it for granted that this should be their point of departure. He described these powers as the subjects in respect of which there is so little difference of opinion amongst intelligent men throughout Australia, that they could certainly be dealt with much better by one parliament, and the laws be better executed by one executive than by many.[7] Reminding the delegates that their goal was the establishment of a great Australian nation, Griffith wound up with a mention of the Canadian federal power of assimilating the laws of property and procedure subject to adoption by the legislatures of the several provinces. This, he concluded, would be a means of solving many of the difficulties facing them in attaining their goal.[8]

But if Parkes and Griffith assumed that the Canadian model would be, at least to some degree, persuasive, the Conference thought otherwise. Almost immediately they agreed that the very thing they must *avoid* was a federation upon the type of the Dominion Government of Canada. Thomas Playford, leader of the Opposition in South Australia, followed Griffith. He began by treating the Conference to a little history of the imperatives and the processes whereby Canada had federated. The British North America Act, Playford conceded, was framed under peculiar circumstances, with the American Civil War still raging in the south. But the Canadian federal parliament had far too much power, and in addition had powers over inappropriate matters, matters that should properly be in the hands of the provinces. The framers of the British North America Act, said Playford, did not realize the immense power [they] were giving to the general parliament – an amount of power which [the Australian] colonies will never consent to give.[9] Canada's provincial legislatures had been reduced to mere parish vestries. Playford's conclusion was that, while Canada had had little choice but to adopt its Constitution, I am quite certain that if we are to build up a Federation on the Canadian lines, the colony of South Australia will never agree to it.[10]

Then followed Tasmanian Attorney General Andrew Inglis Clark, setting his stamp on the debate with an account of the superior virtues of the United States Constitution. Clark believed that if the American Union were now constructed on the lines of those of Canada, there would be far more danger, dissension, irritation, and disunion in the future than exist at the present time.[11] South Australian Premier John Cockburn then exhorted the Conference not to follow Canada, for that was a homogeneous union of colonies without a proper amount of differentiation.[12]

After several days of hearing speeches on this theme, Henry Parkes announced to the Conference that he had never alluded to the Canadian Constitution in any way that would justify the inference that I have any intention of copying it.[13] The shape of Australia's federation was now set. The Conference concluded with an understanding that they would follow the United States example (at least as far as they could) under the Crown. Canada, if anything, would serve as the model of what they *did not* want.

When the first Australasian Federal Convention met in Sydney a year later, all but one of the 13 Conference delegates were present. With 33 other colonial representatives, their task was the writing of a Constitution along the lines agreed at Melbourne. Reading material had been prepared, including compilations of federal systems for the Tasmanians and the South Australians.[14] These works informed them, among other things, of the weaknesses of the Canadian Constitution, its authors forced (they learned) by the pressures of the American Civil War to adopt a more centralist parliament than Australians would tolerate.

At the Convention the delegates again took up the theme of *not being* Canadian, although no one was by this stage seriously suggesting that they should be. Richard Baker, author of the *Manual of Reference* for the South Australian delegates, told the Convention that the greatest frictions and the greatest jealousies and contentions characterized the relations between the Canadian provinces, which were held together by better terms: that is, he said, each province of the Dominion of Canada is constantly trying to get the better of its neighbours, trying to obtain more from the federal government. The authors of the Canadian federation, Baker concluded, have laid the seeds of the dissolution of that union.[15]

Two of the delegates, Charles Kingston from South Australia and Tasmania's Andrew Inglis Clark, had prepared draft Constitutions prior to their arrival in Sydney. Clark, who knew the United States Constitution better than any other delegate at that meeting, and loved it probably better than any other Australian, had produced a constitution closely resembling the United States model. Although, in the end, the Convention did not go as far as Clark would have wanted, it set out now to blend the United States and the Westminster models. A lower house modelled on the House of Commons would be put into operation alongside a Senate wielding almost identical powers. The states would retain their own constitutions and the bulk of their powers, and they would acquire the power to force a dissolution of the Commonwealth parliament. Only a minority thought this an impossible scenario. Predictions that responsible government would either kill Federation or be killed by it were simply ignored. The Australians were attempting to do what they would prove so effective at doing: giving everyone a little of what each wanted.

What should this new federal nation be called? Despite Clark's strong preference for the United States, his draft Constitution still referred to the Dominion of Australia. That term featured in the long title to Richard Baker's *Manual*, and it was still used widely in the Convention's early discussions. But they did not adopt the name Dominion. It is inconceivable, given all they had said about Canada, that they would. On a motion moved by Sir Henry Parkes, they named their future nation the Commonwealth.

It is hard to imagine now that this choice of name in 1891 was controversial. But it was. Many objections were raised, both within the Convention and among the public; the main one was that "Commonwealth" smacked of republicanism. Parkes and the other supporters responded by concentrating on the name's English lineage, by-passing the tricky example of Cromwell's Protectorate, and honing in on that reliable standby, William Shakespeare. Shakespeare had used the word for England, and that would do for Australia. A majority was ultimately won over. But even as late as 1897, one Tasmanian delegate warned the second Convention against employing this unusual name. In

Canada, he said, throughout the provinces of Nova Scotia and New Brunswick, the great and general unpopularity of the Dominion Government, when its functions commenced, was due in a large measure to its unfamiliar name.[16]

Over the years between and during the 1891 and the 1897-1898 Conventions, while Canada's social and economic life occasionally got good press, and while the Australians and Canadians met happily at the Colonial Conference in Ottawa in 1894, the litany of complaints against Canada's constitutional system continued. The Ministry of Sir John Macdonald had lasted too long: it was a very dangerous thing to be so successful.[17] The prejudice against states' rights had "seriously interfered with the federal nature of Canadian union".[18] Canadian democracy was undeveloped. The nomination, rather than election, of Canadian Senators was illiberal. Canadian defence was weak. The "system of Government in Canada [would] more and more, day by day, decade by decade, approximate to a unification, wiping out States altogether".[19]

And yet, for all this, Australia's Constitution resembled the British North America Act in a good number of respects, indeed, almost as closely as it resembled the United States Constitution. This occurred in part because, while the Australians chose to write their own Constitution, they did so in the form of a Bill for an Act of the Imperial Parliament, and they employed much of the standard language and legal expression for such Acts. Thus, for example, the words "for the peace, order and good government" appear at the head of the list of federal powers in both Constitutions (as indeed they do for the South African Union Act, 1877). The similarity also arose because the constitutional systems of both countries were to be "under the Crown" and the Australians adopted the wording of provisions relating to reservation and disallowance of bills almost directly from existing colonial constitutions, provisions shared with the British North America Act.

In addition, although they did not say so, the Australians actually liked a number of things about the Canadian Constitution. Sir Samuel Griffith, as we saw, had begun at the 1890 Conference with an enumeration of the Canadian federal powers and Griffith was the chief draftsman of the first draft Constitution in 1891. Of the 39 heads of federal power in section 51 of the Australian Constitution as it stood in 1901, 14 or so are effectively the same as those found in the Canadian. On a similar comparison, only six of the United States' powers are reproduced in the Australian Constitution. One head of Commonwealth power, over marriage and divorce, was directly drawn from the British North America

Act specifically because the Australians rejected the United States example of state jurisdiction over this "subject of such vital and national importance".[20]

There were other resemblances. While Australia's provisions relating to the Judiciary (chapter 3 of the Constitution) are in significant respects modelled on the United States, the appellate structure adopted in Australia was closer to the Canadian. The Australian provisions concerning the Parliament and Executive are almost entirely dissimilar to the United States, notwithstanding the decision to borrow both America's names for Australia's houses of parliament.

The Australian framers in 1898 also adopted what they considered to be a shield against the "heresy" of the American confederate states and the threat of secession, by including the word "indissoluble" – "one indissoluble federal Commonwealth" – in the Constitution's preamble. They were, as we have seen, very aware of importance of the American Civil War as a catalyst to Canadian Confederation, and indeed they explained the Canadians' inadequate Constitution to themselves in this way. In the event, the word "indissoluble" was to prove effective in Commonwealth domination over the states, with the constitutional suppression of Western Australia's secession movement in the 1930s.

If Australia's Constitution comes out as something of a blend of both the Canadian and the United States models, a great deal in it resembles neither, or it has modified the provisions of one or the other in such a way as to make these quite distinctive. To Canada's marriage and divorce power, for example, was added the power over "parental rights, and the custody and guardianship of infants" (section 51 (xxii)). Some of Australia's provisions were entirely original: the power of the states to "refer" a matter to the Commonwealth Parliament for legislation; the power of the Parliament not only to create federal courts, but to invest state courts with federal jurisdiction; the "double dissolution" and joint sitting provision for resolving deadlocks between the houses of parliament. In addition, the Australian Constitution borrowed a couple of provisions from the two other available federal Constitutions, the German and the Swiss, respectively, the old age pension power (to which invalid pensions were added) and the referendum for constitutional alteration. Australia's was a "platypus" Constitution, "a perfectly original development compounded from familiar but previously unassociated types," in the words of Australia's second Prime Minister, Alfred Deakin.[21] It made almost as little sense to describe the Australian Constitution in terms of what it was not, as it did to describe the platypus (duckbilled, webfooted, egg-laying, but fur-covered, pouched, long-bodied and lactating) as a creature that does not have feathers.

Why, then, were the Australians so insistent that they were not Canadian? There were two main reasons. Where the two Constitutions departed significantly lay in the distribution of powers between federal and provincial parliaments and in the powers of the Canadian Governor General over the appointment of provincial lieutenant-governors and in the right to disallow provincial bills. In the Australians' eyes, this fatally weakened the provinces and threatened ultimate unification. Australia's smaller colonies were ardent champions of states' rights and utterly ill-disposed to such a scheme. In their opposition, they cast Canada in an almost entirely unsympathetic light, fearful that any favourable mention might be the thin end of the wedge, allowing the large colonies (New South Wales and Victoria) to construct a Constitution along the lines of what were assumed (not without reason) to be their centralist ambitions. The larger colonies went along with this interpretation of Canada's Constitution, once it had been set down at the 1890 Conference, because to do otherwise would have effectively meant an end to any progress on federation. For the most part, they left the distribution of federal powers alone, and attempted (although largely unsuccessfully) to gain supremacy in other, more subtle ways, through the allocation of powers to the House of Representatives.

But the Australians went even further than they needed in denouncing the Constitution of their "sister colony". They kept up the criticism long after it had been well and truly established that Australia would not follow Canada's system of allocating powers, long after the platypus had been authenticated and identified as a creature of its own. They did this for the second reason: because they were doing more than writing a Constitution. They were, in their own minds, constructing a "great nation". Thus they marked out their territory as Australians, defining themselves as different from other members of both the imperial and the federal families, determined to show that they would not merely be a copy of others. There was not too much danger that they would be mistaken for Germany or Switzerland, or even for the United States. But Canada was their big sister. She was the only member in common with both sides of the family. They shared a mother; they would both be Federations "under the Crown".

However much the Australians chose to borrow of their sister's style and habits, they were determined to show that their way of going about federating would not only not be a copy; it would be superior. Mr. Parkin from the Imperial Federation League might have tried to tell them otherwise in 1899, but the Australians spent the rest of the decade telling themselves that he was mistaken.

In the end, when the Constitution writing was completed, Canada was allowed to be the sister again. Prime Minister Sir William Laurier telegraphed his congratulations on the success of the 1899 referendums. Canada's troops were invited to join the imperial contingents sent to Australia for the Commonwealth's inauguration. Neither they nor the Canadian prime minister were able to get there in time. In Sydney, however, a committee of Canadian residents joined with Mr. Larke, the Canadian Trade Commissioner, to organize a contribution to the celebrations. It was a horse-drawn float, its driver wearing a "Yukon" fur coat (on a day in which the temperature came close to 40 degrees centigrade) in the inauguration procession on January 1 1901. On its platform, under a blue silk canopy surmounted by a crown, stood two classically draped women holding hands. At the front, gold letters announced: "Canada Welcomes her Sister Australia". The younger sister had now grown up and was launched into the world of adult federations, with her own Constitution.

One hundred years later, more through evolution than alteration, Australia now has a Constitution that permits the Commonwealth to exercise almost the same degree of power over the states as the framers found so alarming in the Canadian example, and that they believed themselves so effectively to have resisted. And, with the defeat of Australia's republican referendum in 1999, Australia and Canada have both reached the end of the 20th century, as they began, still 'sisters' under the Crown.

Notes

1. *Sydney Morning Herald* (June 19 1899).

2. *Bulletin* (June 29 1899).

3. Ibid.

4. J.A. La Nauze, *The Making of the Australian Constitution* (Melbourne: Melbourne University Press, 1972), 6.

5. Ibid., 14.

6. *Official Record of the Proceedings and Debates of the Australasian Federation Conference* (Melbourne: Government Printer, 1890), 21-22.

7. Ibid., 57-58.

8. Ibid., 59.

9. Ibid., 72.

10. Ibid, 71.

11. Ibid., 107.

12. Ibid, 133-134.

13. Ibid, 212.

14. Richard Chaffey Baker, *A Manual of Reference to Authorities for the Use of the Members of the National Australasian Convention* (Adelaide: W.K. Thomas and Co., 1891); Thomas Just, *Leading Facts Connected with Federation, Compiled for the Information of the Tasmanian Delegates to the Australasian Federation Convention, 1891* (Hobart, 1891).

15. *Official Record of the Debates of the Australasian Federal Convention*, vol. 1, Sydney, 1891 (Sydney: Legal Books, 1986), 110.

16. *Official Record of the Debates of the Australasian Federal Convention*, vol. 2, Adelaide, 1897 (Sydney: Legal Books, 1986), 618.

17. Ibid., 222.

18. R.R. Garran, *The Coming Commonwealth* (Sydney: Angus and Robertson, 1897), 128.

19. See Helen Irving, *To Constitute a Nation: A Cultural History of Australia's Constitution* (Cambridge: Cambridge University Press, 1997 and 1999), 65-66.

20. J. Quick and R.R. Garran, *The Annotated Constitution of the Australian Commonwealth* (Sydney: Angus and Robertson, 1901), 610.

21. Alfred Deakin, "The Federal Council of Australasia", *Review of Reviews*, (February 20, 1895).

3

Democratic Pluralism: The Foundational Principle of Constitutionalism in Canada

ERROL P. MENDES

Introduction

Canada is potentially the global model of a peaceful country that has adopted democratic pluralism as its foundational principle of constitutionalism within its legal order. Canada is both a very new country, less than 200 years old and also a very old country, since its first inhabitants, the aboriginal people of Canada, have lived here from time immemorial. We have, in comparison to many European nations, a very diverse population. Over one-third of Canadians can trace their origins from France and are concentrated in the province of Quebec, where they form a powerful majority. Increasingly, Canadian society is becoming a mirror of the global society as we welcome immigration from all over the world. Very soon our major cities – Toronto, Montreal and Vancouver – could become majority non-European in origin, creating calls by racial and ethnic minorities for collective rights to equality.

The founding architects of the Canadian nation had little choice in developing a democratic pluralist state. By the late 1850's, conflicts between the French and English in Canada East and West brought government in the United Province of Canada almost to a standstill. Slowly the idea of a revision of the union that would consist of a looser federal structure began to take hold. The idea of a federalist pluralist structure where local matters in Canada East and West would be in the hands of provincial governments and matters of common concern would be given to a central government would grow in popularity. George-Étienne Cartier persuaded his French co-citizens that federation was essential to survival of French culture and that a Canadian federation would benefit Francophones economically as the Canadian West was opened up to eastern migration. In the Maritimes, the leaders of those communities also felt their economic and cultural specificities would be in danger unless they could secure land and rail connections to central Canada and the larger markets to be found there. These desires for cultural and linguistic survival dominated the conferences at Charlottetown and Quebec City in 1864. Indeed, the strongest concern for cultural survival came from Prince Edward Island and Newfoundland. Prince Edward Island did not come into confederation for these reasons until 1873 and Newfoundland resisted confederation until the 1949 referendum gave a small majority in favour of joining the rest of Canada. The resolutions at the Quebec City conference spelled out the division of powers and the structure of the union that was to be the basis of the British North America Act of 1867, which was finalized at Westminster in 1867. This foundational act of the Canadian State is replete with provisions related to democratic pluralism. Examples include the guarantee of 75 seats for Quebec in the Canadian Parliament (section 37), the entrenchment of the provinces' jurisdiction over property and civil rights in section 92 (13), the protection of denominational schools in Ontario and Quebec (section 93) and the official use of English and French in the Canadian and Quebec legislatures (section 133).

The collective rights of the growing diversity of Canadian society have been guaranteed in the Canadian Charter of Rights and Freedoms entrenched in our Constitution in 1982.[1] In the Constitution, we recognize the collective rights of our aboriginal peoples, and our multicultural and multiracial communities. Through court decisions and provisions of the original Constitution and the Charter of Rights, we recognize the collective rights of our French-speaking population.

The wording of some of the provisions in the Canadian Charter, which recognize collective rights, poses some interesting dilemmas for those who are steeped in the natural rights philosophy of western classical liberalism. To give some examples:

- Section 23(3), which entrenches minority linguistic education rights in Canada, states:

> The right of citizens of Canada under subsections (1) and (2) to have their children receive primary and secondary school instruction in the language of the English or French linguistic minority population of a province
>
> (a) applies wherever in the province the number of children of citizens who have such a right is sufficient to warrant the provision of them out of public funds of minority language instruction; and
>
> (b) includes, where the number of those children so warrants the right to have them receive that instruction in minority language educational facilities provided out of public funds.

This is a curious type of right to be found in a constitutional document in a western liberal democracy where the exercise of the right is contingent on the number of people who wish to exercise it! Imagine a similar contingent right related to the freedom of speech. This entrenchment of linguistic rights in Canada points to the fact that collective rights require an examination of the sociological, economic and cultural backgrounds from which they arise.[2]

- Section 35(1), which entrenches the rights of the aboriginal peoples of Canada, states:

> The existing aboriginal and treaty rights of the aboriginal peoples of Canada are hereby recognized and affirmed.

The case law on this section has clearly indicated that included in this right is the right of the Aboriginal peoples of Canada to their traditional means of subsistence and development, including their inherent right to self-government.[3]

- Finally, in section 27 of the Charter, one finds an interpretive section that reinforces the view that racial and ethnic minorities in Canada have sociocultural collective rights. It states:

> This Charter shall be interpreted in a manner consistent with the preservation and enhancement of the multicultural heritage of Canadians.

This section requires that all rights and freedoms in the Charter be interpreted in a manner that not only ensures the survival of the collectivist principle of cultural pluralism, but also promotes its actual enhancement. Does it not seem paradoxical that individual rights found in other sections of the Charter must be interpreted in a way that not only preserves but enhances the collectivist principle of cultural pluralism?

Let us examine what this collectivist principle of multicultural heritage of Canadians consists of as set out in section 27. For the purpose of the ensuing discussion, I am assuming that the concept of multiculturalism is equivalent to the concept of multicultural heritage of Canadians. It is imperative to define multiculturalism first. Attempts to define multiculturalism have usually set out a historical evolution of Canadian nationhood accompanied by what the concept means or should mean today. The 1987 House of Commons report entitled *Multiculturalism*[4] arrives at the following essential features of multiculturalism:

> Multiculturalism is a principle applicable to all Canadians and it seeks to preserve and promote a heterogeneous society in Canada. The principle refutes the idea that all citizens should assimilate to one standard paradigm over time.
>
> Multiculturalism is today most fundamentally concerned with ensuring substantial equality for all Canadians regardless of what cultural groups they belong to.

If this is correct, then the interpretive rule in section 27 is a mandate for Canadian courts and governments to interpret all rights and freedoms in the Charter, even those focussed on individual rights, in a manner that preserves cultural pluralism and substantive equality among all citizens in Canada. This is a fundamental principle of distributive justice. Distributive justice is at the core of the concept of democratic pluralism.

As others have expounded, distributive justice encapsulates every aspect of all human societies because all human societies are also institutions of distribution. Different political and legal systems promote different distributions of society's most valued assets, such as power, knowledge, wealth, security of the person, health and education. In human history, some societies have either expressly (e.g., the former apartheid regime in South Africa) or de facto (including many so-called Western liberal democracies) allowed full and equal access to the above-mentioned societal goods only to those who conform to a singular and dominant racial, ethnic, linguistic or cultural paradigm. This has been the root cause of much of the racial and ethnic strife that we see around the world today. The multicultural principle denies that such societal distributional criteria can ever be just. Such a collectivist principle maintains that all manifestations of race, language, ethnicity or national origins are equally worthy. The multicultural principle aims at the establishment of a society where no one segment of society can claim that it has the singular and dominant racial, cultural, ethnic or linguistic paradigm and on that basis has the predominant access to society's most valued goods. This is also the predominant value behind the equality guarantee in section 15 of the Canadian Charter of Rights and Freedoms as confirmed by the jurisprudence of the Supreme Court of Canada.[5]

The most relevant and controversial conclusion from this analysis of section 27 is that there will be situations when the exercise of individual rights will, in some circumstances, have to give way to the collectivist principle of cultural pluralism, where the exercise of such rights impedes the equal access by minority groups to the most important goods in our society. This has been illustrated in the area of hate propaganda, as will be discussed below.

But the Canadian Charter of Rights and Freedoms and Canadian Society also recognize the equal value of civil and political rights based on the dignity of the individual human being. Many of the civil and political rights are stated in absolute terms that seem to allow little room for abridgement. For example, section 2 of the Canadian Charter of Rights and Freedoms states:

> Everyone has the following fundamental freedoms:
>
> (a) freedom of conscience and religion;
>
> (b) freedom of thought, belief, opinion and expression, including freedom of the press and other means of communication;
>
> (c) freedom of peaceful assembly; and
>
> (d) freedom of association.

The jurisprudence of the Canadian Supreme Court has imposed a two-step approach to interpreting rights such as these in any litigation process. First, the complainant who is alleging that his or her rights have been infringed upon must establish a *prima facie* case that the government has violated the guaranteed right. This first step is almost a process in natural law thinking. No governmental justification for abridgement of the right is permitted at this stage. For example, even the curtailment by government action or legislation of the vilest forms of hate propaganda has been ruled a violation of section 2. The Supreme Court has held that any form of communication has expressive content and government restriction of any such form of expression is a violation of section 2(b).[6]

However, despite this seemingly initial natural law approach to civil and political rights, we do not put collective rights and interests of groups and society always in a subordinate position to individual liberty and freedom. Rather, we attempt to balance the categories of rights by what I call "the fundamental justice and law of proportionality".

This concept of proportionality is introduced in the first section of our Charter. This section states:

> The rights set out in the Charter are subject to reasonable limits demonstrably justified in a free and democratic society.

The section comes into operation after the plaintiff has proven that there is a *prima facie* violation of his or her rights, as described above. The burden of proof then switches to the government to show that it can justify such a violation on the basis of the criteria set out in section 1. If it can, its actions will be deemed constitutional and valid. In effect, the Canadian Supreme Court will allow governments to override rights to promote the "general average welfare" of the people, where the fundamental justice and law of proportionality is satisfied.

The law of proportionality entrenched in section 1 of the Canadian Charter has been interpreted by the Canadian Supreme Court to contain fundamental principles of justice. The rest of this chapter will:

- discuss the birth and evolution of section 1;
- examine each of the requirements embodied in the distinct phrases in section 1, namely "reasonable and demonstrably justified", "prescribed by law" and "free and democratic society";
- analyze the four branches of the *Oakes* test which set out the requirements that must be fulfilled for a limit to be "reasonable and demonstrably justified in a free and democratic society"; and
- discuss how the Supreme Court of Canada seems to be rejecting a strict and rigid interpretation of the *Oakes* test in favour of an analysis that searches for a background theory of social justice.

Origins of Section 1

Section 1 was included in the Charter of Rights and Freedoms as a reaction to the fact that the American Bill of Rights guaranteed individual rights absolutely, without any limitations.[7] Fearful of creating a society that may guarantee its liberty, but lose its values of community and democratic pluralism, the constitutional drafters sought to wrap the guaranteed rights and freedoms with an extremely flexible limitation clause. Such a clause would offer society, through its legislative and executive representatives, a recourse to avoid liberty and freedom, undermining the very community whose rights and freedoms the Charter was supposed to protect.

Section 1 was amended to its present form, as set out above, in April 1981. The original 1980 version provided that Charter rights were "subject only to such reasonable limits as are generally accepted in a free and democratic society with a parliamentary system of government".[8] This original draft came under severe criticism by, among others, the Canadian Human Rights Commission. The Commission issued a statement to the Hays-Joyal Committee submitting that the original version offered "unacceptably broad excuses for the limitation of rights and freedoms any general limitation clause in the Charter should accord with the accepted clauses in the International Bill of Rights (i.e. the Universal Declaration of Human Rights, the International Covenant on Economic Social and Cultural Rights, the International Covenant on Civil and Political Rights, and the Optional Protocol to that Covenant)".[9]

In the face of such opposition to the original version of section 1, amendments were made to harmonize the wording with Canada's obligations under international human rights instruments and customary international law. However, opinion was still divided as to the efficacy of including a limitation clause, since some feared that it might water down the Charter.[10]

Distinct Phrases in Section 1

The reasonable and demonstrably justified standard: two requirements articulated as one standard

While section 52 seemingly grants courts the wide latitude to deem legislation to be of no force or effect, section 1 limits this power of judicial review, stating that legislation that contravenes a right can still be preserved if it is reasonable and demonstrably justified in a free and democratic society. Thus, the court will not proceed to a section 1 analysis unless the legislation in question is deemed to have violated one of the rights or freedoms guaranteed by the Charter.

Although the rights and freedoms guaranteed by the Charter are not absolute, in order for a court to uphold a law that limits a right, it must balance the value of that individual freedom against the value of the collective goal. A court must be satisfied that a limit on such a right is *both* reasonable and demonstrably justified. These two requirements, however, have not been dealt with separately by the courts but rather have been treated as a single standard. This may be explained by the fact that logic dictates that in order for a limit to be demonstrably justified it must also be reasonable, therefore making a double inquiry redundant.[11]

Prescribed by law

The addition of this phrase in the April 1981 amendment meant that a law that violates a Charter right cannot be upheld as a "reasonable limit" if it has not been "prescribed by law". The Supreme Court first elaborated upon this term in *R. v. Therens,*[12] when Mr. Justice Le Dain stated:

> The requirement that the limit be prescribed by law is chiefly concerned with the distinction between a limit imposed by law and one that is arbitrary. The limit will be prescribed by law within the meaning of s. 1 if it is expressly provided for by statute or regulation, or results by necessary implication from the terms of a statute or regulation or from its operating requirements. The limit may also result from the application of a common law rule.[13]

The Supreme Court in *R. v. Therens* held that the failure of a police officer to inform the accused of his right to retain and instruct counsel, when demanding a breathalyzer test pursuant to section 235 of the Criminal Code, was a violation of section 10(b) of the Charter. Furthermore, this violation resulted from the officer's own failure to pay attention to the guarantees expressed in the Charter rather than from any limit prescribed by Parliament.[14]

Justice Sopinka in *R. v. Butler*[15] adopted the test set out in *Osborne v. Canada (Treasury Board),*[16] namely "whether the law is so obscure as to be incapable of interpretation with any degree of precision using the ordinary tools".[17] The legislation at issue was section 163(8) of the Criminal Code, which provided that 'any publication a dominant characteristic of which is the *undue* exploitation of sex, or of sex and any one or more of crime, horror, cruelty and violence, shall be deemed to be obscene (emphasis added).[18] Justice Sopinka cited *R. v. Morgentaler,*[19] in which Justice Beetz found that a provision can still be prescribed by law even though terms contained therein may be subject to different legal interpretations by the courts. Since the term "undue" had been given meaning in prior judgments, it was considered to be "prescribed by law" despite the lack of a precise technical definition.[20]

It should be noted that the idea of the paramountcy of "law", that is, formal executive and legislative action over the arbitrary acts of private individuals and government officials, is not a new concept unique to section 1, but rather a fundamental principle articulated as "the rule of law".[21]

Put another way, the phrase "prescribed by law" requires that "the legislature [provide] an intelligible standard according to which the judiciary must do its work".[22]

In recent years, however, the courts have ascribed less and less importance to this requirement to the extent that in *Canada (Human Rights Commission) v. Taylor,* Justice McLaughlin did not consider "prescribed by law" as part of the section 1 inquiry. She first concluded that Section 13(1) of the Canadian Human Rights Act, S.C. 1976-77, c. 33, constituted a limit prescribed by law and then proceeded to a section 1 analysis.[23]

Free and democratic society

Chief Justice Dickson, in *R. v. Oakes* focussed upon the final words of section 1 as they were seen as "the ultimate standard against which a limit on a right or freedom must be shown, despite its effect".[24] Because Canada is a free and democratic society, the courts must be guided by the values inherent in these concepts such as:

> respect for the inherent dignity of the human person, commitment to social justice and equality, accommodation of a wide variety of beliefs, respect for cultural and group identity, and faith in social and political institutions which enhance the participation of individuals and groups in society.[25]

Justice Lamer gave further meaning to these principles in *Reference re ss. 193 & 195.1(1)(c) of the Criminal Code (Man.)*[26] when he stated that citizens living in a free and democratic society should be "able, as far as possible, to foresee the consequences of their conduct, in order that persons be given fair notice of what to avoid, and that the discretion of those entrusted with law enforcement is limited by clear and explicit legislative standards".[27] In addition, Justice McIntyre in *Irwin Toy* stated that freedom of expression is "a principle of vital importance in a free and democratic society".[28]

These interpretations of a free and democratic society are open-ended and may possibly conflict with each other.[29] However, inherent in the discussion about the meaning of the phrase is a struggle to find a background theory of social justice that would form the basis of the interpretative task set by section 1. Yet these pronouncements seem to have fallen into the dark recesses of Charter precedent, while formalistic tests that form the basis of the rest of the interpretation of section 1 have taken overwhelming prominence. These formalistic tests were to be subsumed under the name of the first case in which the Supreme Court undertook to wrap the open-texture of section 1, *R. v. Oakes*.[30]

The Oakes Test

The Four Requirements

Chief Justice Dickson, speaking for a unanimous court in *Oakes* adopted a formalistic approach to the interpretation and application of section 1. He articulated the following four requirements that must be satisfied to prove that a law limiting a right is reasonable and demonstrably justified in a free and democratic society:

1) Sufficiently Important Objective

Chief Justice Dickson stated:

> "the objective, which the measures responsible for a limit on a Charter right or freedom are designed to serve, must be "of sufficient importance" to warrant overriding a constitutionally protected right or freedom".[31]

The remaining three requirements set out "a form of proportionality test," which evaluates the means adopted to achieve the objective. Defined by C.J.C. Dickson in *Oakes*, they are as follows:

2) Rational Connection to the Objective

> "the measures adopted must be carefully designed to achieve the objective in question. They must not be arbitrary, unfair or based on irrational considerations. In short, they must be rationally connected to the objective".[32]

3) Least Drastic Means

> The law in question "should impair as little as 'possible' the right or freedom in question".[33]

4) Proportionality Between Effects and Objective

> there must be a proportionality between the effects of the measures which are responsible for limiting the Charter right or freedom, and the objective which has been identified as of sufficient importance.[34]

Analysis of the Four Requirements

1) Sufficiently Important Objective

C.J.C. Dickson in *Oakes* outlined the criteria necessary to demonstrate that the objective of the impugned law is of sufficient importance to justify limiting a Charter right:

> The objective must be consistent with the "principles integral to a free and democratic society at a minimum an objective [must] relate to concerns which are pressing and substantial in a free and democratic society".[35]

These requirements appear at first sight to place a rather onerous burden on the party wishing to have the limitation upheld since, for example, the term "pressing" denotes only those goals which are immediate in nature. Thus, an objective designed to combat unfairness or injustice over the long term could be rejected,[36] because it impacts on rights and freedoms in the present. Such was the case in *National Citizen's Coalition Inc. et al. v. Attorney General for Canada,*[37] where the court held that sections 70.1(1) and 72 of the Canada Elections Act, which prohibited third-party campaign spending during elections, violated section 2(b) and could not be saved by Section 1. The court reasoned that:

> Fears or concerns of mischief that may occur are not adequate reasons for imposing a limitation. There should be actual demonstration of harm or a real likelihood of harm to a society value before a limitation can be said to be justified.[38]

However, in *Andrews*, Justice McIntyre of the Supreme Court of Canada[39] recognized the difficulties inherent in requiring that the objective be "pressing and substantial". He stated that such a test may deny Canadian society the benefits of "sound social and economic legislation".[40] In its place, he would apply a less stringent test:

> In my opinion, in approaching a case such as the one before us, the first question the Court should ask must relate to the nature and the purpose of the enactment, with a view to deciding whether the limitation represents a legitimate exercise of the legislative power for the attainment of a desirable social objective which would warrant overriding constitutionally protected rights.[41]

In general, the courts have often been reluctant to second guess the legislature's choice of objective, if the legislation can be championed as having a social justice agenda.

There is one notable exception in the jurisprudence to such deference to the legislature, namely the landmark decision in *R. v. Big M Drug Mart Ltd.*[42] In that case, the Supreme Court held that the objective of the *Lord's Day Act*,[43] the federal Sunday closing law, was to "compel the observance of the Christian Sabbath".[44] Given the fact that the purpose of the impugned legislation was clearly religious (thereby contravening the Charter right of freedom of religion) rather than the secular objective of providing a common day of rest for employees, it could not be said to justify limiting that constitutionally guaranteed freedom.

Perhaps the anomaly that this case represents could be explained on the basis that where the Supreme Court finds no secular social justice agenda involved in the impugned legislation, they will apply a more formalistic interpretation of the "pressing and substantial" test.

In order to discover the true objective of the Act, the Supreme Court in *Big M* focussed on its legislative history and noted that an objective cannot evolve with the passing of time or change with the social climate. In the words of Dickson C.J.C.: "Purpose is a function of the intent of those who drafted and enacted the legislation at the time, and not of any shifting variable".[45]

However, in *R. v. Butler*,[46] Justice Sopinka writing for the majority, failed to give credence to the shifting purpose rule as argued by the challengers to the obscenity provisions of the Criminal Code. They argued that the original purpose was to safeguard society from the corrupting influence of obscene materials but the government was now characterizing the objective as preventing violence against women and children. Justice Sopinka deferred to the legislature by framing the objective in general terms as preventing harm to society. Thus, it did not matter whether the harm was immorality or violence.

Conversely, if the court wishes to take an activist stance to strike down legislation that does not have a defendable social agenda and find the impugned legislation invalid it will define the objective very narrowly. For example, in *Andrews*, the majority defined the purpose of section 42 of the Barristers and Solicitors Act,[47] which limited membership of the bar to Canadian citizens as restricting entry to the legal profession. However, as we have seen in the *Butler* decision, the court seems to have shied away from this activist position and has, more often than not, interpreted the impugned legislation as having a defendable social agenda. *Rodriguez v. British Columbia (A.G.)* is yet another example of this trend away from the activist position. In that case, the objectives of the Criminal Code provisions against assisted suicide were construed very broadly as preventing human life from being devalued.[48]

Justice McLachlin in *R.J.R.- MacDonald Inc. v. Canada (A.G.)*, however, cautioned against stating the objective too broadly when she concluded that the objective should be phrased in terms of the impugned measure rather than the whole legislative and policy scheme.[49]

It is interesting to note that the courts have frowned upon the legislature citing administrative convenience as a justification for limiting a Charter right. For example, Justice Lamer stated in *Reference re s. 94(2) of Motor Vehicle Act (British Columbia)*[50] that "administrative expediency [should only be considered a legitimate objective] in cases arising out of exceptional conditions, such as natural disasters, the outbreak of war, epidemics and the like".[51] This opinion was reiterated by Justice Wilson in *Singh v. Minister of Employment & Immigration*,[52] by Chief Justice Lamer again in *Schacter v. Canada (Employment and Immigration Commission)*[53] and by Chief Justice Dickson in *R. v. Schwartz*, who stated that "administrative convenience is rarely if ever an objective of sufficient importance".[54] The legislation in *R. v. Edward Books and Arts Limited* fell within this exception for the Chief Justice because "alternate forms of business regulation do not generally impinge on the values and provisions of the Charter of Rights and the resultant legislation need not be tuned with great precision in order to withstand judicial scrutiny".[55] In addition, in *R. v. Lee*[56] the majority upheld a section of the Criminal Code that provided that an accused lost his or her right to be tried by a jury if he or she did not appear for trial and had no legitimate excuse. Thus, in that case, the majority considered cost efficiency and the reduction of administrative inconvenience to be a legitimate objective.[57]

2) Rational Connection to the Objective:

This second step can only be reached when the objective of the law has been deemed to be of sufficient importance to justify limiting a Charter right.

The requirement that the means by which the law is implemented be rationally connected to the objective "calls for an assessment of how well the legislative garment has been tailored to suit its purpose".[58] To illustrate, at issue in *Oakes* was the validity of section 8 of the Narcotic Control Act,[59] which placed the onus on the accused to prove that he or she was not in possession of an illegal substance for the purpose of trafficking when it had been proven that he or she was in possession. Although the objective (to curtail drug trafficking) was held to be legitimate, no "rational connection between the basic fact of possession and the presumed fact of possession for the purpose of trafficking"[60] could be found. Put another way, the means used were too heavy-handed or too extreme given the objective since a person could be charged with the serious offence of trafficking even though he or she was in possession of a very small quantity of drugs.

It is rare that the courts will find that a law is not rationally connected to the objective. However, Justice McLaughlin, speaking for the majority in *Miron v. Trudel,* found that excluding unmarried partners from receiving accident benefits available to married couples was not rationally connected to the legislative goal of reducing the economic hardship on families when one member is injured in a motor vehicle accident.[61] Justice L'Heureux-Dubé and Justice Iacobucci, in their respective dissents in *Egan v. Canada,* found that the exclusion of same-sex couples in the Old Age Security Act was not rationally connected to the objective of ensuring that when one partner retires, the couple will continue to receive income equivalent to the amount that would be earned if both were retired.[62]

Generally, however, the court seems to apply a standard of "minimal rationality"[63] requiring the government to only demonstrate that the means chosen will further the objective. This standard is reflected in cases such as *Rocket v. Royal College of Dental Surgeons of Ontario*,[64] where Justice McLaughlin, writing for the majority, found that legislation that limited the ability of dentists to advertise was rationally connected to the objective because the "objectives of promoting professionalism and avoiding irresponsible and misleading advertising will clearly be furthered by s. 37(39)".[65] Another example of this relaxed standard used in the civil context can be found in *Edmonton Journal v. Alberta (A.G.)*,[66] in which Justice Wilson found it sufficient to state, without further explanation, that legislation that limited media coverage of matrimonial proceedings was rationally connected to the objective of protecting privacy.[67] Furthermore, in *R.J.R.-MacDonald*, Justice McLaughlin stated that scientific evidence was not required to establish a rational connection between the impugned measure and its objective where the legislation in question is aimed at changing human behaviour.[68] In the recent cases of *Ross v. New Brunswick School District* and *Butler*, the Supreme Court further developed the relaxed standard. For example, in *Ross*, Justice LaForest accepted that it was "reasonable to presume" a causal relationship between a teacher's public discriminatory statements and the harm to students thus, the Board of Inquiry order removing him from his teaching position was found to be rationally connected to the objective of ensuring discrimination-free educational services.[69]

It should be noted that this more flexible approach has not been limited to the civil context. For example, the Supreme Court held in the *Prostitution Reference*[70] that Criminal Code provisions that prohibited communication for the purpose of solicitation in places open to public view were rationally connected to the objective of preventing "the public display of the sale of sex and any harmful consequences that flow from it."[71] Justice Lamer had no difficulty justifying this finding on the basis that the legislation "reduce[s] or limit[s] the mischief"[72] by criminalizing the conduct that produces it. In addition, Chief Justice Dickson, writing for the majority in *R. v. Keegstra*,[73] found that the hate propaganda sections of the Criminal Code would satisfy the rational connection test unless the party challenging the provisions could demonstrate that they had either an adverse or no impact on the objective.[74]

3) Least Drastic Means

Once the legitimate objective and rational connection requirements are satisfied, only then can the legislation in question proceed to the third step of least drastic means, which was adopted from American jurisprudence dealing with the First Amendment.[75]

While the courts have been quick to conclude that a legislative objective is sufficiently important and that a law is rationally connected to the objective, the same "rubber stamp" has not been applied to the requirement of least drastic means.[76] Indeed, this requirement has been the focus of the section 1 inquiry. For example, Justice Lamer speaking for the majority in *R. v. Généreux*,[77] focussed his decision upon the least drastic means requirement and effectively ignored the other branches of the test.[78]

Chief Justice Dickson, in *Oakes*, described this branch of the test as requiring that the impugned legislation impair the right or freedom "as little as possible".[79] This definition placed an unreasonable burden on those seeking to uphold the legislation because it was easy to imagine an alternative that may have been less effective but that impaired the right to a lesser extent.[80] For example, requiring the exclusive use of French in commercial signs was deemed to be far too drastic a means of promoting and maintaining the French language.[81] Prohibiting the media from covering matrimonial proceedings was held to be too drastic a means of protecting privacy.[82] The rape shield provisions of the Criminal Code restricting the defence's right to cross-examine and lead evidence of a complainant's sexual conduct during a sexual assault trial was held to be too drastic a means of preventing false inferences that the complainant may have consented or is lying.[83]

In *Edward Books*, Chief Justice Dickson seemed to recognize that too high a standard was demanded of the legislature since he reformulated the test to require that the law impair the freedom in question "as little as is reasonably possible".[84] The inquiry focussed on "whether there is some reasonable alternative scheme which would allow the province to achieve its objective with fewer detrimental effects".[85] A certain amount of deference to the legislature was implied when he further stated that the Court was "not called upon to substitute judicial opinions for legislative ones as to the place at which to draw a precise line".[86] Justice LaForest also observed that "a legislature must be given reasonable room to manoeuvre".[87] In a later case, he reiterated that this branch of the *Oakes* test must be characterized by flexibility.[88] In so doing, he criticized Chief Justice Dickson's statement in *Oakes* that the means should impair "as little as possible": "The difficulty I have with this approach is that it seeks to apply the *Oakes* test in too rigid a fashion, without regard to the context in which it is to be applied".[89]

In *Irwin Toy*, the majority held that the courts should practice judicial restraint only in cases where the government is "mediating between the claims of competing groups" or safeguarding the interests of vulnerable groups.[90] In those cases, the government need only demonstrate a reasonable basis for believing that the means employed were the least drastic means possible. In contrast, the courts must adopt a hard-line approach in those cases in which "the government is best characterized as the singular antagonist of the individual whose right has been infringed".[91] In other words, in criminal cases, the court recommends a rigid application of the *Oakes* test. As the legislation in question in *Irwin Toy* banned commercial advertising aimed at children under the age of 13, it could be seen as protecting a group vulnerable to media manipulation and thus merited a more relaxed application of the *Oakes* test. This analysis was applied by Chief Justice Lamer in his dissent in *Rodriguez v. B.C. (A.G.)*.[92] While the impugned legislation was a criminal code provision, the state could not be seen as the "singular antagonist of the individual" because the case had not been generated by a criminal prosecution.[93]

The trend toward deference to legislative decisions was taken a step further in *R. v. Chaulk*,[94] in which Chief Justice Lamer formulated the test as "whether Parliament could reasonably have chosen an alternative means which would have achieved the identified objective as effectively".[95] In formulating this question, Lamer looked to *Irwin Toy* and *The Prostitution Reference* as the basis for the conclusion that Parliament has no obligation to choose the "absolutely *least* intrusive means" of meeting its objective.[96] It is sufficient that Parliament has chosen from a "range of means" that infringe the Charter right 'as little as is reasonably possible".[97] While he listed several hypothetical provisions that might infringe upon the Charter to a lesser extent, he acknowledged that these may or may not achieve the desired objective as effectively as the legislation already in place.[98]

This much less demanding test of efficacy is also reflected in the majority decision of Chief Justice Dickson in the *Prostitution Reference*, in which he phrased the question as "can effective yet less intrusive legislation be imagined?"[99] Thus, the government is not obligated to devise "the perfect scheme that could be imagined by this Court or any other Court"[100] to satisfy this branch of the test.

Yet another variation of this more deferential approach to *Oakes* can be found in *Tétreault-Gadoury v. Canada (Employment and Immigration Commission)*, where the court asked whether the government could "show that it had a reasonable basis for concluding that it has complied with the requirement of minimal impairment".[101]

4) Proportionality Between Effects and Objective

Even if the impugned legislation satisfies all three previous steps, "it is still possible that, because of the severity of the deleterious effects of a measure on individuals or groups, the measure will not be justified by the purposes it is intended to serve".[102] Thus in theory, even if the least drastic means are employed, they may still be too severe to maintain. Indeed, the more severe the deleterious effects, the more important the government objective must be in order to satisfy this branch of the *Oakes* test. As Chief Justice Dickson stated in *Edward Books*, the "effects [of the legislation] must not so severely trench on individual or group rights that the legislative objective, albeit important, is nevertheless outweighed by the abridgement of rights".[103]

It is often the case that once the court finds that the least drastic means requirement is satisfied, it will deem there to be proportionality between effects and objective as well. Indeed, in certain cases such as *RWDSU v. Saskatchewan* and *McKinney v. University of Guelph*[104] and *Rodriguez*,[105] this latter requirement was not analyzed as a component separate and apart from the least drastic means test.

However, in *R. v. Morgentaler*,[106] Madam Justice Wilson began her section 1 analysis by focussing on this last branch of the *Oakes* test and virtually ignored the least drastic means requirement. The pivotal question for her was: "at what point in the pregnancy does the protection of the foetus become such a pressing and substantial concern as to outweigh the fundamental right of the woman to decide whether or not to carry the foetus to term?"[107]

Professor Peter Hogg has described this fourth step as a test of the objective of the law rather than of the means since it weighs the benefit of the objective against the cost of the violation of the Charter right.[108] As such, it is seen as merely reiterating the "sufficiently important objective" test. In fact, Professor Hogg surmises that if an objective is held to be sufficiently important, the effects of the legislation will not be deemed to be too severe.[109]

Other authors, such as Pierre Blache and the Honourable Mr. Justice Roger P. Kerans, have commented on how ineffectual this last branch of the *Oakes* test seems. The former advanced the view that "the third step has no real weakening impact on the first two steps. It comes too late in the process it seems that it is a step that should almost never be reached".[110] The latter argued that the last two branches of the *Oakes* test are really in fact one: "One requires that the limit "impair the right as little as possible"; the other that it not "so severely trench" that its legislative objective is outweighed by the abridgment of rights".[111]

Burden and Standard of Proof

The burden of proof in a section 1 defence "rests upon the party seeking to uphold the limitation"[112] and the civil standard of "proof by a preponderance of probability"[113] is to be applied "rigorously". However, in *Edward Books*, Chief Justice Dickson advocated a more relaxed approach when he stated that "[b]oth in articulating the standard of proof and in describing the criteria comprising the proportionality requirement the Court has been careful to avoid rigid and inflexible standards".[114]

Conclusion

While the Supreme Court continues to cite *Oakes* in an almost ritualistic fashion, various judges have expressed a discomfort with the rigid and inflexible test that originated from one criminal case involving legal rights. Thus, as we have seen, the test had to be reshaped and moulded carefully to adapt to changing needs, the nature of the interests in question and the particular circumstances of the case. Indeed, Dickson C.J.C., the creator of the test, recognized this and wished to make it "clear that a rigid and formalistic approach to the application of Section 1 must be avoided".[115]

Justice LaForest offered an alternative to *Oakes*: "I prefer to think in terms of a single test for s. 1, but one that is to be applied to vastly differing situations with the flexibility and realism inherent in the word 'reasonable' mandated by the Constitution".[116]

From the analysis of the Canadian Constitutional principles on the justice and law of proportionality, we see that there is a possible universal approach to reconciling individual freedoms with the collective rights and goals of groups and societies. Such an approach respects all societies' right to development and fundamental social and economic rights, but insists on minimal safeguards when the pursuit of such collective rights and goals infringe on fundamental individual rights and freedoms. These minimal safeguards, which comprise the justice and law of proportionality, can be summarized as follows:

- Any limitation on rights, individual or collective, must be prescribed by law. This essentially means the Rule of Law. Limits on rights must be clear, precise and not based on administrative discretion or government policy. Citizens must have certainty and predictability in how their governments behave toward them.
- The limit on rights (whether individual or collective) must invoke an urgent and substantive societal interest, not just a desire to keep a particular government or party in power.
- The limit on rights (whether individual or collective) must be done in the least intrusive way. In other words, the government's action to promote the general average welfare of the people must be proportionate, not excessive.
- If the government's actions to promote the people's general average welfare has excessively damaging consequences (whether intended or not), such action may become disproportionate to the government's objectives and so violate the law of proportionality.

The Supreme Court of Canada has applied this law of proportionality on many occasions to show that civil and political rights can be balanced with collective rights inherent in the concept of democratic pluralism.

Democratic pluralism can be reconciled with traditional notions of constitutionalism through the law and justice of proportionality. The justice of proportionality makes law and governments the servants of the people. This is the true meaning of democracy. It is when the people become the servants of the law and governments that tyranny and injustice begin.

Notes

1. Canadian Charter of Rights and Freedoms, part 1 of the Constitution Act, 1982, being Schedule B of the Canada Act, 1982 (U.K.), chap. 11 (hereinafter the *Charter*).

2. For example, in *Mahe v. Alberta*, [1990] 1 S.C.R. 342, it was held that the number of Francophone students in the Edmonton area justified the establishment of a separate Francophone school and the representation by Francophone parents on the school board, with a measure of management and control of the school. However, there were not enough Francophone students to justify an independent Francophone school board. Where the numbers warrant, section 23 confers upon minority language parents a right to management and control over the educational facilities in which their children are taught, to ensure their language and culture flourish.

3. In *R. v. Sparrow*, [1990] 1 S.C.R. 1075, the Court had to determine the status of aboriginal or treaty rights that had been extinguished or regulated before 1982. The Court held that the word "existing" in section 35 meant "unextinguished". Therefore, a right that had been validly extinguished before 1982 was not now protected by section 35. However, in *Sparrow*, the Court refused to imply an extinguishment of the aboriginal right to fish by the Fisheries Act, despite its extensive regulatory scheme because it did not demonstrate "a clear and plain intention to extinguish the Indian aboriginal right to fish" (1099). An unextinguished aboriginal right should be treated as existing in its unregulated form. An existing aboriginal right cannot be read so as to incorporate the specific manner in which it was regulated before 1982. The phrase "existing aboriginal rights" must be interpreted flexibly so as to permit their evolution over time. The Court further held that section 35(1) is to be construed in a purposive way. A generous liberal interpretation is demanded given that the provision is to affirm aboriginal rights. However, although section 35 is not part of the Charter and therefore not subject to a section 1 analysis, *infra*, the Court held that these section 35 rights were not absolute, but were subject to regulation, provided that any impairment must be a justified impairment, pursuing an object that was "compelling and substantial" (1113).

4. House of Commons Standing Committee report on *Multiculturalism; Building the Canadian Mosaic*, 2nd Sess. 33rd Parl., 1987, 22-23.

5. Section 15 of the Charter provides:

> 15.(1) Every individual is equal before and under the law and has the right to the equal protection and equal benefit of the law without discrimination and, in particular, without discrimination based on race, national or ethnic origin, colour, religion, sex, age or mental or physical disability.
> (2) Subsection (1) does not preclude any law, program or activity that has as its object the amelioration of conditions of disadvantaged groups including those that are disadvantaged because of race, national or ethnic origin, colour, religion, sex, age or mental or physical disability.

For example, in *Andrews v. Law Society of British Columbia*, [1989] 1 S.C.R. 143, Andrews, a British subject permanently resident in Canada, met all the requirements for admission to the British Columbia bar, except that of Canadian citizenship. He sought a declaration that this statutory requirement violated section 15(1) of the Charter. The Supreme Court of Canada found that a rule that barred an entire class of persons from certain forms of employment, solely on the grounds of citizenship status and without consideration of educational and professional qualifications or the other attributes or merits of the individuals in the group, infringed section 15 equality rights. The Court found that the impugned section 42 of the Barristers and Solicitors Act was such a rule.

6. *Irwin Toy Ltd. v. Quebec (Attorney General)*, [1989] 1 S.C.R. 927 (hereinafter *Irwin Toy*); *R. v. Keegstra*, [1990] 3 S.C.R. 697 (hereinafter *Keegstra*).

7. See J. Cameron, "The Original Conception of Section 1 and its Demise: A Comment on *Irwin Toy Ltd v. Attorney General of Quebec*", *McGill Law Journal* 35 (1989) 254, 257, and H. Marx, "Entrenchment, Limitations and Non-Obstante", *The Canadian Charter of Rights and Freedoms: Commentary*, ed., W.S. Tarnopolsky and G.-A. Beaudoin (Toronto: Carswell, 1982), 63-66.

8. *Proposed Resolution for Joint Address to Her Majesty the Queen Respecting the Constitution of Canada*, Tabled in the House of Commons and the Senate, October 6, 1980, as cited in A.F. Bayefsky, *International Human Rights Law: Use in Canadian Charter of Rights and Freedoms Litigation* (Toronto: Butterworths, 1992), 39.

9. Ibid. Indeed, Dickson stated in *Reference Re Public Service Employee Relations Act (Alberta)*, [1987] 1 S.C.R. 313, at 349: "I believe that the Charter should generally be presumed to provide protection at least as great as that afforded by similar provisions in international human rights documents which Canada has ratified."

10. P.W. Hogg and R. Penner, "The Contribution of Chief Justice Dickson to an Interpretive Framework and Value System for Section 1 of the Charter of Rights", *Manitoba Law Journal*, 20, no. 2 (1991): 431.

11. P.W. Hogg, "Section 1 Revisited", *National Journal of Constitutional Law,* 1 (1991): 2.

12. [1985] 1 S.C.R. 613. Le Dain's definition was approved by the Court in *R. v. Thomsen*, [1988] 1 S.C.R. 640, 650-651.

13. *R v.Therens, id.* at 645.It should be noted that previous lower court decisions articulated the meaning behind "prescribed by law." For example, the Divisional Court in *Re Ontario Film & Video Appreciation Society and Ontario Board of Censors* (1983), 41 O.R. (2d) 583, 592,(affirmed by C.A. [1984] 5 D.L.R. [4th] 766), held that the censorship provisions of the Theatres Act violated the applicant's freedom of expression and were not "prescribed by law." Although the board had been granted the power by the legislature to prohibit the exhibition of any film to which it disapproved, these limits were not prescribed by law due to their discretionary character." [L]aw cannot be vague, undefined, and totally discretionary; it must be ascertainable and understandable. Any limits placed on the freedom of expression cannot be left to the whim of an official; such limits must be articulated with some precision or they cannot be considered to be law." In addition, the Federal Court of Appeal in *Re Luscher* (1985), 17 D.L.R. (4th) 503, held that a law that prohibits the importation of obscene and immoral material is too vague and imprecise to constitute a reasonable limit prescribed by law. Serge Gaudet sees these judgments as "formalistic" rather than "legalistic" interpretations. Whereas the former focusses on the form/content of the law or regulation, etc. and requires that it be reasonably accessible and sufficiently precise, the latter simply gives a rubber stamp to any legislation that has come into effect in conformity with the judicial system in place (in S. Gaudet, "La règle de droit au sens de l'article premier de la Charte Canadienne des droits et libertés: Commentaires sur l'affaire *Slaight Communications Inc. c. Davidson*, [1989] 1 *R.C.S.* 1038" [1990], 20 *R.D.U.S.* 448, 456, 458-461, 463).

14. Ibid, 662.

15. [1992] 1 S.C.R. 452.

16. [1991] 2 S.C.R. 69, 94.

17. *Supra*, note 15 at 490.

18. *Criminal Code*, R.S.C. 1985, chap. C-46.

19. [1988] 1 S.C.R. 30, 107. *Butler, supra*, 491, note 31.

20. Ibid.

21. For example, in *Re Resolution to Amend the Canadian Constitution*, [1981] 1 S.C.R. 753, 805-806, the Court referred to the rule of law as "a highly textured expression conveying, for example, a sense of orderliness, of subjection to known legal rules and of executive accountability to legal authority". In addition, the majority in *Reference re Manitoba Language Rights*, [1985] 1 S.C.R. 721, 748-749, described the rule of law as a "fundamental principle of our Constitution" and defined it as meaning that "the law is supreme over officials of the government as well as private individuals, and thereby preclusive of the influence of arbitrary power". Further, "the rule of law expresses a preference for law and order within a community rather than anarchy, warfare and constant strife". See also: L.E. Weinrib, "The Supreme Court of Canada and Section One of the Charter", *Supreme Court Review*, 10 (1988): 475-477.

22. *Irwin Toy, supra*, note 6 at 983.

23. [1990] 3 S.C.R. 892, 954. See also Chief Justice Dickson's comments agreeing with Justice McLaughlin, 915-916.

24. [1986] 1 S.C.R. 103, 136 [hereinafter *Oakes*].

25. Ibid.

26. [1990] 1 S.C.R. 1123 (hereinafter *Prostitution Reference*).

27. Ibid., 1152. Justice Lamer indicated that in the criminal law context, this takes on an added importance.

28. *Supra*, note 6 at 1008.

29. The Supreme Court seems to have valued the "commitment to social justice and equality" over the other principles, as this can be reconciled with the inherent dignity of the human person. See E.P. Mendes,"In Search of a Theory of Social Justice: The Supreme Court Reconceives the Oakes Test", *La revue juridique Thémis*, 24, no. 1 (1990): 6, note 15.

30. *Supra*, note 24.

31. Ibid., 138, quoting *R. v. Big M Drug Mart*, [1985] 1 S.C.R. 295, 352 (hereinafter *Big M*).

32. Ibid., 139.

33. Ibid., quoting *Big M, supra*, 352, note 47.

34. Ibid.

35. Ibid., 138-139.

36. Mendes, *supra*, note 79 at 7.

37. (1985), 11 D.L.R. (4th) 481 (Alta. Q.B.).

38. Ibid., 496.

39. *Andrews v. Law Society of British Columbia*, [1989] 1 S.C.R. 143.

40. Id., 184.

41. Ibid.

42. [1985] 1 S.C.R. 295.

43. R.S.C. 1970, chap. L-13.

44. *Supra*, note 42 at 351.

45. Ibid., 335. See also the Honourable Mr. Justice Roger P. Kerans, "The Future of Section One of the Charter", *University of British Columbia Law Review*, 23, no. 3 (1989): 573.

46. *Supra*, note 15.

47. R.S.B.C. c.1979, chap. 26.

48. [1993] 3 S.C.R. 519, 613.

49. [1995] 3 S.C.R. 199, 335. Justice McLaughlin stated that the objective of the impugned provisions of the Tobacco Products Control Act (which prohibited advertising and promotion of tobacco products unless the package included prescribed health warnings and a list of the toxic contents) was to prevent Canadians from being persuaded by advertisements to use tobacco products. However, the objective of the general legislative and policy scheme was to safeguard Canadians from the risks of tobacco use.

50. [1985] 2 S.C.R. 486.

51. Ibid., 518.

52. [1985] 1 S.C.R. 177. This case revolved around the question of whether every refugee arriving to Canada had to be given a full hearing. The Attorney General of Canada justified limiting rights under section 7, as this would save the government time and money. Justice Wilson rejected these utilitarian considerations when she wrote:

> Certainly the guarantees of the Charter would be illusory if they could be ignored because it was administratively convenient to do so... The principles of natural justice and procedural fairness which have long been espoused by our courts, and the constitutional entrenchment of the principles of fundamental justice in s. 7, implicitly recognize that a balance of administrative convenience does not override the need to adhere to these principles. (218-219)

53. [1992] 2 S.C.R. 679, 709. Justice Lamer emphasized that budgetary considerations are not a legitimate objective and thus cannot justify an infringement under section 1.

54. [1988] 2 S.C.R. 443, 472.

55. [1986] 2 S.C.R. 713, 772. (hereinafter *Edward Books*). Chief Justice of the Court Dickson stated that "simplicity and administrative convenience are legitimate concerns for the drafters of such legislation".

56. [1989] 2 S.C.R. 1384.

57. Justice Wilson, in her dissent, remained true to form when she held that the objective of reducing administrative inconvenience and expense was not a sufficiently important objective that could justify limiting section 11(f), i.e., the Charter right to a trial by a jury. (Id, 1420).

58. *Edward Books, Supra*, note 55 at 770.

59. R.S.C. 1970 chap. N-1.

60. *Supra*, note 24 at 141.

61. [1995] 2 S.C.R. 418, 503.

62. (1995), 124 D.L.R. (4th) 609 (S.C.C.), 680.

63. R. Elliot, "Developments in Constitutional Law: The 1989-90 Term", *Superior Court Law Review* (2d), 2 (1991): 142.

64. [1990] 2 S.C.R. 232.

65. Ibid., 250.

66. [1989] 2 S.C.R. 1326.

67. Ibid., 1367.

68. *Supra*, note 49 at 339.

69. [1996] S.C.J. no. 40, 49.

70. *Supra*, note 26.

71. Ibid., 1212.

72. Ibid., 1195-1196.

73. *Supra*, note 6.

74. Ibid., 768.

75. P.A. Chapman, "The Politics of Judging: Section 1 of the Charter of Rights and Freedom", *Osgoode Hall Law Journal*, 24, no. 4 (1986): 883.

76. *Supra*, note 11 at 17.

77. [1992] 1 S.C.R. 259.

78. Ibid., 313-314.

79. *Supra*, note 24 at 139.

80. Chapman, *supra*, note 75 at 883. David Beatty is quoted as stating: "All of its [the Supreme Court's] most famous decisions in which it rules that laws were unconstitutional can be explained as instances in which the Court, or at least a majority of its members, were satisfied that there were alternate policies available to the Governments involved in those cases which would have interfered with

important aspects of human freedom less." David Beatty, "The End of Law: At Least as We Have Known It" (University of Toronto, 1990 [unpublished]), cited in H. Stewart, "What Is a Social Critic? Or the End of Beatty (At Least as We Have Known Him)", *University of Toronto Faculty of Law Review*, 49 no. 1 (1991): 189.

81. *Ford v. Quebec (Attorney General)*, [1988] 2 S.C.R. 712 (hereinafter *Ford*). The Court held that the Charter of the French Language, R.S.Q., chap. C-11, did not impair freedom of expression as little as possible:

> whereas requiring the predominate display of the French language, even its marked predominance, would be proportionate to the goal of maintaining a French "visage linguistique" in Quebec, and therefore justified under the Quebec Charter and the Canadian Charter, requiring the exclusive use of French has not been so justified. French could be required in addition to any other language or it could be required to have greater visibility than that accorded to other languages. (780)

See also *Irwin Toy, supra*, note 22, where the Court commented on *Ford*, stating that the government failed to introduce any evidence "to show that the exclusion of all languages other than French was necessary to achieve the objective of protecting the French language" (999).

82. *Edmonton Journal, supra*, note 80.

83. *R. v. Seaboyer*, [1991] 2 S.C.R. 577, 626. (Justice McLaughlin).

84. *Supra*, note 55 at 775.

85. Ibid., 772-773.

86. Ibid., 782.

87. Ibid., 795.

88. *United States of America v. Cotroni*, [1989] 1 S.C.R. 1469, 1489 (hereinafter *Cotroni*). In support of this view, he cited *R. v. Jones*, [1986] 2 S.C.R. 284, 300; *Edward Books, supra*, note 55 at 768, 769, 772. Justice LaForest, speaking for the majority in *Cotroni*, held that section 6 (mobility right) was infringed as little as possible by the extradition of a Canadian citizen to the United States.

89. *Cotroni*, ibid.

90. *Supra*, note 6 at 993-994.

91. Ibid., 994. Also see Elliot, *supra*, note 63 at 146-147.

92. [1993] 3 S.C.R. 519.

93. Ibid., 563.

94. (1991), 2 S.C.R. (4th) 1. The impugned legislation was section 16(4) of the Criminal Code, the presumption of sanity, which the challengers argued was contrary to section 11(d) of the Charter (the presumption of innocence).

95. Ibid., 31.

96. Ibid., 33.

97. Ibid., Justice McLaughlin, in *R.J.R.-MacDonald*, affirmed this principle. *Supra*, note 49 at 342-343.

98. *Chaulk, supra*, note 94 at 32-33.

99. *Supra*, note 26 at 1137, Chief Justice of the Court Dickson emphasized that the Fraser Committee and the Justice and Legal Affairs Committee had presented many alternatives that were considered less effective than the legislation in question (1137-1138). Justice Lamer reiterated this view and further stated that because prostitution is "an especially contentious and at times morally laden issue", the Court has an obligation to defer to the choice Parliament made after it weighed the "competing political pressures" (1199). Chief Justice of the Court Lamer reiterated this position in *Rodriguez* and cited the *Prostitution Reference*, when he stated that assisted suicide may also be seen as "contentious" and "morally laden" requiring a certain amount of deference toward the state's choice of policy options (564; Justice Sopinka concurring, 614). However, Chief Justice of the Court Lamer still found that section 241(b) of the *Criminal Code*, which prohibited aiding a person to commit suicide, failed the least drastic means test as it "encompass[ed] not only people who may be vulnerable to the pressure of others but also persons with no evidence of vulnerability" (567).

100. *Prostitution Reference*, ibid., 1138. Madam Justice Wilson, in her dissent, adopted a hard-line approach to the least drastic means test when she asserted that prohibiting any and all means of communication with a person in a public place for the purpose of prostitution was broad and overinclusive, as it could criminalize even communication for a lawful purpose (1210-1211). See also D. Stuart, "Will Section 1 Now Save Any *Charter* Violation? The Chaulk Effectiveness Test Is Improper", *C.R.* 2 (1991), (4th): 111.

101. [1991] 2 S.C.R. 22, 44.

102. *Supra,* note 24 at 140.

103. Ibid.

104. [1987] 1 S.C.R. 460 and [1990] 3 S.C.R. 229, respectively. Justice Laforest, for the majority in *McKinney,* concluded that it was "evident" from his analysis of the minimal impairment test that the effects of the university's mandatory retirement policy did not outweigh the objective and that "the same factors have to be balanced in dealing with deleterious effects and I need not repeat them" (289).

105. *Supra,* note 48 at 615. Justice Sopinka speaking for the majority, felt that no analysis was necessary as "[i]t follows from the above [analysis of the least drastic means test] that I am satisfied that the final aspect of the proportionality test, balance between the restriction and the government objective is also met".

106. *Supra,* note 19.

107. Ibid., 181.

108. *Supra,* note 11 at 23.

109. Ibid., 24.

110. P. Blache, "The Criteria of Justification Under Oakes: Too Much Severity Generated Through Formalism", *Manitoba Law Journal,* 20 (1991): 443.

111. *Kerans, supra,* 570, note 61.

112. *Oakes, supra,* note 45 at 137. Chief Justice Dickson points to the word "demonstrably" as indicating that the burden of proof will be shouldered by those wishing to limit the Charter right.

113. Ibid. The Court did not adopt the more onerous criminal standard of "proof beyond a reasonable doubt" because "concepts, such as "reasonableness", "justifiability" and "free and democratic society" are simply not amenable to such a standard." However, section 1 demands a very high degree of probability, considering that the party is attempting to justify an infringement of a right guaranteed by the Charter (138). It is interesting to note that in *Andrews, supra,* note 12, Justice Wilson for the majority, seemed to indicate that the weight of the burden of proof would vary according to which section of the Charter has been infringed: "Given Section 15 is designed to protect those groups who suffer social,

political and legal disadvantage in our society, the burden resting on government to justify the type of discrimination against such groups is appropriately an onerous one" (154).

114. *Supra,* note 55 at 768-769.

115. *Keegstra, supra,* note 6 at 737. Chief Justice Dickson writing for the majority.

116. *Andrews, supra,* note 5 at 198.

PART II

Colonialism

4

"Obnoxious Border Customs": A Catalyst for Federation

JEFF BROWNRIGG

The earliest stirrings of Australian federalism occurred in the 1850s as the colonies divided. Driven at first by a desire to abolish the transportation of convicts, and having achieved success in this matter throughout the continent by the late 1860s, colonists turned their attention to the meaning of borders. How might these changes affect the trading relationships of people who had, in the past, been able to cross the Murray in order to trade between what had become New South Wales and the new colony of Victoria? An emerging paradox was clear. The creation of borders forced those who lived along them to discover the difficulty of feeling no different from people in another colony, forcing the recognition that European Australians were, in most respects, one people. The emerging codification customs duties presented another picture. There were different rules in different colonies and it was this issue more than any other that initially carried Australia toward federalism.

It was an issue that encouraged formal and informal discussion and, not surprisingly, quickly focussed on the need for colonies to draft individual constitutions. What did these colonists know about making constitutions? Could it be reasonably assumed that they knew something? In northern Tasmania, a pioneering newspaper delivered what it thought the local people required to make an informed decision about their future.

Australian Colonies Search for Constitutional Precedents

The *Launceston Examiner* for May 24, 1853 carried the first instalment of a draft Canadian Constitution, together with a preamble setting out an overview of the general structure of Canadian government. "In this constitution", argued the writer of the preamble, probably the Reverend John West,[1] "it will be evident that all real power rests with the representative assembly, elected by the people". For the *Examiner* the issues were clear. How might the Tasmanian people maximize their power? How might their will be politically applied and what sort of assembly might best represent their needs and desires?

John West, (if it was West, and this seems almost certain) pressed the issue in the *Examiner*, publishing, for example, a complete draft of a constitution for New Zealand[2] as well as ideas drawn from proposals for a constitution for Cape Colony. Through the *Examiner* West pursued his goal of providing readers with the sort of information they would need to make intelligent, informed choices about their destiny. The particular emphasis he put on this information had evolved over time. A Congregationalist minister, he came to Australia in 1839 from a depressed rural region in England where he had ministered to poor rural workers in East Anglia. In the early 1840s he became an active, vocal member of the Tasmanian Anti-Transportation League. A successful intercolonial conference of anti-transportationists held in Melbourne in 1850 adopted the motto "The Australians Are One". The idea and the language of an Australian federal union emerged, encouraged by commentators such as West.

A successful and influential public speaker, West (by 1853) was well established as the editor of the *Examiner*. Fanning the winds of change with his leading articles, in August of that year he published a draft Tasmanian Constitution to which was appended a dot point summary of the areas that were the fundamental concerns of nation builders.

It is not clear just how much the publication of the Canadian and other drafts affected popular thinking, although newspapers and politicians continued to refer to Canada in the lead-up to the referendum of 1898-99, suggesting areas of constitutional thinking that an Australian constitution might examine, accept or reject. But the formulation of constitutions for individual colonies was undertaken with reference to existing precedents such as the Canadian one, and with energy generated by popular movements such as the anti-transportation leagues of the

1840s and 1850s and their antecedents. The actual transition from colony to state took more than 50 years, the popular controversy no longer transportation after the mid-1850s, when transportation to the eastern Australian colonies ceased to be a serious issue. By the middle 1860s the abolition of border customs replaced transportation as a popular cause, raising the issue of the need for an Australian federation once again.

Accounts of Early Australian Federalism

Commentators have tended to neglect the earlier history of Australian federalism by focussing upon the end of the 19th century. This has skewed our understanding and, apparently, our willingness to cite records of Australian federalism before 1880s. Perhaps John Ward's *Earl Grey and the Australian Colonies*, a benchmark in this area of scholarship, as it was in 1958, continues to discourage a fresh examination. Ward commenced his chapter "The Anti-Felon Confederation" with a powerful epigraph drawn from the *SA Register* of November 19, 1850:

> "That federation of the Australian colonies which Earl Grey could not accomplish by legislation, a common concurrence against a common danger seems likely to achieve."

Popular movements in the middle part of the century included Launceston's Anti-Transportation League (after March 1844, its goals reaffirmed on January 24, 1849). Contemporary movements with similar goals were the Victorian Anti-Transportation Association (Melbourne, September 1850), the New South Wales Association for Preventing the Revival of Transportation (Sydney, September 16, 1850) and the Australian League for the Abolition of Transportation (Melbourne, February 1851). Toward the end of the century the issues identified as a "common danger" had changed, the Women's Christian Temperance Union, for example, carrying much of the burden of what would become universal suffrage. But in the period between these popular movements, other "common dangers" emerged as the colonies, some of them already asserting a powerful sense of their separate identity, came to grips with differences engendered by borders and (often) distant colonial legislatures.

The lead taken by Launceston and the Reverend John West probably stimulated the formulation of the earliest draft of an Australian federal constitution. It was made by William Smith O'Brien and published in the *Launceston Examiner* in 1853. I have made a case for Smith O'Brien elsewhere: in essence, his interest at this time grew out of discussions with Michael Fenton (also an Irishman) who became the member for New Norfolk in the first Tasmanian Parliament and who was on the drafting committee for the first Tasmania Constitution.[3] Smith O'Brien knew Charles Gavan Duffy well and between them they generated an extensive correspondence. Gavan Duffy, like Smith O'Brien, was an Irish nationalist, editor/writer of polemical pieces for *The Nation* and an 1848 Irish rebel. With good reason John Ward calls Duffy "the first advocate of Australian Federation who deliberately set out to cultivate national feeling and use it in order to promote federal union".[4] The true position is less clear. We need to add, for example, that Smith O'Brien not only published ideas for a federal constitution in 1853 but also proselytized among Tasmanians. With the publication of his *Principles of Government or Meditation in Exile* in Dublin in 1856, his political theories were disseminated to a much wider audience before Duffy articulated similar ideas (after 1857). Like O'Brien before him, Duffy had joined the British House of Commons in 1852 soon after the British Government reduced the level of animosity it had initially directed toward the 1848 Irish rebels. He watched with interest various debates and the passage of legislation that followed the enactment by the British Parliament of the Australian Colonies Government Act of 1850. He was especially taken with the various constitution bills of 1855 and suggested, later, that the promise of a fresh start and boundless opportunity for nation building attracted him to Australia in 1856. He left Ireland too early to bring with him to Australia Smith O'Brien's political treatise. Smith O'Brien was, by this time, back in Europe but his Australian legacy was already tangible.

There were, then, at least two distinct channels of federalist energy evident as the colonies secured individual identities. Anti-transportation movements focussed one of these streams but faded with the cessation of large-scale transportation after the 1840s. The second stream was generated by the forces anticipated in the thinking of Smith O'Brien and Gavan Duffy.

Smith O'Brien's Australian Constitution

Smith O'Brien proposed 15 areas of shared concern for the Australian colonies.[5] His list of issues that would need to be addressed in a federal constitution is headed by "border/intercolonial tariffs". As the 1860s progressed, tariffs became an issue of serious concern for people along the northern and southern banks of the Murray. (Once the Murray developed eastern and western banks and was enveloped by South Australia, the problem no longer existed). Attempts to find a collective method of dealing with customs rose and fell, like the river, from year to year and would continue to be a problem throughout the later 19th century.

Colonial legislatures were established in the mid-1850s and with them the borders and differences that Smith O'Brien imagined might lead to trouble. These differences in customs duty payable, together with perceived tardiness and suspected lack of interest in matters outside Sydney and to a lesser degree away from Melbourne, resulted in frustration and incomprehension, especially along the Murray River. The high levels of feeling, festering as they did as the 1850s, changed in the 1860s into genuine popular political action and a call for agitation along the Murray. This action foreshadowed the methodologies of the Australasian Federal Leagues and was conceived well before December 1892 by David Arnott, the blacksmith at Yarrawonga, possibly in collaboration with Alexander Sloane, a farmer from Savernake and Mulwala. Within a couple of months, new, vigorous League branches developed along the Murray and in the Riverina. Edmund Barton, sometimes touted as the father of these leagues, established the Sydney branch on July 23, 1893, shamed, according to one commentator, by the vigour and determination of the border-region branches, 15 of which predated Barton's Sydney group.[6] The differences between the bodies established in the 1860s and those of the 1890s present an incremental adjustment of vision but, initially at least, exactly the same impetus. The passion for unity, the insistence that Australians were one people, even the stirrings and subsequent outright rejection of republicanism were all there in the meetings and the rhetoric of the 1860s. The call for the abolition of border customs became loud and insistent along the Murray, the most densely settled border.

Border Customs Abolition Leagues

The first Border Customs Abolition League was convened in Albury toward the end of 1866, although there is much evidence of concern in other places over a long period. The League's intention was to identify and rectify the problems presented by what a delegate at the Corowa's People Convention of 1893 – an event precipitated as much by discontent caused by cross-border trade as any other issue – called "these obnoxious

Customs duties. (Hear, hear)".[7] In 1866, disgruntled citizens of Albury set about enlisting widespread regional support.

The aims of the League were clearly explained to a largely sympathetic gathering by Albury citizens S.F. Blackmore and George Mott when they addressed a public meeting at Echuca on December 15, 1866. This was one in a series of town meetings intended to widen support for the League throughout the border country. An earlier spirited assembly, on December 12, had established Echuca's enthusiasm to embrace the League's agenda, preparing the way for the upriver emissaries and to some degree pre-empting their call. The people of Echuca (in Victoria) and its sister community Moama (in New South Wales) brought the matter to a head for themselves, calling local people together to support the Albury visitors. Echuca's *Riverine Herald* for December 12, summarized the call to arms from Blackmore and Albury as well as a summary of the League's concerns:

> Firstly, the shutting out of local producers from markets heretofore available to them, by a tariff equalling the full value of the articles they produce; thereby throwing upon their hands the crops of the previous years, and rendering them unable to employ the requisite labour to develop the full resources of the soil and climate.
>
> Secondly, the taxation of all articles of consumption at a rate so exorbitant as to amount in many cases to double taxation; thereby still further impoverishing those whose ruin had been nearly accomplished, in preventing them by prohibitive duties from selling their products.
>
> Thirdly, the scarcity of employment, the scarcity of money, the extinction of local industries and the general decline in all interests, caused by the double hardship of cutting off incomes at the same time increasing taxation of the people of the border districts.

Blackmore and Mott came to Echuca to illustrate these three general points with graphic stories from other places, some collected on their progress from Albury. They would reinforce what people already knew, adding to the local catalogue of outrageous incidents with stories drawn from other border communities. As a precaution, prepared motions were planted with local League Committee members. Clearly there had been a high level of informal communication and preparation before each public meeting. Audiences were usually overwhelmingly in favour of what was forcefully proposed: the abolition of border duties and – although it was not official policy of the League and generally not popular at Echuca – the possible abolition of the system of bonded stores. Regardless of this unexpected general concern, there was little dissension, the single exception being a challenge from Echuca auctioneer Jem (Jim) Shackell. Shackell was alarmed by a number of things he heard from what he considered these upriver interlopers. He approved of the bonded stores system and desired no change. When Mott, for example, hinted that in the event of negotiations with Sydney and Melbourne breaking down, some violent action might provide the leverage necessary to effect a change, Shackell could hardly contain himself. Clearly Mott envisaged an armed rising, an option apparently favoured by the German community of Albury. In 1867, this group, with a powerful separate identity and its own subbranch of the League, took part in an Albury street march in Prussian military uniforms. Mott tempered the idea of open revolt with examples that must have stirred both republican and contemporary racist sentiment, although Blackmore, contradicting his partner, insisted that it was the League's job to secure a peaceful way of achieving its goal:

> Some Albury residents were not of such a pacific way of thinking as others, and proposed violent remedies and these persons adduced in support of their argument Magna Charta [*sic*], the decapitation of the first Charles, and the colonial history of Ballarat [Eureka rising, 1854] and Lambing Flat [the anti-Chinese riots of 1861 under the banner of the Miner's Protective League]. This, the holding of these turbulent spirits back, was a task of the League.[8]

One of the Albury visitors' stories bordered on farce with a tincture of personalizing to engage sympathy as well as to amuse:

> It is not going too far to say that if a resident of Moama died in Echuca and wished to be buried in the former place, a package duty would have to be paid on his coffin, and an *ad valorem* duty on his body. Failing the payment the Customs Officer would keep him for a month, according to the act, and advertise the sale of the lot by public auction.[9]

Jem Shackel bristled with indignation. The meeting at Echuca on December 15 was not the first time he had raised objections to the League's agenda. His opinions were obviously well known and not recently formed. On December 12, on the morning of the first Echuca meeting, *The Riverine Herald* carried a poem clearly intended for singing and based upon the Victorian children's song "Who Killed Cock Robin". It failed to become a local anthem regardless of its sombre resonances and ringing last verse.

Original Verses Anent the Border Duties Question

Who'll put the League down?
I, said Jem Shackell,
With my crow and cackle,
I'll put the League down.

Who'll help Jem Shackell?
I, said Fred Payne,
For my ends and gain,
I'll help Jem Shackell.

Who'll tackle Shackell?
I, said Bill Disher,
The peoples well-wisher,
I'll tackle Shackell!

Who'll back Bill Disher?
I, said E Homan,
I'd have you know man,
I'll back Bill Disher!

Who'll stand by Homan?
We the community,
Firm and with unity,
We'll stand by Homan!

And so they did. At the public meeting with the Albury delegates Jem stressed that the system of tariffs was just and equitable and that Mott, in particular, was simply a gifted orator whose "little stories [such as the one about the duties on a corpse] would have reflected great credit on any low comedian [*sic*] on a provincial stage". It was the familiar call of the status quo: if it ain't broke, don't fix it. But the League prevailed in Echuca. Bill Disher, who is mentioned in the Shackell song, moved the first resolution: "That this meeting cordially approve of the steps taken by the Border Customs Abolition League to procure the abolition of Border Customs and reiterate [*sic*] its determination to support the League". In speaking to the motion, he indicated that too much praise could not be given to Albury for her exertions in this matter. The resulting cheers affirmed the League's next step.

A second resolution followed: "That inasmuch as local agitation has hitherto proved unsuccessful it is hereby resolved that the subject be ventilated in Melbourne and Sydney by mean of a deputation appointed to communicate with both Governments." Jem Shackell proposed an amendment calling for a Royal Commission, the amendment was put and lost and the second resolution carried in its original form "amidst great cheering". Blackmore then read the League's draft petition intended for presentation to the Legislative Assembly of New South Wales. It was all carefully orchestrated and meticulously controlled but it had grown out of popular concern and more than this, it was taken forward in individual communities by people who were blacksmiths or butchers or farmers.

For the guests from Albury the situation was clear. Politicians in general, and Colonial Secretary Henry Parkes in particular, could not be trusted to understand and respond to the needs of border/country folk. Parkes fulsomely paraded his apparent interest, sympathy and support when he visited Albury. Once he was back in Sydney, he quickly forgot the cause. His promises were hollow. The Albury delegation and its carefully planned progress drumming up support in the principal population centres put beyond doubt the seriousness of the issue and the determination of local people to solve it. There was a glimmer of the familiar dichotomy of the city and the bush: Sydney and Melbourne were distant and haughty, the Riverina imbued with common sense and practical pastoral wisdom. It was a divide that emerged again in the 1890s in exchanges such as those between the poets Paterson and Lawson in the pages of the *Bulletin*: "the bush'll never suit you, And you'll never suit the bush"Paterson concluded in what appears to have been a staged disagreement where Lawson upheld city values. They felt neglected, identified ignorance of and, perhaps, indifference to their plight. The League needed to make its case in Sydney and in Melbourne. But the number of concerned petitioners needed to be large. The lobby group must be credible and representative of a substantial concerned community, displaying where possible widespread local municipal support.

On December 12, the day of the preliminary meeting at Echuca before the visit of the Albury delegates, the *Deniliquin Chronicle* concluded an article about "The Albury League" by setting out a source of discontent in the district:

> The Riverine population, interested in forms of industry other than those of a direct pastoral character, are now sufficient in number to take a considerable share in political movements. And if these, in conjunction with the pastoral tenants could but meet on a common platform and develop a liberal programme of well recognized principles, *the combined energy and intelligence of the Border people would soon be more than equal to the trickery and indifference of Sydney and Melbourne.*[10]

It was a conviction shared by many people.

Having canvassed opinion along the Murray River and in the more populous centres in the Riverina, determining the level of support they might demonstrate to politicians in Melbourne and Sydney, the League's Central Committee convened a special meeting at Albury in the Lecture Hall of the Mechanics Institute for January 16, 1867. Two appointed delegates from each branch of the League were called to assemble at 3 p.m. and in the evening (at 7:30) there was a "Public Meeting of Inhabitants" at the Exchange Theatre. Alexander Sloane, who had chaired the foundation meeting of the League at Mulwala's Hill's Hotel, did not go to Albury as requested. On December 11, 1866, with Blackmore and Mott present, Sloane presided over a gathering where "the facts adduced by local men showed in a very forcible manner the prejudicial effect of Customs in this portion of the district". In Sloane's place a Mr. D. Reid from Mulwala, who was not a Mulwala Committee member, went to the Albury meeting. But feelings ran high at Mulwala. The Reverend Ware, in a manner not unlike the Reverend West of Launceston, speaking as the mover of the second motion (common to all of Blackmore and Mott's meetings, the "comprehensive agitation" motion), had first addressed the issue of the possible annexation of the Riverina by Victoria. He continued:

> As to customs, he thought [the people of the region] wanted uniform tariff, so that once landed in any part of the continent could be sent across to Carpentaria or anywhere else. He was in favour of a modified system of separation so as to cut up the whole country into convenient sized *states* and to unite these under one Federal Government. By this mean they could have one tariff, one postal system &c.
>
> Mulwala (and Yarrawonga) had suffered the particular indignity of not having a customs capability. Stories of a New South Wales farmer having to drive from Yarrawonga, eastward across the Ovens River and on to Wahgunyah (almost 50 kilometers) in order to cross the border legally at Corowa and then having to drive down the New South Wales side of the River to his home at Mulwala (21 kilometers) were not uncommon.[11]

It was hardly surprising that colonial parliaments noticed the growing discontent. The separation of the Riverina or, worse, its annexation by Victoria were, in New South Wales at least, intolerable thoughts. In fact, things would get much worse. At Denilquin, during the visit of Blackmore and Mott, an attempt had been made to move an unexpected and unwelcome motion "that border customs questions had no interest for the people of Deniliquin".[12] It was seconded but quickly defeated, with the mover, Mr. Filson, leaving the meeting in high dudgeon. "The usual resolutions proposed at all meetings of the League were", the local paper noted, "carried unanimously". Deniliquin recognized its affiliations with and dependence on the border and Victorian markets and marketing infrastructure. A railway line through Moama, Echuca and Bendigo linked Deniliquin to Melbourne. The line reinforced a perception that Sydney remained a remote entity, different in its way of thinking and out of touch with country folk, regardless of its stature and responsibility as Colonial Capital. But Deniliquin, too, was not represented in Albury for the League's Conference.

It was in the Junction Hotel at Moama, a stone's throw from that vital and symbolic rail link to Melbourne, that the League met (December 14) on the evening before the Echuca gathering and included the usual addresses from Blackmore and Mott: "Numbers of grievances of a most galling and oppressive character were exposed". But later, regardless of the depth of the wounds exposed on the 14 December, Moama selected Mr. Moffit from Albury as its nominee, citing distance as a factor in its absence from the Albury meeting. That might have been true, but on

January 12, a Memorandum of Agreement between New South Wales and Victoria was signed off in Melbourne by representatives from both colonies. This had the effect of deflating the significance and hence the drawing power of the Albury meeting scheduled for January 16, obviously reducing attendance and, in some degree, enthusiasm. Blackmore had announced the impending Melbourne Inter-Colonial Customs Conference (New South Wales and Victoria only) in his address to the people of Deniliquin on December 12. By that time he and Mott had spoken in several other places between Albury and Echuca but they were not moved to cancel further meetings. It must have been a difficult decision but clearly they chose to continue to gather support in the event that the proposed January 12 meeting fail to materialize or to achieve what they would have considered a reasonable outcome.

The League's origin in Albury, the improvement in its resources and infrastructure there (reported in *The Border Post* on November 5, 1866), its willingness to provide leadership and its clear tactical and strategic skill all supported Albury as the site for what at first appeared to be a meeting of considerable significance. Accounts of the Albury meeting of January 16 note that representatives came from Albury, Bungowannah, Corowa, Eight Mile Creek, the Albury German Committee (without their Prussian uniforms), Howlong, Mulwala and Wodonga, with nominees from Albury for Echuca, Moama and Mullengandra. It must have disappointed the organizers, who were probably resigned to receiving a smaller group than might have been expected had New South Wales and Victoria not acted to make changes. New arrangements for customs had been agreed to by the two colonial governments and it was expected that these would be in place within weeks. They were projected for February 1, 1867. This intelligence was quickly conveyed to the citizens of Albury on the day the decision was made in Melbourne. With an unmistakable smell of damp ashes, the Albury meeting went ahead, with sittings over two days that moved through the motions ensuring that the League's interests continued to be served. *The Albury Border Post* (January 23) noted:

> It is as well we should be prepared for any emergency, and therefore we are glad to notice that the League and the Congress are still vigilant on behalf of the public interests.

This was not the end of the problem. Echuca's celebratory bonfire and its ambiguously separatist call for a speech from their own "King Hopwood" (the town's founder – Echuca was originally Hopwood's Punt/Ferry) were premature. More difficulties would follow in the coming decades yet the League had proved that audible, popular agitation could bring colonial parliaments together. Also, many ideas that would surface later as important issues for federationists germinated in the hothouse of this spirited response to border tariffs. One of the shortcomings of the League's achievements was flagged in Albury after the publication of an article from *The South Australian Register* concerning South Australia's discontent with the Melbourne Memorandum. Appended to the *Register*'s piece was a riposte from the editor of the *Albury Border Post*:

> This may be [Chief Secretary of Victoria] Mr. McCulloch's notion as to the best way of bringing about federation, but it looks like the first deliberate attempt to place the two larger colonies in bitter opposition to the smaller one.
>
> (South Australia has only herself to blame. She had timely notice of the intention to hold the Inter-Colonial Conference, and her Government thought it a matter of so small importance that they refused to send delegates until some time after the treaty was agreed to. People who allow judgement to be against them by default, cannot reasonably complain of the verdict. Ed. B.P.)[13]

It was an argument from the smaller colonies that would ring out again in the 1890s, but the *Post*'s rejoinder was of the sort that smaller colonies would later heed. And by the 1890s Victoria and New South Wales had heightened levels of awareness of the need to keep the smaller colonies happy.

Border Customs in the 1890s

The generation of the 1890s included James Sloane of Mulwala (son of Alexander), who, gazing south across the Murray, could see the flour mill at Yarrawonga. To his chagrin, it was still cheaper for him to transport his wheat to the north rather than pay border duty on each bag. His generation must have heard about the stirrings of 1866 from their parents, who would have described the mobilization of popular opinion among the "borderers". The extent to which the League was directly responsible for the Memorandum of January 12, 1867 is not yet clear, but it is fair to say that they were noticed. More than this, the League established a modus operandi that would result in the most important of all of the federation gatherings, the People's Federal Convention, at Corowa in 1893. The motivating force for the Corowa meeting was, without question, the hated border duties. It drew in this new generation who continued to suffer what they considered an illogical, iniquitous and in some respects random dividing line that followed the Murray's south bank.

Other things came out of the League. The idea of being a single people with a shared destiny is there in the assumptions that the same rule should apply to people on both sides of the Murray River. "Unity" is used in much the same way in 1866 as it would be in the 1890s. The citizens of Echuca heckled Shackell. This was a community standing together in a just cause ("firm and with unity") claiming the same ground as those who in 1899 used Melbourne's *People's Federation Songbook* and roared in unison, "Unity is strength". The League gave rise to sentiments more usually associated with events 30 years in the future. As the dust settled after the Inter-Colonial Conference and the League's Albury Anti-Customs Conference of 1867, the editor of the *Border Post* mused about what the future might hold, discovering metaphors to reflect his enthusiasm:

> It may seem presumptuous for an inland community like ours to bind the whole continent of Australia by its operations but it appears to us that we must now go in for nothing less than FEDERAL UNION, with the proviso that the Riverina should be formed into a sovereign *State*, having a local legislature of her own.
>
> Federation be it then! The League must extend its Branches throughout the colonies and, of course, must change its name. A little leaven will leaven the whole lump, and when the small snowball, by constant rolling, has become an avalanche, its further progress will be irresistible.[14]

An anonymous letter to the editor of the *Border Post* on December 19, 1866, dealing mainly with "separationism" and "annexation" and pointing to the flaws in argument for both, concluded with sentiments that hint at a sympathy for North America and her solution to colonialism.

> Unity! Ah! that is our remedy. Therein lies the secret of our future welfare.
>
> Union is strength. By such alone we may hope to make of this our adopted country one truly great, that our children some day, may well feel proud of the United States of Australia.

Toward a More Complete Genealogy of Australian Federation

In the 1860s, colonial borders came to symbolize the sturdy independent character of the emerging colonies. By 1893, almost 30 years later, they remained potent symbols of the deeply felt discontent and rancour, especially along the Murray River. Breaking down some of the barriers between the colonies, allowing their independent spirits to flourish without destroying the integrity of individuality was quickly recognized as crucial in an Australian union and remains so. The Reverend John West moved from Launceston, taking up the position of first editor of the *Sydney Morning Herald* on November 16, 1854. In this capacity he was able to continue his campaign for colonial union from Sydney and published a series of 18 articles under the general rubric "Union Among the Colonies" and using the resonant pseudonym "John Adams". West passed on a solid tradition of support for federal union to the paper's second editor, Andrew Garran, who in turn imbued his son Robert with a powerful commitment to federalism. The young Robert Garran not only helped to draft the present Constitution, but in 1901 he wrote what is still considered the most illuminating commentary on the Australian Constitution's evolution and meaning. The lineage is clear. The roots of West's thinking were buried deep in the issues that provoked Australian colonists to find their own way, to establish whatever society they could imagine.

Another line through Smith O'Brien to Charles Gavan Duffy and then Andrew Inglis Clark also leads inexorably to Robert Garran and the other drafters of the Constitution. Garran and Duffy's son (who was also Charles Gavan Duffy) were the last two people to polish the Australian Constitution draft that went to the printer on March 17, 1898, being presented to the Australian people later that year in a referendum. Without people such as West, it might not have happened or would certainly have taken longer. He presented his readers with the issues he thought important in a democratic society beginning to make its own way. Border customs, at the head of Smith O'Brien's list of what a federal Constitution would need to address, identified the issue that would, more than any other, make or break the Commonwealth. The severity of the difficulties that tariffs would bring took a decade to emerge, then seemed to be solved only to emerge again as virulent as before, remaining a running sore until uniform customs laws saw the old customs posts along intercolonial borders closed with the advent of federation. Like West, Blackmore and Mott, Arnott and Sloane and many others along the colonial borders who styled themselves "agitators", are the hidden fathers of federation. National significance was denied them, regardless of their energy. The emergence of Federation Leagues late in 1892 and the first months of 1893 established regional hubs. These would carry the federal cause forward, delivering to federalists in Melbourne and Sydney the opportunity to capitalize on clearly delineated issues, the rhetoric of union expressed in terms of tangible grievances and evident national support. Border tariffs, as much as any other issue and more than most, stimulated the push to federate.

Notes

1. West was near the end of his tenure in Launceston. He moved to Sydney to become the editor of the *Sydney Morning Herald* the following year, a position he held until 1873, when Andrew Garran, himself a committed and active federationist, succeeded him. Garran was the father of Robert Randolph Garran, Edmund Barton's lieutenant in the Sydney Branch of the Australasian Federation League after 1893. See John Reynolds, *Launceston: History of an Australian City* (Melbourne: Macmillan of Australia, 1969), and John Ward, *Earl Grey and the Australian Colonies, 1846-1867* (Melbourne: Melbourne University Press, 1958).

2. *Launceston Examiner*, (Saturday, June 18, 1853). Subsequent editions of the newspaper carried further instalments, concluding on June 30. On June 28, 1853 the editor noted: "We again give up the leading columns to the Act for the government of New Zealand. It is important it should be placed in the hands of the public, suggestive as it is of improvements in the Australian constitution".

3. See, for example, Jeff Brownrigg, "An Early Proposal for a Federal Constitution: William Smith O'Brien, Launceston, 1853", *The New Federalist: The Journal of Australian Federation History*, No. 4, (December 1999): 84-89.

4. See Ward, *Earl Grey*, 372 ff.

5. See Jeff Brownrigg , "An Early Proposal for a Federal Constitution", and John Andrew La Nauze, *The Making of the Australian Constitution*, (Melbourne: Melbourne University Press 1972): 293-294. Smith O'Brien posited half of what Inglis Clark proposed in this draft, including most of the crucial things incorporated into section 51 of the present Constitution.

6. A forthcoming paper first presented at the "Meeting the Challenges of the Border" conference at Albury, September 24, 1999, by historian Brendan O'Keefe explores this aspect of the emergence of the Federation Leagues.

7. See *Proceedings* of the People's Federal Convention Corowa, 1893, 26-29.

8. See *Riverine Herald*, 17 December 1866.

9. Ibid.

10. *Deniliquin Chronicle*, 12 December 1866.

11. "Mulwala" (from a Correspondent), The border Post, December 19,1866.

12. Report of Deniliquin Meeting 11 December 1866 reported in *The Albury Border Post*, 19 December 1866.

13. "Meeting at Deniliquin" (from the *Deniliquin Chronicle*), reported in T*he Border Post* December 19, 1866.

14. "The Border Treaty South Australia Omitted", *The Border Post*, February 20, 1867.

5

Planting British Legal Culture in Colonial Soil: Legal Professionalism in the Lands of the Beaver and Kangaroo

W. WESLEY PUE[1]

> *We are met here for the purpose of expressing the views which we take as our obligations as members of the Bar of the British Empire. It is first of all the Bar of Australia, but the traditions which we have had descended upon us from the Bar of Great Britain and if we recognize that and act upon those traditions we will never depart very far from the paths of rectitude... the first aim was to establish and vindicate the supremacy of the law.*

H. E. Manning, Address to the First Conference of Australian Legal Societies, 1933.[2]

The theme of "shaping nations" draws together a number of threads in contemporary historical, cultural and legal scholarship. It resonates deeply with important themes in the cultural histories of legal professions, in postcolonial studies and in comparative legal history.[3] Despite considerable scholarly interest in both imperialism and in the construction of national identities, there has been surprisingly little work on the role of law in relation to either. Law was, however, both the means and the end of Empire. Lawyers and *their* cultures were present at every level as Empire, colony, dominion and state formed in the British diaspora lands – including, of course, the United States.

In this essay I offer a preliminary exploration of the works of law in British Imperialism's project. It was centrally concerned with establishing the preconditions for the successful implantation of Britishness into new colonies: the preadaptation of its human subjects for eventual self-governance. Law and lawyers had a major role to play in this respect. This was a much harder task than merely wrestling land from its original occupants, harder even than asserting sovereignty against other "Christian princes". The colonies were remote and dangerous places.

I focus in particular on the attempt of a fraction of the organized legal professions to write Canada and Australia as "British" in certain key ways. I do not attempt to evaluate their success in either place. In fact, I don't even know how one would set about to do so.

Britishness

Any attempt to make sense of the processes by which Britishness was inscribed in Canada and Australia requires some appreciation of the British baseline.

In that regard, it is important to note that by the 19th century British Imperialists had absorbed a number of important lessons. Some were taken from "home" understandings of a remote charivari and its consequences. The Boston Tea Party and all that followed in the Americas permanently warped British Imperialism. Other lessons were learned closer to home in the French Revolution and in the various tensions within the United Kingdom. Still others were taken from the British anti-slavery campaigns, from problems of governance in Ireland, India or other parts of the Empire and from an evolving political culture at large. Jonathan Parry has commented, for example, on the lessons Lord John Russell derived from the radical political activity of English Chartists. Chartism, Russell thought, had arisen because the manufacturing population had grown up in appalling conditions, lacking "early instruction... places of worship" and the chance of having "their opinions of property moulded by seeing it devoted to social and charitable objects". It was to "religious and moral instruction" that one should look to "knit together the inhabitants and classes" and ensure "a fair and gradual subordination of ranks". Chartism heightened a need which to Liberals was already obvious – to supply a system of morality to accompany and enrich the rationalised system of order which [was] being established. The key battle to be fought in order to strengthen the state was the spread of "enlightened religious and moral principles". Hence the centrality of religious questions – of church, education and Irish reform – to Russell and like minds.

No equivalent period seemed to have taught more terrible lessons about human sinfulness than that since 1790. Liberty was endangered by infidelity, aristocratic luxury and working-class indiscipline.[4]

More broadly, developing literatures in many disciplines have pointed to important linkages between the seemingly disconnected spheres of projects relating to moral self-governance and larger state projects of establishing peace, order and good government within national or colonial territories.[5] The attainment of proper moral self-governance was the essence of Britishness. Its *substance* included all that the respectable British both at home and overseas valued, encompassing understandings of British history and constitutionalism, appreciation for the rule of law and social understandings over matters as diverse as table manners, conventions relating to marriage and child rearing, diet, dress, gender roles, sports, farming, high culture, popular culture, war and "character" among many, many others.

Dominion Deviations

Many British Canadians shared such concerns. From at least the time of Confederation in 1867, the hegemonic fraction of Canadian society sought to establish what Canadian historians call a "moral dominion". Their peculiar character as overseas British profoundly affected the exercise.

Colonial and dominion proto-state iconography serves to illustrate larger cultural currents flowing between and among the imperial centre and its colonies. Recurrent patternings of imagery underline a number of self-understandings that leaders of the various dominions came to share. A deep ambivalence lay at the core. While Canadians and Australians celebrated their Britishness, they aspired to more than derivative status. They refused to accept a future role limited to imitation of "home". As Angelika Sauer illustrates, the wattle and the maple came to symbolize widely held beliefs that "the fringes of the Empire, rather than its core, were becoming the locus of its greatness and that it was the progressive young nations that would carry the civilization of the future".[6]

Within the realm of state iconography this is nowhere clearer than in the representations appearing on British, Dominion and USA coinage. The reverse of British coinage typically invokes pageantry, royalty, history, symbols of royal power and imperial authority. When one surveys the coinage of former British colonies, however, zoology, botany and anthropology substitute for history. Wildlife, plants, "bush" or empty space and native peoples predominate. The imagery of coinage and bank notes in the dominions and former colonies include beavers, maple leaves, elk, voyageurs' canoes, loons, landscapes (in Canada), aboriginal motifs, kangaroo, platypus, images of aboriginal peoples (in Australia), "Indian heads", eagles, buffalo and so on (in the USA) and Maori designs or kiwi birds (New Zealand).[7]

One obvious point of all this is simply to underline a negative assertion of *what we are not*. We are not British. More accurately, perhaps, we are not *merely* British.

Establishing this with some degree of certainty and clarity was seen as the condition precedent to the development of any more rounded historical self-understanding of what colonial peoples are. The exotic zoology, botany and anthropology communicate the distinctiveness of the peoples and lands of the British diaspora both from "home" and one from another.

Nonetheless, an ongoing Britishness of sorts was always taken for granted by the respectable classes. No one actually wanted to be taken for aboriginal, African, Indian or French![8] Within what came to be known as the old Commonwealth, the obverse of coinage has always dramatically and unequivocally marked the Dominions' ongoing Britishness with a display of their common monarch's image.[9] As the most rebellious of Britain's children, USA could hardly explicitly endorse either royal inheritance or Britishness as such on its coins. Nonetheless, a celebration of the "freedom loving" traditions of the English-speaking peoples also pervades American self-understandings. Americans recorded their Europeanness explicitly by means of visual references to Greek architecture, Latin tags (E Pluribus Unum) and explicit invocation of Judaeo-Christian inheritances ("in God we trust"), among others.

Taken together, such iconography invokes themes of newness, freedom and strength developing from secure foundations: Britishness confronted with new circumstances, new challenges and new opportunities. The power of imagery and of place were linked through complex cultural slippages to then-prominent environmental determinist theories of geography and human evolution. The power and the freedom of indigenous animals or birds (the bald eagle, for example) provide a series of associations sustaining a faith in a future greater still than the past. And, make no mistake about it, the past of the "mother country" has been glorious. The elk, the kangaroo, the "Indian head", the beaver, the buffalo, the voyageurs' canoes invoke histories, associations and self-understandings of powerful, adventurous, daring, hard-working men. British virtue liberated from the confines of a small, overpopulated isle knew no bounds. Britishness was valued for its amalgam of heavily mythologized histories of humane empire, understandings of progress, faith in an ancient heritage of "free Britons", confidence in economic and military prowess, gentlemanliness, combined virtues of fidelity to inheritance and flexibility to confront the future and "fair play": in sum, British law.

If many feared Britain was in danger of race suicide, Canadians and Australians emphatically need not follow. In point of fact, in the decades spanning the turn of the last century, colonials simply would not keep in their place. John Kendle's remarkable book on *The Round Table Movement and Imperial Union*[10] demonstrates this clearly: a profound attachment to Imperial Union and a common Britishness co-existed with a distinct lack of deference to the mother country. To similar effect, Carl Berger describes "the customary attitude of Canadian imperialists to England" as admiring in many aspects but as being characterized by "a curious mixture of affection and anxiety, resentment and solicitude" and "very little of the deferential spirit". Respectful of their heritage, they were positively utopian in their expectations and it was exactly this overestimation of Canadian capacities which enabled them to believe that their country would become "the future centre and dominating portion of the British Empire".[11]

Establishing Dominion Leadership of British Civilization

If the leaders of the various British dominions perhaps "overestimated" their capacities to establish leadership of the Empire, they were nonetheless well aware of the challenges they faced. The dominions were, after all, very much a foreign space in every way.

The first challenge was obvious. The sheer space of the major dominions was daunting. Australia is huge, approaching the size of the United States.[12] Measuring some 7,682,300 square kilometers[13], it is equivalent in size to all of Western Europe and then some. Canada, at

9,970,610 square kilometers,[14] is 129 percent the size of Australia. The difference, relatively minor on the scale of these huge land masses, is not inconsequential by the standards of most other places. To make up Canada's size, Australia would need to acquire additional territory equivalent in size to more than the combined totals of France, Germany, Austria, the United Kingdom, Italy, Portugal and Spain.[15] *Everything* about land masses on this scale is complicated: exploration, mapping, settlement, defence, traversing it, communications, resource exploitation, trade, governance. Planting British civilization required massive investment in infrastructure and institutions – but the prior condition on which all rested was European settlement.

The problem of excessive space was compounded by the problems encountered when Imperial authorities or colonial leaders addressed the problem of filling the void: who was to live here? Where should they come from? And how could they be socialized? Canada, always under threat from its rebellious southern neighbour, perhaps felt particularly pressured to quickly fill its interior with European settlers, but Australia also felt the need. In both cases it was thought desirable to fill "empty continents" with the right kinds of people if only in order to prevent the "wrong" kind from filling the vacuum.

These were considerable challenges. The area that forms the contemporary Prairie Provinces of Manitoba, Saskatchewan and Alberta alone covers some 1,963,085 square kilometers (larger than the combined area of Germany, France and Spain in Europe or the U.S. states of Texas, New Mexico, Arizona and California – or approximately one quarter the size of Australia).[16] Faced with a need for huge numbers of immigrants and the ever-present threat of U.S. annexation, the Canadian government actively sought immigrant settlers in unorthodox places. Policies established by Clifford Sifton, the federal Minister of the Interior from 1896 to 1905, transformed Canada. Though Sifton shared common assumptions that "blacks, Italians, Jews, Orientals and urban Englishmen would not succeed on farms", his department otherwise actively encouraged a wide and diverse range of non-British to immigrate. An enormous influx of Eastern Europeans followed. Sifton's waves of immigrants transformed Prairie Canada. Population growth was explosive.[17]

Now, the attempt torecreate *instantly* the culture, institutions and ethos of another place is inherently problematic. The problems are all the more acute when new settlers come from somewhere other than the place whose culture, institutions and ethos one seeks to reproduce. Any new society lacks the cultural gravitational force that anchors "governance" in older societies. The dominions' organic intellectuals knew this full well. Both Australia and Canada felt pressured in this regard. On the one hand, the influx of settlers to the Canadian West illustrates the extent to which "the promise of the west became the promise of Canada".[18] At a cultural level, Canada sought "to reproduce" in the West "the best characteristics of Eastern Canadian life." More precisely, Old Canada viewed the West as a place in which the nation's mission was "if not to create a new Jerusalem, at least to build a better Ontario".[19] Sifton's immigration policies, however, rendered the region ethnically diverse, polyglot and altogether both "unBritish" and "unOntarian". At the outbreak of the First World War nearly half of the region's residents had been born in another country. The existing Prairie population traced its origins variously to First Nations, Métis, French, Québécois, British, American, or Icelandic ancestry. During the "Sifton" years and their aftermath they were joined by Germans, Poles, Scandinavians, Ukrainians, Hutterites, Mennonites, Jews, Doukhobours, Maritimers[20] and, of course, more British, Ontarians and Americans, among others. Huge ethnic block settlements developed. Even today, a "little Ukraine" stretches almost uninterrupted from near Winnipeg to the outskirts of Edmonton. The ethnic map of the rural Prairies, past and present, reveals a pattern of sizable, discrete, often barely overlapping ethnic block settlements. A trip through the region in 1920 or even as late as 1960 took the traveller through extensive areas where English was rarely spoken. T.C. Byrne reported that in 1937 "knowledge of Ukrainian [was] as indispensable" in east central Alberta "as French in Quebec or English in Ontario".[21] Icelandic, Cree, German, Dakota, Ukrainian, Sarcee, Polish, French, Swedish, Dene, Dutch and Russian, among others, predominated in other areas. By 1931 only about 50 percent of the population of the prairies claimed "British" origins.[22]

Social diversity begat legal pluralism. A multitude of "informal" legal regimes occupied this new Canadian space, even in its urban core. In some variants, alternative legalities were barely "informal" at all. Many First Nations communities remained significantly self-governing, living in accordance with their own norms, values, political structures and legal systems long after the colonial state formally asserted authority over them.[23] The same was true of most immigrant communities. Long after the Canadian state imagined itself to have asserted effective legal control over its entire territory, Doukhobours and Mennonites, for example, enjoyed territorial integrity, shared language, religion, ethnicity and distinct economic structures. Both groups were surprisingly resilient in sustaining "legal" systems that governed almost all aspects of life. They did so without deference to the Canadian state or its norms.[24]

Issue after issue, time after time and place after place, leaders of diverse communities across the Prairie region worked to preserve their "nationality". Religious organizations, alongside more secular forms of association, provided institutional habitats within which informal law flourished. A dense associational life existed. It was oriented, variously, around gender, ethnicity, religion, interests, debt, politics, business, sports, song, labour, cultural activities, economics and class. In the face of such diversity, Canada and Australia confronted the problem of securing Dominion Britishness for the future, of fashioning the moral dominion through a mixture of repressive and educational (or ideological) strategies.

Containing Diversity

The repressive policies of the two dominions are well known and well studied. These included racist immigration policies, eugenics programs, social welfare programs aimed as much at governance as economic subsistence, residential schools, prohibitions on First Nations political organization, temperance, discriminatory vice law enforcement, cultural policies aimed at the destruction of non-British cultures and so on. I need not labour these here. They are well known and well researched in both Canada and Australia.[25]

Many of the ideological strategies are equally well researched. A burgeoning of research on educational policies in both countries – both at the school level and elsewhere – is significant in this regard.[26]

Curiously, however, many researchers have overlooked another, central strategy for the incorporation of these foreign spaces and foreign peoples into a world-spanning Britishness: Law.

This cartoon appeared in the ***Vancouver Sun*** *on August 18, 1938. Captioned "Our Priceless Heritage", it illustrates the central role that colonists thought "British Law" played in the Imperial project.*

Eminent post colonial legal scholar Peter Fitzpatrick has argued that enlightenment European law actively defined itself in *opposition* to the "other".[27] In common with other Western legal regimes and in presumed contradistinction to the laws of the "other", British law makes peculiar claims to its own secular rationality.

Native law may amount only to "Khadi" justice. It may be irrational, inconsistent, corrupt, unwholesome, biased, unpredictable, founded on superstition or charisma, parochial, incompetently administered, primitive and unreliable. British law, however, defines itself *against* these. It represents itself as the accumulated wisdom of the ages, the pinnacle of civilization, the summit of liberty and the reconciliation of freedom with order. Superior even to the laws of other European peoples, British law has often appeared to its subjects as the key to "progress". A common juridical terrain resting on "a rational method, a unified science and an exact language" (misappropriating here Rorty's words[28]), British law was thought of as a very special social tool uniquely capable of transcending the fragmenting and destructive centrifugal forces of religion, class, ethnicity and locality. Viewed from within, the common law appeared to offer a truly transcendental secular rationality.[29]

This not inconsiderable gift had to be carefully transported, implanted and nurtured in foreign soils. Inconveniently, not all peoples were immediately preadapted to appreciate the liberties, freedoms and progress British law held out to them. Recalcitrant individuals and entire populations often failed to even perceive the superiority of British ways over their own superstitions and rituals – failed to understand that "[u]niversal becoming is the prerogative of the West".[30] And not all of the European immigrants to British colonies or indigenous French fully appreciated the superiority of British law either. In the early 20th century knowledge of the intrinsic superiority of British ways, the virtues associated with British law and confidence in the transformative vision of Empire virtually *defined* respectability. But many of the actual inhabitants of the dominions needed to be persuaded on all counts.

The task of transforming unruly peoples around the world into civilized individuals capable of assuming the privileges, rights and responsibilities of self-governance was the central mission of Empire. Complexly, British justice was both a tool used to achieve this result and the desired end itself. "Law" and Britishness were co-extensive, the apex of cultural evolution. "Law", like "English literature", studies sought nothing less than the transformation of souls.[31]

Law's Embodiment in Empire's Outposts

How, then, was law to reach into all the nooks and crannies of the two largest dominions? How was it to be planted in inhospitable soil, grafted onto exotic peoples? How was it to conquer individual souls? Canadian research about these matters is clearer than Australian, though a few indicators hint of equivalent processes at work. Crudely, lawyers' professional projects sought to constitute legal professionals as secular missionaries in the cause of civilization, rationality and righteousness. In a word, the objective was to make them zealots in the cause of Britishness. Transformed legal professionals were to carry their own Great Commission to the furthest reaches of the dominions, over time transforming all with whom they came into contact. In order to attain this, however, lawyers' souls, not just their minds, needed to be converted to a deep and abiding inner affinity with law's majestic project. Patterns of legal education were of central importance.

Before turning to the education of lawyers, however, one more connection must be made. That concerns the relationship between what lawyers thought – or what sort of men they were – and the law's integrative functions. At century's end it is difficult to perceive any connection at all between, for example, a belief that the substantive law should be anti-Bolshevist, British or whatever and an educational mission aimed at the preselection and gentlemanly socialization of lawyers. *Our* habits of thought intrude, creating the sense that a conceptual Berlin Wall of sorts exists between positive law (what the law is) and the personnel of the legal system (who the lawyers are). Separating these, we imagine that the substance of the law exists independently of the actions, values or thoughts of lawyers. In *our* world it seems logical to assume that, while "law" is very obviously made by judges and legislatures, ordinary lawyers are more or less irrelevant to the state of the law. Crudely, we tend to think of lawyers as mechanics of legality, picking bits of law off neatly arranged parts-shelves and sticking the parts where they need to go in order to serve the client's objective best interest. To call such a task value-neutral seems overly fancy: there are no values involved.

If we fail to perceive any connection between "law" and "lawyers", however, it may be that we suffer from too simple-minded a notion of law and law-work. In sharp contrast, the generation that developed the template for modern Canadian legal education was fully aware of law's embodiment, that it has no meaning whatsoever other than that which is absorbed, reflected by and exuded from lawyers.[32] University of Saskatchewan professor and lawyer Ira MacKay, for example, told the Alberta Law Society in 1913 that "[t]he law is what the consensus of legal opinion in the community believes it to be, first the judges, next the lawyers and finally the mass of intelligent laymen who direct the organized activities of the state".[33] Recognizing that law writ large is not self-enacting, does not implement itself, controls no one and influences nothing, MacKay's understanding of the social roles and functions of law approach those we now think of as legal pluralism.[34] The real law – living law – existed, he thought, in consensus of opinion. Without professional consensus both case-law and statute were mere abstractions ("Statute law is as much a creation of the judiciary and the lawyers as case law"[35]). Hence, British law was brought into place not by assertions of sovereignty or legal reception but rather as part of daily routine wherever lawyers acted. Its values were inculcated in the community at large as lawyers went about their work, participated in community life, acting as stabilizing influences in all their multitudinous individual formal or informal, big or small, legal interventions. Early 20th century legal reformers believed that order, community, State were the cumulative result of infinite, repeated, micro-level interventions:

> The lawyer's office is unquestionably the most important office in the community and that for the obvious reason that the lawyer is really the only man in the community who really makes it his business to understand the delicate and complex organization of government and law by which the community directs its activities for common ends. The state itself is an edifice constructed solely out of legal material. It is literally made of law.[36]

Clearly, if the state is made of law and "law" is made of professional "consensus", then it matters tremendously not only what lawyers know in their minds but also what they know in their hearts.[37] Informed gentlemen of MacKay's era felt that a consensus of legal opinion was necessary in order to "create the state; allow it to perish and peace, good order and good government must perish with it".[38] Professional consensus, in short, was the condition precedent to everything they held dear.

Clearly, the geographic and cultural circumstances of early 20th century Canada – huge spaces, a diverse and under-socialized population – militated against the development of professional consensus.[39] Professional consensus, indispensable yet seemingly incapable of spontaneous generation, had to be consciously transplanted, nurtured and developed if British civilization was to flourish in this new land (as Europeans considered it). Crudely and admittedly taking something of a shortcut through the logic involved, if the imminent demise of "peace, good order and good government" was the problem, then legal education was the answer.[40] Only the creation of the right kind of law schools could ensure a "uniform standard of legal opinion," a "professional consensus of opinion and a professional esprit de corps".[41]

Views such as MacKay's held sway among the most active and most influential Canadian lawyers in the years spanning the turn of the past century.[42] The law school mission was but one part of an all-encompassing professional project, oriented not toward economic monopoly nor even toward the pursuit of status as such, but toward pro-social goals. The project of ensuring a purity of mission and uniformity of focus among lawyers, recast now as secular evangelists in the cause of Britishness, spawned ethical codes and gave birth to the Canadian Bar Association, transformations of provincial law societies, monopoly protection and novel professional discipline regimes.[43]

If similar efforts existed whereby Australian lawyers attempted to remake their profession as part of a larger effort to "plant" Britishness safely in their soil the case has not yet been made out. There is, to be sure, a good deal of evidence pointing to apparently similar projects being in play and to parallel developments taking place in the antipodean dominion. The origins of the Queensland Law Society Inc. are found in a period when important professional restructuring was taking place in Canada and its early objectives resembled those of contemporary Canadian legal professions.[44] Similarly, the educational objectives of influential individuals and law teachers such as Jethro Brown, Samuel Way, W.E. Hearn or John Salmond, among many others, were akin to those of their Canadian counterparts. The University of Melbourne's first Dean of Law, W.E. Hearn, invoked themes familiar in Halifax, Montreal and Winnipeg when he stressed the need to teach students about Roman law and jurisprudence as a sort of inoculation against the corrupting influence of practice. The "undue regard to petty details and to mere machinery" that preoccupied lawyers' day-to-day lives tended, he thought, to produce "neglect of those great ends which these details and the machinery were meant to subserve".[45] Some such tradition persisted under his successors and was actively promoted nationally.[46]

The record of association building too suggests parallel trajectories at either end of the Pacific. A number of Australian lawyers worked toward creating a national organization and in doing so they employed languages of public service, of nation building and of professionalism similar to those of professional reformers in Canada. The Law Council of Australia emerged in 1936, just over two decades after the Canadian Bar Association was created. One of its founders, John G. Latham,[47] thought that one of the "most useful functions" of the legal profession was that of "providing legal, as distinct from political, criticism of the judgments and statutes which make the law under which the people of Australia live".[48] In an intriguing address to the First Conference of Australian Legal Societies in 1933 he spoke at length about the virtues of lawyers, their potential for service to the community and the noble ideals for which the profession had "always stood in a British community".[49] Echoes of the larger project of British diaspora lawyers also reverberate in Robert Menzies' view that "the future civilization" of Australia rested on "the purity and the independence of justice" and that "every member of the legal profession" had "a properly vested interest in maintaining that purity and that independence".[50] Again, L.O. Martin (then Minister of Justice for New

South Wales) spoke of the professions' obligation to preserve "legal authority in British communities". In cautioning that "we will not sustain that authority unless we show ourselves as worthy ministers to discharge that authority,"[51] he too seemed to make the preservation of civilization itself dependent upon the contours of legal professionalism. In a surprisingly frank assessment of the end result of the law and, inferentially, the objective of British civilization, Eugene Gorman asserted in 1936 that "the main purpose of the law has been the protection and preservation of those class-relations which result from the private ownership of the means of production". He called for a broad education of future lawyers in fields such as economics, sociology and social sciences. This, he thought, would help them to appreciate fully the necessity of containing social conflict by working to ensure that the gap between law's inertia and social progress did not become unmanageably great.[52]

Despite many such similarities of discourse, association building, project and vision, there do seem to be significant divergences between Canadian and Australian trajectories of legal professionalism. A much fuller professionalization project – or at least a much more successful one – developed in Canada. In part the difference can be gauged by reference to the traces forward from the shared ideals of the past. Australian lawyers today have very little sense of their profession as part of a tradition of British liberties, as a body that exerts collective influence for the community good or as a component of the division of labour which has special roles to play in relation to constitutional governance, freedom and liberty. Whereas the organized legal professions in common law Canada routinely pulls out all the stops in order to resist seemingly modest changes to the structures of their governance – always on the grounds that such changes would threaten the "independence of the bar" (and, by extension, the future of civilization itself),[53] Victoria lawyers had nothing at all to say when the legal profession in that state was effectively abolished as a self-governing profession.[54] Their professional publications spoke of technical concerns only. The ownership of property and the management of liability insurance, for example, registered large but no larger claims could be invoked in defence of the principle of self-governance.

If, as it seems, there is an important difference of kind or of degree here, this raises the question as to why legal professions in similar British dominions responded to the challenges of Empire in such different ways. Why did Canadian lawyers seem more directly concerned, more powerfully motivated to rework their profession with a view to sustaining the mission of inscribing Britishness?

Research in these areas is insufficiently advanced to permit any confident response. Taking the apparent divergence at face value, however, several hypotheses seem to merit further investigation. These relate to the relative insecurity of Britishness in Canada, the divisions of the Australian legal professions and the cultural assets of Canadian lawyers.

Britishness seemed far less secure in Canada in the first half of the 20th century than it did in Australia. Whereas Australians took pride in being 98 percent British in origin,[55] the massive Sifton-era immigration presented peculiar challenges to the imperial project. So too did the French Fact. The Riel Rebellion was still recent history in the formative period of common law Canada's legal professions. Moreover, Quebec, as always, was a force to be reckoned with. The Republic to our south was a cultural, economic and political force of considerable importance. Its proximity rendered many "British" patterns of development culturally improbable in Canada. Britannia may have fancied itself as ruling the seas and, hence, its far-flung island colony. She clearly did not rule the Americas.

Canada also had a more widely dispersed population than Australia and much larger agricultural hinterlands. While extensive habitable territory and productive land are significant assets, they rendered the awareness of space and the sense of threat from distance and difference all the more acute. Comparatively speaking, British Australia could afford a greater degree of complacency: in the early 20th century Australia would have seemed more familiar, more "knowable" than Canada. Anyone inclined to underestimate the challenges of governance in turn-of-the-century Canada would have been jarred by a series of dramatic events. The tenuous hold of Britishness was underlined in the Riel Rebellions, the Winnipeg General Strike of 1919 and in the very visible linguistic, cultural and religious diversity of the West and its metropolis.

Each of these social factors would tend to sharpen the sense of national mission among reforming Canadian lawyers. By another quirk of history related to the sociology of the legal profession, lawyers turned out to be easier to organize in Canada than in Australia. Australia's legal professions were severely divided along several fault lines. The formal division between barristers and solicitors, long abandoned in Canada, made it difficult to develop a coherent, sustained, cultural project of professionalization in Australia.[56] Intersecting with this, another cultural overlay militated against professional unity. Most of Australia's rural settlement is considerably older than that in the Canadian West and North. Consequently, Australia's rural lawyers were better established, well organized on 19th century patterns and resistant to the claims of a metropolitan leadership that they should coalesce around a new vision of professionalism emanating from colonial capitals. The social and structural fluidity of Canada's newest lands, in contrast, may have allowed a hegemonic fraction of Canadian lawyers more freedom to move. Rob McQueen's forthcoming work on Victorian lawyers describes patterns of remarkable and effective resistance to metropolitan control by rural practitioners which finds no equivalent in twentieth century Canada.[57]

The Australian federation itself may have had less coherence than Canada's. Fully 34 years newer as a political unit, Australian lawyers may not have developed a sufficiently "national" frame of mind to make professionalization projects of the Canadian sort palatable. Moreover, no Australian state was the creature of any other. This stands in marked contrast to Canada, where Manitoba, Saskatchewan and Alberta were created as part of Old Canada's (read: "Ontario") reach westward. Patterns of collaboration and co-operation among lawyers in different regions may well have been harder to establish across the recently united colonies of Australia than in Canada.

While reforming lawyers in both Canada and Australia were heavily influenced by the example of the American Bar Association and the "Bar Association" movement in that country, the U.S. influence was more immediate and much stronger in Canada. Proximity, frequency of contact and similarity of social conditions made the U.S. model seem particularly relevant in Canada. The U.S. example was a significant cultural asset to Canadian lawyers bent on remaking their own profession. The Canadian project bears marked similarity to projects of professionalization in the United States at this time and in many ways is derivative of cultural currents in the U.S. The model would have seemed less immediately relevant, less important in Australia. It did not necessarily "stand for" the future in the antipodes as fully and unequivocally as it seemed in North America.

Finally, it is possible that differences in leadership account for differences in professional patterns in the two dominions. The Canadian professionalization project was spearheaded by individuals of extraordinary commitment, energy and ability and in the absence of further research it remains possible that the necessary components of timing, ideas, opportunities and leadership did not coincide in Australia in the way they did in Canada.[58]

Caveats

Two caveats need to be registered in conclusion. It bears re-emphasis that secondary literatures in these areas are insufficiently developed to allow firm conclusions to be put forward – or even to permit relatively sound hypotheses to be developed. Second, it needs to be noted that this has been merely a descriptive project aimed at presenting the professionalizing ambitions of certain professionals. Theirs was an undertaking that *they* understood to be involved in central ways with the expansion of British civilization and, hence, with the colonization projects of the 20th century.

I have not however sought to pass judgment on that project, to evaluate the net effect of this lawyerly vision on twentieth century processes of imperialism, nor to speculate on its subsequent influences on the cultures, politics and societies of either Canada or Australia. Those rather large inquiries are well beyond the scope of the present essay.

Notes

1. A version of this paper was presented at the University of Adelaide on August 17, 1999, as part of the "Distinguished Historians Public Lecture Series", in celebration of the University of Adelaide's 125th anniversary. The University of Adelaide Department of History, Faculty of Law and Centre for British Studies provided an outstanding environment for research and writing during my term as "Distinguished Visiting Scholar" from May to August, 1999. Thanks to Wilfrid Prest, Rob Foster, Ian Duncanson and Rob McQueen for sharing ideas, insights and enthusiasms.

2. H.E. Manning, "Fraternity of the Bar", *The Australian Law Journal,* (1933): 23.

3. See, for example, W. Wesley Pue and David Sugarman, eds., *Lawyers and Vampires: Cultural Histories of Legal Professions,*(Oxford: Hart Publishing, 2001, forthcoming); Robert McQueen and W. Wesley Pue, eds., *Misplaced Traditions: The Legal Profession and the British Empire,* Symposium Issue, *Law in Context, 16, no.1 (1999);* John McLaren, Hamar Foster and Chet Orloff, eds., *Law For the Elephant, Law for the Beaver: Essays in the Legal History of the North American West* (Regina and Pasadena: 1992)

4. Jonathan Parry, *The Rise and Fall of Liberal Government in Victorian Britain* (New Haven: Yale University Press, 1993), 134.

5. See, for example, Alan Hunt, *Governing Morals: A Social History of Moral Regulation* (Melbourne: Cambridge University Press, 1999); Mariana Valverde, *The Age of Light, Soap and Water: Moral Reform in English Canada, 1885-1925* (Toronto: McClelland and Stewart, 1991); Mariana Valverde, ed., Special Issue on Moral Regulation, *Canadian Journal of Sociology / Cahiers canadiens de sociologie,*19, no. 2 (1994): i-xii, 145-255; Mariana Valverde, "Moral Capital" *Canadian Journal of Law and Society/Revue Canadienne Droit et Société,* 9, no. 1 (1994): 213-232.

6. Angelika Sauer, "The Wattle and the Maple Tree in the Garden of the Empire", in this volume, note 28.

7. A developing literature on coinage, paper notes and state iconography is richly promising. See Emily Gilbert, "'Ornamenting the Facade of Hell': iconographies of 19th century Canadian paper money", *Environment and Planning D, Society and Space,* 16 (1998): 57-80; Emily Gilbert and Eric Helleiner, eds., *Nation States and Money: The Past, Present and Future of National Currencies* (London: Routledge, 1999). There is a brief discussion of the appropriation of aboriginal images on Australian currency in Chapter 3, "The Aboriginal Copyright Cases", of Sally Peata McCausland, "Protecting Aboriginal Cultural Heritage in Australia:

Looking for Solutions in the Canadian Experience" LL.M. Thesis, (unpublished), University of British Columbia, (1997). For a discussion in the parallel realm of court dress see Rob McQueen, "Of Wigs and Gowns: A Short History of Legal and Judicial Dress in Australia", Rob McQueen and W. Wesley Pue, 31-58. The paintings of Canada's nationalist Group of Seven painters: (http://www.mcmichael.com/group.htm) and of Australia's Heidelberg school also register large in the realm of state iconography. The deployment of images of first nations peoples in U.S. society is discussed in passing in Rosemary J. Coombe, "Embodied Trademarks: Mimesis and Alterity on American Commercial Frontiers", *Cultural Anthropology*, 11, no. 2 (1996): 202-224.

8. For a sensitive treatment of Canada's ambivalence toward First Nations peoples, see: Eva Mackey, *The House of Difference: Cultural Politics and National Identity in Canada* (London: Routledge, 1999).

9. It is arguable that at some point in the late 20th century, the Queen's image on Canadian coinage became more important as a marker of distinctiveness as against another colonial power – the United States – rather than as a sign of imperial identification.

10. John Kendle, *The Round Table Movement and Imperial Union* (Toronto: University of Toronto Press, 1975).

11. Carl Berger, *The Sense of Power: Studies in the Ideas of Canadian Imperialism, 1867-1914* (Toronto: University of Toronto Press, 1970), 260-261.

12. The 50 states and District of Columbia total 9,629,091 km^2 Source: CIA World Factbook, 1999: http://www.odci.gov/cia/publications/factbook/ushtml#geo

13. Australian Embassy in Washington D.C., Website, http://www.austemb.org/geography.htm

14. Government of Canada Website: http://canada.cio-bic.gc.ca/ (About Canada, Facts).

15. According to the CIA *Factbook*, ibid., the size of these countries is as follows: France (547,030 km^2), Germany (356,910 km^2), Austria (83,858 km^2), United Kingdom (244,820 km^2), Italy (301,230 km^2), Portugal (92,391 km^2), Spain (504,750 km^2).

16. Compton's Online Encyclopedia (http://www.optonline.com/) records the size of the Prairie Provinces of Canada as follows: Alberta, 661,185 km^2; Saskatchewan, 651,900 km^2; Manitoba, 650,000 km^2 . Other comparisons from

World Atlas 3 and *U.S. Atlas 3* (1991-1992) *The Software Toolworks Atlas Pack MPC.* Software Toolworks.

17. See generally G. Friesen, *The Canadian Prairies:* A History (Toronto: University of Toronto Press, 1987), 162. Some aspects of this history are covered in Dale Gibson and Lee Gibson's ground-breaking study *Substantial Justice*: Law and Lawyers in Manitoba, 1670-1970 (Winnipeg: Peguis Publishers, 1572). On Clifford Sifton see also "*TimeLinks*, Sir Clifford Sifton", http://timelinks.merlin.mb.ca/refernc/db0053.htm. See also J.M., Bumsted The Peoples of Canada: A Post-Confederation History (Toronto: Oxford University Press, 1992).

18. G. Friesen, ibid., 340.

19. R.C., Macleod "Canadianizing the West", as excerpted Daniel Francis and Howard Palmer, eds., *The Prairie West: Historical Readings*, 2nd ed. (Edmonton: Pica Pica Press, 1992), 226.

20. That is, residents of Canada's Atlantic provinces: Nova Scotia, P.E.I. and New Brunswick (Newfoundland had not yet joined the Canadian confederation).

21. T.C., Byrne, "The Ukrainian Community in North Central Alberta.", University of Alberta, 1937, M.A. thesis, unpublished, 41.

22. For discussions of prairie ethnicity and settlement patterns see C.A., Dawson, *Group Settlement - Ethnic Communities in Western Canada.,* (Toronto: Macmillan, 1936); Friesen, *supra*, note 33, 242-273; W., Eggleston, "The People of Alberta," *Canadian Geographical Journal* 15 (1997): 212-222; V.L. Hull, "A Geographic Study of the Impact of Two Ethnic Groups on the Rural Landscape in Central Alberta". University of Alberta, M.A. thesis (unpublished), 1965; Jackson, W.H., *Ethnicity and Areal Organisation among French Canadians in the Peace River Region, Alberta.*University of Alberta: (1970) M.A. thesis (unpublished); V.J. Kaye, *Early Ukrainian Settlements in Canada, 1895-1900* (1964); Kaye "Three Phases of Ukrainian Immigration", Y. Slavutych, R.C. Elwood, V.J. Kaye, and J.M. Kirschbaum, eds. *Slavs in Canada;* proceedings, National Conference on Canadian Slavs Inter-University Committee on Canadian Slavs, Edmonton Vol.1, (36-43); Stibbe, H.L.P. *The Distribution of Ethnic Groups in Alberta, Canada, According to the 1961 Census*, University of Alberta: M.Sc. thesis (unpublished); Stubbs, G.M. *The Geography of Cultural Assimilation in the Prairie Provinces.*Oxford University: D.Phil. thesis (unpublished).

23. See, for example, James Youngblood Henderson's contribution to *Canada's Legal Inheritances*. Symposium Issue, *Manitoba Law Journal*, 23 (1995). For an extraordinary study on the complex relations between First Nations peoples and

the state's police during the early twentieth century see T, Loo "Tonto's Due: Law, Culture and Colonization in British Columbia", *Essays in the History of Canadian Law:British Columbia and the Yukon* ,eds., H. Foster and J. McLaren, (Toronto: University of Toronto Press and Osgoode Society, 1995), 128-170; also reproduced in C. Cavanaugh and J. Mouat, eds., *Making Western Canada: Essays on European Colonization and Settlement,* (Toronto: Garamond Press, 1996), 62-103.

24. See, for example, J. Peters, *The Waisenamt: A History of Mennonite Inheritance Custom* (Steinbach, Manitoba: Mennonite Village Museum, 1985); Harold Dick, (1993) *Lawyers of Mennonite Background in Western Canada Before the Second World War* (Winnipeg: Legal Research Institute, 1993); Harold Dick, "Cultural Chasm: Mennonite Lawyers in Western Canada, 1900-1939", W. Wesley Pue and David Sugarman, eds. (forthcoming); John McLaren "Creating "Slaves of Satan" or "New Canadians"? The Law, Education and the Socialization of Doukhobor Children, 1911-1935", *Essays in the History of Canadian Law*: British Columbia and the Yukon, eds., H. Foster and J. McLaren, (Toronto: University of Toronto Press, 1995), 352-385.

25. For example, Andrew Marcus, *Australian Race Relations,* (Sydney, 1994), Alastair Davidson, *The Invisible State: The Formation of the Australian State, 1788-1901* (Sydney: Cambridge University Press, 1991); W. Wesley Pue, "Revolution by Legal Means"; Tina Loo and Carolyn Strange, *Making Good* (Toronto: University of Toronto Press, 1997). John McLaren speaks of a general "deployment of law to produce social or cultural homogeneity" in "Creating "Slaves of Satan" or "New Canadians"?, op. cit, *352.*

26. Carl Berger, *The Sense of Power: Studies in the Ideas of Canadian Imperialism, 1867-1914* (Toronto: University of Toronto Press, 1970), 227 observes that Canadian imperialists, while "highly conscious of racial differentiations. Tended to assume that the unprogressive peoples could be improved but only over a very long period of time.". Among a very extensive body of literature illustrating this mentality and documenting its implementation see, for example, Alastair Davidson, op. cit., who covers this ground as well. See also N. McDonald and A. Chaiton, eds., *Egerton Ryerson and His Times* (Toronto: Macmillan, 1997); J.T.M. Anderson, *The Education of the New Canadians: A Treatise on Canada's Greatest Educational Problem* (London: J.M. Dent, 1918).

27. Peter Fitzpatrick, *Mythology of Modern Law,* (London: Routledge, 1992).

28. R. Rorty, *Philosophy and the Mirror of Nature* (Oxford: Blackwell, 1986), 1063, as cited in I., Duncanson, "Cultural Studies Encounters Legal Pluralism: Certain Objects of Order, Law and Culture", *Canadian Journal of Law and Society. / Revue Canadienne Droit et Société,* (1997): 122 ff.

29. The character of law's engagement with the Enlightenment project is developed and critiqued in Fitzpatrick "Desperate Vacuum", *supra,* note 10. See also Peter Fitzpatrick,«'The Desperate Vacuum': Imperialism and the Law in the Experience of Enlightenment», *Post-Modern Law: Enlightenment, Revolution and the Death of Man* (Endinburg: Endinburg University Press, 1950), 90-106.

30. P. Fitzpatrick *Mythology,* op. cit., 41.

31. See for example, Viswanathan *Masks of Conquest, supra,* 55-56 note 7; Duncanson, I. "The Ends of Legal Studies" *Web Journal of Current Legal Issues* (1997) http://webjcli.ncl.ac.uk; Duncanson "Cultural Studies", *supra,* note 19.

32. Curiously, this makes early 20th century moral reformers in the cause of masculine Britishness conceptual allies of sorts with late 20th century feminists and poststructuralist researchers at large. Margaret Thornton's outstanding book *Dissonance and Distrust: Women in the Legal Profession"* (Melbourne: Oxford University Press, 1996), addresses the embodiment of law (reviewed by Sara Ramshaw and W. Wesley Pue in "Feminism Unqualified: Margaret Thornton's, *Dissonance and Distrust: Women in the Legal Profession", Law in Context,* 15, no. 1 (1997): 166-178; cf. W. Wesley Pue, "Lawyering for a Fragmented World: Professionalism after God", *International Journal of the Legal Profession,* 5, nos. 2-3 (July/November, 1998), (symposium issue on "Lawyering for a Fragmented World", ed., W. Wesley Pue): 125-140.

33. I.A. MacKay, "The Education of a Lawyer" speech delivered December 1913, to the Third Annual Meeting of the Law Society of Alberta, *Alberta Law Quarterly,.* 108. See also J.C. Gray's 1883 observation that "the opinions of judges and lawyers as to what the law is *are* the law" as quoted in R.W. Gordon "Case For (And Against) Harvard", *Michigan Law Review,* 93 (1995): 1239.

34. Though he assigned greater urgency to bringing "one law" into being than most contemporary legal pluralist scholars consider necessary or desirable.

35. I.A. MacKay, op. cit.., 108.

36. Ibid., 115.

37. Contemporary scholarship is returning to a focus on similar understandings, albeit motivated by rather different concerns. See the essays collected in Wesley Pue, ed., (1998), op. cit.

38. I.A. MacKay, op. cit., 115. There are cross-border parallels that are interesting and deserving of further exploration. These include the American Law Institute's Restatement projects, which "supposed that disinterested legal minds could identify a core of national common law principles that rose above both variations in state law and mere politics." This and similar views suggest an integrative or state-formation function of the legal profession, albeit not as explicitly as among the Canadian professional reformers. See Gordon, "Case for Harvard", *supra,* 1235, note 11 (source of quotation; referencing LaPiana *Logic and Experience;* see also G.E. White, "The American Law Institute and the Triumph of Modernist Jurisprudence", *Law and History Review,* 15, no. 1 (1997): 1-47.

39. I.A. MacKay, op. cit., 107-108.

40. Ibid, 110.

41. Ibid, 110-111.

42. I have developed such themes at greater length elsewhere: "British masculinities", op. cit.; "Common Law Legal Education in Canada's Age of Light, Soap and Water", *Canada's Legal Inheritances,* eds., W. Wesley Pue and D. Guth, Symposium Issue, *Manitoba Law Journal,* 23 (1995): 654-688; *Law School: The Story of Legal Education in British Columbia* [Vancouver: Continuing Legal Education Society of British Columbia and Faculty of Law, University of British Columbia, 1995] (xxvii + 285 pages); also published at: http://www.law.ubc.ca/handbook; "The Disquisitions of Learned Judges: Making Manitoba Lawyers, 1885-1931", *Essays in the History of Canadian Law: In Honour of R.C.B. Risk,* eds., Jim Phillips and G. Blaine Baker, (Toronto: Osgoode Society, 1999), 825-914; "Revolution by Legal Means", op. cit.; "Locating Hurst", forthcoming in James Willard Hurst Special Issue, *Law and History Review,* 18, no. 1 (2000): 187-195.

43. See W. Wesley Pue, "Legal Culture and Professional Structures: Cultural Projects of Structural Transformation among Canadian Lawyers", eds., W. Wesley Pue and David Sugarman; W. Wesley Pue, "Becoming 'Ethical': Lawyers' Professional Ethics in Early Twentieth Century Canada", *Manitoba Law Journal,* 20 (1991): 227-261 (also published in Dale Gibson and W. Wesley Pue, eds., *Glimpses of Canadian Legal History* (Legal Research Institute, University of Manitoba, Fall 1991), 237-277).

44. Helen Gregory, *The Queensland Law Society Inc., 1928-1988: A History* (Brisbane: Queensland Law Society Inc., Continuing Legal Education, 1991).

45. As quoted in Ruth Campbell, *A History of the Melbourne Law School, 1857 to 1973* (Melbourne: Faculty of Law, University of Melbourne, 1977), 48.

46. Generally, see Ruth Campbell, *A History of the Melbourne Law School, 1857 to 1973*, op. cit. See also K. H. Bailey (Dean, University of Melbourne Faculty of Law), "University Law Course", *Law Institute Journal*, 3 (1929): 168-169 (letter explaining relationship of "cultural", "professional" and "arts" components of the curriculum); "Reviews and Notices", "A Defence of Jurisprudence", *Law Institute Journal*, 3 (1929): 178 (account of a pamphlet from University of Melbourne on the inaugural address of the Chair in Jurisprudence). On the roles of other law teachers see also Alex Frame, *Salmond: Southern Jurist* (Wellington, 1995); Michael Roe, *William Jethro Brown, An Australian Progressive, 1868-1930* (University of Tasmania Occasional Paper 7, 1977); Alex Castles, Andrew Ligertwood and Peter Kelly, *Law on North Terrace, 1883-1983* (Adelaide: Faculty of Law, University of Adelaide, 1983); Marion Dixon, *Looking Back: A Short History of the UWA Law School, 1927-1992* (Perth: University of Western Australia, 1992); J.B. Peden, "Legal Education", *Australian Law Journal*, (1933), 25-28.

47. "Current Topics: Law Council of Australia – Legal Convention", *Australian Law Journal*, 9, no. 7 (1935): 245, which reported on the Australian Legal Convention, organized by the Law Council of Australia. Following up on earlier ideas that had come to nothing, Federal Attorney General J.G. Latham proposed the "formation of an Australian Law Association" in 1927. See "An Australian Law Association", *Australian Law Journal*, (1927): 184-185.

48. "Foreword" by J. G. Latham, *Australian Law Journal*, 1, no. 1 (May 5, 1927): 1.

49. John G. Latham, "Duties and Opportunities of the Legal Profession in Australia", *Australian Law Journal*, (1933): 18.

50. R.G. Menzies, Attorney General, Commonwealth, reply to toast at banquet, "Supplement to the Australian Law Journal – Australian Legal Convention, 1936", *Australian Law Journal*, 10: 25.

51. L.O. Martin, "The Methods of Protecting the Public and the Legal Profession Against Defaulting Solicitors", *Australian Law Journal*, (1933): 20.

52. Eugene Gorman, K.C., "The Legal Profession and the Community", supplement, *Australian Law Journal*, 10, (1936): 30, 31-32.

53. For a review of professional apologetics, see W. Wesley Pue, "In Pursuit of Better Myth: Lawyers' Histories and Histories of Lawyers", *Alberta Law Review* 33, no. 4 (1995): 730-767. (Symposium issue on legal profession).

54. This was the effect of the Victoria Legal Practice Act 1996 (Act No. 35/1996).

55. A. Sauer, chapter 6 in this volume, note 41.

56. J.R.S. Forbes, *The Divided Legal Profession in Australia: History, Rationalisation and Rationale* (Sydney: The Law Book Co., 1979).

57. Rob McQueen, "A Not So Golden Age: Australian Lawyers During the Great Depression, 1930-1936", eds., W. Wesley Pue and David Sugarman.

58. Messrs. Aikins, Thorson, MacKay, Robson, Mather, Farris, Edward Ludlow Wetmore, Charles Frederick Pringle Conybeare, W. Kent Power and others come to mind. Some of their contributions are canvassed in Lou Knafla, "From Oral to Written Memory: The Common Law Tradition in Western Canada,", *Law and Justice in a New Land: Essays in Western Canadian Legal History, ed.,* Louis A. Knafla, (Toronto: Carswell, 1985), 31-77; and in W. Wesley Pue, "British Masculinities", op. cit.; "Common Law Legal Education in Canada's Age of Light, Soap and Water," in W. Wesley Pue and D. Guth, eds. *Canada's Legal Inheritances,* Symposium Issue, *Manitoba Law Journal*, 23 (1995): 654-688; "Becoming `Ethical'", op. cit.,; *Law School: The Story of Legal Education in British Columbia* (Vancouver: Continuing Legal Education Society of British Columbia and Faculty of Law, University of British Columbia, 1995); also at: http://www.law.ubc.ca; "Legal Culture and Professional Structures", op. cit., "`The Disquisitions of Learned Judges': Making Manitoba Lawyers, 1885-1931", *Essays in the History of Canadian Law: In Honour of R.C.B. Risk, eds.,* Jim Phillips and G. Blaine Baker, (Toronto: Osgoode Society, 1999), 825-914.

6

The Wattle and the Maple in the Garden of the Empire

ANGELIKA SAUER

Duke Lawless was the heir to the title and estates of Trafford Court, which belonged to his uncle, old Admiral Lawless. One fine summer day, Duke fell in love with Miss Emily Dorset, a woman like himself of limited income but in line for a big inheritance. Lawless was devoted to Emily but thought it prudent to make a home first before taking a wife. He leaned toward either ranching in Canada or a planter's life in Queensland, but lacked the eight to ten thousand pounds necessary for a successful start in either position. The romance went awry when Lawless mistakenly assumed that he had seen Emily in a compromising situation with his cousin. Heartbroken and angry, he disappeared into the interior of Australia, where he went searching for gold. After five years he resurfaced in the Canadian Rockies. It was here that, by happenstance, he was reunited with his cousin. The two men cleared up the old misunderstanding and Duke returned to England to be reunited with the lovely and still virtuous Emily.

This story,[1] written by Canadian novelist Gilbert Parker in 1894 as part of the series *Pierre and His People: Tales of the Far North,* illustrates the place that Canada and Australia held on the British horizon. As lands of opportunity and adventure, or as exiles of the misfits and the broken-hearted, these two places were equals: parts of the male frontier of young middle and upper-class Britain. Young Britons – often second sons who had lost their place in British society – sought the primordial wilderness, the vast unconquered lands that had not yet been transformed by civilization, to prove their manhood and national dominance throughout the Empire. Some came as remittance men, equipped with generous allowances and hopes of preserving social status and privilege by settling in a new land.[2] Others pursued the quest to colonize and civilize in hunting and fishing parties; by the late 19th century they descended upon Western Canada in such numbers that the Canadian Pacific Railway's guidebook *Fishing and Shooting* required annual reprinting.[3] "We were mad and keen to kill", one member of a 1898 hunting party in Alberta remembers. His group brought down 47 brace of duck in one morning. One young man ran out of ammunition and flung his empty gun at some geese flying past.[4] Nor were geese and other birds the only targets. The incongruous image of red-coated hunting parties on horseback surrounded by purebred foxhounds is the stuff of Canadian Prairie lore.[5] Harvests were delayed to stage the annual fox hunt week at Cannington Manor in Saskatchewan, yet the frontier wilderness, whether in Canada or Australia, did manage to extract some concessions from the imperial sportsmen. They had to adapt to hunting coyotes and kangaroos rather than British foxes, and instead of the green meadows of England, they traversed buffalo grass and kangaroo grass.

At home, young Britons at the turn of the century were bombarded with these and other frontier images hitching their own task of finding a manly purpose in life to the dominions' images of youthful vitality and promise. In weekly publications such as Howard Spicer's *Boys of the Empire* schoolboys encountered virile men struggling and succeeding in the wilds of Canada, Australia and other far-off lands. At least one such magazine was sold throughout the Empire but packaged with a different title for each country. Recognizing the importance of children in immigration recruitment campaigns, the dominion governments initiated essay contests and distributed maps and other educational material in British schools. *Boys of the Empire* promptly defined juvenile migration in imperial terms, sponsoring the "Free Start Out West" prize competition to stimulate a "manly effort to some purpose and to bring the opportunities and duties of Imperial Citizenship within the reach of all British Boys".[6]

It is obvious that the settler colonies, as British offshoot societies, played a special role within the Empire. Much has been written about how Britain, the metropolitan centre, perceived the self-governing dominions. Age underlies any metaphor for this relationship and cements the British claim for authority: the colonial mother is surrounded by obedient children – strapping sons and dutiful daughters. As Rudyard Kipling extolled Canada in 1897: "Daughter I am in my mother's house, but mistress in my own. The gates are mine to open, as the gates are mine to close, and I abide by my Mother's House, said our Lady of the Snows." Similarly, English poet Alfred Tennyson appealed to Australia's filial loyalty in 1888: "To all the loyal hearts who long to keep our English Empire whole! To all our noble sons, the strong New England of the Southern Pole!"[7]

As has been demonstrated for both Canada and Australia, there were strong segments in society who, at the turn of the century, heeded the call for a united Empire despite being strong advocates of separate nationhood for the dominions. Luke Trainor suggests that "the Australian colonies had their part to play in British imperialism ... [and] worked to encourage imperialism" by fostering the idea of "independent Australian Britons".[8] Similarly, Carl Berger has argued that Canadian imperialism "was one variety of Canadian nationalism".[9] His student Doug Owram later added another facet to this thesis by proving that expansion in the Canadian West was a concerted nationalist-imperialist drive.[10] Western Canadian writers complain that "millions of acres of western real estate were expected to serve the interests of 'old Canada'". Western Canada was to be a new investment frontier and an agricultural hinterland for the manufacturing plants of central Canada, which, in turn, was the hinterland of Britain.[11]

In the framework of imperial-national thinking, which centres around a narrative of colonial progress, Canada served as a model for Australian federation. In British discussions in the 1870s and 1880s, Canada was the most commonly cited colonial prototype; British officials hoped that the Australian colonies would "move toward the Canadian position".[12] Arthur Jose, one of the British-Australian historians who interwove national historiography and the imperial theme, wrote in the early 20th century that Australia was "now a single great colony like Canada". The *Manitoba Daily Free Press* reported in January 1901 that the new Australian government was designed like that of Canada and Britain[13], while the Calgary paper *The Albertan* suggested in July 1900 that the success of Canadian Confederation was confirmed by the fact that "another part of the British Empire is to be federated in a somewhat similar way".[14] Liberal institutions, a conservative social order and the British flag – these were the visions that many members of the ruling elites in Britain, Canada and Australia shared.

It is in a direct comparison of the two hinterlands and in their perceptions of each other that both similarities but also differences become most apparent.[15] As this essay will suggest, the British imperial garden provided the soil: the racialist, gendered definition of the new nations. In this soil two saplings developed – in direct competition with each other – into self-consciously nationalistic and substantially different trees. Symbolizing this development was the logo of the maple leaf, which appeared on all Canadian posters and ads in Britain around the turn of the century as part of a modernized, more competitive immigration campaign.[16] Around the same time, the initiatives of various Australian Wattle Leagues came to a head. As Richard White writes, "Theirs was a conscious effort to inspire patriotic feeling, and imitated the Canadians' promotion of the maple leaf".[17] Clearly, the two siblings were watching each other closely and with mutual jealousy.

Canadians tended to comment on Australian culture and the Australian environment with a mixture of wonderment and condescension. To some, the island continent was a distant jail for which the Canadian colonies had supplied their share of political prisoners after the failed rebellions of 1837-38.[18] There were other reasons to be somewhat disdainful. Canadian intellectuals judged Canadian poets to be superior to their Australian counterparts in purity and elegance of language. Canadians, argued noted journalist and historian Sir John George Bourinot in 1893, were grounded in their writing by a love of their country, its scenery and its long history. Australians, on the other hand, had a less varied and picturesque scenery, and a shorter history devoid of dramatic 18th-century battlegrounds. Australians could only counter with the assertion that Australian authors were "cheerful and vigorous, as becomes the pioneer writers of a young and hopeful country".[19] One detects in Canadian comments the sense of cultural superiority vis-à-vis the "new countries" that is usually associated with the British metropolitan centre.

In the Canadian imagination, the Australian landscape was dominated by two things, the ubiquitous shoreline and vast sheep pastures. For example, one of Canada's "superior" poets described Australia this way: "...as she stands, fanned by sea-winds all around, and sends a voice to swell the sound, from fertile fields and pasture lands".[20] Fortunately, comments on Australia's fauna were less purple. One promotional pamphlet attempted to ward off negative publicity about

Western Canada's abundance of mosquitoes with a reference to Australia having not only "troublesome insects but centipedes, poisonous snakes and other venomous reptiles, totally unknown in Canada". "The man who lacked courage to do battle against a mosquito", the pamphlet added, "had better allow others to precede him. We require pioneers of sterner stuff in Canada".[21]

That pioneers in the great Canadian Northwest had to be of stern stuff was obvious to all but the grievously foolish, but Canadians went further and made virtue of a necessity. As a first step in conquering a new frontier, scholars have argued, language turns an area previously deemed unfit for settlement into something known and inhabitable – the "Great American Desert" turned into the "Great Plains" one step ahead of white agricultural settlement.[22] The Canadian Plains, which in fur trading days had been declared a treeless semi-Arctic wasteland, were similarly reinvented by turning its climate into its main asset. From the 1870s onward, Prairie winters were invariably described as "bracing" and "invigorating" and the climate was praised as one of "unrivaled salubrity" that made Manitoba and the Northwest "the home of healthy, prosperous and joyous people".[23]

By the turn of the century, the northern climate had assumed a much broader and more important dimension. Carl Berger argues in his study that the search for a Canadian identity resulted in the claim that the northern location of Canada gave its inhabitants peculiar qualities and that the northern climate "imparted to it a high degree of energy, vigour and strenuousness". Contemporary experts argued that there would be a Canadian race of "taller, straighter, leaner people; ...muscles more tendinous and prominent and less cushioned". The climate was also held to promote other qualities not to be found in southern climes, which, in turn, were associated with "decay and effeminacy, and disease. The clean and frosty air seemed incompatible with lax morality; the voluptuous living characteristic of southern climes was impossible in the northern zones".[24] Canadians, was the conclusion of the time, "were a strong and serious race, enjoying advantages over Britain as well as the United States. Canada, alone of all the dominions, lay above the forty-fifth parallel and ...was surely predestined to assume an important position in the world".[25]

Linking the northern climate to moral and even political superiority was part and parcel of the British interpretation of Social Darwinism, which not only tied liberty to the blood of northern people but also held that the cold northern climate was responsible for the vigour of the British race. In a time when the self-governing dominions were attempting to define for themselves a new "national type", Canada had a distinct advantage over Australia. The question of whether the British race would degenerate in the debilitating climate of the sunny south loomed large in the Australian mind. Some experts before the turn of the century already argued that "the weakening effect of the climate shows itself more and more strikingly with each succeeding generation" and that the original vigour of physique and mental stamina would have to be maintained by constant addition of new immigrants. However, increasingly Australians, too, built a distinct and superior identity upon the foundation of their climate. Drier climate was said to be healthier and more wholesome while the sun explained the "vigorous frame, manliness of bearing, and stamp of independence of the average Australian"[26]. Evidence of the beneficial effects of the sunny climate and favourable environment was found in the success of Australian products such as wheat, wine, wool and beef, and increasingly in sports victories over British teams. By 1902, the Premier of Victoria could proudly declare: "We are not degenerating but are of that old British bull-dog breed... worthy descendants of that noble stock".[27]

At the turn of the century, then, both Canada, and especially the Canadian West, and Australia located themselves in the framework of the transplanted Anglo-Saxon race. They were, in Luke Trainor's words, "on the conveyor belt of British racial thinking"[28] but developed their own approaches to this racialized discourse. The concept that new types could develop from transplanted British stock was lent extra force at this time by speculations that indeed "the fringes of the Empire, rather than its core, were becoming the locus of its greatness, and that it was the progressive young nations that would carry the civilization of the future".[29] The Empire, as British scholar Catherine Hall argues, "could offer new possibilities for the white men of the future – possibilities which could secure a 'Greater Britain' in which Anglo-Saxon men, linked through blood and culture, could ensure the continued development of the 'race'".[30] Empire settlement thus was celebrated as "a generator of race power".[31] Canada and Australia were quite ready to take on the white man's burden: in 1896, Premier Greenway of Manitoba proudly declared that "the Northwest is one of the greatest factors in the civilization of the world".[32] At the same time C.H. Pearson declared Australia to be "an unexampled instance of a great continent that has been left for the first civilised people that found it to take and occupy. We are guarding the last part of the world in which the higher races can live and increase freely for the higher civilisation".[33]

It was the part of "increasing freely" that gave a role to women in the otherwise masculine nation-building exercise.[34] By the turn of the century, birth rates were declining markedly in established Anglo-Saxon societies and the term "race suicide" gained currency. It was here that white women – needed to mate with white men – gained renewed attention in the metropolitan centre as well as in the settler societies. In their task of prolific childbearing to ward off race degeneration, Australian- and Canadian-born women were cast into a realm of ultra-respectability and domesticity.[35] It was, however, women from the British Isles who were deemed to become the dominant moral force and "race mothers" of the new nations.[36] From the 1880s to the beginning of the First World War, various British emigration societies helped over 20,000 British women to emigrate. They deliberately directed them to sparse and primitive settlements in the Canadian West and the Australian bush. Notions of imperial destiny and class and racial superiority prevailed in the work of these societies. Indeed, as James Hammerton demonstrates, at the turn of the century they primarily hoped that their work, rather than provide career opportunities for single women, would help keep the British Empire for the British race:

> And to you 'tis now entrusted with a meaning larger, higher you, my daughters, as you go to join your kinsfolk o'er the foam 'Tis for you to keep the flaming torch of loyalty on fire In the land of your adoption, for the honour of your home. Yes! for God and for your country now 'tis yours to make the story you, the future nursing mothers of the English race to be In your arms his love will lay them and he looks for England's glory To her loyal sons and daughters in her homes beyond the sea.[37]

Thus, the settler societies and, within Canada and Australia, the expanding frontier – the prairies and the bush – were declared to hold the full imperial and national promise. It has been demonstrated rather convincingly that race and gender ideologies overlapped by the turn of century as worries about Empire and race became inseparable from patriarchal concerns about female cultural assertion.[38] Yet while Canadian and Australian elites largely agreed on the issue of a woman's place, it was in answering the question of the place of the "other", the foreigner, in the new societies that Australian and Western Canadian developments began to diverge well before the new century. To be sure, both countries were fierce competitors for British migrants.[39] Both, equally fiercely, rejected the immigration of Chinese and Japanese. Securing the Australian colonies against coloured migration played some role in the movement for intercolonial federation, with immigration and emigration appearing among prescribed federal powers and exclusion of undesirables among early federal legislation. In Alfred Deakin's words, "we should be one people and remain one people, without the admixture of other races".[39] That to Australians the concept of "other races" was wider than the issue of Asian immigration becomes obvious in Arthur Jose's explanation of the type of "undesirable immigrant" as one "whose traditions and ideals differ substantially from Australian traditions and ideals".[40] The fact that Australia was 98 percent British when other areas of British settlement included large populations of non-British immigrants was emphasized with considerable pride.[41]

The Canadian West took a different view, mostly out of necessity. First there was the French factor and its potential for conflict, well established in the 1880s "race and creed" wars following the execution of Métis leader Louis Riel. Second, the extremely slow rate of settlement of the Prairies in the 1870s and 1880s, and continuing high emigration of Canadians to the United States, led to a new immigration policy designed to recruit Eastern European and Russian farmers by the 1890s. By the new century, Winnipeg was a multilingual "Chicago of the North", and within three decades, the Prairies' population of British origin would be in a minority. Western Canadians, however, were confident of the assimilative power of British institutions. "Canada is now in a position to extend a hearty welcome to the people of every land who are willing to stop old world prejudices, and unite as Canadians in building up and developing a nation on the broad lines of Anglo-Saxon institutions," proclaimed the *Moose Jaw Times.*[42] Foreigners were seen as necessary to progress and prosperity. The fear that Western Canadian culture would become cosmopolitan was confidently rejected: "Of the two evils which is greater – the stopping or rather retarding of our growth as a nation ...or the influx of some tens of thousands of labourers from other lands, lower in the plane of civilization, uneducated and possibly not quite so moral as ourselves but who, with our boasted superiority, we should be able to educate and uplift," asked the *Regina Leader.*[43]

A third element which marks a difference between Western Canada and Australia can be found in existing attitudes toward the Aboriginal population of the region. In Australia, there were no official treaties since legal understanding had constructed the process of white occupation as settling the land rather than conquest. By the turn of the century, Social Darwinism had provided a seemingly scientific explanation for the ensuing destruction of Aboriginal society: within the "doomed race theory" the inferior aboriginal race was simply destined to lose the struggle for survival and disappear.[45] Western Canada operated in a different legal framework, that of the British Proclamation of 1763, which held that the crown must formally extinguish Indian rights and sovereignty through treaties before settlement or other distribution of the land could occur. The necessity of treaties was underscored by the fact that the native presence in Western Canada well into the 1880s was sufficiently strong to constitute a potential military threat or at least a disincentive to white settlement.[46] The Canadian government, by necessity rather than inclination, had to manage Indian-white relations carefully. Here, as in the case of the Central European immigrants, great hopes were placed in the assimilative power of Canadian society and institutions. Through reserve, agricultural and educational policies and through the franchise, the authorities hoped to break the hold of native tradition and create a properly Christianized, civilized, Canadianized "white" Indian.[47]

The final element that distinguished the development of Western Canada from that of Australia around 1900 was the strong American influence on the region. "American capital, technology, and settlers made significant contributions to the development of the Canadian West," a new study concludes.[48] Between 1896 and 1914, over half a million American residents moved to the last plains frontier. Their capital and experience, rather than that of the poorer central European migrants, molded Prairie Canada. This is not to deny the American influence on Australia, which by the beginning of the 20th century was seen as, or feared to be, the "Yankee-land beneath the Southern Cross". As Richard White demonstrates, the United States as an archetypal example of a new society and the standard of modernity was seen as a beacon in 19th-century Australian development and influenced colonial legislation. American themes – the heroic outlaw, the pioneer family – resonated in Australian folklore as American words – the squatter, the bush – crept into the Australian lingo.[49] However, it is difficult to see this influence as nearly as pervasive as the American technological and economic penetration of the Prairies.

Ironically, the American cultural influence on Western Canada lay mostly in the negative themes that the American "wild and wicked West" provided in the ideal construction and actual development of the region's identity.[50] Rudyard Kipling marvelled at the differences between the Canadian and the American side of the border: "On one side of an imaginary line ...Safety, Law, Honour and Obedience and on the other frank, brutal decivilisation".[51] While the economic order with the family homestead as its keystone was directly copied from the American example – the Canadian Dominions Land Act of 1872 with its provision of free 160 acre quarter sections was a virtual carbon copy of the American Homestead Act of 1861 – the social order that was imposed on this agricultural frontier was a direct product of the late Victorian British mind. Government actions, rather than individual initiative, shaped this strange frontier environment where the land was surveyed and divided into plots well ahead of the arrival of the settlers, and the North-West Mounted Police, created in 1873, represented and enforced Victorian notions of respectability and class sensibilities.[52]

Legal historian Wesley Pue has demonstrated the importance that Canadian imperialists attached to British law and institutions in carrying the "civilizing project" to the Canadian West.[53] The red-coated Mountie was but one symbol of British civilization; another was the elevation of the individual ownership of small plots of land into a core value. Anglo-Canadians placed unlimited faith in the assimilative powers of private land ownership, both with respect to Aboriginal and immigrant populations. In Prairie Canada, the freehold farmer was seen as the key unit of society, and the ideal bolstered by the claim that all that was needed for success on the Prairies were the Victorian values of "pluck" and "grit." As Manitoba's Premier boasted in 1896, the Northwest offered "a home in a land where every man can secure a living by his personal exertions, something that no other country can offer today". The imagery presented in immigration or travel literature reflected this theme of the yeoman farmer – hardy, self-reliant and close to nature.[54]

That this fundamentally conservative, anti-modernist agricultural ideal could shape the emerging culture of Western Canada to the degree it did can be explained by the nature of the Western Canadian economy and society at the fin de siècle. In the 1890s the region boasted only two important urban centres: Winnipeg (pop. 26,000) and Edmonton (pop. 4,000). A mining frontier with its company towns was forming ever so slowly. Social class did not become a fact of life until the first decades of the 20th century, while the family farm and the rural village supporting it were indeed the paramount institutions. Certainly, the idea of rural equal opportunity was an illusion: not every farm was a homestead, and the ones on better land almost always had to be bought for a substantial price. Yet, despite apparent distinctions in land-based wealth, social relationships still offered a great deal of flexibility.[55]

The differences to turn-of-the-century Australia are obvious. The emerging agricultural order of the 19th century had been dominated by a landed pseudo-gentry and large pastoral estates. The ideal of the independent smallholder experienced its high point in the 1860s when the "selector", much like the North American "homesteader", dominated the imagination. The process, to be sure, was not unlike the later development in the Canadian West: "Much of what in the opening of the American West was achieved by private capitalist ventures was accomplished in the Australian colonies by government initiative".[56] However, by the 1890s the agricultural frontier seemed to have reached its limits, as the urban centres with their class divisions became the dominant reality of Australian life. As Paul Sharp argued in his 1950s comparative study, the Australian continent did not "provide the geographical base to a nation of small farmers".[57] The essentially North American romantic ideal made a rare appearance in Edward Jenks' 1912 *History of the Australasian Colonies*, which glorified the selector as "the class which is the real backbone of Australia".[58] The popular Australian imagination, however, seized upon the legend of the bushworker, not the farmer, to counter Australia's urban reality.

Were they alike or were they different? The necessary complexity of the answer has become apparent. In the last third of the 19th century both Australia and Western Canada developed within the same set of ideals and ideologies as part of the British Empire. To deny its influence is to ignore the fundamental realities of their respective histories. The persuasiveness of British ideas can be seen even when they were vigorously negated. However, it is also obvious that history, geography and the natural environment produced different responses to similar challenges. There was no coherent imperial frontier. Yet as new societies, the two shared, at least in the perspective of others, similar characteristics: they were materialistic, brash, young, egalitarian, provincial, braggart. And, above all, in their own view, they were bound for greatness. As *The Albertan* editorialized in July 1900: "The close of the century finds the Canadian nation on the threshold of a great career". Australian papers echoed the sentiment.

Notes

1. Gilbert Parker, "Shon McGann's Toboggan Ride", *Pierre and His People: Tales of the Far North series* (London: Methuen, 1892).

2. Mark Zuehlke, *Scoundrels, Dreamers and Second Sons: British Remittance Men and the Canadian West* (Vancouver and Toronto: Whitecap Books, 1994).

3. Karen Wonders, "A Sportsman's Eden," 2 parts, *The Beaver* 79, 5 (September-October 1999): 26-32 and 79, no. 6 (December 1999-January 2000): 30-37. See also John M. MacKenzie, *The Empire of Nature: Hunting, Conservation and British Imperialism* (Manchester: Manchester University Press, 1997).

4. Mark Zuehlke, *Scoundrels, Dreamers and Second Sons,* 10-11.

5. Ronald Rees, *New and Naked Land: Making the Prairies Home* (Saskatoon: Western Producer Prairie Books, 1988), 83-84.

6. Patrick A. Dunae, "'Making Good': The Canadian West in British Boys' Literature, 1890-1914," *Prairie Forum* 4, no. 2 (1979); Richard White, *Inventing Australia: Images and Identity, 1688-1980* (Sydney: Allen and Unwin, 1981), 83-84.

7. Deirdre David, *Rule Britannia: Women, Empire and Victorian Writing,* (Ithaca: Cornell University Press, 1995), 168-177.

8. Luke Trainor, *British Imperialism and Australian Nationalism: Manipulation, Conflict and Compromise in the Late Nineteenth Century* (Cambridge: Cambridge University Press, 1994), 4-5.

9. Carl Berger, *The Sense of Power: Studies in the Ideas of Canadian Imperialism 1867-1914* (Toronto: University of Toronto Press, 1970), 9.

10. Doug Owram, *Promise of Eden: The Canadian Expansionist Movement and the Idea of the West 1856-1900* (Toronto: University of Toronto Press, 1980).

11. Gerald Friesen, *The Canadian Prairies: A History* (Toronto : University of Toronto Press, 1987), 162.

12. Luke, Trainor, *British Imperialism and Australian Nationalism,* 8, 11.

13. "Australia Rejoicing", *Manitoba Daily Free Press,* January 2, 1901.

14. *The Albertan* and *The Alberta Tribune*, July 4, 1900.

15. Paul F. Sharp, "Three Frontiers: Some Comparative Studies of Canadian, American and Australian Settlement", *Pacific Historical Review*, 24, no. 4 (November 1955): 369-378. See also K.A. MacKirdy, "Conflict of Loyalties: The Problem of Assimilating the Far West into the Canadian and Australian Federations", *Canadian Historical Review*, 32 (1951): 337-55.

16. Patrick A. Dunae, "Promoting the Dominion: Records and the Canadian Immigration Campaign, 1872-1915," *Archivaria, 19* (1984-85): 89.

17. Richard White, op. cit., 117.

18. This theme appears in the writings of Gilbert Parker. See also Jack Cahill, *Forgotten Patriots: Canadian Rebels on Australia's Convict Shores* (Toronto: Robin Brass, 1998).

19. Patrick White,op. cit., 117.

20. Jean Blewett, *Heart Songs* (Toronto: G.Morang, 1897), 79.

21. Sanford Fleming, *Canada and Its Vast Undeveloped Interior* (n.p., 1878).

22. John Greenway, *The Last Frontier: A Study of Cultural Imperatives in the Last Frontiers of America and Australia* (London: Davis-Poynter, 1972), 42.

23. Doug Owram,op. cit., 11-15, 116ff.

24. Carl Berger, op. cit., 129-130.

25. Ibid., 133.

26. Richard White, op. cit., 75.

27. Ibid., 72-75.

28. Luke Trainor op. cit., 81.

29. Richard White, op. cit., 78-80.

30. Catherine Hall, "Going a-Trolloping: Imperial Man Travels the Empire", *Gender and Imperialism*, ed. Clare Midgley (Manchester: Manchester University Press, 1998), 197.

31. Michael Roe, *Australia, Britain and Migration, 1915-1940: A Study of Desperate Hopes* (Cambridge: Cambridge University Press, 1995), 9.

32. Quoted in Karel Denis Bicha, *The American Farmer and the Canadian West, 1896-1914* (Lawrence, Kansas: Coronado Press, 1968), 45.

33. Patricia Grimshaw et al., *Creating a Nation 1788-1990* (Melbourne: McPhee Gribble Publishers, 1994), 178.

34. Marilyn Lake, "Australian Frontier Feminism and the Marauding White Man," *Gender and Imperialism*, ed., Clare Midgley (Manchester: Manchester University Press, 1998), 123-136.

35. Patricia Grimshaw, op. cit., 193; Luke Trainor, op. cit., 74.

36. Patricia Grimshaw, op. cit., 188.

37. A. James Hammerton, *Emigrant Gentlewomen: Genteel Poverty and Female Emigration, 1830-1914* (London: Croom Helm Ltd., 1979), 142, 157-164. Poem "To England's Daughters" (1904) quoted in ibid., 198.

38. Deirdre David, op. cit., 158.

39. Patrick Dunae, op. cit., 76-77.

40. Michael Roe, op. cit., 6; Patricia Grimshaw, op. cit., 191-192.

41. Arthur Jose, *History of Australia: From the Earliest Time to the Present Day*, 11th ed. (Sydney: Angus and Robertson, 1925), 207n.

42. Richard White, op. cit., 71.

43. *Moose Jaw Times*, September 16, 1890.

44. *Regina Leader*, July 19, 1910.

45. Ibid., 69; Luke Trainor, op. cit., 83-84; Patricia Grimshaw, op. cit., 134, 147.

46. Gerard Friesen, op. cit., 136-137.

47. Jim Miller, *Skyscrapers Hide the Heavens: A History of Indian-White Relations* (Toronto: University of Toronto Press, 1997).

48. Randy W. Widdis, *With Scarcely a Ripple: Anglo-Canadian Migration into the United States and Western Canada, 1880-1920* (Montreal and Kingston: McGill-Queen's University Press, 1998), 34, 306; Bicha, 9-10.

49. John Greenway, op. cit., 26, 33; Richard White, op. cit., 49-51.

50. Desmond Morton, "Cavalry or Police: Keeping the Peace on Two Adjacent Frontiers, 1870-1900", *The Mounted Police and Prairie Society 1873-1919*, ed. William M. Baker (Regina: Canadian Plains Research Center, 1998).

51. Quoted in Richard White, op. cit., 56.

52. See the contributions in William Baker, op. cit.

53. See Wesley Pue's contribution in this volume, chapter 5.

54. Patrick Dunae and Karl Bicha, op. cit., 45, 78.

55. George Friesen, op. cit., 274, 301-320.

56. Patricia Grimshaw, op. cit., 109-13.

57. Paul Sharp, op. cit., 371.

58. Edward Jenks, *A History of the Australasian Colonies* (Cambridge: Cambridge University Press, 1912), 323.

PART III

Relations Between Australia and Canada

7

Parties Long Estranged: The Initiation of Australian-Canadian Diplomatic Relations, 1935-1940

GALEN ROGER PERRAS

In their introduction to this volume, Linda Cardinal and David Headon have made reference to the Reverend John Dunmore Lang's 1852 comment about the existence of "a secret sympathy between" Australia and Canada. One hundred and thirty years later, Canadian academic T.H.B. Symons remarked that there were "few countries in the world which have as much in common as Australia and Canada". Both states were settler societies and "federations of continental dimensions", and they had "moved to self-government and nationhood by a process of evolution rather than revolution".[1] Yet Australia and Canada established formal bilateral diplomatic relations only in late 1939. This delay might be explained in part by the confusion that was engendered by constitutional change within the British Empire after the First World War. However, even when it became clear that Britain's self-governing dominions could appoint diplomatic representatives to other nations, Australia, claiming that its interests overseas were best handled by Britain, resisted Canadian overtures for several years. Australians also resented the role Canada had played in loosening imperial ties and therefore felt no need to "reward" Canada by establishing diplomatic relations until the advent of the Second World War. Sympathy, secret or otherwise, was sorely lacking.

The origins of this problem lie in the First World War. Canada and Australia had achieved self-government in 1867 and 1901, respectively, but no British dominions controlled their foreign policies. Though Canada, especially during Wilfrid Laurier's prime ministership (1896-1911), had expressed considerable doubts about a common imperial foreign policy, few disputed British Prime Minister H.H. Asquith's assertion in 1911 that with the Empire's foreign policy "authority cannot be shared".[2] The loss of 125,000 Australian and Canadian soldiers on the First World War's bloody battlefields altered that equation. As T.O. Lloyd aptly put it, those troops had gone to war in 1914 certain that they were British but they came away from that horrendous conflict certain they were Australian or Canadian.[3] Regulation IX in 1917 was the best example of rising dominion nationalism. Frustrated that Britain was demanding more troops while not granting the dominions a substantial say in the imperial war effort, Canadian Prime Minister Robert Borden and South African Minister of Defence Jan Smuts compelled a reluctant Prime Minister David Lloyd George to recognize that the dominions were "autonomous nations of an Imperial Commonwealth" with the right to an adequate voice in the formulation in imperial foreign policy making.[4] But at war's end the dominions found that their martial sacrifices counted for little as the great powers settled down to the complex and divisive task of dictating peace to a beaten Germany. American President Woodrow Wilson objected to granting the dominions separate standing at the Versailles negotiations, though Lloyd George, facing strident protests from Borden and Australian Prime Minister William (Billy) Hughes, eventually granted Australia and Canada limited representation within Britain's delegation and allowed the dominions to separately sign the final peace treaty with Germany.[5]

The real problems emerged in a series of imperial conferences held in the 1920s. First, imperial leaders gathered in London in 1921 to debate the renewal of the Anglo-Japanese alliance. Isolated and alone in the vast Pacific Ocean and fearful of Japanese military power, Australia and New Zealand favoured renewal. But Conservative Canadian Prime Minister Arthur Meighen, pushed by Department of External Affairs adviser Loring Christie, argued that the alliance's reaffirmation would alienate the United States. Recalling Foreign Secretary Lord Roseberry's comment in 1888 that the voices of Canada and Australia "must sound very loud" in matters that related to their interests, Meighen argued for the right to veto renewal on the grounds that Canada would suffer most in an Anglo-American confrontation. Desperately afraid of Japan, Hughes bitterly condemned Meighen as the "voice of America" but as many British officials also opposed renewing the alliance, the imperial conference agreed to seek broader multilateral security agreements with the United States and Japan that would limit armaments in the Pacific, achieving them at the Washington Conferences of 1921–1922.[6]

Though it was Britain's decision to seek the shelter of a broader security pact and not Meighen's opposition which had killed the Japanese alliance, R.G. Casey, Australia's liaison officer to Britain, noted bitterly in 1928 that "Canada alone was for the break (owing to her United States complex)".[7] Nor did subsequent events make Canadians any more popular among their antipodean cousins. In early 1923 Canadian Prime Minister William Lyon Mackenzie King's Liberal minority government, pushed by Ernest Lapointe of Quebec, signed the Halibut Treaty with the United States, the first bilateral treaty negotiated and ratified by a dominion without British input. Britain had objected, only to back down when King threatened to open a Canadian legation in the United States.[8] When imperial leaders reconvened in London in 1923 to discuss foreign and defence policy centralization, King stubbornly blocked closer imperial co-operation on the grounds that it would irreparably damage Canadian domestic unity and complicate relations with the United States. After Maurice Hankey expressed confusion as to why Canada was abandoning Borden's wartime demands for a real share in shaping imperial foreign policy, Skelton made Canada's position quite clear: Borden's policies had been an aberration and a reversal of the previous 50 years of constitutional change, an aberration that Canada now intended to correct. Thus the conference's closing statement, at King's insistence, argued that its views on foreign policy were "necessarily subject to the actions of the Governments and Parliaments of the Empire". Additionally, joint defence of the Empire gave way to an emphasis on local defence, while the Halibut Treaty set a precedent in that Britain agreed that its dominions had the exclusive right to enter into bilateral treaties with other nations.[9]

King's stand in 1923 remains controversial. Foreign Secretary Lord Curzon found King "obstinate, tiresome and stupid, nervously afraid of being turned out of his own Parliament when he gets back". To British historian Correlli Barnett, King, abetted by an Anglophobe Skelton, intended "to break up the 'white' empire as an effective alliance; not directly and deliberately, but as the by-product of achieving complete freedom of action" domestically. Barnett's compatriot Philip G. Wigley has alleged that Skelton deliberately ascribed a sinister and inaccurate interpretation to Britain's attempts to effect better imperial co-operation in the early 1920s. Canadian historian W.L. Morton, writing in the 1960s, was even less kind. Averring that "the present condition of Canada, in which the country is so irradiated by the American presence that it sickens and threatens to dissolve in cancerous slime," was King's fault for his persistent pursuit of autonomy without any positive counterundertaking to balance America's influence, Morton argued also that 1923 paved the way for more extreme South African and Irish nationalism that "killed" Borden's desire for an adequate dominion voice in the formulation of imperial policy.[10]

King and Skelton boast their defenders too. Noted historian Nicholas Mansergh has credited a politically masterful King with playing a major positive role in Commonwealth development, while Skelton (Canada's Undersecretary of State of External Affairs from 1925 to 1941) has been praised as an ardent Canadian nationalist who believed that Canada and Britain would not always have complimentary national interests-rather than as an isolationist Anglophobe.[11] Australian officials, however, would have sided with the more negative historical assessments. Acutely conscious of their reliance upon British military power for security, Australians had accepted Billy Hughes' comment in 1921 that some continuing dependency status "was the price we pay for Empire".[12] Thus in 1926, Australian Prime Minister Stanley Bruce had pushed hard at the Imperial Conference for Common Foreign and Defence Policies for fear that disunity would prompt the Empire's disastrous disintegration or a loss of British interest in Australian affairs and defence. But when King's position won out, a position that Casey regarded as "selfish" given "Canada's practically guaranteed immunity of aggression," the Australians realized that the old imperial order was gone and with it the old certainties about Australian reliance upon the entire Empire in a crisis.[13]

The Imperial conference further complicated matters. South African nationalist Prime Minister J.B.M. Hertzog demanded more autonomy, threatening to pull his nation out of the Empire if he did not get his way. King mediated between Hertzog and the British, massaging egos and watering down more strident stipulations within Lord Balfour's Committee on Inter-Imperial Relations. King had no inherent objection to increased autonomy, but total independence and perhaps the Empire's demise would be politically dangerous domestically and internationally. Intent on retaining the Empire as a counterweight to America's gravitational pull and hoping to carve himself a role as interpreter between Britain and America,[14] King helped to redefine the dominions as "autonomous Communities within the British Empire, equal in status, in no way subordinate one to another in any aspect of their domestic or external affairs, though united by a common allegiance to the Crown, and freely associated as members of the British Commonwealth of Nations".[15] Britain's acceptance of this "Balfour Declaration," accompanied by an admission of equality of status between Britain and its dominions, and a re-assertion of dominion rights to pursue foreign relations as long as those relations did not commit Britain or the dominions "to the acceptance of active obligations except with the definite assent of their own governments," was tempered by an assertion that equality of status did not necessarily signify equality of stature. Britain would continue to act internationally as if it still assumed the major share of responsibility for imperial security.[16]

Some Australians had anticipated these events, and their advice had been clear. On September 26 the Melbourne *Argus* had urged Bruce to stand against South African and Canadian attitudes as Australian "self-preservation and Empire unity stand for the same thing", given that Australia could not afford to defend itself. Furthermore, Walter Henderson, head of the small External Affairs Branch within the Prime Minister's Department, had cautioned that Australia should not associate itself with any proposal to present the dominions as independent; that would compel Australia to conduct its own foreign affairs, create its own foreign service and might deprive Australia of an automatic security guarantee from Britain. Bruce, though, had been unable to stem the radical dominion tide,[17] but far worse than Balfour's Declaration was on the way. In October 1925, King, seeking to avoid a vote of censure that would have toppled his minority government, had asked Governor General Lord Byng for Parliament's dissolution and an election. To King's horror, Byng opted to let Arthur Meighen's Conservatives form an administration without an election, but when Meighen admitted failure after just three days, Byng granted him an election. King's Liberals won a clear majority at the ballot box, partly due to King's insistence that Byng had exceeded his powers. Though Byng had not acted improperly, King and many Canadians felt that he had, and at the 1926 imperial conference King used the so-called "King-Byng" affair to press for alterations to the Governor General's role. The Governor General would remain the representative of the British Crown, but Britain would appoint a High Commissioner to Canada to handle diplomatic and political duties.

A Canadian High Commissioner had been present in Britain since 1880, but that position, while important for economic and immigration matters, had no diplomatic status. Foreign Secretary Austen Chamberlain had told Casey in 1925 that he favoured one day seeing dominion High Commissioners accredited to the Foreign Office and authorized by their governments to maintain touch on foreign relations. Most importantly, Leo Amery, the head of the newly created Dominions Office (set up in 1925 to differentiate between the self-governing dominions and Britain's other colonies, who remained under the Colonial Office's aegis), engaged in a power struggle with the Foreign Office and sought to use King's proposal to facilitate imperial unity via economic co-operation and directed immigration. But when King and Skelton, worried about Amery's motives, vetoed regular consultative meetings between dominion High Commissioners and British officials, Britain's Cabinet had second thoughts about the initiative. Only in April 1928 did Britain appoint Sir William Clark to be its first High Commissioner to Canada, with Chamberlain describing the new office as a means "of keeping the different Gov'ts of the Empire in step" and combatting America's growing economic influence in Canada.[18]

Britain likely felt compelled to act, as Canada had begun taking advantage of its new diplomatic freedoms. In 1926 King had approached the United States about exchanging legations. Ireland had done so already in 1924, but Canada had set the precedent in 1920 when it had convinced Britain that the sheer volume of business with America demanded a separate Canadian Minister in Washington. Britain had agreed but had insisted that Canada's Minister be safely housed in the British Embassy. The appointment, though, was delayed until 1926. The United States failed to show much interest; Canadians in general regarded foreign affairs with distaste after the war; the Conservatives were anything but united on the issue; few suitable candidates of appropriate financial and political pedigree were obvious; and, once the Liberals took over in late 1921, their minority position and internal dissent ensured that a Canadian Minister for America was relegated to the diplomatic back burner.[19] But with King's hold over his own party and government much firmer in 1926, and the imperial conferences of 1923 and 1926 behind him, King felt confident enough to move. After some initial British reluctance – they insisted that all matters that might affect the Empire would have to be handled by the British Embassy, and though Skelton protested, King thought that a small price to pay – Canada sent Vincent Massey to the United States in February 1927; in June, William Phillips presented his diplomatic credentials in Ottawa.[20] Then, in early 1928, King announced Ministers for France and Japan. The former appointment, King admitted, was designed to appeal to French Canadians, while the initiation of relations with Japan in 1929 was intended to address British Columbia's anxiety about Japanese immigrants and Canada's desire to expand trade with Asia.[21]

Australians regarded all of these changes with concern. Australia had established a High Commissioner in Britain in 1910, but like his Canadian counterpart, the Australian official had enjoyed no diplomatic status. At the 1926 imperial conference Bruce had considered the possibility of a wider role for the High Commissioner, but then decided in January 1927 that dominion missions would be appropriate only when there were "special relations" between a dominion and another foreign nation "involving consideration of so many questions that it was desirable that there should be a special representative"; Canada might have such a connection with America, but Bruce was certain that Australia enjoyed no such relationship. Lord Stonehaven, Australia's Governor General, objected to a British High Commissioner to Australia on the grounds that the Governor General's position would be weakened. He therefore was happy to report to London in November 1927 that various resolutions regarding imperial relations and the status of the Governor General had "aroused no enthusiasm in Australia." Indeed, Australian legal expert Sir Robert Garran had raised concerns that allowing the federal government to act in the realm of external relations might jeopardize state roles in the Australian federation. Britain would not dispatch a High Commissioner to Australia in 1936; Australia announced in January 1928 that it would not emulate Canada's diplomatic expansion.[22]

Certainly Bernard Attard is correct in his assertion that Australian officials viewed the 1926 resolutions as largely irrelevant sops to the more radical dominions. Casey thought that the conference had "meant very little to Australia. We are not much concerned about what may be the pure milk of constitutional theory in Imperial relations",[23] It is clear too that Australians resented Canada and King. Casey picturesquely noted in early 1928 that "surely no one man can claim credit for having done so much as Mackenzie King to damage what remains in these autonomous days of the fabric of the British Empire. His efforts to make political capital out of his domestic nationalism are analogous to a vandal who pulls down a castle in order to build a cottage".[24] And once Canada began extending diplomatic relations with the United States, France and Japan, Casey gleefully reported that Japan seemed uneager to reciprocate, adding that Canada's enthusiasm for diplomatic exchanges could lead to embarrassment, a reference to rumours that China too desired diplomatic recognition. Additionally, Casey worried that Canada would attempt to bypass the Dominions Office in order to deal directly with the Foreign Office.[25]

Australian officials must have been surprised then when Canada made an overture in November 1927 regarding an informal diplomatic connection. Skelton and Jean Desy, commenting upon their need to gather more foreign policy-related information after Canada's election to a non-permanent seat on the League of Nations' Council, asked William Hodgson of the Australian Department of External Affairs for non-official telegraphic communications between their respective governments. Though Hodgson thought that the Canadians were "sincere", he saw "difficulties and dangers" in accepting the Canadian proposal; therefore he convinced Skelton and Desy that such requests would be handled best via personal correspondence between relevant officials.[26]

Almost eight years passed before Canada would approach the Australians again. One reason was that after establishing legations in America, France and Japan, King told Amery that he intended to make no additional diplomatic appointments.[27] Then King lost the election in 1930 to R.B. Bennett's Conservatives. Bennett's timing could not have been worse. With the Great Depression gathering strength, as a self-made millionaire philosophically opposed to massive government intervention Bennett was ill-equipped to deal with the economic disruption. Famously described by a Liberal adversary as a man who "often exhibits the manners of a Chicago policeman, and the temperament of a Hollywood actor," even his sympathetic biographer had described Bennett as enjoying "probably, the worst reputation of any Canadian prime minister".[28]

One of Bennett's bugbears was the Department of External Affairs. Bennett vigorously had opposed the Washington legation, arguing in 1927 that the step was a "doctrine of separation" that foreshadowed the undesirable end of Canada's British connection. He also had condemned the diplomatic exchanges with France and Japan as a serious threat to the Empire's ability to speak with one voice.[29] Bennett had intended to fire Skelton immediately upon taking office, and Ottawa was rife with rumours that the new prime minister might scrap the Department of External Affairs altogether. But Bennett did neither; having failed to dump Skelton within 48 hours of taking control, he found that he could not do without the knowledgeable and workaholic Undersecretary.[30] As for Canada's legations, Bennett informed Parliament in 1931 that while he doubted that the existing missions could be "justified from purely diplomatic usefulness," he planned to maintain them in the hope that they might contribute "in the field of commercial activities".[31]

Indeed, trade and economic growth were Bennett's obsessions until he met his electoral Waterloo in 1935. In 1932 he pursued a comprehensive system of imperial preferences at the Imperial Economic Conference in

Ottawa, an attempt that engendered considerable intra-imperial acrimony as Bennett bullied the other negotiators to accept positions highly favourable to Canada.[32] Bennett had far more success dealing directly with the Australians. Australia had dispatched a trade commissioner to Canada in 1929, 34 years after Canada had sent its first trade commissioner to Australia. Progress had not come easily, with Trade Commissioner D.H. Ross reporting back to Ottawa in 1910 that "from several successive Ministers I have heard [such] strong expressions of sympathy towards the desires of the Canadian Government in regard to preferential trade that I am almost inclined to think that such sentiments are nothing more than empty platitudes".[33] Canada and Australia had reached a trade agreement in 1925 only to see King effectively gut that pact in 1926. Eager for a better deal from Bennett, Australia signed a new agreement in 1931 that tripled Canadian exports to Australia in just four years while Australian exports to Canada rose less than 50 percent.[34]

That imbalance was not warmly greeted in Australia, while Bennett had poisoned the well further by failing to oppose Britain's ratification of the Statute of Westminster on December 11 1931. At the 1930 imperial conference Britain had recommended extending full legislative freedom to the dominions subject only to voluntary restrictions. This was not an entirely sincere effort as Britain had sought to assuage more radical South African and Irish demands in the hope that an imperially minded Bennett would scuttle the process. But while Bennett had been unenthusiastic about the Statute, he also knew that Canadians favoured the change and therefore declared himself bound by an earlier House of Commons resolution accepting the constitutional alteration.[35] Australian and New Zealand opposition could not block Britain from passing the Statute, but Prime Minister J.H. Scullin, before his electoral defeat in December 1931, described the Statute as having "little importance" and refused to introduce enabling legislation in Australia's Parliament. After Scullin's loss, Prime Minister J.A. Lyon's coalition government also declined to acknowledge the Statute as successive conservative Australian administrations in the 1930s (Australia would not ratify until the Second World War) "pretended that independence simply had not happened and kept their electorate ignorant".[36]

Rather than pursuing foreign policy independence from Britain, Australian leaders, worried about growing Japanese power and an opposition Labour party that castigated involvement in world affairs as the dangerous product of elitist, class-driven and militarist motives, sought instead to reconcile the "clash between imperial idealism and national responsibility by trying to maximize the Australian contribution to the foreign policy of the Empire" via improved consultation and closer ties with Britain.[37] In this environment, proposals regarding diplomatic exchanges were received coolly. Though Australia had appointed a Trade Commissioner to New York City in 1918 and acknowledged his status as "the recognized link between Australia and the States",[38] American attempts to open direct diplomatic relations with Australia stalled. Bruce had declined in 1928 on the grounds that Australians would not countenance the high cost of an American mission when their limited bilateral business could be readily handled by Britain. Then when President Franklin Roosevelt, who had a keener interest than most of his compatriots in developing economic and security ties with the dominions, personally invited Lyons in 1935 to appoint a Minister to the United States, Lyons respectfully declined. He was willing to consider dispatching a trade commissioner to Washington, D.C., but a ministerial placement was "impracticable" and would set a precedent for appointments in other countries.[39]

Roosevelt subtly altered his tactics; he made State Department star and noted Anglophobe Jay Pierrepont Moffat the American Consul in Sydney to defuse a growing crisis in Australian-American economic relations and to prepare the way for the initiation of formal diplomatic relations.[40] Subtlety, however, was not Bennett's strong suit. In January 1935, with the Great Depression retaining a stranglehold on Canada's dismal economy and Bennett's political future, the Canadian leader surprised even his closest allies by abandoning his archconservatism in favour of a sweeping reform package that would transform the nation's capitalist economic system. Though Bennett's emulation of Roosevelt's "New Deal"would run aground on the shoals of constitutional difficulties and the perception that this was a cynical deathbed conversion, it is not coincidental that Bennett contacted Lyons on January 11 1935, about exchanging High Commissioners. Bennett advised that "such an arrangement would be of distinct advantage in effecting exchange of views and development of closer relations". But Bennett could not mask his impatience, closing the brief nine-line telegram with the pithy comment that "as we are at present framing estimates for the current year, I should particularly appreciate an early reply".[41]

Bennett got his timely reply but it was not to his liking. The Australians blamed Bennett for the Statute of Westminster, believing that he had refused to block that legislation because Britain had not purchased more Canadian wheat. Neither had it helped that Arthur Meighen, in Australia the previous November to celebrate Melbourne's centenary, had remarked publicly that Canadian indifference toward Australia could be ascribed to the fact that "Canada is on the highway of the nations while Australia is a nation alone".[42] So when the Australian Cabinet considered the matter, it briefly surveyed the history of imperial High Commissioners and paid particular attention to the expense of maintaining trade commissioners in North America. Finally on February 13 Lyons notified Bennett that while Australia appreciated the "desirableness" of promoting a closer relationship with Canada, after "careful consideration" his government had concluded "that the present time is inopportune for exchange of High Commissioners".[43]

Bennett would not get a second chance; he was soundly trounced by King's Liberals at the ballot box in October 1935. After five years out of power, King, having witnessed Adolf Hitler's emergence and increasing Italian and Japanese aggressiveness, desperately wanted to ensure Canada's prosperity and security. He therefore speedily signed a reciprocity agreement with the United States, repudiated Canada's League representative for supporting sanctions against Italy over that nation's conflict with Ethiopia, declined to make any automatic security commitments to Britain and, concerned about American intervention in British Columbia if the United States fought Japan, initiated a substantial rearmament program in 1936 that emphasized home defence rather than an expeditionary force for another European war. Canadian historians have long argued whether such policies reflected "a low and dishonest decade" or "a self-evident national duty," but King believed his path was clear: "in respect to all the great issues that come up," he told Parliament in 1936 that his first duty to the Empire and League was to "keep this country united".[44]

King also wanted to limit Canada's interaction with the other dominions. Before making Vincent Massey Canada's High Commissioner to Britain in November 1935, King ordered him not to be drawn into 'imperial councils, commitments, or policies and to avoid becoming a member of any conference of dominions. Canadians, King averred, could not become "subordinate or subject ourselves to any combined influence of Australia – New Zealand, Newfoundland etc. in our policies".[45] Skelton had some other ideas. Though he too desired a safe policy distance from Britain, the Undersecretary began examining the widening of the Department of External Affairs' roles and powers in 1936, presenting a final report in October 1937. Two Australian initiatives had played a substantial role in shaping Skelton's recommendations. In late 1936, Australia had installed a Counsellor in Britain's Embassy in Washington to liaise with the Americans. Then, most controversially, the Australian government decided also in 1936 to kick-start its sagging economy by dramatically limiting imports from the United States and Canada. Skelton's bitter response had been to condemn Australia as "colonial" and to label its trade diversion policy "economic nationalism with a vengeance" (American Secretary of State Cordell Hull acidly had remarked "that the nature and extent of the deliberate policy of Australia to discriminate against [America] had given us an even worse jolt than the discriminations of Germany and other countries").[46] Drawing attention to imperial constitutional changes as well as expanding trade, Skelton advocated establishing diplomatic missions in Australia, New Zealand and South Africa. Trade considerations also made diplomatic relations with Denmark and Argentina desirable as Skelton doubted that British representatives could be relied upon to secure any advantages for their Canadian economic competitors in overseas markets.[47]

Response to Skelton's recommendations was mixed. Having been informed by Department of External Affairs officer Lester Pearson, in early 1936 that Canada would appoint a High Commissioner to Australia "within the next two years," the Dominions Office worried that Canada was far more serious than originally thought. Britain's High Commissioner in Canada had heard similar rumours but unlike his London masters, F.L.C. Floud thought that given the recent difficulties between Canada and Australia "an appointment of this kind may well be found desirable." Loring Christie, who had recently returned to the Department of External Affairs after leaving the service in the 1920s, disliked Skelton's emphasis. A former imperialist who had converted to anti-imperial isolationism, Christie wanted to open relations with Germany, Italy and the Soviet Union. Doubtful that there was much to be gained politically from appointing High Commissioners to the dominions, Christie suggested instead converting existing trade commissioners to consular agents in order to cultivate dominion markets.[48]

But Prime Minister King's opinion was the one that mattered, and King did not like Skelton's plan. Meeting with the Undersecretary on December 9, 1937, a tired King made clear that "representation in any foreign country" in such uncertain times was almost certain to drag Canada into difficult situations. Rather than expanding the Department of External Affairs and adding to the government's responsibilities, King advised Skelton that more attention should be paid to properly organizing the Prime Minister's office and dealing with domestic problems. Skelton counterattacked in January 1938 by appealing to King's national pride. Pointing out that Canada had not done much to demonstrate its independence from Britain as opposed to South Africa and Ireland (eight and seven foreign missions, respectively), and arguing that Canada had to have an infrastructure capable of combatting foreign trade restrictions, Skelton asked for missions in Belgium (the Belgians already had announced they were sending a Minister to Ottawa), South Africa, Ireland, Argentina and Australia. Most of the Canadian Cabinet opposed this idea, and when Ernest Lapointe recommended appointing a Minister to Belgium but delaying the accreditation of High Commissioners to the dominions, King backed his Quebec lieutenant. A delay was in order, and if South Africa insisted upon sending an emissary to Ottawa, Canada would not reciprocate and would insist that the South African official be referred to as an accredited representative and not a High Commissioner.[49]

King's reluctance to act may have stemmed, as he later explained to Floud, from "his experience of political life which had taught him that any success he had attained had been due far more to avoiding action rather than taking action".[50] Australians did not much appreciate such sentiments. In September 1936 Australia's Toronto-based Trade Commissioner L.R. Macgregor had explained that nearly 5 million Canadians of non-British stock (from a total population of 11 million), especially 3 million French Canadians, had an isolationist and anti-imperial outlook. But Australian Minister of Defence George Pearce, who had criticized the other dominions in 1932 for not spending as much on defence as Australia even though the seaborne trade of the other dominions exceeded Australia's, commented in early 1937 that Canada's initiation of its rearmament program had demonstrated that it was finally "awaking to a realization of the dangers of the situation".[51] Yet when imperial leaders met in London in spring 1937, King, as in 1923, would not budge. Though King knew that Canada would not stand idly by if Britain went to war with Germany, he refused to commit to Britain for fear that Neville Chamberlain's government would then adopt a harder line against Hitler. So as Lyons and New Zealand Premier M.J. Savage lobbied for a statement that emphasized a common imperial foreign policy, King gave the antipodean leaders "no quarter". King would not agree, believing that such a blanket statement would injure Canadian unity, and in his mind there could be no greater threat to the Empire than if Canada fell apart.[52]

So as Skelton sought to convince his political master to dispatch a High Commissioner to Australia, the Australians were sending signals that such an appointment was unwelcome. When the Montreal *Gazette* claimed in July 1937 that Canada was considering dispatching High Commissioners to all the other dominions, the Australian Counsellor in Washington was in Ottawa for a short visit. But Skelton informed Keith Officer that the story had no foundation beyond King's statement earlier in the year that such representation was "desirable". A year later when Macgregor met with Skelton, the Australian confirmed that his government remained opposed to exchanging accredited representatives or High Commissioners "with Canada or any other Dominion at the present time" because Britain could ably handle Australian affairs overseas. Moreover, Attorney General Robert Menzies, whom Macgregor expected to be soon moved to the external affairs portfolio, "was strongly Imperialistic and violently opposed to separate diplomatic representation" because it would make it far more difficult for Australia to deny formal relations with Japan and the United States.[53]

Though Skelton had admitted that the decision was Australia's to make, privately he did not understand why imperialist Australians could not explain to America or Japan "the tremendous difference between sending a representative to a part of the Empire and to sending one to a foreign country." Skelton may have had a point, as Menzies' violent opposition may have been more apparent than real. Though Menzies had written in late 1935 that the average Australian trusted Britain and found the notion of a "British Commonwealth of Nations something of a mouthful and not altogether self-explanatory," in August 1938 he told Officer that he could support swapping High Commissioners with the other dominions as long as Australia did not have to establish legations in foreign nations.[54] Officer had some sympathy for this position. When Casey asked in December 1938 whether Australia should set up a legation in America, Officer admitted that, while the present arrangement of having a Counsellor attached to the British Embassy was working well, it was a "cheap method of doing things". More importantly, that arrangement created the impression that Australians were "imbued" with the British point of view. But while a separate Australian legation would satisfy Roosevelt's administration, would allow Australia to present its views directly to the State Department without British intermediaries and might increase British prestige and influence in America, the financial cost would be quite high. Furthermore, with limited department resources back in Canberra and a foreign policy that emphasized information gathering rather than action, Officer was not certain that a Washington legation would be very useful. From his vantage point then, the appointment of an Australian High Commissioner in Ottawa was "at least as important, and, I believe, more important, than the establishment of a Legation here".[55]

Still, Officer was not certain that the Canadian example was necessarily a good one. While he greatly desired a larger and more capable Australian Department of External Affairs, Officer tried to impress upon Canberra that the Canadians:

> have built up a big Department of External Affairs and a numerous series of Missions abroad with very little use or effect, for my very definite impression is that they get little if any more information in spite of their Mission[s] than we get depending as we do on the Foreign Office, and that they have no policy on any subject except to do nothing or say nothing for fear that they may do or say the wrong thing.[56]

But when Britain abandoned appeasement after Germany occupied the rest of Czechoslovakia and issued subsequent territorial demands to Poland, Australian leaders, concerned that war in Europe would leave Australia vulnerable to Japanese aggression, wanted better diplomatic connections. In late April, Prime Minister Menzies (Lyons had died suddenly in April) broadcast a speech to his fellow Australians in which he outlined the need for "full consultation and co-operation" with Britain and the other dominions, as well as America, China, Japan and the Netherlands East Indies.[57]

Canada, though, wanted Australia to make the first move. In late 1938, Skelton again had sought to convince King to widen Canada's diplomatic representation. But in March 1939 a reluctant Cabinet agreed only to accept a new connection with Ireland, ruling that it would wait for the other dominions to take the initiative. Not until August 1939, as fears of a general European conflict mounted, did the notion of a diplomatic exchange between Australia and Canada even come up. In Ottawa on August 2, Officer met with Department of External Affairs second-in-command Laurent Beaudry, plus Christie and N.A. Robertson. Finding the Canadians quite anxious to discuss Britain's worsening relations with Japan, Officer came way with two impressions: that Canada, though it had already agreed in June to appoint High Commissioners to South Africa and Ireland, did not want to send those representatives unless it could dispatch a High Commissioner to Australia too; and that the Canadian Department of External Affairs would be very happy "if an Australian High Commissioner or other political representative in Ottawa and an Australian Legation in the U.S.A. could be established more or less contemporaneously".[58]

But as Officer made clear to the State Department in mid-August, Australia still had not decided upon a legation in Washington even though Bruce, now the High Commissioner to Britain, backed the notion.[59] Germany's invasion of Poland on September 1 altered the equation. When France and Britain declared war on Germany two days later, Menzies immediately informed Australians that they also were at war. Prime Minister King argued that Canada, having accepted the Statute of Westminster, had the right to make its own decision. King had no doubt that Canada would fight, but in the interests of ensuring domestic unity he recalled Parliament to debate a formal declaration of war against Germany, a declaration that Canada made on September 10. Still, just hours after Britain's formal announcement of belligerence reached Ottawa, King cabled Menzies in Australia with a proposal. Anticipating that the British Commonwealth would face difficulties as a result of the new conflict and "desirous of strengthening means of intercourse and co-operation existing between Canada and Australia," King wanted to assign a High Commissioner to Australia and hoped that Menzies would reciprocate in kind as quickly as possible.[60]

Menzies proceeded cautiously upon receiving King's message. Though he and his Cabinet were "strongly in favour" of accepting King's proposal as it would maintain Empire unity, Menzies cabled Bruce in London on September 5 to determine if Britain objected to the initiative. When Bruce wired back that Britain warmly welcomed the exchange, Menzies responded to King on September 6. Australia would "welcome cordially" the appointment of a Canadian High Commissioner "at an early date" and intended to carry out a reciprocal appointment in Canada "as soon as necessary arrangements can be completed".[61]

Completing the necessary arrangements took some doing, though. In Ottawa, King quickly selected Charles J. Burchell, the former law partner of Minister of Finance J.L. Ralston. Certainly not a professional diplomat, as King noted in his offer letter, Burchell had "an active interest in public affairs" and had attended a British Commonwealth relations conference in Sydney in 1938. Still, the appointment obviously smacked of patronage, especially as King noted somewhat sourly that Burchell was "looking forward to the social prominence of the post" and seemed to regard "his sojourn to Australia as a quasi pleasure trip, satisfying a certain social ambition". (Such ambitions probably did not alarm King too much for he had told Massey in 1936 that a High Commissioner was merely "the agent of the government, with no right to raise foreign policy issues or to make public statements about them").[62]

Menzies had to work a little harder. First he had to justify the appointment to the Australian Parliament on September 12. Outlining the initiative's brief history and noting that diplomatic swaps had been considered "from time to time" in the past, Menzies asserted that the current agreement should not "be regarded as resting solely upon war-time needs" but would "have substantial advantages in the period ahead."

Intent on ensuring substantial advantages would accrue to his bureaucratic masters, Officer pushed the Department of External Affairs in Canberra to confirm that the High Commissioner for Canada and any subsequent appointments to the other dominions would fall under departmental control, unlike the High Commissioner in Britain, who reported only to the Prime Minister's Department. Finally, as Macgregor and others campaigned for the job, it took until December 1939 for the Cabinet to select Sir William Glasgow, a veteran of the First World War and a former Minister of Defence in Bruce's government, to go to Ottawa.[63]

As expected, the Canadian-Australian agreement to implement formal diplomatic relations established precedents. Within days Menzies had decided finally to open a legation in America though Cordell Hull did not learn of that decision until Ambassador Joseph Kennedy cabled from Britain at October's end that Bruce might be sent to Washington to prepare the way for a permanent appointee. (R.G. Casey proved to be the new Minister, presenting his credentials to Roosevelt on March 6 1940). Australia announced it was creating a legation in Japan in 1940, established relations with China in late 1941 and sent an official representative to Singapore in September 1941.[64]

But after enduring such a difficult and prolonged birth, did Australian-Canadian diplomatic relations function well? The verdict must be mixed. Certainly bilateral co-operation expanded considerably over the course of the war. Canada provided substantial amounts of money and aid to Australia through its generous Mutual Aid program, and thousands of Australian service personnel spent time in Canada, most under the aegis of the British Commonwealth Air Training Plan (BCATP), the brainchild of Vincent Massey and Stanley Bruce. But Massey and Bruce later argued over who had suggested the BCATP's creation, while Australian Minister of External Affairs H.V. Evatt accused Canada of driving a "hard bargain" and not doing enough to help Australia in the war when Canada in 1943-1944 tried to explicitly link Mutual Aid money to an Australian promise to lower tariff walls in the postwar period.[65]

Much of Evatt's anger derived from Major General Victor Odlum's disastrous intervention in 1942. Sent by King to replace the recalled Burchell, the hyperactive and self-centred Odlum arrived in Australia in January 1942 as Japanese forces were sweeping southward to the antipodes. Intent on creating a meaningful military role for himself and convinced of the validity of his own judgment, Odlum promised the Australians that Canada would send at least one division to save them from the Japanese. King had not authorized such a promise, but he made the matter much worse by taking over three months to finally tell Evatt that no Canadian military aid would be forthcoming. Australian-Canadian relations, at least into the immediate postwar period, would not recover from Odlum's ill-advised initiative. In October 1942, Evatt, "in a very bad temper", accused King of being "tied to Mr. Churchill's apron strings" and complained bitterly about Canada's "empty gestures to Australia".[66] Then in 1945, when Canada declined to support Evatt's very public denunciation of the great power veto in the United Nations' new Security Council (Canada preferred to lobby quietly behind the scenes), the Australian denounced the Canadian representative as "an American stooge" and castigated Canada as "a pawn in the move to defeat the Australian case". In response, Canadian Department of External Affairs official Charles Ritchie labelled Evatt "insufferably megalomaniacal and irresponsible". Finally, in 1947, when Evatt tried to organize a conference to protest American domination of the Japanese peace treaty, the Canadian Department of External Affairs, convinced that Evatt intended only to advance a personal agenda, killed Evatt's hope for a united Commonwealth position.[67]

The various High Commissioners also had their problems. Glasgow did well at his new position until his recall to Australia in late 1944. Though King initially had some doubts – meeting with Glasgow on June 17, 1940, the same day that France capitulated to Germany, King felt that the Australian "seemed completely remote from [an] appreciation of the serious situation" – N.A. Robertson (he had succeeded Skelton upon the latter's death in January 1941) praised Glasgow as "a very much better representative than the other Dominion High Commissioners". When the pleasant and unpretentious Glasgow went home, both Robertson and King agreed that Australia could not have chosen a better candidate for its first High Commissioner to Canada.[68] Burchell too started well though he had to ask for road signs so that visitors could locate the High Commission's offices in Canberra. *The Sydney Morning Herald* welcomed Burchell as a friend "returning to enjoy our renewed hospitality," and Burchell worked hard to make a good impression. The American Legation in Canberra reported that a "very popular" Burchell averaged three speeches a week until his transfer to Newfoundland in July 1941 and judged that had "undoubtedly done a great deal to foster Canadian-Australian relations".[69]

Yet substantial differences had emerged quickly. In June 1940 Glasgow praised Canadian friendliness, hospitality and business acumen. But he also worried about a Canadian tendency to suspect British motives and feared that King lacked either "the ability or the will to rouse the country and provide the lead it has been waiting for", an opinion expressed more picturesquely by Menzies after he visited Ottawa in 1941. Four years later, as he was preparing to depart Ottawa, in the wake of King's refusal in May 1944 to support Prime Minister John Curtin's desire to create an imperial defence framework that would last into the postwar era, Glasgow doubted that Canadians were prepared to make sacrifices to defeat Japan, a fault the Australian placed firmly upon King's rounded shoulders.[70]

Still, Canadian High Commissioners gave way to no one in patronizing attitudes. Though Burchell judged Australians as "exceedingly friendly, sociable people" with a high standard of honesty, he also concluded that Australia was run "really very much on the Colonial basis" and "ruled from Downing Street". This may not have been a necessarily bad thing in Burchell's view given that the average Australian was "a happy-go-lucky individual, who is very haphazard in his plans".[71] Despite his star-crossed tenure, which began badly and ended poorly less than one year later, Odlum found time to criticize his hosts. Highly critical of Australian fighting spirit and indiscipline and scornful of lower-class Australians who were anti-British "with no hope of changing them," Odlum thought that Australians were "like children" suffering from a "definite inferiority complex".[72] Even the diplomatic T.C. Davis, sent to Canberra to repair the damage Odlum's unauthorized promise of Canadian military assistance had inflicted, castigated the Australians for poor eating habits and a leisurely, undisciplined and irresponsible approach to work and responsibilities, sins Davis attributed to a too gentle climate, complacency, class consciousness and a fondness for labour actions. Doubtful that Australians could reform themselves quickly or at all and asserting that Australia was "just a bit of Britain located out of its element in these Southern Seas," Davis still admitted to liking what he called the "spoilt brat of the family"; therefore he advocated giving them "a few beatings and a bit of kicking around and then you couldn't beat them".[73]

One might defend Canadian attitudes by pointing to George Kennan's observation that diplomats are akin to physicians in that they are often frustrated by having to deal with "a shabby and irritating group of patients: violent, headstrong, frivolous, unreasonable". Furthermore, Canadian historian Ronald Haycock has argued that much of the wartime unpleasantness can be attributed to the too rapid expansion of the Canadian and Australian diplomatic corps. This notion had some validity, especially in Odlum's case, but American diplomats in the period prior to 1945 like Moffat and Nelson T. Johnson also shared Canadian concerns about Australian complacency, cultural inferiority and insularity, with Johnson declaring that Australia was a "parasite on the body of the empire" intent on latching on to a new American host.[74] In fact, after his 1940 appointment as the American Minister to Canada, Moffat commented that in terms of political development, Australia was "still in the adolescent stage" while Canada was a "post-graduate who has just completed his doctor's thesis". If a particular process required seven steps, Moffat judged that "the average Australian could never see more than two at most; the Canadian can see at least five, sometimes six and occasionally all seven".[75]

But powerful systemic influences had hampered the initiation of good relations between Australia and Canada. Geography and isolation cannot be underestimated in framing distinctive dominion identities. After decades of distrust and sometimes outright conflict, by the dawn of the 20th century most Canadians did not regard the United States as a serious military threat to their national survival. As Wilfrid Laurier had told Lord Dundonald in 1904, Canada need not bother "with spending any money" on defence as Canada's security was "guaranteed by the Monroe Doctrine".[76] Canada's sense of security was demonstrated most dramatically during the Anglo-Japanese alliance debate in 1921, but strategic differences had emerged long before then. While Canada and Australia had blocked a proposal in 1902 to establish special bodies of troops earmarked specifically for imperial service in favour of letting individual colonies make decisions on a case-by-case basis, an Australian attempt in 1907 to form a centralized council to form and direct imperial foreign policy foundered upon the rocks of Laurier's determined opposition. Thus for Australian politician and diplomat F.W. Eggleston it was very clear by 1914 that the Empire faced a crucial "two ocean" geopolitical dilemma.[77]

Unlike Canada, which lapsed into a safe form of semi-isolationism after the hideous losses of the First World War, Australia's response to the geopolitical dilemma in the absence of a nearby ally was to re-emphasize its British connection, though that decision remains a matter of some contention for Australian and imperial academics. For T.B. Millar, John McCarthy, David Day, W.J. Hudson and M.P. Sharp, Australia's choice was a negative one brought on by an unquestioning reliance upon Britain, apathy, remoteness, perceptions of cultural inferiority and an unwillingness to practise independent defence and foreign policies. But Bernard Attard, Nicholas Mansergh and P.G. Edwards have argued that while Australia was a dependent dominion reliant upon Britain for its security, that fact derived from historical and geopolitical rationales that made sense at the time; moreover, that in no way meant that Australians ever stopped trying to play a real role in that relationship.[78] But regardless of how one interprets the rationale for this policy, Australian hopes for imperial unity and security were simply at odds with King's vision of an Empire functioning "with the complete independence of the parts united by co-operation in all common ends".[79] Therefore, successive Australian governments, though they failed to block the constitutional demands put forward by the more radical dominions, chose not to co-operate when Canada asked for formal diplomatic relations until that option offered Australia concrete advantages.

Many of the problems that plagued Australian-Canadian affairs after the First World War, ironically, had been predicted in 1894. In late 1893 Canada's first Minister of Trade had arrived in the Australasian colonies with a mandate to explore trade prospects in the wake of the initiation of steamship service between British Columbia and New South Wales. But Mackenzie Bowell had returned home from his arduous journey with mixed emotions. Though he believed that he had helped to create an Australian interest in Canadian products where none had existed before, and had found Australians to be "hospitable almost beyond credibility," he also had judged them as "intensely British". He pessimistically predicted then that he did not "anticipate any great immediate results" from the visit as "the parties with whom we have been estranged so long can scarcely be brought into a close relationship at a moment's notice".[80] As subsequent events amply demonstrated, perhaps Bowell, a short-lived Prime Minister later in the 1890s, might have pursued a more efficacious career as a professional psychic.

Notes

1. T.H.B. Symons, "Closing Remarks: Two Federations," *Public Policies in Two Federal Countries: Canada and Australia* ed., R.L. Mathews, (Canberra: Centre for Research on Federal Financial Relations, Australian National University, 1982), 10.

2. H.H. Asquith quoted in W.J. Hudson and M.P. Sharp, *Australian Independence: Colony to Reluctant Kingdom* (Melbourne: Melbourne University Press, 1988), 43.

3. T.O. Lloyd, *The British Empire, 1558-1983* (Oxford: Oxford University Press, 1989), 276-277.

4. H. Duncan Hall, *Commonwealth: A History of British Commonwealth of Nations* (London: Van Nostrand Reinhold, 1971), 156.

5. Dominion attempts to gain a real say in the peace talks are explored in W.J. Hudson, *Billy Hughes in Paris: The Birth of Australian Diplomacy* (Melbourne: Nelson, 1978); Peter Spartalis, *The Diplomatic Battles of Billy Hughes* (Sydney: Hale and Iremonger, 1983); R. Craig Brown, *Robert Laird Borden: A Biography, volume 2* (Toronto: University of Toronto Press, 1980); and C.P. Stacey, *Canada and the Age of Conflict. Volume 1: 1867-1921* (Toronto: University of Toronto Press, 1984), chap. 9.

6. Lord Rosebery quoted in Hall, 47; Spartalis, 218-229; and Stacey, 332-348. See also Loring Christie, "The Anglo-Japanese Alliance: Recapitulation of Points", June 1, 1921, published in *External Affairs,* 18 (September 1966): 402–413; and Michael Graham Fry, "The Pacific Dominions and the Washington Conference, 1921–22", *The Washington Conference,* 1921–22: *Naval Rivalry, East Asian Stability and the Road to Pearl Harbor* eds., Erik Goldstein and John Maurer, (Ilford: Frank Cass, 1994), 60–101.

7. R.G. Casey to S.M. Bruce, January 12, 1928, *My Dear P.M.: R.G. Casey's Letters to S.M. Bruce, 1924–1929* eds., W.J. Hudson and Jane North, (Canberra: Australian Government Publication Service, 1980), 241-242.

8. John Hilliker, *Canada's Department of External Affairs. Volume 1: The Early Years, 1909-1946* (Montreal and Kingston: McGill-Queen's University Press 1990), 92; and John MacFarlane, *Ernest Lapointe and Quebec's Influence on Canadian Foreign Policy* (Toronto: University of Toronto Press, 1999), 51-54.

9. See Minutes and Final Report of the 1923 Imperial Conference, Imperial Conference Records, CAB 32/9, Public Record Office (PRO); "The Negotiation, Signature and Ratification of Treaties: Resolution of the Imperial Conference of 1923", in Hall, 983-988; and Skelton quoted in Ramsay Cook, "J.W. Dafoe at the Imperial Conference, 1923", *Canadian Historical Review*, 41 (March 1960): 36–37.

10. Lord Curzon quoted in Norman Hillmer and J.L. Granatstein, *Empire to Umpire: Canada and the World to the 1990s* (Toronto: Copp Clark Longman, 1994), 94; Correlli Barnett, *The Collapse of British Power* (London: Eyre Methuen, 1972); Philip G. Wigley, *Canada and the Transition to Commonwealth: British-Canadian Relations, 1917-1926* (Cambridge: Cambridge University Press, 1977), 186-190; W.L. Morton, "Review of William Lyon Mackenzie King. II. The Lonely Heights, 1924–1932", *Canadian Historical Review*, 45 (December 1964): 320-321; and W.L. Morton, *The Kingdom of Canada* (Toronto: McClelland and Stewart, 1969), 441.

Skelton's briefing notes to King, "The Imperial Conference. Preliminary Notes," 1923, are found in the W.L.M. King Papers, Memoranda and Notes, vol. 81, National Archives of Canada (NAC).

11. Nicholas Mansergh, *The Commonwealth Experience* (London: Weidenfeld and Nicolson, 1969), 378; Norman Hillmer, "The Anglo-Canadian Neurosis: The Case of O.D. Skelton", in Peter Lyon, *Britain and Canada: Survey of a Changing Relationship* (London: Frank Cass, 1976), 61-84; and H. Blair Neatby, *William Lyon Mackenzie King: The Prism of Unity, 1932-1939* (Toronto: University of Toronto Press, 1976), 134-135.

12. Hughes quoted in W.J. Hudson and M.P. Sharp, op. cit., 68.

13. Casey to Bruce, February 5, 1925, in Hudson and North, 20; and Hudson and Sharp, 76. Bruce's position at the 1923 conference can be read in E. 4th Meeting minutes and E. 9th Meeting minutes, October 8 and 17, 1923, CAB 32/9, PRO.

14. Diary, March 7, 1925, W.L.M. King Papers, Diaries, NAC.

15. "Status of Great Britain and the Dominions [The Balfour Declaration], 1926", in Hall, 978-979.

16. Duncan Hall, op. cit., 415-416.

17. Quoted in W.J. Hudson and M.P. Sharp, op. cit., 87-89.

18. Casey to Bruce, November 5, 1925, in W.J. Hudson and Jane North, op. cit., 102–103; Norman Hillmer and Jack Granatstein, op. cit., 104; and John Hilliker, op. cit., 114.

19. J.L. Granatstein and Norman Hillmer, *For Better or For Worse: Canada and the United States to the 1990s* (Toronto: Copp Clark Pitman, 1991), 75. Dr. Michael Clark, an Alberta Member of Parliament, had noted after the First World War that Canada "and the world have had all the foreign policy they want for a number of years"; quoted in Robert Bothwell and John English, "The View from Inside Out: Canadian Diplomats and Their Public", *International Journal* 39, (Winter 1983–84): 51; W.S. Fielding, King's Anglophile Minister of Finance from 1921–25, had opposed sending a Minister to America. He viewed Washington, D.C., as a very expensive city, believed Britain's embassy could handle Canadian affairs and worried that such a step would injure imperial unity; James Eayrs, "The Diplomatic Eye", *Dalhousie Review*, 56 (Summer 1976): 206-207.

20. John Hilliker, op. cit., 111-112. President Calvin Coolidge initially had shown little interest in opening formal diplomatic relations with Canada, believing that consular agents could handle anything that might arise. But the American State Department was quite interested, though it had to convince its employees that an Ottawa posting was "a real job" that would not injure their careers: Coolidge quoted in Peter Charles Kasurak, "The United States Legation at Ottawa, 1927–1941: An Institutional Study", Duke University: 1967, Ph.D. dissertation, 17–18; and William R. Castle to Ferdinand L. Mayer, February 21, 1929, William R. Castle Papers, Herbert Hoover Library, box 2, file Canada 1929–1932. That worry might explain William Phillip's selection. A diplomatic high flier, Phillips accepted a demotion from ambassadorial rank in Europe to take up the position in Ottawa.

21. Diary, October 18, 1927, King Papers, NAC; and Hilliker, 112-113. See also Tou Chu Dou Lynhiavu, "Canada's Window on Asia: The Establishment of the Tokyo Legation in 1928–1931", *Journal of Canadian Studies*, 31 (Winter 1996–97): 97-123.

22. Bruce quoted in P.G. Edwards, *Prime Ministers & Diplomats: The Making of Australian Foreign Policy, 1901-1949* (Melbourne: Oxford University Press, 1983), 77; Hall, 595–601; Lord Stonehaven to the Dominions Secretary, November 16, 1927, Dominions Office Records, DO 35/22/12498, PRO; Robert Garran quoted in *Towards a Foreign Policy: 1914-1941, ed.*, W.J. Hudson, (Melbourne: Cassell, 1967), 24; and Casey to Bruce, February 23, 1928, in Hudson and North, 294.

23. Bernard Attard, *Australia as a Dependent Dominion, 1901–1939* (London: Sir Robert Menzies Centre for Australian Studies, University of London, 1999), 15; and Casey quoted in E.M. Andrews, *The Writing on the Wall: The British Commonwealth and Aggression in the East 1931-35* (Sydney: Allen and Unwin, 1987), 24.

24. Casey to Bruce, April 26, 1928; Hudson and North, 337.

25. Casey to Bruce, January 19, 1926, ibid., 252; and Casey to Bruce, June 6, 1929, ibid., 520. Australian intelligence also reported in April 1928 that Japanese newspaper *Yamato* wanted Japanese concerns about Canadian anti-Japanese sentiment satisfied before any diplomatic exchange took place; excerpt of "Australian Station Intelligence Report Part II R.4.28," in memorandum by Keith Officer, April 21, 1928, Series A981/4 Item IMP73, National Archives of Australia (NAA).

26. William Hodgson memorandum, "Canada," November 17, 1928, Series A981/4 Item CAN32, NAA.

27. Casey to Bruce, March 8, 1928, in W.J. Hudson and Jane North, op. cit., 311.

28. C.G. Power and P.B. Waite quoted in P.B. Waite, *The Loner: Three Sketches of the Personal Life and Ideas of R.B. Bennett, 1870-1947* (Toronto: University of Toronto Press, 1992), xiii.

29. R.B. Bennett speech, 13 April 1927, *Debates of the House of Commons 1927, Volume 2*, 2472; and "Canadian Ministers Abroad", *The Times of London*, 16 June 1928.

30. John Hilliker, op. cit., 137.

31. Foreign Office memorandum, "Canadian Legations," August 7, 1931, Series A981/4 Item IMP67, NAA.

32. Chancellor of the Exchequer Neville Chamberlain claimed that Bennett "strained our patience to the limit" and "alternately blustered, sobbed, bullied, prevaricated, delayed and obstructed, to the very last moment"; Keith Feiling, *The Life of Neville Chamberlain* (London: Macmillan, 1946), 215.

33. O. Mary Hill, *Canada's Salesman to the World: The Department of Trade and Commerce, 1892–1939* (Montreal and Kingston: McGill-Queen's University Press, 1977), 78.

34. Greg Donaghy, *Parallel Paths: Canadian-Australian Relations Since the 1890s* (Ottawa: Department of Foreign Affairs and International Trade, 1995), 7–8.

35. Norman Hillmer and Jack Granatstein, op. cit., 114-115.

36. Scullin quoted in David Day, *Great Betrayal: Australia & the Onset of the Pacific War* (New York: W.W. Norton, 1989), 3; and W.J. Hudson and M.P. Sharp, op. cit., 4.

37. P.G. Edwards, op. cit., 67-68.

38. M. Ruth Megaw, "Undiplomatic Channels: Australian Representatives in the United States, 1918-1939", *Historical Studies*, 15 (October 1973): 611.

39. Department of State Division of Western European Affairs memorandum, "Direct Diplomatic Relations with Australia," July 27, 1933, Department of State Records, RG84, Foreign Service Posts, Australia Canberra Legation, Entry 2033, file 124, National Archives and Records Administration (NARA); and J.A. Lyons to Franklin Roosevelt, August 31, 1935, Franklin Roosevelt Papers, Official Files, box 11, file OF48d Australia 1933–40, Franklin Delano Roosevelt Library (FDRL). In 1934 Roosevelt, concerned that Britain would appease Japanese demands for a larger navy than allowed by the Washington Agreements, made very clear "that

if Great Britain is even suspected of preferring to play with Japan to playing with us, I shall be compelled, in the interest of American security, to approach public sentiment in Canada, Australia, New Zealand and South Africa in a definite way to make these dominions understand clearly that their future security is linked with us in the United States". Britain promptly disavowed any deal with Japan; Roosevelt to Norman H. Davis, November 9, 1934, *Franklin D. Roosevelt and Foreign Affairs. Volume II: March 1934–August 1935*, ed., Edgar B. Dikon, (Cambridge: Belknap Press, 1969), 263.

40. P.G. Edwards, ed., *Australia Through American Eyes, 1935-1945: Observations by American Diplomats* (St. Lucia: University of Queensland Press, 1979), 4; and Raymond Esthus, *From Enmity to Alliance: U.S.-Australian Relations, 1931-1941* (Seattle: University of Washington Press, 1964), 16-17.

41. Bennett to Lyons, January 11, 1935, Series A461/8, Item A348/1/1, NAA.

42. W.J. Hudson and M.P. Sharp, op. cit., 113; and John Armitage, "Warning to Australia", *The Winnipeg Free Press*, December 22, 1934.

43. Prime Minister's Department to Cabinet, "High Commissioners – Question of Exchange Between Australia and Canada", January 24, 1935, Series A461/8, Item A348/1/1, NAA; and Lyons to Bennett, February 13, 1935, Department of External Affairs Records, RG25, vol. 1724, file 117, NAC.

44. James Eayrs, "'A Low and Dishonest Decade': Aspects of Canadian External Policy, 1931–1939", *The Growth of Canadian Policies in External Affairs*, ed., Hugh Keenleyside, (Durham: Duke University Press,1960), 59–80; and J.L. Granatstein and Robert Bothwell, "'A Self-Evident National Duty': Canadian Foreign Policy, 1935-1939", *The Journal of Imperial and Commonwealth History*, 3 (January 1975): 212-233; and diary, October 29, 1936, King Papers, NAC. King's concerns about America are explored in Galen Roger Perras, *Franklin Roosevelt and the Origins of the Canadian-American Security Alliance, 1933–1945: Necessary But Not Necessary Enough* (Westport: Praeger, 1998).

45. Diary, November 2, 1935, King Papers, NAC.

46. Skelton memorandum, "Visit of Mr. Keith Officer", July 22, 1937, King Papers, Memoranda, vol. 149, C108237; Skelton to Herbert Marler, February 6, 1937, RG25, vol. 1834, file 1937–319, NAC; Skelton to King, May 28, 1937, in John A. Munro, ed., *Documents on Canadian External Relations (DCER), Volume 6* (Ottawa: Department of External Affairs, 1972), 331; and Cordell Hull memorandum, "Commercial Relations with Australia", January 17, 1938, Cordell Hull Papers, box 58, file Great Britain 1936-38, Library of Congress.

47. Skelton to King, "Extension of Canada's External Affairs Service", October 5, 1937, King Papers, Memoranda, vol. 158, file 1415.

48. E.J. Harding to F.L.C. Floud, January 13, 1936, DO35/187/7102A/1, PRO; Floud to Harding, 30 January 1936, DO35/187/7102A/2, PRO; and Christie memorandum, "Notes on the Placing of New Legations", September 23, 1937, RG25, vol. 791, file 428. Christie's conversion is described in J.L. Granatstein, *The Ottawa Men: The Civil Service Mandarins, 1935–1957* (Toronto: Oxford University Press, 1982), chap. 4.

49. Diary, December 9, 1937, King Papers, NAC; Skelton memoranda, "Resumption of Development of Canadian Representation Abroad, Summary of Memorandum", January 11, 1938, "Memorandum re Establishment of New Offices, Finance and Personnel", January 17, 1938, and "Extension of the Canadian Service Abroad", January 21, 1938, RG25, vol. 791, file 428.

50. Floud to Sir Harry Batterbee, May 24, 1938, DO35/586/G88/55.

51. L.R. Macgregor to Secretary Department of External Affairs, "Some Influences Upon Canada's Foreign Policy", September 29, 1939, Series A981/4, Item CAN65, NAA; Paul Hasluck, *The Government and the People, 1939-1941* (Canberra: Australian War Memorial, 1952), 40; and George Pearce to Lyons, 26 January 1937, in R.G. Neale, ed., *Documents on Australian Foreign Policy, 1937-1949. Volume I: 1937-38 [DAFP]* (Canberra: Australian Government Publishing Service, 1975), 5.

52. Diary, June 7 and 10, 1937, King Papers, NAC; and extract of minutes of 10th meeting of the Principal Delegates to the Imperial Conference, E (PD) (37) 10, June 1, 1937, *DAFP*, 98-99. King's performance is explored in Norman Hillmer, "The Pursuit of Peace: Mackenzie King and the 1937 Imperial Conference", *Mackenzie King: Widening the Debate* eds., John English and J.O. Stubbs (Toronto: Macmillan, 1978), 149–172.

53. "F.C. Mears, "Canada to Send Commissioners to Represent Her in Dominions", July 22, 1937; Keith Officer to Secretary Department of External Affairs, "Canada Representation Abroad", July 27, 1937, Series A981/4, Item IPM67, NAA; and Skelton memorandum, June 25, 1938, RG25, vol. 2959, file B-80, NAC.

54. Skelton memorandum, June 25, 1938, RG25, vol. 2959, file B–80, NAC; R.G. Menzies, excerpt of "The Relations Between The British Dominions", December 1935, in Hudson, *Towards a Foreign Policy*, 26; and Edwards, *Prime Ministers & Diplomats*, 123.

55. Edwards, *Prime Ministers & Diplomats*, 118; and Officer to Casey, January 25, 1939, *Documents on Australian Foreign Policy, 1937-49. Volume II: 1939* ed., R.G. Neale, (Canberra: Australian Government Publishing Service, 1976), 24-26.

56. Officer to Casey, January 25, 1939, *DAFP Volume II*, 26.

57. Menzies speech, April 26, 1939, Ibid., 97-98.

58. John Hilliker, op. cit., 189-190; and Officer to Hodgson, August 2, 1939, *DAFP Volume II*, 163.

59. Diary, August 14, 1939, Jay Pierrepont Moffat Papers, MS Am1407, vol. 43, Houghton Library (HL), Harvard University; and Moffat memorandum, "Establishment of an Australian Legation in Washington", December 23, 1938, State Department Records, RG59, Political Relations Between the United States and Australia 1910–1944, T–1191, reel 1, NARA. Passages from the manuscript material of Jay Pierrepont Moffat, shelf mark MS Am1407, used by permission of Houghton Library, Harvard University.

60. No. 7, King to Menzies, September 3, 1939, Series A461/8, Item B348/1/16, NAA.

61. Cabinet minute extracts, "Exchange of High Commissioners", September 5, 1939, Series A461/8, Item B348/1/16; Menzies to Bruce, September 5, 1939, Series A981/4, Item AUS151 Pt. 1, NAA; no. 412, Bruce to Menzies, September 5, 1939, ibid.; and Menzies to King, September 6, 1939, ibid.

62. King to Charles J. Burchell, October 17, 1939, RG25, vol. 1944, file 763, NAC; diary, October 31, and November 24, 1939, King Papers, NAC; and King to Massey, January 25, 1936, W.L.M. King Papers, Correspondence, vol. 223, NAC.

63. Menzies speech to the House of Representatives, September 12, 1939, Series A981/4, Item AUS151 pt. 1, NAA; Hodgson to the Minister of External Affairs, "Australian High Commissioner, Canada", September 13, 1939, Ibid.; and Edwards, *Prime Ministers & Diplomats*, 123. Menzies did not inform King of Glasgow's selection until late December; Menzies to King, December 23, 1939, Series A461/8, Item A348/1/15, NAA. Letters from the various petitioners can be seen in Series A461/9, Item B348/1/15, NAA.

64. No. 2225, Joseph Kennedy to Hull, October 31, 1939, Department of State Records, Foreign Service Posts, RG84, Australia Canberra Legation, Entry 2033, file 124 Legation, NARA; no. 1350, Hull to Kennedy, November 1, 1939, Ibid.; Hull to American Consul Sydney, November 2, 1939, ibid.; and Edwards, *Prime Ministers & Diplomats*, 121-126.

65. Vincent Massey, *What's Past Is Prologue: The Memoirs of the Right Honourable Vincent Massey, C.H.* (Toronto: Macmillan, 1963), 303-304; Cecil Edwards, *Bruce of Melbourne: Man of Two Worlds* (London: Heinemann, 1965), 277-278; and T.C. Davis to King, December 18, 1943, King Papers, Correspondence, vol. 339, NAC.

66. E.B. Rogers to King, October 13, 1942, *Documents on Canadian External Relations. Volume 9: 1942-1943,* ed., John F. Hilliker, (Ottawa: Department of External Affairs, 1980), 376. See also Ronald G. Haycock, "The 'Myth' of Imperial Defence: Australian-Canadian Bilateral Military Co-operation, 1942", *War & Society,* 2 (May 1984): 65-84; and Galen Roger Perras, "She Should Have Thought of Herself First: Canada and the Provision of Military Aid to Australia, 1939–1945," presented at the 1999 Australian Studies Association of North America Conference. Odlum admitted in 1944 that he had "learned to see things, not as they are, but as they ought to be, or, rather, as my fancy would like them to be"; Kim Richard Nossal, "Chungking Prism: Cognitive Process and Intelligence Failure", *International Journal,* 32 (Summer 1977): 559-576.

67. Evatt quoted in Paul Hasluck, *Diplomatic Witness: Australian Foreign Affairs, 1941–47* (Melbourne: Melbourne University Press, 1980), 195; Charles Ritchie, *Diplomatic Passport: More Undiplomatic Diaries, 1946-1962* (Toronto: Macmillan, 1981), 2; Evatt to King, April 20, 1947, Series A1068, Item P47//10/61 ii, NAA; Hume Wrong to D. Johnson, May 6, 1947, in Norman Hillmer and Donald Page, eds., *Documents on Canadian External Relations. Volume 13: 1947* (Ottawa: Department of Foreign Affairs and International Trade, 1993), 202-203; Lester Pearson to Louis St. Laurent, "Japanese Peace Settlement", May 23, 1947, ibid., 204-205; and Pearson memorandum, "Japanese Peace Settlement: Commonwealth Conference; Canberra", July 18, 1947, ibid., 209.

68. Diary, June 17, 1940, King Papers, NAC; N.A. Robertson to King, September 23, 1943, King Papers, Memoranda, vol. 234, NAC; Robertson to King, October 28, 1944, ibid.; and King minute, December 2, 1944, ibid.

69. Burchell to J.A. Carrodus, February 5, 1940, Series A292/1, Item C19591, NAA; "Australia and Canada", The Sydney *Morning Herald,* December 28, 1939; and no. 155, John R. Minter to Hull, July 22, 1941, Military Intelligence Division Regional File 1922-1944, RG165, file 3600 Australia, NARA.

70. T.W. Glasgow to the Governor General of Australia, June 4, 1940, Series A3095/2, Item 17/1; and Glasgow draft memoranda, September 1944, Series A3095/1, Item 35/9. In 1941 Menzies had found King to be "pleasant and cooperative" but thought that King "possesses no burning zeal for the cause, and is a politician who possibly prefers to lead from behind"; Diary, May 8, 1941, in A.W. Martin and Patsy Hardy, eds., *Dark and Hurrying Days: Menzies' 1941 Diary* (Canberra: National Library of Australia, 1993), 124-125. Canada's reluctance to fight in the Pacific is discussed in Galen Roger Perras, "Once Bitten, Twice Shy:

The Origins of the Canadian Army Pacific Force," *Uncertain Horizons: Canadians and Their World in 1945*, ed., Greg Donaghy, (Ottawa: Canadian Committee for the History of the Second World War, 1997), 77-99.

71. Burchell to Skelton, April 24, 1940, RG25, vol. 1944, file 763; and Burchell to Skelton, November 14, 1940, King Papers, Memoranda, vol. 383.

72. Odlum to Douglas MacArthur, June 25, 1942, Victor Odlum Papers, vol. 7, file Macarthur Douglas, NAC; no. 129, Odlum to King, May 11, 1942, J.L. Ralston Papers, vol. 38, file Australia Gen. (Secret), NAC; Odlum to King, June 1, 1942, King Papers, Correspondence, vol. 331, NAC; diary, September 23, 1942, King Papers, NAC; and Odlum to King, July 28, 1942, King Papers, Correspondence, vol. 331.

73. Davis to Robertson, January 25, and February 8, 1943, June 23, and September 11, 1944, King Papers, Memoranda, vol. 234, NAC; Davis quoted in J.F. Hilliker, "Distant Ally: Canadian Relations with Australia During the Second World War", *The Journal of Imperial and Commonwealth History*, 13 (October 1984), 57; Davis to King, October 16, 1943, King Papers, Memoranda, vol. 234, NAC; and Davis to Robertson, December 29, 1945, James Garfield Gardiner Papers, reel 4210, Saskatchewan Provincial Archives.

74. George Kennan quoted in Elmer Plischke, *United States Diplomats and Their Missions: A Profile of American Diplomatic Emissaries Since 1778* (Washington, D.C.: American Enterprise Institute for Public Policy Research, 1975), 277; Haycock, 80; Moffat to Hull, October 14, 1935, Moffat Papers, vol. 8, HL; Moffat to Hull, January 18, 1937, RG59, T–1190, reel 2, file 847.00/248, NARA; Nelson T. Johnson to Mrs. Van Santvoord Merle-Smith, Nov. 20, 1941, Nelson T. Johnson Papers, box 39, file 1941, LC; and Johnson to Stanley Hornbeck, December 11, 1941, box 66, file Stanley Hornbeck Correspondence Aug. 1941-1942, ibid. P.G. Edwards has explored American attitudes in *Australia Through American Eyes, 1935-1945: Observations by American Diplomats* (St. Lucia: U. of Queensland Press, 1979).

75. Moffat to Minter, May 2, 1941, Moffat Papers, MS Am1407, vol. 46, HL.

76. Richard A. Preston, *Canada and "Imperial Defense": A Study of the Origins of the British Commonwealth's Defense Organization, 1867-1919* (Durham: Duke University Press, 1967), 327.

77. "Extract from the Summary of Proceedings, Colonial Conference, 1902", *Documents on Australian International Affairs 1901-1918*, ed., Gordon Greenwood and Charles Grimshaw, (Melbourne: Nelson, 1977), 224-225; Edwards, *Prime Ministers & Diplomats*, 4; and F.W. Eggleston quoted in Andrews, 195.

78. T.B. Millar, *Australia in Peace and War: External Relations, 1788-1977* (Canberra: C. Hurst, 1978); John McCarthy, *Australia and Imperial Defence, 1918-1939: A Study in Air and Sea Power* (St. Lucia: University of Queensland Press, 1976); Day, *The Great Betrayal*; Coral Bell, *Dependent Ally: A Study in Australian Foreign Policy* (Melbourne: Allen and Unwin, 1988); W.J. Hudson and M.P. Sharp, op. cit., 126; Bernard Attard, op. cit., 3; Nicholas Mansergh, *Survey of British Commonwealth Affairs: Problems of External Policy 1931-1939* (London: Oxford University Press, 1952), 138–39; and Edwards, *Prime Ministers & Diplomats*, 3.

79. Diary, September 10, 1939, King Papers, NAC.

80. Bowell quoted in Hill, 28; and Greg Donaghy, *Parallel Paths*, op. cit., 1.

8

Throwing Out the Baby with the Bathwater? Huntington's "Kin-Country" Thesis and Australian-Canadian Relations

KIM RICHARD NOSSAL

Introduction

The end of the Cold War between 1989 and 1991 forced many students of international relations to rethink their theoretical perspectives to account for the profound changes so obviously underway in world politics. Among the theoretical newcomers in the early 1990s was the civilizational perspective advanced by Samuel P. Huntington. In an article in *Foreign Affairs* in 1993, entitled "The clash of civilizations?" and expanded in 1996 in a book (which lost the question mark of the article along the way), Huntington argued for a fundamental retheorizing of international relations. Asserting that world politics had entered a "new phase," he suggested that international politics in the post-Cold War era was no longer going to be dominated by nation-states or even collectives of states organized into four compass points along ideological or economic lines (North, South, East, and West). Rather, he hypothesized that the world consisted of a number of civilizations, and suggested that the major conflicts of 21st century world politics were going to be found along what he called the "fault lines" between these various civilizations. Huntington's civilizational theory was not without its normative implications: he argued that the world's dominant civilization, the West, was in danger of declining against other civilizations – unless, that was, it moved to maintain its economic and military power.

Huntington's theory, while original, is not without deep empirical and normative problems, as I will argue. This chapter will examine the civilizational perspective as outlined by Huntington, and will suggest that for a variety of reasons civilizational theory can be dismissed as so much bathwater, richly deserving to be pitched. At the same time, however, I will argue that there is one aspect of the civilizational perspective – the Kin-Country thesis – that is analytically useful and provides an explanation for a particular phenomenon not well explained by orthodox international relations theory: relationships between some kinds of countries, such as Australia and Canada, that do not at all conform to the predictions of orthodox international relations theory.

The Bathwater: Civilizational Theory and its Discontents

Huntington's theory rests on the idea that the crucial unit of analysis for world politics in the 21st century will be civilizations rather than nation-states. Like other civilizational theorists, such as Fernand Braudel[1], Huntington defines civilizations as being amalgams of culture, language, ethnicity, religion, customs and "ways of life". But, importantly, Huntington argues that civilizations are not just cultural entities, but essentially *political* entities as well. While civilizations do not replace or supplant the main political entities that have dominated world politics since the 17th century – Westphalian nation-states – they co-exist with them. Indeed, most civilizations in Huntington's view have a "core state"– the acknowledged centre of the civilization, around which other kin countries rally in order to support the civilization in its struggles against other civilizations. In other words, civilizations as political entities have an overt political component. They inspire the same kind of political loyalty as nation-states did in the past. Most importantly, people will, in Huntington's view at least, put themselves in harm's way in defence of the interests of "their" civilization. It is this political loyalty that gives rise to Huntington's idea of civilizational "fault lines". In this view, civilizations do not have clear cut borders. Where they "meet" – on "fault lines" – conflict is likely to develop; and these conflicts between civilizations will be the dominant source of war in the 21st century.

The civilizational perspective advanced by Huntington almost immediately generated a wave of objections and criticisms. In fact, both the article and the book provided grist for a variety of mills. Some critics, including Fouad Ajami and Binyan Liu, focussed on Huntington's misreading of other civilizations, particularly the Islamic and Confucian (or, as he was to rename it by the time he wrote the book, the Sinic)[2]. Others fixed on his underestimation of the durability of the sovereign state as the primary actor in world politics, and the difficulties of ascribing political control to amorphous "civilizations".[3] Others still criticized the civilizational perspective as inappropriately encouraging the creation and maintenance of artificially constructed notions of "fault lines" between civilizations.[4]

These objections alone would be grounds enough to call into serious question the civilizational perspective as advanced by Huntington. But there is an even more basic problem: the very characterization of the civilizations deemed to exist in contemporary global politics is, it can be argued, deeply flawed. In Huntington's view, there are nine extant civilizations: Western, Latin American, Islamic, Sinic, Hindu, Orthodox, Buddhist, Japanese and African – though an African civilization exists only "possibly" in his view.[5] As will be immediately evident from this list, it is not entirely clear which criteria Huntington sees as most important for defining a "civilization." Religious beliefs obviously play an important part in Huntington's view of what constitutes a civilization, since four civilizations are identified with religious beliefs (Buddhist, Hindu, Islamic and Orthodox). Two – Latin American and African – are coterminous with continents. In Huntington's view of the world, the Sinic civilization includes all the territory of the People's Republic of China, excluding Tibet, but including not only the predominantly Muslim areas of China's Far West but also Vietnam, the two Koreas and the northern islands of the Philippines. One civilization is entirely coterminous with a contemporary nation-state – Japan is the territorial repository of the "Japanese" civilization.

Huntington argued in response to his many critics that because he was proposing a new paradigm for the analysis and understanding of world politics, he had to rely on "simplified pictures of reality".[6] While it is true that any paradigm must necessarily rely on a certain degree of simplification, there is a difference between making things simple and getting things simply wrong; and it can be argued that Huntington's portraiture of contemporary civilizations is indeed simply wrong.

A look at the map that Huntington uses to illustrate the world of civilizations[7] reveals how deeply problematic his definitions of contemporary civilizations are. Virtually every region of the world features some exceedingly odd, if not outright bizarre, characterizations. Perhaps the most striking is the inclusion of Papua New Guinea as a country of the West. The map also features a razor-sharp line between the putative "West" and Islamic civilization running down the 141st parallel that forms the boundary between Papua New Guinea and the Indonesian *propinsi-propinsi* of Irian Jaya. Perhaps Huntington or the cartographers at Simon and Schuster thought that the eastern half of the island was part of Australia, like Tasmania. But how can we explain his characterization of Irian Jaya as Muslim? In fact, except for the Javanese and others who have been purposely settled in Irian Jaya by the government in Djakarta, the people of that territory are predominantly Melanesian and not at all Muslim. Far from feeling any "civilizational" links to their nominally fellow Indonesians, many people in Irian Jaya are deeply opposed to the rule of Djakarta and the central government's policy of granting land to settlers from other parts of the country. And the line that runs so cleanly down the centre of New Guinea along the 141st has little actual significance to people on the ground on a day-to-day basis: the international boundary that divides all Melanesians on the island is important mainly in the minds of elites in Port Moresby and Djakarta and the world's cartographers.

Or consider his characterization of the Philippines in Map 1.3 as half Sinic and half Muslim. This is surely an odd way to paint a country where 84 percent of the population are Roman Catholic, 10 percent are Protestant, and only four percent are Muslim. And it is not clear what Sinic civilizational connections contemporary Philippine society is supposed to have; it has been several hundred years since Sinic influence was felt in the Philippines, and the only clear Sinic connection at present is that the Philippines are located in the South China Sea.

Other oddities include the characterization of Hong Kong as a little dot of Westernness on China's underbelly. Was this because, at the time he was writing, Hong Kong was technically a British Crown Colony, even though the vast majority of Hong Kong people are Chinese? One wonders how Huntington would colour Hong Kong today, after its return to the sovereignty of the People's Republica of China. Would he paint Hong Kong "Sinic", thus denying the very Western nature of the polity and its people? Singapore suffered a similar fate in Huntington's portraiture. Just as Huntington ignored Hong Kong's mixed character, so too did he cause Singapore simply to disappear into Islamic crosshatching, masking completely the particular mix of "civilizations" evident in that island state.

A different oddity is Huntington's treatment of Japan. That country is given its very own "civilization," the only country where the nation and the civilization are deemed by Huntington to be in perfect coincidence. Importantly, by declaring Japan its own civilization, Huntington ensures that Japan cannot be deemed in any sense part of the "West," thus in a stroke denying some unmistakable Western characteristics of contemporary Japanese society, culture, economics and politics.

Japan is not the only country that has numerous Western characteristics to be denied membership in Huntington's "West". Huntington also denies the Westernness of Israel; indeed, his treatment of that country is nothing short of bizarre. While in the map of the Cold War era, Huntington painted Israel as a "Free World" country, in his civilizational portrait Israelis simply disappear into the crosshatching of Islamic civilization, a religious relocation that would no doubt come as a surprise to Israeli Jews. But this is no cartographic slip: Huntington's discussion of Israel throughout the book leaves in no doubt that he does not consider Israel a "Western" country.

Other odd characterizations include the fact that in Africa, neither Madagascar nor South Africa receive treatment different than those of all other "African" states south of the Sahara, despite the considerable differences in origins and culture that mark both these countries from other African states. And with the exception of the Guyana coast – which is painted a mixture of Hindu, African and Western civilizations (but does not include any reference to Islamic civilization, even though some 15 percent of Guyanese are Muslims) – everything south of the Rio Grande, including the Caribbean, is characterized as part of a "Latin American" civilization. This simply does not reflect reality: there are considerable "civilizational" differences among the peoples of the Caribbean, and between the Caribbean and Central America, and between Central America and South America, and in South America between the Spanish-speaking countries and Portuguese-speaking Brazil, but also *among* Spanish-speaking Latin Americans.

More importantly, perhaps, even when Huntington's characterizations of a civilization are nominally accurate, there is no hint at all of the deep cleavages and cultural divisions *within* these "civilizations". For example, the black colouring that comprises "the West" constitutes a huge black box: it reveals nothing of the deep fissures within and between the various communities that make up this supposedly unitary political actor. There are deep cultural divisions between national groups – one need not do more than reflect on the marked politico-cultural differences between Americans and French, for example – but also within national groups. For example, all of the so-called "immigrant nations" – Australia, Canada, Britain, France, New Zealand and the United States itself—are portrayed as homogeneously "Western", masking the huge diversities of race, ethnicity and religion that exist in these communities.

Likewise, in the "Islamic civilization", the crosshatching sweeps unperturbed across North Africa, the Middle East, Southwest Asia and into Southeast Asia, offering no hint of the fundamental lack of cultural similarity between those at the eastern and western reaches of this "civilization." There is no hint of the deep divisions between Sunnis and Shiites that is at the heart of so much violence, both between nations (for example, between Iran and Iraq, or between Iran and Saudi Arabia) and within nations (for example, Pakistan or Iraq). Nor is there any hint of the deep cleavages between those Muslims who tend to be described in the Western media as "fundamentalist" and those who have a rather more secular perspective.

And in all the civilizations painted by Huntington, all Aboriginal peoples simply disappear into the dominant "civilization", There is no recognition in the civilizational perspective that Aboriginal peoples occupy numerous countries of the Western, Latin American, Orthodox, Sinic, Buddhist and Japanese civilizations, despite the fact that many Aboriginal peoples have "civilizational" claims of their own, and that those Aboriginal claims are deeply entrenched politically, not only in the national politics of many states, but also at the international level.

Finally, the "fault lines" that Huntington paints between civilizations run suspiciously along the borders of existing sovereign states. We have already noted the amazingly sharp fault line between Islam and the West that supposedly runs through the jungles and highlands of New Guinea along the 141st parallel. But this is not the only example of such coincidences between existing nation-states and civilizational fault lines. Likewise, there is no hint, for example, that the "fault line" that is supposed to exist between the southern part of the United States and the northern reaches of Mexico cannot be neatly drawn along the Rio Grande. On the contrary, as Robert D. Kaplan has put it evocatively, the Southwest and the Pacific Coast is where "America sheds its skin".[8] The border between the United States and Mexico takes a more concrete form than many international borders, but neither the U.S. Border Patrol nor the electronic sensing devices have been able to stop the fundamental transformation of the American Pacific Southwest into what Kaplan claims is the world's first "multicultural civilization". Even if it can be argued that the language of civilizations is inappropriate to describe the transformation of American society in this region, there can be no denying that Huntington's clean line drawn along the present international border is even less appropriate.

How important are Huntington's oversimplified, idiosyncratic, bizarre or simply erroneous portraits of the world? Do they take away from the broader civilizational argument? Do they render the new paradigm meaningless? The short answer, in my view, is 'yes'. For if the descriptive portraiture of the civilizations is flawed – and the critiques outlined above suggest that the civilizational paradigm is riddled with errors – then it can be suggested that the project must also have deep analytical flaws.

If we accept Robert W. Cox's wise observation that international relations theory is always purposeful – "theory is always *for* someone and *for* some purpose"[9] – we might ask whether there might be a relationship between the flawed portraiture of civilizations and the normative purpose of the exercise. One is left to wonder whether the "theoretical" purpose of the civilizational paradigm is in fact little more than the creation – and legitimization – of an Other for Westerners to hate and fear. For certainly Huntington can be read as a late 20th century variant of that oldest of dichotomies in human affairs – the dichotomy between the Civilized Self and the Uncivilized Other. That dichotomy was central to how ancient Greeks, imperial Chinese and Crusading Christians saw the world, and themselves: the Civilized Self was defined in terms of Uncivilized-Other barbarians, *yi ren*, or heathen. As I have argued elsewhere[10], unlike the more traditional forms, however, Huntington's updated variation involves a Civilized Self confronting an "Other-Civilized" Other.

It can be noted that for this dichotomy to work, one does not have to get the other civilizations right. Indeed, one does not need to know very much about other civilizations at all. It is enough to paint the world in such a way as to show one's own civilization surrounded by others, and to characterize those other civilizations as unitary actors seeking dominance over one's own civilization, and thus posing a threat. Moreover, aggregating data from numerous countries into a supposedly unitary "civilization" allows one to add to the visual threat-display by engaging in a further bit of analytical legerdemain, showing how supposedly one's own civilization is "declining" relative to others. Tables with ominous titles like "Shares of World Population Under the Political Control of Civilizations, 1900-2025", "Civilization Shares of Total World

Military Manpower", "Youth Bulge in Muslim Countries" and "Militarism of Muslim and Christian Countries" are served up to give the argument a patina of scientific authority.

And, of course, all of this provides the necessary backdrop to the normative prescriptions offered by civilizational theory: the West is in decline relative to other civilizations; the West needs to guard against the decay that has always threatened civilizations in the past; if it wishes to retain the dominant position it has enjoyed for the past several centuries, the West needs to devote serious resources to defending itself against other civilizations seeking dominance over the West. Indeed, Huntington goes so far as to suggest that war may be necessary to defend the West's position: he sketches out a scenario (described by Huntington as "highly improbable but not impossible") in which the West and the Sinic civilization go to war in 2010.[11] There are at least two problems with this scenario. First, the scenario ironically reveals the emptiness of the contention that conflicts in the future will be between civilizations, not states: for in fact, the 2010 scenario is all about *states*, all acting in their own *national*, not *civilizational*, interests. Second, and more important, little evidence is adduced by Huntington to demonstrate the *intent* of other "civilizations" to dominate the West, much less oppose it. On the contrary: Hungtington simply glosses over the homogenization, modernization and Westernization that so marks contemporary world politics. Such evidence is ignored, downplayed or reinterpreted to fit the civilizational thesis.

In sum, the civilizational paradigm reveals itself to be deeply flawed. It appears to have been based primarily on one particular conflict in the early 1990s – the collapse of the Federal Republic of Yugoslavia – and then extrapolated to a broader set of international conflicts. It is true that there were some important elements of "civilizational" identity politics at work in the Balkans throughout the 1990s. Likewise, it is possible to interpret the intercommunal violence that broke out in Indonesia in the late 1990s using the civilizational perspective, and interpret the rapes of Chinese women during the Djakarta riots, the killings of Timorese or the violence against Christians in the Moluccas in 1999 as the struggles of the Islamic, Sinic and Western civilizations. But ethnic, religious or nationalist violence, when it occurs within a political community, does not necessarily imply a broader civilizational struggle. Moreover, the extrapolation to something more global founders badly, no more clearly than when one considers that there seem to be so few "civilizationalist" enthusiasts in the supposed "core" states. In short, when one looks at the holes in

Huntington's "paradigm", it appears little more than a very old-fashioned enemy-creation exercise dressed up in academic clothing.

The Baby: The Kin-Country Thesis

One of the phenomena in the new world of clashing civilizations identified by Huntington is "kin-country rallying." The term was first used in an article in the *Boston Globe*[12] to describe the phenomenon, observed in the Yugoslav civil war, of who was allying with whom in that conflict. Huntington extended the family analogy, arguing that each civilization had a "core state" that was able to engage in "ordering" the civilization it led. Huntington argued that the core state could perform its ordering function "because member states perceive it as a cultural kin. A civilization is an extended family and, like older members of a family, core states provide their relatives with both support and discipline".[13]

This civilizational "kinship" felt by people in different nations has important political effects, in Huntington's view. In particular, "in civilizational conflicts, unlike ideological ones, kin stand by their kin". This leads to "kin-country rallying," which is marked by "efforts by a state from one civilization to protect kinsmen in another civilization".[14] This rallying involves both governments and peoples: in some cases, diasporas will take the lead in organizing support – financial, military and political – for their civilizational "kin"; in other cases, governments will be the prime movers.

This rallying, Huntington contends, has a critical impact on contemporary conflict. In a world of nation-states, conflicts between states are largely limited to the protagonists or those with a deep and direct interest in devoting blood and treasure to the cause. A1 and B1 might go to war, but the likelihood of widening that conflict is limited. In a world of civilizations, by contrast, the dynamics of kin-country rallying have the effect of widening wars. In fault line wars, A1 fights B1, with each seeking "to expand the war and mobilize support from civilizational kin groups A2, A3, A4 and B2, B3 and B4, and those groups will identify with their fighting kin".[15] Moreover, contemporary transportation and communications make the "internationalization" of kin-country support easier to accomplish: money, goods, services, arms and even people are moved effortlessly across national boundaries.

While the fit is not always perfect, Huntington is able to provide considerably more evidence for the kin-country rallying thesis than for his civilizational thesis more generally. He can point to the quintessential case for the 1990s, the war in Yugoslavia, and the willingness of groups and states to rally around the different warring parties. More importantly, he can point to the growing importance of diasporas, particularly diasporas in Western states, in rallying to support their "kinfolk" back home. We have not only seen this in Yugoslavia, but conflicts in Haiti, Timor and the Middle East.

Such an identification of feelings of "kinship" across borders – the existence of "kin countries" – stands in stark contrast to orthodox theorizing in international politics about the relations of political communities. The orthodox theorizing conceives of political communities as atomistic, self-regarding and fundamentally selfish in their relations with all other political communities. One of the most popular theories of international relations conceives of world politics as little more than the endless struggles of self-interested units seeking to avoid domination by others in an environment that is fundamentally anarchic and comparable to a Hobbesian state of nature, where there was no government, and thus where everyone treated one another as an enemy. In this view, the units may take different forms over time—since 1648, they have predominantly been sovereign nation-states—but the essence of their interaction is unchanging over time: they define their interests in terms of power[16] and struggle with each other to seek a balance of power. This bleak perspective is termed realism, for it purports to offer a realistic (and *Realpolitik*) portrait of world politics. To be sure, there are different strands of realism. For example, Keohane and Nye[17] argued that the classical realist portrait did not fit the relations between the United States and its European allies. Instead of raw power politics determining their relationship, they argued that the "complex" interdependence between the U.S. and Western Europe changed the nature of their relationship: their economic and security relationship altered the way that power was exercised across the Atlantic. Another strand was the elaboration of a "new" realism in the late 1970s, purporting to offer a more theoretically rigorous version of classical realism. "Neorealists" argued that world politics could be understood by its structure.[18] In this version of realism, states were led to dominate others by the anarchic structure of the system in which they found themselves. The only way to avoid domination by others was by seeking power, either singly or in combination with other states.[19] In turn, neorealism (or structural realism) spawned the emergence of a neoclassical realist school that argues that the structure of the system does not have such overweening deterministic power, and that other factors contribute to state behaviour.[20]

What unites the different strands of realism is the belief in the importance of selfishness based on materialist conceptions of interest and the importance of power to advance of those interests. Needless to say, an interest-based, atomistic view of world politics will have important implications for how one understands how foreign policy is made, how alliances and coalitions work,[21] and why states will intervene in some conflicts and not in others. Fouad Ajami put the interest-based argument succinctly in his response to Huntington's 1993 article: "States avert their gaze from blood ties when they need to; they see brotherhood and faith and kin when it is in their interest to do so". He went on to remind us of the lessons of the Melian dialogue:

> Beseiged by Athens, [the Melians] held out and were sure that the Lacedaemonians were "bound, if only for very shame, to come the aid of their kindred." The Melians never wavered in their confidence in their "civilizational" allies: "Our common blood insures our fidelity". We know what became of the Melians. Their allies did not turn up, their island was sacked, their world laid to waste.[22]

This is a common way of interpreting the grim world of world politics, but it is hardly a convincing account to those who would try to understand a whole range of relationships between states that patently are not marked by the atomism predicted by the orthodox theory. For there are a number of state-to-state relationships that do not conform at all to the standard international relations orthodoxy. A partial list would include: Austria-Germany, Australia-New Zealand, Australia-United States, Belgium-France, Britain-United States, Canada-Britain and Canada-United States.

In these cases, a rather different political dynamic is at work, one that bears very little relationship to the predictions of the Waltzian neorealist perspective. On the contrary: ties of "blood" and "sentiment" are very much part of how we understand the relationships of these states (and indeed their governments and peoples). These are not atomistic units, seeking self-interest pure and simple; they are linked by ties of different sorts: economic, commercial, familial, political, diplomatic, strategic, language and culture.

Importantly, there is an "insider" element that comes with such shared attributes as language, culture and history that provides crucial links for peoples of different political communities. Such shared attributes provide the basis for widely shared *cultural* understandings that tend not be present when such critical elements are absent. The existence of a common "culture" is often mentioned in discussions of Canadian-American relations, for example.[23] Indeed one could not imagine trying to understand relations between the other dyads mentioned above without reference to culture.

To be sure, often these links are only inchoately understood. Consider, for example, the case of Canadian ties to Britain in the late 1930s. Technically, with the passage of the Statute of Westminster in 1931, Canada was a sovereign nation-state, an independent member of the League of Nations, and subordinate to no other state. It existed, in short, in an atomistic environment. But this is not how many Canadians conceived of that environment. Stephen Leacock, the Canadian humorist, put it this way in the summer of 1939: "If you were to ask any Canadian, 'Do you have to go to war if England does?' he'd answer at once, 'Oh, no.' If you then asked, 'Would you go to war if England does?' he'd answer 'Oh, yes.' And if you asked 'Why?' he would say, reflectively, 'Well, you see, we'd have to'".[24]

But in Leacock's vignette lies the essence of kin-country sentiment identified, more or less, by Huntington: a willingness to identify with another community that is manifestly not one's own, but to which one nonetheless has considerable cultural and – dare one say? – civilizational links. Such links prompt one to devote treasure – and indeed on occasion blood – to a cause that might be objectively "foreign" and "alien," but that one believes to be (or *constructs* as being) one's own, and hence in one's self-interest. It should be noted that it is not necessary for the materialist interests, economic or geostrategic, which are so important for realists of different stripes, to be present. Indeed, this kind of "kin-country" identification is consistent with the constructivist school of international relations that is emerging in the American academy in the post-Cold War era to challenge the dominance of the rationalist-materialist approaches.[25]

Conclusion: The Kin-Country Thesis and Australian-Canadian Relations

The argument in this paper has important implications for how we understand the Australian-Canadian relationship. Certainly there are few students of the relationship between the two countries who would try to understand the dynamics of the relationship in the stark terms favoured by American neorealists. On the other hand, we lack solid analytical tools for interpreting a relationship that is marked by an unusual closeness despite the marked distances, both physical and cultural. Analyses of the relationship tend to favour familial analogies: for example, a recent collection edited by Margaret Macmillan and Francine McKenzie relies heavily on sibling analogies.[26]

The argument here is that there are international relationships, such as the Australian-Canadian relationship, that are not well explained by orthodox international relations theorizing. By contrast, the kin-country thesis advanced by Huntington – focussing on "civilizational" links – does provide a fuller and richer account of certain relationships. Pitching the links at a putative "civilizational" level seeks to go beyond attributes like politico-strategic or economic interests, language, common historical origins or political institutions, culture, religion or "way of life," each of them on their own important variables but not as fully explanatory as the "civilizational" variable.

Needless to say, embracing the kin-country thesis to analyze Australian-Canadian – or, for that matter, the Australian-American, or the Canadian-American – relationship is problematic, since the kin-country thesis is so closely identified with Huntington's broader civilizational paradigm. Yet it can be argued that while the "clash of civilizations" perspective may richly deserve to be pitched as so much shonky dreck, the "baby" – the kin-country thesis – deserves closer consideration for the light that it can shine on certain international relationships.

Notes

1. Fernand Braudel, *A History of Civilizations*, trans. Richard Mayne (Harmondsworth: Penguin, [1987] 1983).

2. Fouad Ajami, "The Summoning", *Foreign Affairs*, 72 (September/October 1993); Binyan Liu, "Civilization Grafting", *Foreign Affairs*, 72 (September/October 1993).

3. See F. Ajami, ibid.; Stephen Blank, "A New World Order: Simple, Elegant – and Flawed", *Literary Review of Canada*, 6 (September 1997).

4. See Richard A. Higgot and Kim Richard Nossal, "The International Politics of Liminality: Relocating Australia in the Asia-Pacific", *Australian Journal of Political Science* 32, (July 1997); Vilho Harle, "Identity Politics in Borderlands: The Case of Finland, Karelia, and Lapland", Paper to the International Studies Association, Washington, D.C., February 1999.

5. Samuel P. Huntington, *The Clash of Civilizations and the Remaking of World Order* (New York: Simon and Schuster, 1996), 47.

6. Samuel P. Huntington, "If Not Civilizations, What?", *Foreign Affairs*, 72 (November/December 1993): 186.

7. Samuel P. Huntington, 1999, op. cit., 26-27, map 1.3.

8. Robert D. Kaplan, "Travels into America's Future", *The Atlantic Monthly*, (July/August 1998).

9. Robert W. Cox, "Social Forces, States and World Orders: Beyond International Relations Theory", *Neorealism and Its Critics*, ed. Robert O. Keohane (New York; Columbia University Press, 1986), 207.

10. Kim Richard Nossal, *The Politics of Canadian Foreign Policy*, 3rd ed. (Scarborough, Ontario: Prentice Hall Canada, 1997), 469-471.

11. Samuel P. Huntington, op. cit.

12. H.D.S. "War in Yugoslavia", *Boston Globe*, (December 3 1992): 19.

13. Samuel P. Huntington, op. cit., 156.

14. Ibid., 208-217.

15. Ibid., 254.

16. Hans Morgenthau, *Politics Among Nations: The Struggle for Power and Peace* (New York: Alfred A. Knopf, 1998).

17. Robert O. Keohane and Joseph S. Nye, *Power and Interdependence. World Politics in Transition* (Boston: Little, Brown, 1977).

18. See Robert O. Keohane, ed., *Neorealism and Its Critics* (New York: Columbia University Press, 1986).

19. Kenneth Waltz, *Theory of International Politics* (Reading, Mass.: Addison Wesley, 1979); Stephen Walt, *The Origins of Alliances* (Ithaca: Cornell University Press, 1986).

20. See Gideon Rose, "Neoclassical Realism and Theories of Foreign Policy", *World Politics*, 51 (October 1998).

21. Stephen Walt, op. cit.; Randall L. Schweller, "Bandwagoning for Profit: Bringing the Revisionist State Back On", *International Security*, 19 (Summer 1994); Andrew Bennett, Joseph Lepgold and Danny Unger, eds., *Friends in Need: Burden Sharing in the Gulf War* (New York: St. Martin's Press, 1997).

22. Fouad Ajami, op. cit., 9.

23. Anette Baker, Fox Canada and the United States: Transnational and Transgovernmental Relations. (New York: Columbia University Press 1976); John Herd Thompson and Stephen J. Randall 1994, p. 302-303.

24. Quoted in Kim Richard Nossal, op. cit. 149.

25. Ole Wæver, "Figures of International Thought : Introducing Persons Instead of Paradigms", *The Future of International Relations: Masters in the Making?*, eds. Iver B. Neumann and Ole Wæver (London/New York: Routledge, 1997); John Gerard Ruggie, *Constructing the World Polity* (New York: Routledge, 1998).

26. Margaret Macmillan and Francine McKenzie, eds., *Parties Long Estranged: Canada and Australia* (Vancouver: University of British Columbia Press) forthcoming.

9

Canada and Australia: An Ocean of Difference in Threat Perception

DESMOND MORTON

Canadians and Australians have a lot in common. They shared the same Empire and Commonwealth and similar parliamentary and federal systems in which defence and foreign affairs are almost wholly within the federal domain.[1] Both countries have largely European populations, and residual pre-contact Aboriginal populations which, due to law, health and education, have begun to make their interest felt to a degree astonishing to their parents – and ours. In Canada and Australia, English is the prevailing language, though Australians have no clear counterpart to Canada's French Fact. British traditions have dominated many aspects of life, but they have also been fiercely and resentfully contested. The political, economic and cultural power of the United States, unmedicated by translation, has had even greater influence on these countries than on those with deeper roots or a distinct language.

Australia and Canada have also shared most of the same wars and a common heritage of British military traditions, modified by postwar adaptation to the tactical and strategic doctrines of their newly dominant ally, the United States. Both countries have depended for most of their history on the Militia or Citizen forces, officered by lawyers, engineers, businessmen and prosperous farmers, whose chief struggle has been the despised "professionals" of the small permanent-force instructional cadres. Both countries established military colleges, at Kingston in 1876 and Duntroon (shaped by a Kingston graduate in 1911, to give young men a chance to start a military career. Both countries had to leave more advanced training to be acquired somewhere else. Duntroon's designer, Lieutenant-General W.T. Bridges, was a graduate of the RMC of Canada who went on to command the Australian and New Zealand Army Corps at Gallipoli. By the end of the war, both Australia and Canada had found native-born officers to command their respective army corps and the similarities and differences between Monash and Currie would make a fascinating paper in itself. A valuable article already compares Canadian and Australian naval experience and, in a paper that is already long, I have gratefully left most maritime issues to James Goldrick.[2]

Even more than Canada, Australia's heritage has been shaped by the experience of foreign wars: Anzac and the Canadian Expeditionary Force, Gallipoli and Vimy, Dieppe and Hong Kong or Malaya and Singapore, have shaped national memories. Both Canada and Australia have centrally located memorials to the First World War in the heart of their respective capitals but there is no doubt which is more imposing. Similarly, the 12-volume official history of the 1914-1918 war directed by C.E.W. Bean may be contrasted with the lonely volume produced by Canada's official historian, in 1938.[3] Both countries have been postwar peacekeepers. Both countries experienced conscription crises in the First World War, though in different circumstances and with different outcomes. Both have felt the strains and possibilities of a primary-products economy in wartime and both have used war to expand industrial self-sufficiency. Both emerged with a conviction, perhaps earlier in Canada, that the traditional notion of Imperial Defence was a failure in actual practice.[4]

In a phrase Canadians and perhaps Australians used in the 1920s, both countries were providers, not recipients, of security. It was a smug phrase, a reminder of shiploads of young men dispatched to assist an embattled mother country by colonies self-governing enough that they might have done little or nothing if they preferred. They had preferred to do a great deal, and there was a strong feeling in the 1920s that young Australians and Canadians had been sacrificed to the imbecility of British generals and the folly of British politicians. Australians remembered Helles and Anzac, Pozières and Passchendaele; Canadians matched them with Second Ypres and the St. Eloi craters, Courcelette and Regina Trench, and the 15,000 dead and wounded they, too, had lost at Passchendaele. The Great War cost both countries about 60,000 lives, a heavier burden on Australia's 5 million than on Canada's 8 million.

In the Second World War, there were more disasters and even more resentment. Was the Australian fleet sacrificed in the early phases of the Pacific War by the inadequacies of the Royal Navy in the Far East? Should the British have allowed Canada to squander 2000 soldiers at Hong Kong? Would 30,000 Australians have suffered Japanese captivity if the British had supplied adequate resources or a better general? Some harsh questions might also have landed in Ottawa or Canberra but the colonial mind is spared responsibility.

Australia and Canada survived the 20th century without being invaded, dismembered or widely devastated. Has this been due to the alliances both countries have contracted and, on the whole, upheld, at some cost to internal unity? Both Canada and Australia shifted from British to American dependence at about the same time and for the same reason. If Great Britain had ever had the will to defend its major English-speaking dominions, it lacked the means in 1940-42. The sense of abandonment was infinitely greater in Australia than in Canada two years earlier. In 1940, the senior dominion found itself the second largest adversary of the Third Reich. No one had the faintest notion whether the Führer had targeted Canada. The Japanese thrust that ended at Darwin on February 19th, 1942, and lapped around the coast as far as Sydney, was absolutely serious and incarnated an almost century-old Australian nightmare. Despite similarities, Canadians and Australians militarily have had little to do with each other. Geopolitical reasons sent Australians to Suakin in 1885 and to Vietnam in the 1960s; for their geopolitical reasons, Canadians did neither. Young Australians came to Canada in the early war years as part of the British Commonwealth Air Training Plan; Canadians who went to the Korean War benefited from the British Commonwealth Forces, Korea (BCFK), the Australian-managed administrative base in Kure, Japan.

Canadians and Australians had limited contact in the South African War and no significant common experience. In 1914-18, relations between the Canadian Corps and Anzacs were, reputedly, poisonous. At the Somme and at Passchendaele, Canadians inherited Australian positions, never an endearing experience. The two corps shared only one major battle, the secret offensive at Amiens. Australians and Canadians made August 8, 1918, "the Black Day of the German Army", according to General Erich von Ludendorff, but Canadian historians will not let Australians forget that their corps advanced eight miles and the Australians only managed seven! [5] Without conscription, the ranks of the five Australian divisions were thin and brigades had been cut to three battalions. Canada had supported conscription, as had the C.E.F. The political consequences would be agonizing but the Corps in the summer of 1918 was full of volunteers from a disbanded fifth Division and brigades retained a full four battalions. The benefits for the second- phase of a two-part offensive were obvious. Conscripts ("MSA Men", in official terminology) did not arrive until late September. The result was a Corps that, for the next hundred days, broke the Hindenberg Line and fought all the way to Valenciennes, while the Australians after Amiens were worn out for their next valiant battles.

Apart from some mixing of B.C.A.T.P. aircrew in R.A.F. squadrons, there was little operational contact between Canadians and Australians in the Second World War. Canada's wartime prime minister, W.L. Mackenzie King, refused an invitation to send Canadians to the Western Desert. Embarrassment at this refusal weakened resistance to the Hong Kong gambit in 1941, providing Canada with a much smaller version of the disaster that befell Australians in Malaya and Singapore. Apart from two transport squadrons in Burma and some warships with the Pacific Fleet, coast defences and a bloodless invasion of Kiska, Canada left others to fight Japan until Germany surrendered. A cautious contribution was being prepared when Japan surrendered.[6]

In Korea, Canadians served with Australians in the First Commonwealth Division and after the Battle of Kap'yong. A Canadian battalion, the Second PPCLI, shared the honour of a U.S. presidential citation with the Third Royal Australian Regiment for holding the shoulders of a Chinese assault.[7] In the ensuing years, Canadians, Australians, New Zealanders and British troops battled the tough and resourceful Chinese Communist Forces (CCF) as part of the First British Commonwealth Division. Canadians and Australians have also shared British and American professional courses, exchanges and secondments, though, outside peacekeeping or peace-restoration operations in Cambodia and East Timor, contacts have been rare.

There are other reasons for divergences in the Canadian and Australian defence experience. The most significant may be the nature of threat. For much of its history, Canada was invulnerable on three sides and indefensible on the fourth. Until the development of the long-range bomber in the 1940s, Canada's Arctic was virtually impassable and, so long as the two most powerful navies in the world controlled the Atlantic and Pacific Oceans, no invasion could come by sea.[8] The southern frontier, in contrast, had been an invasion route in pre-contact times, and it continued under the French, the English and the Americans. In the 19th century, the United States border ranked with the Northwest Frontier as the two great problems of British imperial defence. Between Fenians, Alabama claims and a huge Union army, in the 1860s the risk of war was immense and a British officer later involved in Australian defences, W.F.D. Jervois, warned that the prospect of victory or even a draw in a future War of 1812 was hopeless.[9]

From a British perspective, Confederation in 1867 was a means of liquidating the problem. In 1865, the colonial secretary, Edward Cardwell, assured anxious Canadians that, if Canada was "ready to devote all her resources, both in men and money to the maintenance of her connexion with the Mother Country", then "the Imperial Government fully acknowledged the reciprocal obligation of defending every portion of the Empire with all the resources at its command".[10] This and a guarantee for a $2 million fortification loan made helpful arguments in the Confederation debates. Reality arrived afterward. Sent to the War Office in W.E. Gladstone's first government, the same Edward Cardwell announced that British garrisons would leave all self-governing colonies. Canadians paid no heed, but on November 11th, 1871, after a brief delay to enforce the transfer of the Red River colony to Canadian ownership, the last British soldier left Quebec.[11] Britain might or might not respect Cardwell's earlier commitment but there would be no hostages to enforce performance.

Bemoaned at the time, Cardwell's decision benefited all sides. The British were liberated from a hopeless military commitment. They made no plans to meet the 1865 commitment. Free to invade Canada whenever they chose, Americans never would unless they felt threatened. And Canadians had enough sense not to provide that threat. In 1871, the British took Sir John A. Macdonald to Washington, where they "wiped the slate" of outstanding Anglo-American issues, often at Canada's expense. The lesson was obvious. Keeping peace with the Americans could sometimes be costly and annoying but the alternatives were infinitely worse. The fortification loan was used to build the Intercolonial Railway. When an unsettled prairie frontier threatened to bring U.S. cavalry north, Canada created a police force and sent it west, literally to keep the peace.[12] Imagine the cost if Canadians had ever seriously undertaken their own defence against the Untied States, or if the Americans had responded?

Canada was neither entirely defenceless nor entirely confident about its big neighbour. After all, no major American election passed without bloodcurdling threats – mainly to Irish voters – against the British and their shabby, unhappy North American dependency. In Canada, the Fenians were not forgotten – as late as 1900, they tried to blow up the Welland Canal. In 1896, a dispute over the border of Venezuela led to the last real risk of an Anglo-American war climax – and Canada would have been the prize. To win his Alaska boundary dispute, President Theodore Roosevelt moved troops and threatened to use them.[13]

Not that Canada did much. In 1872 small artillery schools moved into the British fortresses at Kingston and Quebec, and they were followed, a decade later, by company-sized training schools for the cavalry and infantry. A British colonel was given command of a 40,000-member volunteer militia that got as much equipment, clothing and training as the balance of a $1-million defence budget could afford. A Royal Military College opened in 1876 as a conspicuous but cheap way to show that Canadians cared about defence. They didn't. Never acknowledged save by tactless British officers, the ostensible enemy was the United States but in the militia's sham battles, the sides were represented by rival colonels. During the Venezuela Crisis, Canadians were preoccupied with the Manitoba School Question and a successful attempt by fellow Tories to get rid of a bumbling prime minister. The current militia commander, too keen for his own good, was sent home to England and replaced by someone guaranteed to cause no trouble. The Venezuela Crisis – the last possible Anglo-American war – is not a salient part of Canada's history.[14]

The American menace in the 1860s had seemed remote to the lower provinces in the 1860s – at least until Fenians staged a minor raid – but it was real enough to the British, and they had forced the marriage. There was much less need of outside agency when Australians formed their Commonwealth in 1900. A vast island, set in the South Seas, on the other side of the world from Europe, may have looked safe enough from Whitehall, but not to the few million who lived there. The common view from Melbourne, Sydney, Brisbane or even Hobart was of the teeming masses of Asia, exploding their boundaries much like Europeans and, by sheer numbers, doing to Australians what they and their forebears had done to Aborigines. The "White Australia" policy, on which the Commonwealth was founded, breathed defiance and demanded defence. A navy was a logical response to a perceived danger, no less real for being limited, of neighbours with real territorial and population-related demands. So was an army for home defence. Unlike his Canadian counterpart, the defence minister of the Australia created in 1901 was expected to do more than distribute patronage. Australia's first Defence Act was passionately debated, demolished by frequently informed critics and entirely replaced.

For a few early years of the 20th century, some Canadians believed in universal training but, by 1909, they had been fobbed off with compulsory cadets in the high schools of most provinces. Their movement died in the pre-1914 depression.[15] Australia was different. Over predictable resistance, pressure for Universal Military Training, cadet corps and reserve service had succeeded by 1911 and weeks of training and subsequent service in the Citizen Force became a part of male socialization. And who could argue, given publicly espoused attitudes, that Asia's hostility would be a surprise?

Long before 1914, both Canadians and Australians had volunteered for imperial wars. Fighting Dervishes or Boers was an obvious outlet for adventurous and ambitious romantics. In 1885 and 1899, at least some Australians could insist on the need to safeguard the lifeline "Home"; most Canadians could see no argument at all. In 1899, enthusiasts for a Canadian contingent argued that it would create a debt of gratitude for the British to repay with support for Canada's Alaska boundary claim. Teddy Roosevelt scored higher in Whitehall by staying sympathetically neutral in the Boer War and by sending real troops to the Alaska panhandle.[16] Canadians blamed Britain, not the United States, for the humiliation. An audience in Toronto, a presumed bastion of imperialism, heard Henri Bourassa demand that Canada set its own foreign policy and gave him a standing ovation. It would not happen often.

Australians and Canadians both depended on British professionalism, naval and military, and both suffered their disillusionments too. General Edward Hutton brought his experience of New South Wales directly to Canada in 1898 and returned to the young Commonwealth after commanding "Imperials" in South Africa. Neither country would remember him with unmixed admiration.[17] Colonials also had direct conflicts with British authority. Among the best known was the Breaker Morant affair – an Australian officer shot by firing squad for the killing of a German missionary. The experience helped convince Australians that, henceforth, they would control discipline and administration.[18]

With a serious naval defence problem, Australia needed British professionals; Canada insisted on a Canadian like Rear Admiral C.E.

Kingsmill, whatever his professional limitations. It gained more than it deserved from Royal Navy officers like Commander Walter Hose of H.M.C.S. *Rainbow* and the Halifax Patrol of 1917-18. As postwar Chief of the Naval Staff, Hose and the French-Canadian deputy minister, George Desbarats, were the saviours of Canada's tiny interwar fleet.[19] Australians have been more critical of their British professionals. Neither country paid its British officers adequately.[20]

Contrasting defence perspectives help explain why Canadians urged, over Australia's protests, that Britain abandon its Anglo-Japanese alliance. Reducing American antipathy was central to Ottawa; Australians had had recent reason to appreciate the Japanese as allies. The decision, with its direct link to the Pacific War of 1941-45, reflected Canada's preoccupation with American opinion and Britain's desire to have a unified imperial foreign policy, even a foolish one.[21] Australians and New Zealanders were uncomfortable with appeasement in the 1930s and Canada's government adored Neville Chamberlain's cautious policies. Not only did Mackenzie King positively hate the idea of war; so did his party's key bases of support, Quebec and the Prairie Provinces.

Superficial similarities in Canadian-Australian experience of the two wars conceal some differences. In the 1914-18 war, Australia deployed a significant navy and organized its own air force. Canada's wartime government had come to power in 1911 intent on throttling an infant navy, and the demoralized survivors managed little except a largely helpless anti-submarine patrol out of Halifax when U-boats finally reached the far side of the Atlantic, long after the *Sydney* had sunk the *Emden* and given Australia's sailors a tradition. Nor was there any comparison between the 1939-45 experience in Canada and Australia's desperate struggle in home waters and in the jungles of New Guinea. Canada's counterpart to Darwin was a few shells lobbed at the Estevan Point lighthouse by a Japanese submarine.

Not Hitler but Stalin changed Canada's sense of invulnerability. So did the nuclear weapons Canada had played a significant role in developing during the war. In the 1930s, designers had envisaged bombers that, with a single refuelling, could leap the Arctic icecap and return. The Pacific War made the B-29 a reality and its successors, the B-36 and B-52, practical possibilities. In American or Soviet hands, nuclear weapons gave bombers a payload worthy of a one-way trip. Instead of frozen isolation, Canada's Arctic became the buffer zone between two increasingly hostile superpowers. Suddenly, Canadian air space became as important to the United States as it was to its official owner. Canadian soil became the "killing ground" for the nuclear bombers of either side that "did not get through".[22]

In return for nominal recognition of Canada's sovereignty in the Arctic, Washington defended Canada as if it were its own territory. Unable to do the job themselves without bankrupting the treasury and exasperating the United States, Canadian politicians in the 1950s made a virtue of what they could not change. Indeed, military leaders in Canada (and perhaps Australia) found that allies became their own best agents in promoting both a general defence effort and the interests of a specific service.[23] For the first time, Canadians in peacetime had to co-exist with the prospect of unimaginable levels of destruction. Perhaps it could happen to Australia, too, but a popular film of the era, based on a Nevil Shute novel, suggested that Australians would outlive us all.

Indeed, Australia was also changed by the Cold War. Few strategists ever claimed that Sydney or Melbourne appeared on Soviet target lists, though the Commonwealth inspired a richer vein of Communist spy legends than most countries. Marxist-style decolonization across Southeast Asia, the triumph of Mao Tse-tung in China and the emergence of Chinese-backed armed revolutionary movements brought Asia very much closer. Indonesia was no longer the Dutch East Indies. Australians might be in urgent need of their new American friends at any moment. Sending troops to South Korea, Malaya and Vietnam were not idealistic commitments to collective security but pragmatic premium payments to an alliance system that, under different management in 1942, had failed Australia and its other members disastrously. They also seemed like practical ways of shoring up resistance to Asian revolutionaries with a potential appetite for the region's richest and emptiest offshore islands. Long accustomed to pretending to be an extension of Britain, magically endowed with sunshine and warmth, Australians, found themselves geopolitically, if not emotionally, a part of Asia. Canada might feel linked to Europe, and to Asia too but nothing as traumatic as the memory of 1942 has yet forged that mental link.

A few years ago, at a lunch with the then defence minister in the Chrétien government, the Honourable Doug Young regaled me with the latest wisdom acquired on a visit to the North American Aerospace Defence Command (NORAD) mountain at Colorado Springs. Canada, he discovered, must ready itself for the latest triumph of North Korean technology, a rocket called the Dong. Polite giggling ensued, at the temerity of a starving people, at the resourceful imaginations that kept

NORAD alive and, as intended, at a weapon armed with the popular name for a feature of male anatomy. Our minds lightened, we turned to serious business.

Australians, as remote from the Dong as Canada, would not be quite so careless about a major concern for Asian security as their remote northeastern friend.

Notes

1. Both provinces and states have external interests, primarily, though not exclusively, in trade. Responsibility for the maintenance of order involves recourse to defence forces normally under federal jurisdiction. And, as regional politicians, state and provincial leaders have expressed concern for defence and even, as in the case of Sir Richard McBride of British Columbia in 1914, taken explicit initiatives.

2. James Goldrick, "Strangers in Their Own Seas: A Comparison of the Australian and Canadian Naval Experience, 1910-1982", *A Nation's Navy: In Quest of Canadian Naval Identity*, eds. Michael L. Hadley, Rob Huebert and Freed W. Crickard, (Montreal and Kingston: McGill-Queen's University Press, 1996), 325-338.

3. See Dudley McCarthy, *Gallipoli to the Somme: The Story of C.E.W. Bean* (London: Leo Cooper, 1983); C.P. Stacey, "The Life and Hard Times of an Official Historian", *Canadian Historical Review*, (March 1, 1970); *A Date with History: Memoirs of a Canadian Historian* (Ottawa: Deneau, 1982).

4. The best overall account of both Canadian and Australian roles in "Imperial Defence" is still R.A. Preston's *Canada and "Imperial Defence": A Study of the Origins of the British Commonwealth's Defence Organization, 1867-1919* (Durham: Duke University Press, 1967).

5. See Daniel Dancocks, *Spearhead to Victory: Canada and the Great War* (Edmonton: Hurtig Publishers, 1987), 20-88; C.E.W. Bean, *The Australian Imperial Force in France During the Allied Offensive, 1918* (Sydney: Angus and Robertson, 1942).

6. Desmond Morton, *A Military History of Canada: From Champlain to Kosovo*, 4th ed. (Toronto: McClelland and Stewart, 1999), 223-224.

7. H.F. Wood, *Strange Battleground: Official History of the Canadian Army in Korea* (Ottawa: Queen's Printer, 1966), 72-79.

8. Though Arctic overflight was discussed in *Popular Mechanics* and kindred magazines in the 1930s, the region is not mentioned in the relevant volume of the official history of the R.C.A.F., W.A.B. Douglas, *The Creation of a National Air Force: The Official History of the Royal Canadian Air Force*, vol. 2 (Toronto: University of Toronto Press, 1986).

9. On Canada's insecurity at Confederation, see C.P. Stacey, *Canada and the British Army, 1846-1871: A Study in the Practice of Responsible Government* rev. ed. (Toronto: University of Toronto Press, 1963); J.M. Hitsman, *Safeguarding Canada, 1763-1871* (Toronto: University of Toronto Press, 1968); R.A. Preston, *The Defence of the Undefended Border: Planning for War in North America, 1867-1909* (Montreal and Kingston: McGill-Queen's University Press, 1977), 9-67.

10. Public Record Office (PRO) C.O. 42/693, 380-1: *Papers Relating to the Conferences that have taken place between Her Majesty's Government and a deputation from the Executive Council of Canada*; Cardwell to Monck, June 17 1865.

11. On British defence of Canada, see Kenneth Bourne, *Britain and the Balance of Power in North America, 1815-1908* (London: Longman's, 1967).

12. See Desmond Morton, "Cavalry or Police: Keeping the Peace on Two Adjacent Frontiers, 1870-1900", *Journal of Canadian Studies*, 12, no. 2, (Spring 1977): 27-37.

13. R.A. Preston, op. cit., 125-148.

14. The period is summarized by the author's *Military History of Canada*, 93-129.

15. See Desmond Morton, "The Cadet Movement in the Moment of Canadian Militarism, 1909-1914", *Journal of Canadian Studies*, 13, no. 2, (Summer 1978): 56-68.

16. R.A. Preston, op. cit., 169-174 *passim*.

17. See ibid., 229-230, 243-245; Desmond Morton, *Ministers and Generals: Politics and the Canadian Militia, 1868-1904* (Toronto: University of Toronto Press, 1970), 133-162; and a much more sympathetic view from Norman Penlington, *Canada and Imperialism, 1896-1899* (Toronto: University of Toronto Press, 1965), 132-182.

18. R.A. Preston, *"Imperial Defence"*, op. cit., 274-275; see also 279. Canada showed no such determination to protect its soldiers from British discipline. See Desmond Morton, "The Supreme Penalty: Canadian Deaths by Firing Squad in the First World War", *Queen's Quarterly*, LXXIX, no. 3, (Winter 1972).

19. Hose and Desbarats emerged as heroes of the RCN's survival struggle in James Eayrs, *In Defence of Canada: From the Great War to the Great Depression* (Toronto: University of Toronto Press, 1964).

20. James Goldrick, "Australian and Canadian Navies", 329.

21. See C.P. Stacey, *Canada and the Age of Conflict: A History of Canadian External Policies, vol. 1, 1867-1921* (Toronto: Macmillan, 1977), 334-351.

22. Brian Crane, *An Introduction to Canadian Defence Policy* (Toronto: Canadian Institute of International Affairs, 1964); Melvin Conant, *The Long Polar Watch* (New York: Harper, 1962); James Eayrs, *Northern Approaches: Canada and the Search for Peace* (Toronto: Macmillan, 1961); General Charles Foulkes, "The Complications of Continental Defence", *Neighbours Taken for Granted*, ed. Livingstone Merchant, (New York: Praeger, 1966).

23. See, for example, Peter T. Haydon, "Sailors, Admirals and Politicians: The Search for Identity After the War", *A Nation's Navy*, eds. Hadley, Huebert and Crickard, 221-235; and German, *The Seas Around Us*, 233-248: Joseph T. Jockel, "The Canada-United States Military Co-operation Committee and Continental Air Defence, 1946", *Canadian Historical Review*, LXIV, no. 3 (September 1983): 352-377; Douglas Bland, *The Administration of Defence Policy in Canada, 1947 to 1985* (Kingston: n.p., 1987).

10

The Great War Soldier as "Nation Builder" in Canada and Australia

JEFFREY KESHEN

In the 1999 Canada Day edition of *Maclean's* magazine, two of the country's most prominent historians, J.L. Granatstein and Norman Hillmer, selected the Battle of Vimy Ridge as first among 25 events that contributed to the formation of modern Canada. Although lamenting more than 3,000 dead and 7,000 wounded and though noting, in contrast to most earlier work, that this victory by the Canadian Corps did not produce a great breakthrough for the Allies, still they wrote of a stupendous triumph that forged a national spirit that "ma[de] Canada into a nation".[1]

Writing in the *National Post* about half a year later, the well-known Canadian literary critic Robert Fulford, in a review of a British book, *The Pity of War*, by Biall Ferguson, who cast the 1914-18 conflict as the "greatest error of modern history,"carped that "all my life I have been reading that Canada became a nation on the battlefields of France". In light of the deep and long-lasting French-English divide over conscription and the loss of so many young and promising lives, Fulford contends the Great War should be reclassified as "the unmaking of Canada as much as the making".[2] Responding to Fulford, historians David Bercuson and Jonathon Vance correctly argue that Canadian historians have not glossed over the divisiveness caused by the Great War – a plethora of work testifies to that[3] – and that the link between this conflict and the flowering of Canadian nationalism is undeniable. "What did happen", asserts Bercuson, "was that the sacrifices, and the triumphs, of the Canadian Corps gave Prime Minister Borden the leverage to win constitutional equality for Canada within the Empire",[4] a process evident, for example, in Resolution IX declared by the Imperial War Cabinet in 1917 classifying Canada and the other self-governing dominions as autonomous members of the Empire with a right to ongoing consultation. This paper does not dispute that link. Canada's mammoth contribution of 600,000 men and its loss of 60,000 young lives out of a population of 8 million did generate national pride and the determination that Britain respect Canadian concerns and views, and certainly helps explain the rapid growth of Canadian autonomy following the war. However, it is also a link constructed upon glorified accounts of Canada's Great War soldiers, accounts first articulated by wartime propagandists, that still calls forth the use of romanticized high diction and, by ascribing transcendent and often superhuman characteristics to these men, obscures this part of Canada's past.

While trade and migration flows between Canada and Australia have always remained weak, this is not the case with respect to national memories of the Great War. A new nation – only 13 years old in 1914 – had something to prove both to the mother country and to itself. This was achieved through Australia's Great War soldiers who, according to the standard story, through stupendous feats of arms, particularly at Gallipoli, generated the type of sentiment that transformed the new federation into a true nation.

Both Canada and Australia possessed a disposition toward the advancement and acceptance of this pumped up view. A strong imperialist creed prevailed in each country that was very much evident, for example, from their enthusiastic response to assist Britain during the Boer War.[5] But linkages to Britain, besides being built upon blood, cultural and trade ties and the perceived need for military protection, were also premised upon the notion of demonstrating national qualities, gaining respect and thus rising in status within the Empire. There prevailed in Canada and Australia the belief that their population possessed *the stuff* to make important contributions to imperial campaigns. Canadian imperialists often emphasized the country's northern qualities, namely how a rough and demanding climate produced a people characterized by "energy, strength, self-reliance, health and purity".[6] In Australia, the prototype was the bushman or digger (i.e., miner or prospector), "a person whose roots lie in the outback," and was portrayed as "improvising, tough, taciturn [and] who will stick to his mates through thick and thin".[7]

Such young men, and many others who were rather less impressive, flocked to recruiting booths in August 1914 to prove their mettle, seek out adventure, defend the Empire, preserve democracy or simply obtain a job. However, to buoy patriotism and the willingness to sacrifice among all people as the scope of the conflict and the demands it placed upon citizens expanded rapidly, each country created an apparatus for information control. In these lands so distant from the front, the ability of censorship and propaganda to maintain the currency of romantic beliefs had tremendous impact. It was impossible for Australian and Canadian soldiers to get home on leave and most wounded men did not return home until the latter stages of or after the war. Messages transmitted over censored underwater cables, in censored newspapers and in censored soldiers' letters (which were often self-censored since men did not want to worry loved ones), all tended to confirm romantic stereotypes. Journalistic dispatches, photographs and moving pictures from the front destined for Canada and Australia were first perused by military personnel in France attached to General Headquarters and often again in London by Press Bureau officials or the British Board of Film Censors.

On August 18 1914, Britain's Colonial Office informed dominion governments that they could each send one correspondent to the front. But 10 days later this offer was withdrawn after the London *Times*, in an effort to spur more men into service, reported upon a desperate retreat from Mons by Allied forces. To Britain's War Minister, Lord Kitchener, such material demonstrated the necessity of keeping the press on a short leash. Brief journalistic tours were started in December, but correspondents were prohibited from travelling within 20 miles of the front. Initially, practically every front-line report carried throughout the Empire came from Colonel Ernest Swinton, formally of the London *Daily Chronicle*, who was given the title of official *eyewitness*. His dispatches, aptly termed "eyewash" by several newsmen, described the war in terms of "plucky cavalry charges".[8]

The demand in Canada for front-line press representation intensified after its troops first saw action in March 1915 at Neuve Chapelle. Also that month, General Headquarters accredited six British journalists and appeared ready to accept an official press emissary from Canada. The result was Ottawa's appointment of William Maxwell Aitken to perform *eyewitness* duties. By the Great War, Aitken, a Canadian expatriate, had acquired a substantial piece of the London *Daily Express* and ran successfully for parliament in the Manchester suburb of Ashford-Under-Lyne. The immediate stepping-stone to his emergence as Canada's official press representative was his January 1915 appointment as director of the Canadian War Records Office, a job that involved gathering documents relating to the country's war effort. It was a task that Aitken saw as recording for posterity how Canadian heroism won for the nation a new level of respect and status within the Empire.[9]

On March 27 1915, Aitken began issuing a stream of press dispatches that appeared primarily in Canadian, but also in British and American, newspapers. Most of the information for his reports came from unit war diaries that he and a small writing staff at the Canadian War Records Office twisted into inspiring tales of triumph.[10] Aitken provided material not only to raise spirits in Canada but also, as an imperialist, to promote the country's image in Britain. Such an aim was evident in the coverage he provided, both in article and book form, of the April 1915 battle of Second Ypres.[11] To at least 40,000 Canadians and Britons who bought volume 1 of *Canada in Flanders*,[12] Aitken juxtaposed French colonial soldiers, who "fled before the German gas attack" with Canada's stalwart warriors, who stood firm, "saved the day" for "liberty and civilisation" and in the process ensured that "the mere written word Canada glow[ed]... with a new meaning before all the civilised world".[13] *Canada in Flanders* also underlined the powerful "physique and soldierly swing" of these men who came not just from "shops and offices" but, Aitken emphasized, "from the lumber camps... the vast wheat fields... the slopes of the Rocky Mountains... the shores of Hudson Bay... the banks of the Yukon... the reaches of the St. Lawrence"[14] – a portrayal that contrasted sharply with the fact that, as of March 1 1916, 18.5 percent of Canada's volunteers were former office workers, 64.8 percent manual labourers and only 6.5 percent farmers and ranchers.[15]

By 1916, the Canadian Press Association (CPA) was complaining loudly over not having its own representation in France. John Bohn of *The Toronto Star* charged that Aitken possessed no journalistic qualifications and had likely acquired the *eyewitness* post through his friendship with Canada's Militia Minister, Sam Hughes. A principal assistant to Aitken at the Canadian War Records Office, Henry Beckles Willson, assured his chief that his eventual replacement by a CPA reporter would change little. Besides being subject to censorship rules, Willson noted that British and Australian correspondents had demonstrated "a keen sense of patriotism".[16] Aitken had also likely reached such a conclusion not only from the conduct of other country's journalists, but also from his role, starting in September 1915, in bringing over small parties of Canadian reporters for brief visits to France, nearly all of whom, in one manner or another, emphasized Canadian soldiers "who have become famous through their prowess and heroism".[17]

By March 1917, CPA members, who had long bickered over who to select as their overseas representative, finally settled upon Stewart Lyon, managing editor of *The Toronto Globe*.[18] After seven months, this job was rotated to W.A. Willison, the son of *The Toronto News'* editor and proprietor, J.S. Willison, and then in August 1918 to J.F. Livesay, former president of the Western Canadian Press Association. Although the messengers changed the message did not. Typical was the press coverage given to the bloody encounter at Passchendaele. Unit diaries focussed upon "waist deep" mud in which some of Canada's 16,000 casualties drowned.[19] The last thing needed by Ottawa, then in the midst of a conscription crisis, was a faithful recounting of this debacle. Willison did not disappoint. Mud was mentioned in his dispatches, but only as a means of reinforcing the idea that nothing could deter Canadian soldiers from their objective. Despite casualty lists running on for several newspaper pages, Willison maintained that only "enemy losses" were "frightful," describing, for instance, "a veteran machine gun officer...having had as a target for an hour and a quarter [German] reinforcements coming up in columns of four for use in counter-attacks".[20]

From the first shot to the final salvo, the vast majority of publishers and editors in Canada, eager to pitch in patriotically but also aware of a domestic censorship network and the severe penalties for breaking its rules as stipulated in the 1914 War Measures Act,[21] overwhelmingly reflected and augmented imperialist and romantic notions of duty, honour and warfare, buttressed virulent sentiment against Germany and boosted the reputation of Canada's men in khaki. Especially acclaimed in newspaper columns was the grit displayed by Canadian lads. "They seem... to have something heroic and almost divine about them," declared the Toronto *News* after Second Ypres.[22] In its reaction to Canada's 6,000 casualties in this clash, the Manitoba *Free Press* insisted that "above the tears... there rose steady and clear the voice of thankfulness to God... that they were permitted in their death to make so splendid a sacrifice".[23] Through several bloody encounters this romanticized pattern persisted and was most evident following the April 1917 battle at Vimy Ridge, where the newly formed Canadian Corps captured 54 large guns, 104 trench mortars, 4,000 soldiers and an objective that some military men, following failed French and British assaults, described as unattainable. *The Winnipeg Tribune* was certainly accurate in describing "citizens [who] thrill[ed]" over the triumph but, given Canada's 10,000 casualties, was hardly being forthright in depicting "German troops... scattered like chaff before the vigour of the... attack".[24] Yet, with glowing tributes from British and American newspapers, thus validating for many Canadians the importance of this victory, those in the dominion spoke more about their country as providing the "finest troops in the world",[25] something supposedly confirmed by their use in several subsequent attacks, particularly during the final hundred days of the Great War.

Australia's contribution of men during the war was remarkable: some 400,000 volunteers out of a population of fewer than 5 million. These men were presented to Australians as being physically powerful, exceptionally brave, independent-minded, democratically inclined and as possessing undying loyalty to their mates – attributes said to be derived from the nation's bushman or digger background that called for strength and adaptability and that brought out the best in people.[26] Yet, by the Great War, the distribution of Australia's population was clearly one in which such a background did not apply to most Australian males.[27] As K.S. Inglis concludes, the "unromantic fact" was that more Australian soldiers experienced an urban, or even suburban, upbringing rather than one connected in any way to the outback.[28]

No matter, the image of rugged, courageous and highly effective soldiers who harboured the qualities of the bushman or digger prevailed. Such was strikingly evident in reports from Gallipoli, in the Dardanelles, where, on April 25 1915, the Australia New Zealand Army Corps (Anzac) experienced its *baptism of fire* and, so goes the story, Australia was psychologically transformed into a nation. As Australia's first major battle, a tremendous amount of emotional investment was placed in this clash. "The men who waded ashore on that April morning carried with them... the hopes and self-doubts of those at home", wrote D.A. Kent.[29] Then and in years to follow, Gallipoli was cast in Australia as being solely an Australian undertaking when, in fact, besides New Zealanders, British and French soldiers were also present. Indeed, following Gallipoli, the term "Anzac" became viewed in Australia as signifying solely Australian troops.[30] So celebrated was the event that forgotten was the fact that Gallipoli was actually a military defeat with the Anzacs suffering 7,600 casualties among the initial invading force of 50,000 and then withdrawing after eight months.

The first reports from Gallipoli were actually filed by British reporter Ellis Ashmead-Bartlett. To a nation soon bursting with pride, he wrote: "These raw colonial troops in these desperate hours proved worthy to fight side by side with the heroes of Mons, the Ainse, Ypres and Neuve Chapelle".[31] More so than Ashmead-Bartlett, however, it was Australia's official *eyewitness*, Charles Bean, who influenced the home front. Bean possessed strong imperialist sympathies (having attended British private schools and Oxford University) and, to promote the status of Australia within the Empire, he stressed the special qualities of its people, which he believed traced to the bushman past. In 1908, Bean, who had "dabbled" in teaching and law in the outback, joined the staff of *The Sydney Morning Herald*.[32] While at Gallipoli, he articulated what became, and to this day still persists, as the "Anzac legend": the physically powerful, independent-minded and adaptable product of the outback who never abandoned their mates and who always prevailed in combat no matter the odds. It was a depiction that often contrasted sharply with Bean's personal wartime diary which told of men who sometimes retreated in panic and who hoped for (and on occasion gave themselves) wounds in order to escape the carnage.[33]

Bean fashioned the "Anzac legend" not only through press reports, but also by editing in 1916 the *Anzac Book*, a commemorative album of the Gallipoli landing largely comprised of submissions from soldiers. Over 100,000 copies were sold in Australia. Bean permitted some sarcasm against military authorities and even a little black humour about combat to appear – realizing this was necessary if the work was to retain any legitimacy among soldiers – but overwhelmingly the book celebrated Anzac heroism especially since Bean sliced out enough critical material to create an "alternative" *Anzac Book*. The only direct reference left to Australian soldiers being scared was found in the story of Icy, "the 'cold foot,' who flinche[d] at each shell-burst but ultimately redeem[ed] himself with a solo raid on a machine-gun post".[34]

The impact of information control upon Australians, which included an extensive system of domestic censorship created under the 1914 War Precautions Act,[35] was evident during the October 1916 conscription referendum, playing, according to some historians, the ironic role of having helped produce a narrow defeat – 51 to 49 percent – for the pro-draft forces. This is not to dismiss the importance of other factors, including the opposition of organized labour to the conscription of men before wealth, the strong reluctance among Australia's large Irish-Catholic population to fight alongside Britain following London's brutal suppression of the Easter 1916 Republican uprising in Dublin and the absence of an identifiable group such as Québécois upon whom pro-conscription forces could focus as not carrying their weight in the war effort and thus as requiring compulsion to serve. But also tipping the balance was censorship. After an endless stream of sugar-coated front-line reports, and with authorities unwilling to jolt people toward conscription through alarmist accounts, many Australians, perhaps enough to decide the tight outcome, simply failed to appreciate the need for conscripts. One Brigadier General returning to the country to help the pro-conscription campaign was "so distressed by the rosy picture given in the papers" that he visited the New South Wales premier to urge him to use his influence to reverse the tone.[36] Rather than symbolizing a population having gone sour on the war, the defeat of conscription in October 1916, and again 14 months later, was also linked to Australia's disconnection from depressing information.

In Canada and Australia, well-entrenched imperialism, geographic isolation and a patriotic press corps all provided the impetus for and perseverance of effective information control. Moreover, the ability of censors and propagandists to shape opinion derived from the fact that their unrealistic depictions were usually confirmed by soldiers in their letters home. Fearing consequences from military censors, some men hid the grim realities of front-line life. Others, perhaps, could not find words to express their feelings, believed that there was no point in trying to enlighten people who could never comprehend their predicament, tried to shield loved ones from worry, and sought to reflect the masculine stereotypes that had prompted so many to enlist.

This is not to cast civilian populations in Australia and Canada as unaffected by nearly a half decade of unprecedented sacrifice. Hundreds of thousands were distraught over the loss of family and friends while conscription debates and hyper wartime inflation intensified ethnic- and class-based cleavages. Still, in no manner did civilians approach the level of disillusionment, or several other disturbing emotions, they often discovered among repatriated soldiers. Several barometers of public opinion demonstrate that among most civilians in 1919, the Great War in general, and the part played by soldiers in particular, still constituted causes for celebration and not sadness.

From several quarters in Canada came the declaration that from its participation in the war, the dominion had obtained worldwide respect. "This country is 'on the map' so to speak as never before," said The

Calgary Herald.."[37] Deemed as the cause of such progress was the magnificent record of Canadians in combat. Typical were the words in *The Hamilton Spectator* that, in reporting upon the 19th Battalion's return, dwelt upon a "path of glory... across the craters of St. Eloi... up the scarred heights of Vimy Ridge and the slopes of Hill 70, through Passchendaele's slough and mud and blood to the epic days of 1918... which released the world from the yoke of Prussian militarism".[38] Towns – Vimy, Alberta, being one – ships, mountains and even children were named for battles in which Canadians participated. Those who did not join were often made to feel shame. Throughout his political career, William Lyon Mackenzie King, though 39 years old in 1914, had to fend off attacks that he was a shirker. In 1921, Canada's parliament declared Armistice Day, November 11, as an official day to commemorate Canada's fallen soldiers. The determination that the country not "break faith" with its heroes resulted in 1931 in its re-naming as Remembrance Day and the splitting away of Thanksgiving from November 11 to create a separate holiday devoted to soldiers.[39]

As Jonathon Vance argues in *Death So Noble: Meaning, Memory and the First World War,* to believe that the carnage of the Great War prompted Canadians to adopt what Paul Fussell identifies as a sardonic "ironic mode" in the place of high diction and romanticism is to miss the essence of postwar discourse, especially with respect to the portrayal of Canadian troops. Civilians and most soldiers were simply unwilling to accept a view of the war as having been fought for false ideals and that, by implication, so much suffering and death had been in vain.[40] If nothing else, the need for emotional healing required a more upbeat interpretation. During the interwar years, sources that resonated most with Canadians continued to stress that soldiers fought for high and pure ideals, such as the maintenance of freedom, and that their stupendous performance in combat created a new, strong and internationally respected nation. Certainly, depressing postwar realities such as 175,000 physically – and thousands more psychologically – wounded men along with a sharp economic downturn made it very difficult for Canadian civilians to sustain romantic notions about war itself. Yet, other wartime and postwar milestones such as Resolution IX, separate Canadian representation at the Versailles talks and Canada's signature on the 1919 Treaty, its own seat at the League of Nations and the 1931 Statute of Westminster providing Canada with full self-determination in foreign affairs encouraged the persistence of that romanticized rendering of Great War soldiers whose sacrifices and triumphs bequeathed a proud, esteemed and fully autonomous country.

The existence of such ideas was evident from the reaction of civilians to battle trophies. Tens of thousands flocked to a series of shows during the autumn of 1919 to see those items for which, in capturing, it was stressed, many of the country's courageous lads made the supreme sacrifice. At the Canadian National Exhibition, the best attended pavilion, attracting over 200,000 people in 10 days, was a war trophy display billed by *The Toronto Star* as "living evidence of Canadian valour in France and Flanders".[41] Many artifacts, particularly large guns, were used to help build war memorials that emerged in practically every hamlet that had lost one of its own. Their message remained consistent: a romanticized commemoration of those men who had, through their "heroic sacrifice" and "saintly deaths" on behalf of freedom, earned the eternal gratitude of their country. The tribute erected in Preston, Ontario, portrays a warrior with arms outstretched in the crucifixion position suggesting that he too died for the salvation of civilization, and in the process, achieved everlasting life. In commissioning a National War Memorial in 1925, Ottawa wished to promote "the spirit of heroism... exemplified in the lives of those [who] sacrificed". The result depicts 22 figures from all service branches symbolizing the "great response", while the arch through which they pass represents "peace and freedom".[42] That same year, construction started on a monument at Vimy Ridge to honour those who had not only won a battle but, it was claimed, changed the course of the Great War. On 250 acres provided by the French government, the structure, designed by Walter Allward, has two pillars signifying Canada's European founding races soaring 226 feet upward from a 40,000-square-foot platform set upon the ground's highest point – Hill 145, or the so-called "Pimple," which was the last German position to fall in April 1917 – so that those for miles around could appreciate the significance of the triumph. Between the pillars stands a figure symbolizing the "Spirit of Sacrifice". The long walls at the base signify Canada's rigid line of defence and around that base are "figures representing the Breaking of the Sword, the Sympathy of the Canadians for the Helpless, and Canada mourning her dead".[43] In 1936, 6,200 Canadian pilgrims each paid $160 (at a time when annual salaries averaged around $1,500) to the Canadian Legion to attend the monument's dedication. Before them and French spectators that swelled the crowd to 100,000, King Edward VIII proclaimed Vimy as "a feat of arms that history will long remember and Canada... [could] never forget".[44]

Such themes also characterize much of Canada's postwar literature. H. Napier Moore, a literary reviewer for *Maclean's*, commented soon after the war that citizens were not interested in stories of "gloom" but sought "romance and adventure".[45] *Canada's Hundred Days* (1919), by the former war correspondent J.F. Livesay, chronicled, with heavy doses of high diction, the critical role played by the Canadian Corps during the final stages of the war. In *Canada's Sons and Great Britain in the World War* (1919), Colonel George G. Nasmith, formerly of the Canadian Expeditionary Force, stressed that at places like Ypres and Vimy Ridge, Canadian soldiers proved that "some races of humanity are inferior to others". In the book's introduction, Canadian Corps commander General Arthur Currie, reflecting and expanding upon that theme, emphasized the "rugged strength of the Canadian [soldier]", which was an "invaluable gift of our deep forests and lofty mountains, of our rolling plains and our great waterways, and of the clear light of our Northern skies," a portrayal that ignored the fact, however, that by late-1915, in order to maintain satisfactory recruitment, Canada's military substantially dropped minimum requirements for chest and height measurements.[46] In 1921, in part to make up for the lack of a government-financed *Official History*, there came *Canada and the Great World War*, a compilation of short, largely factual, accounts on different military service branches and campaigns. Yet, here too is manifested the romanticized treatment of Canadian soldiers in 100 pages of photographs and official dispatches describing the heroism of all 64 Canadians who won the Victoria Cross.[47]

The job of writing the planned eight-volume *Official History* of Canada in the Great War was given in 1921 to a new but small Historical Section of the General Staff. Not until 1929 had it sifted through and arranged 135 tons of available documents, and not until 1938 did the first, and what turned out to be the only, volume of the series appear, a 550-page account written by the Director of the Historical Section, Colonel A. Fortesque Duguid, covering the war until September 1915.[48] Duguid's work was exceptionally detailed and without doubt far more balanced than previous efforts, noting, for example, battlefield setbacks by Canadians as well as disturbing facts such as high venereal disease rates among the troops. But even here, in a work that was supposed to strive for objectivity, traces of high diction and national chauvinism remain. For example, in describing the aftermath of the German gas attack at Ypres, Duguid wrote: "The Canadians who had been in this battle were convinced in their own minds that they were equal to the best soldiers in the world. Had they not stood when the French went back? [A]nd the indomitable confidence it engendered was confirmed in every fight – at Mount Sorel and the Somme, at Vimy, Hill 70 and Passchendaele, at Amiens, in the Arras-Cambrai battles, at Valenciennes and in the Pursuit to Mons".[49]

Meanwhile, typical of the initial postwar war novel was J. Murray Gibbon's *The Conquering Hero*, where the author described the exploits of Donald Macdonald of the "fighting 42nd", who, in the process of displaying his unswerving "respect to tradition, King and Country", won the Distinguished Service Medal.[50] Heroic redemption on the battlefield was also a popular theme. In Theodore Goodridge Roberts' *The Fighting Starkleys*, Jim Hammond, who deserted in Canada, overcame his fear, re-enlisted and "return[ed] home a hero with a shattered knee".[51]

Clearly, the Canadian home front was more disposed to welcome back heroes enhanced by combat rather than ordinary men often left physically and mentally scarred. By no means was every veteran stepping off the boat in Halifax Harbour in 1919 embittered and/or maladjusted. Some men recalled their time in uniform fondly; never before had they experienced such comradeship or felt so alive. Countless veterans simply buried any bitterness, obtained a job and got on with life. Yet for thousands it was literally frightening to think about rejoining a society that, they felt, possessed no conception of the ordeals they had endured nor of the torment still often dominating their thoughts. "Friends wanted to hear [glorious] stories of the battlefield", wrote one soldier, "and you felt like vomiting when the subject was mentioned".[52] This chasm often widened after the repatriated discovered that while the home front seemed anxious to canonize those who had perished overseas, it appeared far less eager to extend generosity to troops who had survived the carnage, suggesting an assumption that such *manly men*, by applying their wartime pluck, could, with relatively little public assistance, prosper in the peacetime world.[53]

From some disillusioned Canadian veterans there came antiwar novels. Sir Peregrine Acland, who served as a major with the First Division, published *All Else Is Folly* in 1929; Charles Yale Harrison, previously a machine gunner with the Royal Montreal Regiment, followed in 1930 with *Generals Die in Bed*; and in 1937, Philip Child, formerly a subaltern with a howitzer battery, produced *God's Sparrows*.[54] Not one was a bestseller. Harrison's novel, the most shocking, used the literary device of an anonymous narrator to demonstrate the dehumanizing nature of war. The book dwelt upon the gore of combat and made clear, at several junctures, that Canadian soldiers were often terrified in battle, regarded their officers with contempt, went on drunken rampages and even killed German prisoners. The reviews were scathing. In *Saturday Night*, Nathaniel Benson claimed that most of the disturbing incidents Harrison described "never occurred," while W.B. Kerr condemned the work as "fiction of the blood-curling type".[55] Far better received and published the same year as *Generals Die in Bed*, was Will Bird's *And We Go On*. Formerly with the 42nd Battalion, Bird did not deny the horrors of war nor the fact that the stresses of combat prompted some soldiers to act in a rather shocking manner. Ultimately, however, the message with regard to Canadian soldiers was optimistic. They were "not brutalized or dehumanized by war," because they proved capable of psychologically leaving the trenches behind. For instance, Bird described his former comrades as "boys again, horsing around and bathing in streams" after being moved to the rear.[56]

The use of high diction and romanticized imagery to describe the exploits of Canada's Great War soldiers, and the nationalistic legacy they left the country, grew to become a fixture. During the 1960s, in a decade supposedly dominated by antiwar attitudes, the unparalleled vigour of these soldiers was acclaimed as having forged a self-assured nation about to mark its 100th anniversary. Impossible to "overstress", wrote John Swettenham in his 1965 account, *To Seize the Victory*, was "the quality of the human material making up the [Canadian] Corps".[57] That same year, Kenneth Macksey emphasized the "martial manhood" of those who "saved the day" at Ypres and captured Vimy Ridge.[58] H.F. Wood's narrative, written during Canada's centennial year, made much of the fact that the clash at Vimy Ridge occurred during the dominion's half-century point, thus symbolizing a watershed where heroic men thrust the country from its colonial roots to full national status – it was, he declared, Canada's "Agincourt, no more, and no less".[59]

Only the lasting influence exerted by this "cult of the Canadian soldier" can explain the strong reaction to the 1986 National Film Board production of *The Kid Who Couldn't Miss*. So offended were so many people by its theme that air ace Billy Bishop was psychologically unstable and exaggerated his war record that Canada's Senate launched an official inquiry that ultimately, but unsuccessfully, attempted to pressure the director into labelling the film a "docudrama".[60] Also revealing was that in *Vimy* (1986), Pierre Berton believed it necessary to inform readers explicitly that Canadian soldiers did not, in this battle, fundamentally turn the tide against Germany; for the British, he wrote, Vimy was considered just one episode in the larger and longer Battle of Arras, something that explains why the renowned British historian Liddell Hart, "in his definitive history of the Great War [,]... gave [the encounter] no more than a paragraph".[61]

Over the last generation, as those directly connected to and most interested in protecting the image of Canada's Great War soldiers have died off, the historical portrayal of these men has shown signs of losing some lustre. This pattern also obtained intellectual encouragement from antiwar attitudes growing out of America's unpopular foray into Vietnam as well as from the explosion of graduate-level studies over the past quarter century as there came more scholars trained to question long-held assumptions – factors that produced several critical studies of Canadian tactics and performances upon land, at sea and in the air during the Great War.[62] Moreover, in oral reminiscences collected from Canada's Great War veterans during the late 1970s, a number of men admitted to sometimes becoming overwhelmed by fear, acting sadistically and remaining traumatized long after the conflict ended.[63]

Yet compensating for such inquiries are several popular accounts. Daniel Dancocks, in a bestselling trilogy written during the late 1980s, commented not only upon muddy trenches and costly battlefield strategy, but also upon "noble" sacrifice "not [undertaken] in vain".[64] While the experiences of 10 Canadians permitted Sandra Gwyn's 1992 work, *Tapestry of War*, to reveal much heartache and suffering, there also reverberated a declaration about Canadian soldiers that clearly runs deep in the national psyche: "Thrust for the first time upon the world stage they performed at all times credibly and often brilliantly – holding the line under gas attacks at Second Ypres in 1915, capturing Vimy Ridge in 1917 and... performing in the vanguard in 1918 during the hundred days of the astonishing counter-attack".[65] Also in 1992, to commemorate the 75th anniversary of Vimy Ridge, the Canadian Broadcasting Corporation produced a lengthy report for the "Magazine" segment of its national newscast entitled "Courage and Sacrifice." Slaughter and stalemate on the Western Front was covered but also used to highlight the importance and brilliance of this successful assault that, the film claimed, was seen as "incredible to everyone except the Canadian infantry".[66] This was followed in 1997 by a four-part NFB production entitled *Battle of Vimy Ridge*, which "dramatically reveals how innovative tactics combined with iron courage and heroic self-sacrifice... enable[d] Canadian soldiers to transform a field of slaughter into a field of glory".[67]

Australia's collective memory of the Great War bears striking similarity to Canada's, and it is a memory, also like Canada's, bolstered by events during and after the conflict that pointed to growing nationalism and autonomy. Although an ongoing perceived military threat from Japan slowed Australia's move toward complete independence from Britain (it did not adopt the Statute of Westminster until 1942), it nonetheless came out of the war more self-assured and ready to manage more of its own affairs.[68] By 1918, Australian soldiers were being commanded by Australians, principally by Major-General John Monash, who that year became Australian Corps Commander, something that reflected not only the nationalism generated by battlefield sacrifices but also the belief that British commanders were less innovative than Australians, who harboured the spirit of a frontier society. Following the war, Prime Minister W.M. Hughes strongly supported Canada's suggestion that, in recognition of "blood sacrifice", Britain provide separate representation to its self-governing dominions at the Versailles peace talks; following this concession and upon his return from France, Hughes declared that "Australia became a nation".[69] Furthermore, the ongoing "worship of the digger" (i.e., Australian soldier) drew strength from the massive number of families who experienced personal loss; for them, and for countless others who knew someone among Australia's 60,000 war dead and 160,000 wounded, "the Anzac myth," as Marilyn Lake explained, "turned that terrible loss into a meaningful event".[70]

Given the deluge of inspiring wartime information and years of complete separation from an army that endured the highest percentage of field casualties among imperial forces, many an Australian on Armistice Day stood prepared to greet "strong, heroic [and] undefeated" veterans now ready to thrive in civilian life, as opposed to "real men who needed... support [from] their society".[71] Notwithstanding what some civilians came to see as selfish demands made by ex-servicemen for better postwar support programs[72] and their sometimes violent outbursts,[73] the "Anzac legend" did not diminish. Indeed, the word "Anzac" was even legally protected in peacetime from derogatory statements, initially under the War Precautions Act, and then, after its repeal in 1920, under a new piece of legislation called Protection of the Word Anzac.[74]

Remaining prominent in postwar Australia was the picture of warriors whose deeds exceeded "those done on the field of Troy".[75] In 1927, Anzac Day, the April 25th anniversary of the Gallipoli landing, became an official national holiday. Veterans marched before cheering crowds, then usually drank (sometimes excessively), played various "manly" games and, in the process, reminded the country of the rugged manhood that, it was said, forged a great nation.[76]

Australia's celebration of its soldiers also produced an obsession with war memorials, something built, says Patsy Adams-Smith, "at every crossroads where it was difficult to imagine a squad of men having lived at any time"[77]; though, as in Canada, this also reflected a population that could not easily visit graveyards in far-off Europe. Romanticized themes dominated. The most common figure in local monuments was the Australian soldier, usually in some heroic pose or being offered up in sacrifice by a woman as an expression of the pure, if not saintly, ideals for which he died.[78] Meanwhile, starting in the early 1920s, in order to provide the Anzac with a fitting tribute, the tireless and influential Charles Bean initiated a campaign to construct a national testimonial in Canberra without rival. "We planned", he said in later years, "that just as one had to go to Florence or Dresden to see the finest picture galleries, so people would have to come to Australia to see the finest war memorial". In 1925, the national government allotted a little over £250,000 to this project, then a record for a public building. Financial constraints slowed construction during the 1930s, but when finally completed in 1941 the dedication ceremony invoked images of brave men to raise resolve in the face of a possible Japanese invasion. The monument's centrepiece, the domed Hall of Memory, reproduced Will Longstaff's painting, *Menim Gate at Midnight*, where Australian soldiers rose from graves overseas to make their final journey home. Finishing touches in 1955 included stained-glass windows detailing the country's Great War achievements and a dominating 18-foot bronze statue of a soldier symbolizing "young Australia proudly and courageously giving her all in the cause of freedom and honour".[79]

It was also through postwar literary endeavours that Bean strengthened the "Anzac legend." In 1919, he commenced what became a 23 year-long undertaking to write and edit a 12-volume *Official History* of Australia in the Great War. The result was a massively detailed and, compared to previous works, exceptionally careful study that, according to some scholars, discouraged others from writing similar histories.[80] It was well received: the volumes sold 150,000 copies in Australia. One reviewer called it Australia's "*Iliad* and *Odyssey*," though in England and New Zealand Bean's work was criticized for its nationalistic chauvinism. This bias was established in the first volume, which was released in 1921 and focussed upon the battle at Gallipoli. Here Bean turned to the bushman theory that, he believed, explained the superiority of Australian soldiers. For example, against "huge men from Australia", Bean portrayed "little pink-cheeked lads from the Manchester cotton-mills, who had... volunteer[ed] in the East Lancashire Division."[81] Although the *Official History* mentions Australian defeats and that some men succumbed psychologically to the stresses of front-line life, such as by self-wounding and deserting, there can be no mistake about the general theme: extraordinarily effective and brave soldiers who, for instance, at Gallipoli, displayed "indifference" to the intensity of enemy fire as they rapidly scaled the cliffs. Moreover, lapses within the Anzac were written off as exceptions and, as such, were often buried in footnotes even though, for example, the desertion rate among Australians during the first six months of 1917 was four times the British rate.[82]

Those Australians whose work reflected the depressing messages of Lost Generation writers such as Robert Graves and Siegfried Sassoon – works that a sizable number of Australians wanted banned – like that by Martin Boy, who, in 1939, published *A Single Flame,* barely dented the "literary fortress" protecting the "Anzac myth". Authors could cast the war as intense and ghastly, but when it came to the reputation of the Anzac, it remained essential to present a positive, if not heroic, picture. Such was the approach adopted in Leonard Mann's *Flesh in Armour,* which was awarded the 1932 gold medal from the Australian Literature Society. Mann, a veteran of the Great War who was badly injured and psychologically traumatized at Passchendaele, did not in his story avoid the horrors and high costs of conflict, but in the final analysis still presented a tale of Anzac triumph over adversity. Not as critically acclaimed, though probably more popular as it went through six editions in two-and-a-half-years following its release in 1932, was Ion Idriess' *The Desert Column.* Of the courageous Anzac spirit in Palestine, Idreiss wrote: "It was a grand sight, the thrill, the comradeship, the knowledge that hell would open out". Also reflecting public attitudes was a 12-volume set of war memoirs marketed in 1936 by *Reveille* magazine – in all, some 3,500 pages celebrating the "modern Odysseus" through books such as *Jacka's Mob,* which was described as a "vivid and true picture" of the "gallant men" who landed at Gallipoli.[83]

In the Second World War, several writers turned to the "Anzac legend" to rally the nation. They included Charles Bean, who, in *The Old A.I.F. and the New* (1940), cast the two armies as "father and son".[84] However, controversy during the late 1960s and early 1970s surrounding Australia's involvement in the Vietnam War threatened the "Anzac legend". A predominantly conscript army of 50,000 was viewed by many people, particularly by young Australians whose large antiwar protests received vast media coverage, as helping to carry out American imperialism in Southeast Asia.[85] Starting around that time was the appearance of works critically assessing the "Anzac myth"; no doubt many people believed that the glorification of these soldiers, and hence Australia's military past, contributed to its involvement in Vietnam. In 1974, Bill Gammage, relying largely on wartime diaries and postwar oral testimony provided by Australian Great War veterans, presented in *The Broken Years* men who sometimes cracked in battle, who relished *blighties,* who self-wounded – who, in other words, were not superhuman. In 1980, Suzanne Brugger's *Australia and Egypt, 1914-1919* "unearth[ed] a plethora of misdemeanours, from minor and essentially comical (such as the teaching of unwitting Arab news-boys obscene cries) to various brutalities, including rape, committed on the despised local population".[86] Most recently, Robin Gerster's *Big-Noting: The Heroic Theme in Australian War Writing* (1987) and Alistair Thomson's *Anzac Memories: Living with the Legend* (1994) present the inspirational portrayal of the Anzac as the creation of Great War propagandists.

Yet, the power of this appealing legend persists. Tim Duncan, in a piece entitled "History as a Kangaroo Court", condemned those whom he sneeringly classified as "young, radical historians," including Gerster and Thomson, for denigrating the country while enjoying the fruits of its freedom won by the Anzac.[87] Indeed, despite the unpopularity of Australia's involvement in the Vietnam War, the reputation of the Anzac was never truly imperilled. While controversy over the conflict still saturated the media, the 1972-75 Whitham government told citizens then enduring a recession to face these uncertain times with the same fortitude as had their fathers and grandfathers at Gallipoli. Popular entertainment also paid homage. Peter Weir's 1981 film *Gallipoli,* though showing Anzacs indiscriminately mowed down in battle, made the point that this was the result of failure among British commanders, not Australian soldiers. Not only did Weir evoke empathy for the Anzac, but also "pleasure in... Australian characteristics, and pride in their courage and... achievements." *Gallipoli* was followed by several other productions for the big screen and for television: *1915, Anzacs, The Lighthorsemen* and *The Man from Snowy River*. Each portrayed the Great War as "miserable, bloody and terrifying," but the Australians "endure and emerge with pride in their manhood, their military achievements and their new nationalism".[88] Many popular histories continue to reflect such notions. W.F. Mandle characterized

Australian soldiers "as tough and inventive... a bit undisciplined... [but also] chivalrous and gallant",[89] and in describing those at Gallipoli, Patsy Adams-Smith made comparisons with "the three hundred [Spartans] at Thermopylae" who stemmed the tide against several thousand Persian invaders.[90] Finally, on Anzac Day 1990, in a highly publicized media event, 58 Australian veterans of the Great War returned to Gallipoli. Prime Minister R.J. Hawke, speaking before these old soldiers but really addressing himself to the nation, urged Australians to "follow the Anzac... model of sacrifice, courage and mateship" as a guide for the country as it moved toward its centennial and a new century.[91]

In Canada and Australia the modern memory of the Great War is one not only of muddy trenches and massive death, but also of gallant men scaling the heights at Vimy Ridge or the cliffs at Gallipoli to endow the foundations of modern-day nationalism. The fact that both countries entered the Great War as colonies intent upon demonstrating their worthiness within the Empire predetermined that monumental significance would be placed into each one of their battlefield encounters. However, in addition to prewar desires, there also existed a series of factors ranging from geographic isolation to press corps' patriotism to the "manly" stoicism often displayed in soldiers' letters home, making it easier for authorities to mould the perceptions of civilians. Furthermore, following the war, there emerged the determination among most civilians and soldiers not to accept a version of events that would lead to the conclusion that so much suffering had been in vain. Certainly, the monumental human costs of the war discredited many romantic notions. Not long after the conflict, the view of war as a glorious adventure for the manly and chivalrous lost nearly all legitimacy as indicated by the fact that in both countries few celebrations occurred in September 1939 as most people approached the fight against Nazism as an unpleasant but necessary task. Still, the rapid growth of autonomy in Australia and Canada following the First World War helped retain the depiction of superior, if not superhuman, soldiers who, despite often errant behaviour after repatriation, were and to this day largely remain portrayed as men motivated by the highest of ideals and esteemed as the valiant catalysts behind the appearance of self-confident, progressive, freedom-loving and truly independent nations. No doubt this was a flattering and, in some respects, deserved image for those who had endured so much. Yet, it is a popular memory given birth by wartime propagandists, that conjures the use of high diction, romanticizes events and people, and thus, in the final analysis, obscures the past.

Notes

1. *Maclean's*, July 1, 1999: 22-23.

2. *National Post* (8 February, 2000): B1.

3. See for example, Elizabeth Armstrong, *The Crisis of Quebec, 1914-18* (New York: Columbia University Press, 1938); H. Blair Neatby, *Laurier and a Liberal Quebec: A Study in Political Management* (Toronto: McClelland and Stewart, 1973); Robert Craig Brown and Ramsay Cook, *Canada, 1896-1921: A Nation Transformed* (Toronto: McClelland and Stewart, 1974); Robert Craig Brown, *Robert Laird Borden: A Biography*, vol. 2 (Toronto: University of Toronto Press, 1980); and J.L. Granatstein and J.M. Hitsman, *Broken Promises: A History of Conscription in Canada* (Toronto: Oxford University Press, 1977).

4. *National Post*, February 11, 2000: A18.

5. Canada sent more than 7,000 and Australia more than 16,000 men to the Boer War. See Carman Miller, *Painting the Map Red: Canada and the South African War, 1899-1902* (Montreal and Kingston: McGill-Queen's University Press, 1992); Peter Firkins, *The Australians in Nine Wars: Waikato to Long Tan* (Adelaide: Rigby Limited, 1971), 14; R. Norris, *The Emergent Commonwealth: Australian Federation, Expectations and Fulfilment, 1889-1910* (Carlton: Melbourne University Press, 1975); and M. Dunn, *Australia and the Empire: 1788 to the Present* (Sydney: Fontana, 1984).

6. Carl Berger, *The Sense of Power: Studies in the Ideas of Canadian Imperialism, 1867-1914* (Toronto: University of Toronto Press, 1970), 129.

7. Mick Taussig, "An Australian Hero", *History Workshop*, 24 (1987): 118.

8. Jeffrey A. Keshen, *Propaganda and Censorship During Canada's Great War* (Edmonton: University of Alberta Press, 1996), 28; Kevin Fewster, "Expression and Suppression: Aspects of Military Censorship in Australia During World War I", University of New South Wales: 1980, Ph.D. dissertation 88.

9. A.J.P. Taylor, *Beaverbrook* (New York: Simon and Schuster, 1972), 91; Anne Chisholm and Michael Davie, *Beaverbrook: A Life* (London: Hutchinson, 1992), 127.

10. The CWRO also hired cameramen and artists to record the magnificence of Canadian troops in this struggle. For details, see J. Keshen, op cit., 35-38.

11. Aitken's zeal to champion Canadian soldiers produced some complaints in Britain, especially from British military leaders, over the impression being created of Canadian soldiers as the most capable among the Allies. On this dispute, see Timothy H. E. Travers, "Allies in Conflict: The British and Canadian Historians and the Real Story of Second Ypres", *Journal of Contemporary History*, 24 (1989): 301-325.

12. Volume 2 of *Canada in Flanders* appeared in 1917 under Aitken's new title of Lord Beaverbrook and carried the story forward to mid-1916. Volume 3 was written in 1918 by Theodore Goodridge Roberts, a CWRO staff writer who initially joined Canada's First Division and was part of the famous New Brunswick literary family. In 1918, Aitken, in part due to his successful propaganda work for Canada, became Britain's first Minister of Information. Jonathon F. Vance, *Death So Noble: Meaning, Memory and the First World War* (Vancouver: University of British Columbia Press, 1997), 165. Volumes 2 and 3 were much the same as volume 1. For instance, when writing about trench raids, such as in 1916 at La Petite Douve, Aitken described, "a handful of men of the 7th Canadian Battalion... [who] killed at least fifty of the enemy.... Fame and decorations had been won, and fresh glory for Canadian arms". Lord Beaverbrook, *Canada in Flanders*, vol. 2 (London: Hodder and Stoughton, 1917), xii, 116.

13. *Saturday Night* (May 22, 1916): 8; Ken Ramstead, "The 'Eye-Witness': Lord Beaverbrook and Canada in Flanders", *The Register*, 12 (1984): 309-310.

14. Maxwell Aitken, *Canada in Flanders*, vol. 1 (London: Hodder and Stoughton, 1916), 3-4.

15. Desmond Morton, *When Your Number's Up: The Canadian Soldier in the First World War* (Toronto: Random House, 1993), 278.

16. *The Toronto Star* (August 12, 1916): 6; House of Lords Records Office, Lord Beaverbrook papers, BBK E/1/16, Beckles Willson to Aitken, June 28, 1916.

17. Ibid., BBK E/2/11, Robinson to Beckles Willson, April 29, 1916.

18. National Archives of Canada (NAC), RG 25, Records of the Department of External Affairs, Vol. 262, File P-6/73, C.F. Crandall to Lt.-Col. Hugh Clark, February 7, 1917.

19. NAC, RG 9, Records of the Department of Militia and Defence (MD), Vol. 4688, File 42-21, Operations Report, November 30, 1917; A.M.J. Hyatt, "Corps Commander: Arthur Currie", *Canadian Military History: Selected Readings*, ed. Marc Milner (Toronto: Copp Clark Pitman Ltd., 1993), 109.

20. MD, Vol. 4725, File 186-1, Press Dispatch, December 6, 1917.

21. For a description of domestic censorship see J. Keshen, op. cit., chapters 3 and 4. The War Measures Act provided a maximum penalty of $5,000, five years incarceration, or both.

22. NAC, MG30 D14, J.S. Willison papers, Willison to J.M. MacDonald, July 21, 1915.

23. *Manitoba* Free Press (May 3, 1915): 5.

24. *The Winnipeg Tribune* (April 12, 1917): 9.

25. Pierre Berton, *Vimy* (Toronto: McClelland and Stewart, 1986), 293.

26. Robin Gerster, *Big-Noting: The Heroic Theme in Australian War Writing* (Melbourne: Melbourne University Press, 1987), 14; K.S. Inglis, "Anzac and the Australian Military Tradition", *Revue internationale d'histoire militaire*, 72 (1990): 6.

27. Bruce Ryan, "Metropolitan Growth", *Contemporary Australia: Studies in History, Politics and Economics*, ed. Richard Preston, (Durham: Duke University Press, 1969), 203-204.

28. K.S. Inglis, "The Anzac Tradition", *Meanjim Quarterly*, 24 (1965): 33.

29. D.A. Kent, "The Anzac Book and the Anzac Legend: C.E.W. Bean as Editor and Image Maker", *Historical Studies*, 21, no. 84 (1985): 376.

30. Marilyn Lake, "Mission Impossible: How Men Gave Birth to the Australian Nation – Nationalism, Gender and Other Seminal Acts", *Gender & History*, 4, no. 3 (1992): 308-309.

31. R. Gerster, op. cit., 25; Alistair Thomson, *Anzac Memories: Living with the Legend* (Melbourne: Oxford University Press, 1994), 53.

32. Annabel Cooper, "Textual Territories: Gendered Cultural Politics and Australian Representations of the War of 1914-1918", *Australian Historical Studies*, 25, no. 100 (1993): 416; M. Taussig, op. cit., 126.

33. A. Thomson, op. cit., 60-61.

34. Ibid., 66-70; D.A. Kent, op. cit., 378, 380-381.

35. For an analysis of Australian censorship, see K. Fewster, op. cit., By war's end, the *War Precautions Act*, initially passed in August 1914, established theoretically unlimited penalties against those who "spread false reports... public alarm... or prejudice[d] His Majesty's relations with foreign powers". Ibid., 27-28.

36. Ibid., 108.

37. *Calgary Herald* (March 25, 1919): 8.

38. *Hamilton Spectator* (May 9, 1919): 1.

39. J. Vance, op. cit., 111-114, 121, 201, 213.

40. Ibid., 5. This argument is made about Australian Great War veterans in Alistair Thomson, "Memory as Battlefield: Personal and Political Investments in the National Military Past", *Oral History Review*, 22, no. 2 (1995): 55-73.

41. *The Toronto Star* (September 3, 1919): 3.

42. Allan R. Young, "'We Throw the Torch': Canadian Memorials of the Great War and the Mythology of Heroic Sacrifice", *Journal of Canadian Studies*, 26, no. 4 (1990): 13, 16, 18.

43. Brereton Greenhous and Stephen Harris, *Canada and the Battle of Vimy Ridge, 9-12 April 1917* (Ottawa: Minister of Supply and Services, 1992), 139; J. Vance, op. cit., 66-67; *Guide Book of the Pilgrimage to Vimy and the Battlefields* (Ottawa: Vimy Pilgrimage Committee, 1936), 71.

44. P. Berton, op. cit., 304; Norm Christie, *For King and Empire: The Canadians at Vimy* (Nepean: CEF Books, 1996), 86-89. On the nationalistic imagery surrounding the Battle of Vimy Ridge, also see John Pierce, "Constructing Memory: The Idea of Vimy Ridge", Wilfrid Laurier University: 1993, M.A. thesis; Dave Inglis, "Vimy Ridge, 1917-1993: A Canadian Myth Over Seventy-Five Years," Simon Fraser University: 1995 M.A. thesis.

45. John Herd Thompson and Allen Seager, *Canada, 1922-1939: Decades of Discord* (Toronto: McClelland and Stewart, 1985), 166.

46. J. Vance, op. cit., 94-95; Colonel George G. Nasmith, *Canada's Sons and Great Britain in the World War* (Toronto: John C. Winston Co., 1919), iv, 305.

47. *Canada in the Great World War* (Toronto: United Publishers of Canada, 1921), 274-374.

48. Vance, *Death So Noble*, 172-173; Colonel A. Fortesque Duguid, *Official History of the Canadian Forces in the Great War, 1914-1919*, vol. 1 (Ottawa: Ministry of National Defence, 1938), ix. Despite positive reviews, the extraordinarily long time it took to complete the first volume, its poor sales (due in part to the appearance of so many other war histories by 1938, including some 20 regimental histories) and the diversion of attention in September 1939 to the war against Nazism kept the series to a single entry.

49. Ibid., 421-422.

50. Dagmar Novak, "The Canadian Novel and the Two World Wars," University of Toronto: 1988 Ph.D. dissertation, 22.

51. J. Vance, op. cit., 54.

52. Pierre Van Paasen, *Days of Our Years* (New York: Hillman-Carl Inc., 1939), 91.

53. Although the programs introduced by the Department of Soldiers' Civil Re-establishment constituted a record sum expended by the federal government upon public welfare, there remained, throughout the interwar years, complaints from Canada's Great War veterans that the various initiatives were grossly inadequate. See Desmond Morton and Glenn Wright, *Winning the Second Battle: Canadian Soldiers Return to Civilian Life, 1915-1930* (Toronto: University of Toronto Press, 1987), and J. Keshen, op. cit., 201-206.

54. D. Novak, op. cit., 37, 69, 92; Linda Rae Steward, "A Canadian Perspective: The Fictional and Historical Portrayal of World War One", University of Waterloo: 1983 M.A., thesis, 80.

55. J. Vance, op. cit., 193.

56. Ibid., 196.

57. John Swettenham, *To Seize the Victory: The Canadian Corps in World War I* (Toronto: Ryerson Press, 1965), 247.

58. Kenneth Macksey, *The Shadow of Vimy Ridge* (Toronto: Ryerson Press, 1965), 189.

59. H.F. Wood, *Vimy!* (Toronto: Macmillan of Canada, 1967), 170.

60. Senate Standing Committee on Social Affairs, Science and Technology, *Production and Distribution of the National Film Board Production, "The Kid Who Couldn't Miss"* (Ottawa: Supply and Services, 1986); Winnipeg *Free Press*, (April 16, 1986): 33.

61. P. Berton, op. cit., 295-296.

62. See Desmond Morton and J.L. Granatstein, *Marching to Armageddon: Canadians and the Great War, 1914-1919* (Toronto: Lester and Orpen Dennys, 1989); O. Morton, op. cit.,; Bill Rawling, *Surviving Trench Warfare: Technology and the Canadian Corps, 1914-1918* (Toronto: University of Toronto Press, 1992); Michael Hadley and Roger Sarty, *Tin-Pots and Pirate Ships: Canadian Naval Forces and German Sea Raiders, 1880-1918* (Montreal and Kingston: McGill-Queen's University Press, 1991); Stephen J. Harris, *Canadian Brass: The Making of a Professional Army* (Toronto: University of Toronto Press, 1988); and S.F. Wise, *Canadian Airmen and the First World War: The Official History of the Royal Canadian Air Force*, vol. 1 (Toronto: University of Toronto Press, 1980).

63. See Heather Robertson, ed., *A Terrible Beauty* (Toronto: James Lorimer and Company, 1977), and Daphne Read, ed., *The Great War and Canadian Society* (Toronto: New Hogtown Press, 1978).

64. Daniel Dancocks, *Spearhead to Victory: Canada and the Great War* (Edmonton: Hurtig Publishers, 1987), 240; *Legacy of Valour: The Canadians at Passchendaele* (Edmonton: Hurtig Publishers, 1986); and *Welcome to Flanders' Field: The First Canadian Battle of the War, Ypres, 1915* (Toronto: McClelland and Stewart, 1990).

65. Sandra Gwyn, *Tapestry of War: A Private View of Canadians in the Great War* (Toronto: HarperCollins, 1992), xvii.

66. Canadian Broadcasting Corporation, *News in Review* (May 1992).

67. National Film Board, *Battle of Vimy Ridge*, part 4, "The Battle Joined and Won".

68. Donald Horne, *The Australian People* (Sydney: Angus and Robertson, 1972), 207-208.

69. Peter Dennis, "Introduction", *Revue internationale d'histoire militaire*, 72 (1990): xiii.

70. D. Horne, op. cit., 184; Lake, op. cit., 312.

71. Deborah Hull, "'The Old Lie': Teaching Children about War, 1914-1939", *Melbourne Historical Journal*, 20, no. 1 (1990): 95.

72. Gavin Souter, *Lion and Kangaroo: The Initiation of Australia, 1901-1919* (Sydney: Collins, 1976), 286.

73. A. Thomson, op. cit., 6; Raymond Evans, "Some Furious Outbreaks of Riot: Returned Soldiers and Queensland's 'Red Flag' Disturbances, 1918-1919", *War & Society* 3, no. 2 (1985): 75-95.

74. K.S. Inglis, op. cit., 6.

75. D. Hull, op. cit., 92.

76. K.S. Inglis, "Men, Women and War Memorials: Anzac Australia", *Deadalus*, 116, no. 4 (1987): 53-54.

77. Patsy Adams-Smith, *The Anzacs* (London: Hamish-Hamilton, 1978), 316.

78. K.S. Inglis, op. cit., 49.

79. K.S. Inglis, "A Sacred Place: The Making of the Australian War Memorial", *War & Society* 3, no. 2 (1985): 100-101, 109.

80. P. Dennis, op. cit., viii.

81. Alistair Thomson, "'Steadfast Until Death': C.E.W. Bean and the Representation of Australian Military Manhood", *Australian Historical Studies*, 23, no. 93 (1989): 462-464; K.S. Inglis, op. cit., 26.

82. A. Thomson, Ibid., 470-472.

83. R. Gerster, op. cit., 95, 104, 121, 134-135, 158.

84. Ibid., 173.

85. K.S. Inglis, "Anzac and the Australian Military Tradition", 18. Also see Jeff Doyle, "Dismembering the Anzac Legend: Australian Popular Culture and the Vietnam War", *Vietnam Generation*, 3, no. 2 (1991): 109-125.

86. R. Gerster, op. cit., 53; Bill Gammage, *The Broken Years: Australian Soldiers in the Great War* (Canberra: Australian National University Press, 1974).

87. A. Thomson, op. cit., 261.

88. Ibid., 190-192, 196-197.

89. W.F. Mandle, *Going It Alone: Australia's National Identity in the Twentieth Century* (Victoria: Penguin, 1977), 4.

90. P. Adams-Smith, op. cit., ix.

91. J. Doyle, op. cit., 110.

PART IV

Republicanism and National Identity

11

The Australian Republic: Still Captive After All These Years

MARK MCKENNA

Cause for Celebration?

On the evening of Thursday, November 18, 1999, less than two weeks after the republic referendum was lost on November 6, Australian Prime Minister John Howard stood on a chair under a chandelier in the dining room of Kirribilli House in Sydney. In his speech of thanks to Kerry Jones, head of Australians for Constitutional Monarchy, the prime minister appeared "happy and ebullient" as he described his own role in the campaign as "respectful and dignified". The guests who had gathered at the Prime Minister's invitation had come to celebrate the defeat of the republic. Looking across the blue-green waters of Sydney Cove at dusk toward the Opera House, they sipped their Chardonnay and gave thanks that the British Crown remained the sovereign power in Australia's Constitution. In the words of the Prime Minister, "the good sense of the Australian people" had prevailed, Australia would remain a constitutional monarchy – her people could sleep safe in the knowledge that the dire consequences of a republic had been avoided – at least for the time being.[1]

Missing from Mr. Howard's drinks party were the many republicans who had bedded down with the monarchists during the campaign. Chief among them Ted Mack and Phil Cleary, the two independent MPs who had advocated a No vote on the grounds that the republic model on offer made no provision for a directly elected president. They had argued that a No vote would see a subsequent referendum on a directly elected president, knowing full well that the immediate result of this strategy would see Australia continue as a constitutional monarchy.

Father Frank Brennan, who had publicly supported the bipartisan appointment model, quipped that Mack and Cleary had done such great service to the monarchy during the referendum campaign that they should be knighted. But now, when it came to drinks, this loveless marriage of monarchists and republicans was over before the reception began. Only the monarchists could bring themselves to raise their glasses in triumph. Republicans of all persuasions were left to sift the ashes and contemplate the rebuilding of the Australian republican movement.

Who Were the Winners?

In attempting to understand the referendum result, there are some explanations that come readily to mind and over which few would quibble. The history of referendum questions in Australia is notoriously bleak – at least if you favour constitutional change. Only eight out of 44 have been successful since federation. There seems to be little or no prospect of achieving the necessary double majority of states and voters without bipartisan support and the absence of significant opposition.

The referendum on the republic was opposed most significantly by the Prime Minister as well as a convenient union of constitutional fundamentalists and democratic republicans – a union that only made sense because the referendum question combined two questions in one: Did Australia want to become a republic? – and Did the electorate wish to embrace a president appointed by a two-thirds majority of federal Parliament?

The referendum took place in a political context which could only be described as indifferent. Like many other liberal democracies in the late twentieth century, Australian political culture is marked by a deep cynicism toward elected politicians and their meeting place – in this case, the national capital – Canberra. When this trend is combined with the traditional hard-nosed pragmatism of Australian politics, a tradition that is not renowned for its receptivity to symbolic arguments for change, it might seem remarkable that 5 million Australians actually voted Yes on November 6, 1999. In such political climate, it is difficult to see how any republic that might be represented as one initiated by self-serving politicians could pass the tough test of a referendum. As a monarchist might read the result on November 6, 1999, a republic by the politicians, for the politicians and of the politicians was sensibly rejected by the people. In the words of Kerry Jones on November 8, "The No campaign was the people's protest"[2] While it might be tempting to see the republic referendum as a contest between the forces of popular sovereignty and parliamentary sovereignty, the truth is more elusive.

The bald facts of the result tell several stories. The referendum was lost nationally by a margin of 10 percent: 55 to 45. The state breakdown was not encouraging – not one state voted Yes – although Victoria was lost narrowly. New South Wales, long seen as the strongest support base for the republic, struggled to reach a Yes vote of 46 percent. In Queensland, South Australia, Tasmania, and Western Australia, a 20 per cent gap separated the Yes and No vote – approximately 60 to 40. Only in Canberra did the Yes vote reach the resounding level of 64 per cent - evidence perhaps that contempt for politicians increases steadily with every additional kilometre one drives away from Parliament House.[3] Of 148 federal seats, only 42 voted Yes, 23 of which were Liberal-held seats and 19 Labor held. Every National Party seat voted No. Aside from two seats to the north of Melbourne and Sydney, all the Yes seats were based in the inner suburbs of the major cities. Measured in terms of tertiary education, 19 of the top 20 electorates voted Yes while 93 of the 100 least qualified voted No.[4]

Similar trends were evident in relation to income. It was not until income rose above $50,000 per annum that the Yes vote managed to crawl above 50 percent.[5] The geographic distribution is equally startling. All but nine of the 42 Yes seats were in New South Wales and Victoria, and all but 11 were in the metropolitan areas of Sydney and Melbourne. In the words of *The Sydney Morning Herald* columnist Alan Ramsey, those who voted No most resoundingly were among "the country's least educated, most isolated, most insular, most uninformed, lowest paid, most prejudiced, and more than likely, hardest working anywhere".[6]

In the wake of the referendum results, a consensus emerged among Australia's political commentators in their explaining the extent of the No vote. This view emphasized the sharp divide between city and country, inner city and outer suburbs, rich and poor, the constitutionally informed and the blissfully ignorant. The referendum result cut across party allegiances. The traditional home of Labor, the outer suburbs of the major cities, voted against the republic. With some irony, voters in the Prime

Minister's own seat of Bennelong in Northern Sydney voted Yes. It was the letter boxes of John Howard's constituents in the "republic of Bennelong", which had received the Prime Minister's personal letter explaining his reasons for voting against the republic.[7]

The headline run by *The Australian* on the Monday after the republic referendum neatly captured the now generally accepted interpretation of the vote – "One Queen two nations".[8] As soon as we divide the Australian nation into two categories – the "elites" and "the ordinary people" – as if there were 5.5 million bright "high flyers" who voted Yes and 7 million unwashed dullards who voted No – we have adopted the categories of populism. This is little different from journalists and intellectuals dutifully or unthinkingly employing the Howard government term "mainstream" to describe Australian society. When we use the language of populism to understand political behaviour, the populists have won.

It is also worth remembering that after every referendum, both the victors and the vanquished believe that their supporters cast a "sensible" and "informed" vote, while those who voted against them are "mislead" or "uninformed". For example, when Prime Minister Howard was asked to explain the vote on the republic he had opposed, he praised the good sense of the Australian people. When asked to explain the poor Yes vote on the preamble that he had personally proposed, he blamed the apathy and ignorance of the people.[9]

Another factor that complicates a simplistic reading of the republic vote is the many and varied number of reasons people had for voting Yes and No, reasons that do not necessarily coalesce obediently in tidy geographic clusters. The first group of Yes voters, for example, were republicans who were willing to replace the Queen as head of state with a president appointed by a two thirds majority of federal Parliament. Some in this category believed it would be the first step toward further constitutional reform, (a directly elected President, a bill of rights, a new constitution). Others believed a Yes vote would act as a safeguard against further reform (better to approve the more conservative change now rather than risk the possibility of a complete change to the system in the future). The latter group would have included both conservative republicans and a sprinkling of small "m" monarchists fearful of direct election. Other Yes supporters didn't cast their vote with the future in mind. They were willing to accept the model, perfect or flawed, in order to get the republic through.

Contrary to the belief that all the informed voters were on the Yes side, many of those who voted Yes would have done so without understanding the fine detail of the bipartisan appointment model. They simply believed that it was time – the monarchy had had its day, out with the old – in with the new. Some may even have voted Yes because they felt it was the only refuge for a patriot, others because they didn't want to agree with Prime Minister Howard and a minority perhaps because they didn't like Kerry Jones or the sound of the word No. Finally, there were those who voted Yes for combinations of the above or for none of the above – some of them fully informed, some partially informed, some misinformed, some not carrying information of any particular kind.

No voters, on the other hand, comprised at least seven different groups. First came those "hard core" monarchists who would vote No to any republic. We might call these voters the "monarchy or death" clique. Close on their well-polished heels come the constitutional fundamentalists. These are the "1901ers" – while not attached deeply to the monarchy, they dread the prospect of any change to the sacred text of the founding fathers. While the former may be able to draw the Windsor family tree from memory, the latter are more likely to be found at public meetings with well thumbed copies of the Australian Constitution at the ready, dutifully protecting "the word" of the fundamental law.

Next come those who were republican but voted No because they didn't particularly like the model, either because they were sympathetic to direct election – perhaps without necessarily understanding the constitutional ramifications of a President elected by popular vote ("I want to have a say"!)-or because they were committed to one form of direct election (the Irish, American, Austrian or French for example) and were not willing to accept anything less. There were also republicans who preferred a President appointed by Parliament, but were unhappy with certain features of the bipartisan appointment model put before them on November 6, such as the dismissal mechanism or the public nominations procedure.

While some No voters in the previous categories might also have harboured contempt for politicians, there were many who voted No out of spite. They saw the republic referendum as an opportunity to register a protest against politicians – after all it was the politicians who had "wasted" $120 million on the referendum when there were "real" needs in thousands of local communities across the country – and these same politicians now wanted to appoint the president. There could only be one answer –" Vote No to the politician's republic".[10] This strategy is one that has also proved successful in other plebiscites or referendums held in New Zealand, Canada and Europe over the last decade.

Mixed up with this anti-politician sentiment were No votes sustained by various homilies and clichés that encouraged ignorance and exploited fear. Slogans such as "Don't Know Vote No" and "If It Ain't Broke Don't Fix It" struck a chord with those who could not find the capacity, space or time to understand the issues involved, as well as those who were suspicious of change per se or simply apathetic.[11] The stark reality is that many voted against the republic without understanding the proposal for change and with little or no idea of the system they were pretending to protect.

Yet while it may be true that the more wealthy inner metropolitan areas tended to support the republic, whereas the outer suburbs of the cities and the bush were largely opposed, the "two nations" analysis is still far too simplistic. Given the well-documented ignorance of the Constitution in Australian society, and the many different reasons people had for voting Yes or No, many of which cross the city-bush divide, we should not assume too readily that those who voted Yes did so because they were more informed than those who voted No.[12] We should also refrain from casting Yes voters as an elite. When it comes to the Constitution, the wealthy may be no more informed than the poor.

The reasons that university-educated, upper-middle-class Australians of the inner cities were more likely to support the republic may lie elsewhere. Perhaps it is this class which is more persuaded by the symbolic arguments for a republic, more convinced of the need for a republic as image, brand, identity, an internationally recognized label of independence. Perhaps it is this class which is also more in touch with the production of information, new technology and the continual process of change and invention in a global marketplace – one that encourages and embraces change – and one that does not hold politicians in contempt precisely because it has benefited materially from the economic reforms of the last two decades. It has not suffered at the hands of economic rationalism as those in the outer suburbs or isolated rural communities have done. It is not that the wealthy and more educated Australians are necessarily more informed about the Constitution, but that they have come to see change as positive, while others have come to fear it.

Who Supported the Republic?

The Yes case was backed by a wide cross section of leading figures from the political, legal, corporate, clerical and media environments.[13] The Murdoch press, which comprises almost 70 percent of the mass circulation major metropolitan daily newspapers in Australia, supported the republic. News Corporation chief executive Rupert Murdoch and his son Lachlan both made public interventions in the campaign which were critical of the stance of Prime Minister Howard and supportive of the republic.[14]

The Murdoch broadsheet *The Australian*, Australia's only national daily, led the way with regular pro-republic editorials and comment. *The Australian* even sold car stickers for the Yes case, and organized its own public forums on the referendum that were naturally given maximum coverage.[15] On the day of the referendum, *The Australian's* front page carried a large banner in full colour urging readers to "Vote Yes". The day after the referendum, the Murdoch tabloid *The Daily Telegraph* lamented "Long to Reign Over Us. Queen lives but Our Republic Dies".[16]

The Fairfax stable, most notably *The Sydney Morning Herald* and *The Age*, were fully behind the republic. Like *The Australian*, *The Herald* and *The Age* advocated a Yes vote largely on two grounds. First because the model was conservative, minimal, and safe. Second, because the monarchy was no longer an appropriate or meaningful symbol for Australia in the 21st century.[17]

These arguments were supported by the Australian Labor Party, a majority of Australian Democrats, approximately 35 to 40 percent of the federal Liberal Party, every state premier except Western Australia's Richard Court and every state Opposition leader except Queensland's Rob Borbidge.[18]

Despite all the powerful forces gathered together in favour of the Yes case, the "Manufacturing of Consent" could not be arranged.

"Vote No to the Politicians' Republic"

Four days before the referendum on November 6, *The Australian* carried a photograph of one of the final No campaign rallies in Sydney. The photographer's eye chose to fall on a collection of elderly monarchists. Seated on green plastic chairs, they floated their No balloons and held a placard that read "Vote No to the Red Republic". In the bottom right-hand corner of their placard was the unmistakable sign of the hammer and sickle, appropriately coloured in bright red.[19]

If the caption below the photograph had read "Loyalists rally in favour of Menzies attempt to outlaw the Communist Party", the photograph would have seemed entirely credible. The photographer had caught an almost fossilized form of opposition to an Australian republic – more relevant to the formative years of the generation holding the balloons than the 1990s – and one which had virtually no bearing on the result of the referendum.

The success of the No vote was not explained by popular support for the monarchy but by lack of popular support for politicians. The No Vote succeeded because it tapped into the widespread contempt for politicians in Australian society – "Vote No to the Politicians' Republic". Combined with this empty slogan were a number of contradictory but highly effective messages.

First, cast the republicans as elites, as friends of the politicians, the media, lawyers, academics and other "high flyers" – all republicans are enemies of the people – enemies of the "ordinary Australian". Except, that is, those republicans who intended to "Vote No to This Republic" – such as "politicians" Ted Mack, Phil Cleary and Peter Reith and "lawyer" Jocelyn Scutt. These "elites" were the friends of the people - at least until November 7, 1999.[20]

To convey this populist message the No side was aided by Tony Abbott, Minister for Employment, Rhodes Scholar and a product of struggle town on Sydney's northern beaches. More than any other federal minister, Abbott exploited the class card, fanned fear of the disastrous consequences of the model and encouraged community loathing of his profession. His was an outstanding contribution.[21]

But hounding the elites wasn't enough. The No campaign also concentrated on painting the republic as the end of civilization. If a Yes vote succeeded, the electorate was told the flag would change, Crown land would finally be handed back to the Aborigines, the Weimar commonwealth of Australia would become a fascist republican dictatorship and Perth businesswoman Janet Holmes a Court would "buy the Australian Presidency".[22]

The language of this fear campaign cleverly relied on analogies that evoked the everyday experience of ordinary Australians – that is, cars and their drivers. Hence, the public was told that under the bipartisan appointment model, the Prime Minister could sack the President more easily than "he could sack his driver". After all, "would you buy a used car without driving it first"? – "With no kilometre guarantee"? – just drive away and hope for the best?[23]

This clever mixture of deceit, populism and scare campaign emanated from a range of voices across the political spectrum – everywhere from the right wing One Nation Party to ex-High Court judges, monarchists and radical republicans – something that made the task of the Yes case that much harder. They were attacked from right and left and within their own ranks.

The No campaign was also able to exploit the belief that the referendum would not be the last and only opportunity to vote on the republic. In the middle of the campaign Kerry Jones, a monarchist who opposes all republics, suggested that after the referendum failed "a better republican model, based on a popularly elected President, should be drafted by a new convention and submitted to the people at a subsequent referendum".[24]

Yet there was still a more damaging feature of the No campaign. Since 1991, when Australians for Constitutional Monarchy came into being, the organization has claimed to be a staunch defender of the current system of government, a system that its members frequently describe as "the Westminster system". The essential feature of the Westminster system of government is the supremacy of Parliament. The elected representatives are accountable to the people through Parliament. Yet while monarchists claimed to defend this system of government, a system that places enormous trust in politicians and the institutions of parliamentary democracy, they based their campaign on slogans that sought to denigrate politicians. The only notable exception to this crusade against politicians came from the monarchist prime minister John Howard. In his 3,000-word decree on the republic, which was widely published in the press and covered extensively in the electronic media, Howard made it clear that he did "not support a directly elected Presidency". He stressed the benefits of Australia's stable democratic system and side-stepped the issue of symbolism by claiming the Governor General was Australia's effective head of state. He concluded, "Even among many who intend to vote Yes there is a ready acknowledgement that there are far more important issues on the national agenda. In these circumstances Australians are right to be sceptical about the need for change. I hope they reject the republic. It will not produce a better Australia."[25] Howard's strategy is not to argue against a republic, but to make the issue appear inconsequential and trivial, as if the republic will only have legitimacy when thousands march in passionate rage on Capital Hill.

Yet, regardless of the merit of Howard's arguments, they are markedly different from those presented by the No campaign. Not only had the monarchists given up on the monarchy during the campaign, they also reviled the core features of the very system they claimed to defend: Parliament and its elected representatives. Their slogans did not promote the protection or understanding of the current system of government in Australia. In fact, they suggested that Australia should depart from its current system of government and opt for a republic with a directly elected president.

The result was that monarchists no longer articulated a conservative case for retaining constitutional monarchy. The side defending Australia's current system of government was the Yes case. The bipartisan appointment model allowed for greater popular involvement through a public nomination process, but still retained the supremacy of Parliament.

"Vote Yes for an Australian Head of State"

From 1991 until his fall from power in March 1996, Prime Minister Paul Keating led the republic debate with a singular passion and determination. Yet when it came to the republic referendum three years later, the man who had done more than anyone to push the republic to the top of the national political agenda was absent. Keating was now a political liability and the only service he would be allowed to perform would be to remain silent.

But silence didn't come easily to Keating. On the one occasion he entered the public debate he managed to provide one of the more memorable lines of the campaign. With the same sharpness of wit, and eye for vulnerability in an opponent's position that he had demonstrated when prime minister, Keating described the No side's failure to defend the monarchy as "the love that dare not speak its name". Oscar Wilde would have been pleased.[26]

During the referendum campaign in October and November 1999, Labor leader Kim Beazley stepped into Keating's shoes with limited success. Whereas Keating had made the republic his own, Beazley had never believed the issue should occupy the central position in Australian Labor Party policy that it had claimed under Keating's leadership. After the election of the Howard government in March 1996, the republic debate fractured, losing the clear focus it had maintained under the leadership of Paul Keating. The sentiment for direct election increased at the same time the populist Pauline Hanson and her One Nation party rose to prominence. While the Constitutional Convention of February 1998 captured the public imagination for a brief moment, by the time of the referendum campaign in November 1999, Australians no longer seemed to accept that they were about to vote on a republican model that made no provision for direct election. The Convention, and the compromise model that emerged from it, always struggled for legitimacy. With 50 per cent of its delegates appointed, and only 45 percent of the electorate [in a non-compulsory vote] returning the remaining 50 percent of delegates, the Convention could easily be painted as a device structured by "elite politicians" to ensure "the people" were denied a vote on the republic model they wanted.[27]

When the referendum debate began in earnest in October 1999, the context of the debate had shifted significantly from that of March 1996. Born of a process that could claim only partial legitimacy, hobbled by the necessary compromises forced on the "Keating-Turnbull republic" by the competing interests of the Convention delegates and lacking the prime ministerial support it had enjoyed from 1991 to 1996, the republic model put to the people in November 1999 was weighted with a handicap it could never hope to carry to victory.[28]

The dismissal mechanism in the republic model that allowed for instant dismissal of a President by a Prime Minister, while replicating the existing system, still proved to be the Achilles' heel of the Yes campaign, together with the method of parliamentary appointment. The proposed public nomination system was also little understood, either pilloried as a half-hearted attempt to involve the people, or misunderstood as a feature that would be entrenched in the Constitution.[29]

Added to these factors was the failure of republicans of various persuasions to find common ground before November 6, 1999. Those republicans who supported the bipartisan appointment model could not manage to persuade enough of their comrades who favoured direct election to vote Yes.[30] Much of the referendum debate was drawn to hypothetical scenarios – When would the next referendum be? Would there be another referendum? What would a Yes or No vote mean for the prospect of a further referendum on a republic with a directly elected President?

Predictably, the No case claimed there would be another referendum, while the Yes case stressed that "No meant No" – at least for the foreseeable future. But here was the rub. To attract direct election republicans to vote Yes, supporters of the model were forced to hold out some hope of another referendum in the near future. The result was a contradictory message. On the one hand, "No" meant no for a very long time. On the other hand, Yes didn't necessarily mean there would not be another referendum on popular election. Labor leader Kim Beazley's attempt to capture Labor's traditional "battler" support base – where sympathy for direct election was strong – and his frequent stumbling over the question of future referendums – revealed the impossible position in which the Yes case found itself.[31] There were too many olive branches to hold out and too many fears to allay.

Consistent with the Australian Republic Movement's (ARM) campaign since 1991, the Yes campaign relied heavily on nationalism and the anachronistic nature of the monarchy.[32] Funding and campaign management was controlled from the Sydney headquarters of the ARM. The public face of the campaign was a cavalcade of media-friendly faces that included ex-Prime Ministers Whitlam, Fraser and Hawke, all of whom qualified in their different ways as celebrities. But the procession of stars endorsing the new product failed to have the expected impact. As the Yes case wheeled out more and more celebrities, it seemed merely to reinforce the "elite" persona of the republican movement painted so menacingly by their opponents. It may well have been "time" for a republic, but for many it was also "time" for fewer politicians.

Perhaps it was the last star of the Yes campaign that best reflected the tenor of plan A: photo opportunities for celebrity republicans. On November 4, 1999, a bull stood in front of Sydney Town Hall with an appropriately dull, blank and bullish look on his face. He was led ably by republican stockmen before any available camera or microphone. He was there to tell the world that Prince Charles had just been appointed British beef ambassador. The media spin went as follows: when this Australian bull was put to death, the Prince of Wales, as ambassador for British beef, would probably be somewhere in Europe representing dead British bulls. Australia needed to become a republic so it would have its own head of state to represent its own dead bulls. It is difficult to tell just how many voters were won over by this strategy.[33]

While the television image of the republican case was one dimensional and simplistic – replete with patriotic tunes and the slogans of grab nationalism – the model was explained in detail in other mediums.

In the print media and on ABC Radio, there was much detailed discussion of the model, its merits and its flaws. For anyone willing to find the time to read and listen, there was ample opportunity to come to an informed decision.

The constant claim that there was not enough information concerning the referendum proposal is misleading. There was a surfeit of information, buried among the ever-increasing cascade of information that already inhabits daily life. The truth is not that the public was given too little information, but that it failed to find the time or interest to read and digest the information before it. For any advocate of Constitutional reform in Australia, it is not only necessary to raise community awareness and understanding of the constitution, but to create the space and time for voters to concentrate on the detailed arguments involved.

To achieve a more informed vote, the nation needs to take a collective tea break; empty the mailbox; shut the door on the background noise of advertising, news and entertainment; turn off the TV, the radio and the stereo; take the phone off the hook; log off; and sit down. Then there might be some "quality time" for the details of referendum questions to be closely examined and calmly discussed. Can Singleton Ogilvy and Mather offer us any advice?[34]

Where to Now?

On November 13-14, 1999, the broadsheet that had done more than any other daily paper to push the republic debate in Australia had reached the point of exhaustion. The editorial on this day insisted that *The Australian* was still a "republican newspaper" but that it was time to press "the pause button on the debate". "Enjoy the summer", said *The Australian* – a comment that perhaps begs the question - just how long will the summer of Constitutional monarchy in Australia last? Although Australia's love affair with the monarchy is over, the monarchy will be difficult to remove because it is perceived as being largely a benign presence. The Prime Minister, for example, recently conformed with Governor General William Deane's initiative, that the official toast given on State occasions to be changed from "To Her Majesty Queen of Australia", to "the Queen and people of Australia".[35] This might be seen as yet another step in Australia's long journey to becoming a "crowned republic", or a transparent attempt to band-aid a situation which will become an ongoing embarrassment? For how long will Australian officials continue to propose formal toasts to a head of state who visits her people for a few weeks every five years?

After the failure of the referendum, the anachronism of the monarchy on Australian soil will not be enough to solve the dilemma that Australia now finds itself in – knowing what it is not but not knowing what it wants to become. Nor was it enough to achieve a national majority for the republic at the November referendum. In some ways, the old paradigms of the republic debate – monarchy or republic – independent nation or colonial outpost – King Charles III and an Australian Governor General or "one of us" as head of state – have passed us by. The future debate will be less focussed on symbolism, oaths of allegiance and British beef.

In this sense the referendum has been a crucial turning point. When the republic resurfaces, it is likely to be a more interesting, potentially more invigorating debate, less about the symbols of democracy and more about the substance of democracy. If the November 1999 referendum proved anything, it was that a nation that has never sought to attach its national identity to political institutions still refuses to do so.

The long held belief that the Australian republic promised a new national identity for Australia – a casting off from the imperial motherland toward a new, uniquely Australian identity – has been tested and has failed. Not enough Australians have been persuaded by the traditional republican argument that Australia's identity, confidence and independence is diminished by the monarchical thread. For the majority, the precise nature of the constitutional change involved in the move to a republic matters more than the symbolism associated with the change. As always, Australians seem to assess the merit of proposals for change by placing their heads under the bonnet - the practical machinery matters more than the glossy concept.

Despite all of the misplaced and poorly conceived notions currently attached to the idea of a directly elected Presidency, for many Australians, it is only a popular vote that will allow them to feel "connected" to the process of change. But if the prospect of a directly elected president is the only viable future for an Australian republic, then there are many hurdles to overcome: a political class that is largely opposed to the idea, substantial ignorance of the Constitution as it exists now and an enormous capacity for scaremongers to sharpen their knives once more on the many constitutional changes necessary to introduce a popularly elected presidency.

The powers of any future Australian President elected by popular vote must be codified in the Constitution. The great balancing act required of lawyers and politicians will be to find a way to deal with the 1975 crisis when codifying the president's powers. Do we attempt to deny the Senate's power to block supply, a course of action that would seem destined for political defeat? Or do we entrench the Senate's power to block supply and insert the unpredictable office of a directly elected president as the arbiter of constitutional crises? Either course of action is fraught with political obstacles. Even to adopt the Irish system, and arrange for a Council of State to advise the President in certain circumstances, might be portrayed as an "elite" attempt to control the power of the people's representative. Finally, there is the experience of the deliberative poll held in Canberra, in November 1999, that suggests that support for direct election may well evaporate in the face of prolonged scrutiny.[36] There is every chance that a direct election model will also suffer defeat in a national referendum when subjected to sustained analysis.

To date, the illusion created by proponents of direct election is the suggestion that a national popular vote for a largely ceremonial figure will give the Australian people a greater say in the way they are governed. Perhaps it might afford access to a figure with democratic and moral authority, but as for fostering a more participatory democracy, an informed vote in the local council elections would pay greater dividends. Despite the apparent appeal of a directly elected presidency, we should think carefully before conforming with the accepted view of the 1990s republican movement as a self-serving conspiracy of elites, and pretending naïvely that the new millennium will see a more grass-roots movement for a republic. The flip side of "Vote No to the Politicians' Republic" is "Why bother to participate"? – many of those who hold politicians in contempt also hold politics itself in contempt. There is no evidence that a grass-roots movement for a more radical republic is about to rise in the streets of Liverpool or the dirt tracks outback of Bourke.

The most likely outcome is that future republic models will emanate from the existing players, lobby groups and politicians who have been involved in the present debate. A compromise of sorts, but a compromise that can always be represented as an elite conspiracy by its opponents.

From 1994, when the ARM began to broaden its base beyond Sydney, Melbourne and Canberra, thousands of "ordinary" Australians across the country joined the movement, raised funds, attended meetings and campaigned over a five year period. First for a Constitutional Convention in February 1998, in which less than half of their fellow citizens bothered to vote, and finally for a referendum campaign in November 1999, which took place in a context in which the mood of the electorate could only be described as "anti-politics".

While the media face of the republican movement has been largely that of merchant banker and lawyer Malcolm Turnbull, and the inner party clique of the ARM in Sydney and Melbourne, the bulk of the movement's members came from diverse backgrounds and many different localities. We have an impoverished civic culture if we can do little better than crucify the rich who bother to spend their money and time on issues of national significance, and blindly accept the populist mantra that all those who took the trouble to participate are "elites" bent on self-aggrandizement.

There is no one answer to the problems ahead for republicanism in Australia. But some things are clear. The future debate needs to be more inclusive and relevant – especially to women and younger Australians.[37] It also needs to have the courage to make the republic more meaningful – to write a republican preamble and to forge a republican position on reconciliation – to make these issues central to the republican platform. A version of direct election, most probably designed and vetted by politicians, will not be enough.

Republicans have to rediscover the spirit of the word "Commonwealth" – government for the common good – something that is easy to say but difficult to realize. Republicans will also need to foster a community spirit that is more receptive to constitutional change and more convinced of the benefits that change might bring. The only way to do this is to abandon minimalism and think more broadly. There must be a platform that goes beyond "one of us" to include "all of us". If the republic can be presented as one means of rebuilding a sense of trust in our political institutions, and speak directly to the major political issues of our time – reconciliation and citizenship – then the promise of a new national identity might be more believable. The alternative is a long, hot summer for "the Captive Republic".

Notes

1. *The Australian* (November 19, 1999): 1.

2. *The Australian* November 8, 1999.

3. *Australian Financial Review* November 8, 1999.

4. Ibid.

5. *The Australian* (November 13-14, 1999).

6. *The Sidney Morning Herald* (November 13, 1999). Some safe Labor seats did vote Yes, while others lost narrowly, except in Sydney. In addition 25 out of 35 (7 in New South Wales) of those seats with high ethnic populations voted Yes. However, in political terms, little prominence was given to the multicultural support for the republic as a reason to Vote Yes – perhaps many were fearful of alienating the so-called Mainstream and One Nation.

7. *The Australian* (October 27, 1999) 15. Bob Hawke made the "republic of Bennelong" remark on ABC TV, November 6, 1999.

8. *The Australian* (November 8, 1999).

9. *The Sydney Morning Herald* (November 8, 1999).

10. *The Sydney Morning Herald* (November 6, 1999) David Williamson on Apathy and Contempt for Politicians. Journalists who ventured out into the bush came back with confronting reports of alienation eg *The Sydney Morning Herald* (November 13, 1999): 41 on Gwydir in North west NSW, which registered a 72.5 per cent No vote. The decline in services, high unemployment decline and lower living standards had created much anger, eg one voter claimed "I didn't vote against the republic but against the politicians". Another ALP member and former Mayor of Gunnedah – "our electorate is the classic, they hate politicians; they absolutely hate them. They blame them for the downturn in the rural economy and its every politician every party" rural people never had a chance to be part of the republic process , it was railroaded through by the likes of Malcolm Turnbull and his ilk" Also see similar report *The Sydney Morning Herald* (November 9) on outer western Sydney. Finally see the launch of the No campaign which certainly plays up the anti politician theme, *The Australian* (October 11, 1999).

11. *The Sydney Morning Herald* (October 29, 1999): 7 on apathy.

12. Malcolm Turnbull e.g., believes Yes voters were more informed. See Malcom Turnbull, *Fighting for the Republic* (Hardie Grant Books, 1999), 249.

13. *Australian Financial Review* (October 29, 1999) on business leaders, *The Sydney Morning Herald* (November 4, 1999) Catholic Archbishop George Pell, ex Chief Justices Brennan and Mason and ex Governor-General Cowen in letters page *The Australian* (October 23-24, 1999).

14. *The Sydney Morning Herald* (November 4, 1999).

15. *The Australian* (August 2, 1999).

16. *The Australian* (November, 6 1999) and *Daily Telegraph* (November 7, 1999).

17. See the series of weekly *The Sydney Morning Herald* editorials on the republic beginning (October 11, 1999) and finishing (November 4, 1999).

18. *The Australian* (August 3, 1999) only 10 Out of 29 of Howard Cabinet Support Republic.

19. *The Australian* (November 2, 1999).

20. The populism of the No case emanated as much from the direct election republicans as it did from the monarchists. See Peter Reith's article in *The Australian* (August 3, 1999) 13, where he employs the phrases "high flyers", "backroom committees" and "ordinary Australians". Also see *The Sydney Morning Herald* (August 2), where Reith states his reasons for voting No. See also *The No Case Papers* Standard Publishing Sydney, 1999 – especially Phil Cleary "The Phoney Republic: An Unholy Alliance of Wheeler Dealers" (9-15), and Ted Mack "An Independent's Dissection of the Elitist Model".

21. See Abbott e.g. in *Australian Financial Review* (August 6, 1999), where he likens members of Conservatives for Australian Head of State to aristocrats whom Lenin once called "useless fools" Also see any of the last three weeks before November 6 1999 in the opinion pages of *The Australian* ,where Abbott appears with alarming regularity.

22. *The Australian* (March 3, 1999) Geoffrey Blainey Claims Republic risks dictatorship. *Australian* (August 20, 1999): 1 David Elliot's analogies with Weimar republic and Hitler like dictatorship. Reith in the *Australian* (August 23, 1999) claimed the republic would inevitably lead to a change in the flag.

23. See formal No case in the pamphlet *Yes/No Referendum 99* produced by the Australian Electoral Commission.

24. *The Australian* (October 13, 1999) (Paul Kelly) See also Kerry Jones being caught by Gerard Henderson *The Sydney Morning Herald* (October 19, 1999). During a TV debate a colleague sitting next to Jones had claimed she was opposed to "this model" because "we don't get the right to vote". When she was asked by David Dimbleby of the BBC whether she did in truth support the removal of the Queen for a directly elected president, she appeared uneasy. Jones then whispered in her ear, "Just say you like Australia the way it is". Her colleague then dutifully mouthed the words.

25. *The Australian* (October 27, 1999): 15

26. Ibid.

27. See M. McKenna "The Greatest Show on Earth: The 1998 Constitutional Convention", *Alternative Law Journal,* (April 1998): 82-84.

28. For one perspective on the Keating-Turnbull republic see David Flint *The Cane Toad Republic* (Wakefield Press 1999), Chapter 6.

29. *The Australian* (August 10, 1999). All Party Parliamentary Committee Finds Public Nomination System Not understood.

30. For a more lengthy discussion of this problem see M. McKenna "Shed the Queen", *Eureka St.* (October 1999): 24-29.

31. *The Sydney Morning Herald* (September 27, 1999).

32. On one occasion in July 1999, Malcolm Turnbull argued before a Senate Committee that the ARM preferred no mention of the word "republic" in the referendum question. He was mocked by the media. See *Fighting for the Republic,* 96-101.

33. *The Canberra Times* (November 5, 1999).

34. The firm employed to market the Yes case in the media for the referendum.

35. Judges and parliamentarians still swear an oath of allegiance to Her Majesty, her heirs and successors.

36. See report of deliberative poll in *The Australian* (October 25, 1999). The poll registered a 73 percent Yes vote, an increase of 20 percent. After a weekend's deliberation, support for direct election fell from 51 to 19 percent.

37. For gender gap, see *The Australian* (November 3, 1999) for young see *The Australian* (July 28, 19 99).

12

Mateship, Mayhem and the Australian Constitution's Preamble

DAVID HEADON

On November 6, 1999, Australians went to the polls to vote on what the Australian federal government publicity material called "two... important questions about the Australian Constitution", The first question asked the following:

> Do you approve a proposed law to alter the Constitution to establish the Commonwealth of Australia as a republic with the Queen and Governor-General being replaced by a President appointed by a two-thirds majority of the Members of the Commonwealth Parliament?

It was not by any stretch the simple Yes/No plebiscite question that many republicans had been hoping for; yet, until relatively late in the referendum campaign, cautious optimism remained in the "Yes" camp. History records that the Yes vote mustered less than 45 percent of the count nationwide, the No case 55 percent, and the question was defeated in all states, in Victoria by the narrowest margin. Only the Australian Capital Territory voted Yes, going about 63.5 percent in favour.

Almost lost in the media accounts and recriminations that followed was that the electorate had actually voted on a second question, which sought to establish whether Australians were prepared to approve a proposed law to alter the Constitution to insert a preamble.

Postreferendum, there was scarcely a line written about the fact that the electorate had similarly rejected the second question, by majorities in each state some 5 to 10 percent larger than those for the first question.

While the sheer scale of the rejection of the preamble question would seem commensurate with its virtual disappearance in the last three months of the referendum campaign, it hardly does justice to the lively, at times hostile, debate pertaining to the preamble that occurred on three separate occasions during 1999, and the interest in a new preamble that had surfaced in more general discussion of an Australian republic as early as 1996. A clear problem for the second question was the popular perception that Prime Minister John Howard had played an interventionist role. Howard, an avowed monarchist, had after the Constitutional Convention in February 1998 said he would let Australians make up their own minds and he would stay out of the debate. That he did not is obvious when one considers the short, genuinely bizarre history of Australia's first attempt since 1901 to revisit the set of unadventurous phrases that presently precede the Commonwealth of Australia Constitution Act, the British parliamentary act.

When Australian electors stepped into their booths for the historic republican vote, many recoiled when they were asked to make a judgment on a new form of preamble words – words that were not printed on the ballot paper. This curious absence appeared to them to be an indicator of insider trading, of manipulation. As I will show, the narrative of the new preamble – of mateship, mayhem and a mischievous Prime Minister – might well be taken as an instructive microcosm of the larger republic debate itself. This paper will first expand the chronological parameters beyond the events of 1998, in order to complement Mark McKenna's meticulous account of voter patterns and priorities in the 1999 referendum; second, it will clarify the issues surrounding the referendum's marginalized second question; and, third, it will make a few observations about the question itself.

To contextualize the events of late 1999, a short slice history of the wider republican debate in Australia this decade is needed. When the Australian Republican Movement (ARM) launched itself at the Sydney Opera House in 1991, amidst considerable publicity and led by well-known citizens, such as author Thomas Keneally, businessman Malcolm Turnbull and former premier of New South Wales, Neville Wran, hopes were high that this fourth historical wave of Australian republican sentiment would bring a result never likely in the previous three eras: the actual establishment of an Australian republic. However, despite the potential obvious in this disparate yet talented and publicly respected group, it was not long until the initial enthusiasm of the general public began to fade. Enter, relatively new Prime Minister Paul Keating, who decided that the issue had distinct value for him out there in the electoral marketplace. A former treasurer-turned-Prime-Minister in a relatively bloodless party coup in 1992, Keating had begun to reinvent himself for presentation at his first federal election as the incumbent leader.

In order to describe what happened in 1993–96, and to bridge the culture gap between Canada and Australia, Canadian football terminology might be useful. Keating, early in 1993, pounced on his own republican team's open-field fumble and made a further 20 yards before the opposition (monarchist Australia) could gather him in. When he was finally tackled, instead of giving the football again to his own offensive team – rank and file republican Australians – to continue the downfield march, he decided to do the critical quarterbacking job himself. Hence, in the three years following his election-against-the-odds in 1993, Keating's deteriorating government fortunes resulted in a similar decline in the Australian public's response to the republican debate. Keating would not give up the football when his offensive coaches beckoned. The team's completion rate disintegrated.

What happened, then, in non-football terms? When Keating presented himself for re-election in 1996, his party, the Australian Labor Party, suffered a disastrous defeat. The concomitant slump in republican fortunes was almost palpable. Mike Steketee, senior political journalist for Australia's only national newspaper, *The Australian*, summed up the mood in a long article written in September 1996 entitled "Whatever Happened to the Republic?" The ARM, Steketee wrote, had during the election year witnessed de-stabilizing changes to its staff; Prime Minister elect John Howard, once in the job, vigorously restated his monarchist commitment; and Howard's influential parliamentary secretary, Nick Minchin, had in mid-1996 delivered a speech where he categorically stated that the "Federal Coalition Government [believes] that our current constitutional arrangements have served us well and can continue to do so".[1] It was an ominous warning to all those card-carrying republicans in Australia inclined to think a republic paradoxically just might have a smoother and more rapid political birth in Australia under a conservative government, because the legislation could almost certainly count on Labor Party support.

Two other pieces of republican signage caught the eye in 1996 because of their relevance to this account. The first, an editorial in *The Australian* newspaper on the Australia Day weekend in January 1996, entitled "Time to Commit to a New Preamble", declared its purpose "to provoke a more vigorous debate on constitutional change, in the lead-up to the 2001 centenary, of the Australian Constitution".[2] In the same issue the paper ran a copy of the present preamble ("Whereas... humbly relying on Almighty God... one indissoluble Commonwealth... no Western Australia...") and it ran new preamble drafts written by five prominent Australians: Malcolm Turnbull, former Prime Minister Malcolm Fraser; George Winterton, professor of law; Lowitja O'Donohue, former head of the Aboriginal and Torres Strait Islander Commission; and Zita Antonios, race discrimination commissioner. The editorial and the five drafts were timely, and *The Australian*'s obvious sympathy for an Australian republic anticipated, well before the fact, its strident republican stance in 1998-99.

The second bit of signage that appeared in 1996, in June, emanated from renowned Australian poet Les Murray, who delivered a well-publicized lecture in the Australian Senate's Occasional Series, which he called "A Poet's View of the Republic". Three years further down the track Murray would play, as will later be mentioned, a controversial yet significant role in the events of 1999. In his 1996 Senate talk, Murray made it clear how much he had changed from his radical social and cultural stance of the 1970s, when he was in the business of designing new Australian flags minus the Union Jack. To his Senate audience he declared that "the Marxist takeover of our republic of letters... [was] perhaps never complete... [but it was] powerfully intimidatory".[3] With characteristic hauteur, Murray assumed the high moral (and sporting) ground as he went further: "All of Bradman Australia, we may say, was made to vanish for a long time."[4] Let me translate. Murray was basically saying that in 1996 left-wing urban elites had overwhelmed his vernacular country people, legendary cricketer Sir Donald Bradman's people, if you will. Les Murray's people. This was nonsense, but it told us with clarity where Les Murray was coming from after too many years in the New South Wales scrub at Bunyah near Taree. Murray and his imagined Bradmanians would be back in 1999, writ large. They will recur in this paper, too.

The Howard government won by a landslide in 1996. The republican bone in the throat of the new Prime Minister, however, is that in order to counter Keating's overt republican agenda, during the campaign he promised, in a policy-by-default statement, to hold a Constitutional Convention on the republic. After the election, the promise became a genuine embarrassment. What to do with it? The issue was not about to disappear.

Liberal Senator Nick Minchin was in time given "responsibility for the Constitutional Convention." He was handed the slightly toxic chalice. No doubt with the boss's words ringing in his ears, Minchin immediately equivocated about "Con Con" (as the Convention would come to be called) in a radio interview shortly after the election. He said that he was not sure that voters even remembered that Con Con was a coalition promise, or whether they would be disappointed if it were not kept. Con Con, he asserted, was no John Howard "core" promise. It was not a promise you necessarily kept, or had to keep.

Yet it became difficult for the Prime Minister to maintain Con Con as soft core when his own team, inner circle and outer, started to break ranks. First, in September 1996, Andrew Robb, former Liberal director and the guru responsible for the Howard campaign and election platform, declared himself for a republic; shortly after, some fifty rebel Liberals published a national "coming out" advertisement in November 1996; then NSW Liberal leader Peter Collins, in a much-publicised January 1997 speech to the Young Liberals' National Convention, threw down the gauntlet to his national head:

> Let John Howard, as we prepare to celebrate our nationhood on Australia Day, take up the challenge and show Australia the way to achieve constitutional change in the interests of all Australians.[5]

The Convention eventually materialized over 10 days in February 1998. In its own terms it was a popular success, but hindsight suggests that beyond the euphoria of many of the delegates at Convention's end, two points were critical: first, Prime Minister Howard insisted on, and got, a specific model to be presented to Australian voters (rather than the more representative Yes/No plebiscite option); second, republican Australians – according to polls at the time, anywhere between 50 and 65 percent of all Australians – were divided between those supporting the two-thirds, so-called "bipartisan" model (explained in Mark McKenna's paper in this publication) and direct-election republicans. Some direct electionists at the Convention promoted the ideological clash within republican ranks as a contest between the "battlers", the "rank and file", the "punters" – their group – and the Chardonnay-sipping elites – the bipartisan model supporters. When one of the latter, former New South Wales premier and canny numbers man Neville Wran, had his "battler" credential challenged, he responded with typical dash: "I come from the shit heap. Just because I wear a nice suit now and have a good-looking missus and live in Woollahra, doesn't mean I'm an elitist".[6] The ideological point scoring, expedient policy making on-the-run and the barefaced lies that close observers noted at the Convention, as a worrying undercurrent beneath a number of splendid individual contributions, would return during the rest of 1998 and throughout 1999 to undermine the republican case.

What follows is a postage-stamp account of the last two years, post-Con Con. As early as July 1998 flaws in the bipartisan model were being exposed and this was reflected in the paralysis afflicting organisation of the Yes case, in all states. Continuing slippage in support for the model prompted *The Canberra Times*, on October 18, 1998, to review its support, and to canvass again a Yes-No plebiscite. A year out from the referendum, Yes republicans were already getting very nervous. Indeed, the high-profile reverend Tim Costello, republican and brother of the present federal treasurer, Peter Costello, commented at the beginning of November 1998 that the republican issue had in fact "died".[7] It had not, but there were certainly signs of chronic fatigue syndrome. Passionate Yes republicans held a National Convention in Canberra in February 1999 in an attempt to reinvigorate the issue, a gathering, incidentally, that proved to be a catalyst for widespread national discussion about the preamble. At about this same time, employment minister and monarchist Tony Abbott went searching for a headline with the declaration that "Republicanism has become a kind of national feel-good pill or constitutional Viagra – to be prescribed whether we need it or not".[8] The debate was sliding into farce. Well, farce and apathy and opportunism.

Moir's cartoon in *The Sydney Morning Herald* on Australia Day in January 1999 noted widespread vote apathy as he had the "Don't Know" and "Don't Care" runners in the "Great Republican Race" passing the finishing line, fit and strong, miles ahead of the tired and defeated "republic" and "monarchist" runners.[9] It proved to be a prophetic sketch. As did Kudelka's cartoon, much later, in August 1999 in *The Australian*. In the first of Kudelka's two frames, there was a perplexed voter in his booth, confronted by the complex wording of the republic question, staring rather bemusedly at his two choices. The No box was straightforward. To vote Yes, however, was to tick the box that read, in Kudelka's second frame: "Indubitably I do wish to aver and affirm my partiality to the above proposition and to have recorded for the purposes of this referendum a response indicative of a positive inclination".[10]

If *The Australian* newspaper cartoonists were registering community apathy and distress, the Prime Minister configured much of the opportunism. This is never more evident than in the story of the poor old preamble, or should we say the poor, new preamble. Recalling its brief and brilliant history is nothing if not the recollection of a bright though transient shooting star: dramatic, intense, then gone. While, as I mentioned earlier, discussion of a new preamble occurred fitfully in the years before 1999, it was only during 1999, at three distinct chronological points, that the issue crackled with passion. To understand these three months, some context is again required.

We have in Australia a Constitutional Centenary Foundation headed by former Governor General Sir Ninian Stephen and constitutional history professor Cheryl Saunders. Intended to be strictly politically neutral, the Foundation dithered and dallied for most of the 1990s as the republic issue split along Keating-inspired partisan lines. Yet it did manage to display some initiative in late 1998 when, with the Howard government keeping tight control of the republic referendum question, the Foundation advertised a competition, a quest for a new preamble. In doing so, it was guided by the third resolution of the February 1998 Constitutional Convention, which said that a new preamble to the Constitution should include:

1. Introductory language in the form of "We the people of Australia"
2. Reference to Almighty God
3. References to the origins of the Constitution and acknowledgment that the Commonwealth has evolved into an independent, democratic and sovereign nation under the Crown
4. Recognition of our federal system of representative democracy and responsible government
5. Affirmation of the rule of law
6. Acknowledgment of the original occupancy and custodianship of Australia by Aboriginal and Torres Strait Islander peoples
7. Recognition of Australia's cultural diversity
8. Affirmation of respect for our unique land and the environment

9. Reference to the people of Australia having agreed to re-constitute our system of government as a republic
10. Concluding language to the effect that "[We the people of Australia] asserting our sovereignty, commit ourselves to this Constitution".[11]

The Constitutional Centenary Foundation Preamble Quest eventually resulted in the launch, in February 1999, of a 30-odd page pamphlet, both engaging and topical, called *"We the people of Australia . . .": Ideas for a New Preamble to the Australian Constitution.*[12] The publication reprinted those preambles that the Foundation found "particularly interesting, either because of their overall style, or because of their approach to or expression of particular Con Con proposals".[13] The Foundation also published its own preamble template, developed to "broadly [reflect] the ideas expressed by participants in the Quest". The product of some 375 submissions, the template reads this way:

> We the people of Australia,
>
> Who came together in 1901 as a Federation under the Crown with the blessing of God,
>
> Which has since become an independent nation,
>
> Now renew our Constitution [as a republic].
>
> In the spirit of reconciliation, we acknowledge the indigenous Australians as the original occupants and custodians of our land,
>
> United by pride in our diversity,
>
> Our belief in equality and freedom,
>
> And love of this unique and ancient land.
>
> We commit ourselves to this Constitution.[14]

With the Foundation's Preamble Quest announcement coming only a week or two after the National Convention of Republicans in Canberra, this dual impact stirred the constitutional and civic imaginations of Australians right around the country. This was no mean feat. It was as if a significant number of Australians had decided spontaneously to affirm the comment made at that time by Jesuit priest and social commentator Frank Brennan, who said he was "sick of the doublespeak and embarrassing silences and omissions at what ought to be important moments in the national life".[15]

Mark McKenna had his preamble widely quoted in the media, as did Tom Keneally. But then so did Ronald Duff, a plumber from Morely,

Perth, who was photographed on the front of *The Australian* chattering to his pet pink galah, Pinky. Could it actually be, optimistic republicans intoned, that the debate was, at last, getting to the grass roots? Alas, the sobering note was recorded in *The Australian* the very same day as the appearances of Ronald and Pinky, when Newscorp in-house journalist Richard McGregor quoted the words of the Prime Minister that he could not be accused of having any "Machiavellian desires" regarding the preamble.[16] McGregor disagreed, observing that the Prime Minister "is also a partisan political animal by nature and surely can see the advantages of muddying the republic debate by merging it with the potentially contentious preamble issue".

To the extent that McGregor suspected the Prime Minister's motives, he observed accurately; to the extent that he spoke of the "potentially contentious preamble", he was wrong. It was instantly contentious. Australians would vote on two questions. For one glorious month, albeit one shaped by naïve enthusiasm, mid-February to mid-March 1999, the preamble was the only game in town.

The reason? Prime Minister Howard, monarchist and 1990s misfit, decided – incredibly – on February 16, 1999 to write the new preamble himself. It would be, he said, a "feel good statement".[17] People were outraged at the prospect of a preamble for the present and future written by a man from yesterday. Dumped on by just about everyone, and looking to relieve the pressure, Howard enlisted the support of, you guessed it, poet and renegade republican-turned-full-bottle conservative Les Murray. It was no match made in heaven, two old white blokes putting their heads together to find a form of words to suit and satisfy a proudly plural nation committed to reconciliation and a multicultural, non-sexist future. The partnership was never going to work. Howard knew it.

On March 23, 1999, the pair circulated a form of words that included the highly contentious word "mateship", a word with undeniable Australian resonance but nonetheless a word deeply gendered. If the Murray/Howard preamble received the support of even a handful of Australian citizens, it was not apparent to me. The "Letters to the Editor" columns of all the major Australian dailies howled with protest. Writer and publisher Angelo Loukakis asked: "What do you get when a Prime Minister and a poet-to-the-nation *preamble* together? A dog's breakfast!"[18] Playwright Alex Buzo called it a "Pre-Ramble".[19] "It's full of bum notes... and doubtful values," another critic declared.[20] One particularly pithy response came from an anonymous Internet poet who circulated his or her poem on the screen, "The Post-Amble", which begins (in imitation of a famous Australian poem written earlier this century, Dorothea Mackellar's "I Love a Sunburnt Country"):

I love a sunscreened country
Its ranks of unemployed
Its eyesores built by Seidler
Its art by Arthur Boyd.
Our kids are all drug addicts
Our businessmen are crooks
Our pollies are a bunch of clowns
Who couldn't raffle chooks.
But that is our tradition
We're rugged and we're tough
And because we live in paradise
We couldn't give a stuff.
When first we came from England
We stole it from the blacks
and now we won't apologise
In case they want it back.
But we have a great vision
A great Australian dream
For every bloke a Barbie,
Two cars, a football team.
A fenced-off yard with dogs in
Or else a harbour view;
A school to put the sprogs in
and after, a dole queue.[21]

– and concludes:

So forget your Constitution,
Forget your plebiscite;
Don't fret about the future,
We are Aussies – she'll be right.

An equally trenchant response came from Australian comedian and entertainer Tim Ferguson, who, inspired by his Prime Minister's "stirring" words, produced his own preamble. It begins:

> We, the People of the broad, brown land of Oz, wish to be recognised as a free nation of blokes, sheilas and the occasional trannie. We come from many lands (although a few too many of us come from New Zealand) and, although we live in the best little country in the world, we reserve the right to bitch and moan about it when we bloody like.[22]

– and concludes:

> We the Brain, the Heart and the Nerve of Oz, want the world to know we have the biggest rock, the tastiest pies and the worst-dressed Olympians in the known universe. We don't know much about art but we know we hate the people who make it. We shoot, we vote. We are girt by sea and pissed by lunchtime. And even though we might seem a racist, closed-minded, sports-obsessed little People, at least we're better than the Kiwis. Now bugger off, we're sleeping.

Perhaps the most astute reaction came from Les Murray's literary biographer, Professor Peter Alexander of the University of New South Wales, who suggested Murray's words had clearly been "tinkered with quite a bit".[23] As we would find out, postreferendum, they certainly had been. Richard McGregor wrote at the time that the Prime Minister had applied all his considerable skills to "calibrate a clever position".

It was a very clever position: one is prompted to say it was an expertly manipulated one. Howard would discard the word "mateship" and produce a revised preamble version in August 1999 with the help of the Australian Democrats and Aboriginal senator Aden Ridgeway, but the damage had been done. Australia had a "Clayton's Preamble", a damp squib, to vote on in the referendum's second question. By late August, the preamble had faded almost to invisibility; by October, Ridgeway himself had his say in an article syndicated in the Murdoch tabloids and entitled "The Forgotten Preamble". He had lost his enthusiasm, probably realizing that he, like most of naïve Australia, had been duped.

Referendum Postscript

Tuesday November 9, 1999 – three days after the referendum, in a newspaper article entitled "Poet Heartlessly Used":

> Poet Les Murray – who helped write the constitutional preamble – yesterday said he was heartlessly used by the Prime Minister and now regrets any involvement. Murray said John Howard "gutted" the original text, leaving the poet to rue the day he broke his rule of never having anything to do with politics... It was gutless. The only parts left in that were worthwhile was [sic] the beginning "With Hope in God" and the close about the Aborigines' role... I think I got used. Then I was thrown aside like a banana skin.[24]

If Murray got used, he was not, as we say in Australia, on his Pat Malone. He was not alone. The preamble issue was cunningly piloted by the Australian Prime Minister, virtually from start to finish, to maximize damage to the republican cause. Whether the 70 percent of Australians who want a republic can rebound from last November's internationally embarrassing result will depend on the lessons learned from the last two years. For in that time, Australian republicans were done over by a Prime Minister far from benign, and done over pretty good.

Notes

1. *The Weekend Australian* (September 7-8, 1996).

2. Ibid., January 27-28, 1996.

3. Papers on Parliament, No. 28. *Poets, Presidents, People and Parliament, Republicanism and Other Issues* (November 1996), 36.

4. Papers on Parliament, No. 28, 37.

5. *The Canberra Times* (January 11, 1997).

6. See Miranda Devine, *The Daily Telegraph* (February 5, 1998).

7. *The Weekend Australian* (October 31- 1 November, 1998).

8. *The Daily Telegraph* (January 18, 1999).

9. *The Sydney Morning Herald* (January 26, 1999).

10. *The Weekend Australian* (August 14-15, 1999).

11. See "What the Convention Decided", *Bulletin,* 117, No. 6111 (February 24, 1998): 20.

12. "We the people of Australia . . .", *Ideas for a New Preamble to the Australian Constitution* (Carlton, Victoria: Constitutional Centenary Foundation, 1999).

13. *We the people,* i.

14. Ibid., 17.

15. *The Canberra Times* (February 8, 1999).

16. *The Australian* (December 10, 1999).

17. *The Canberra Times* (February 17, 1999).

18. *The Daily Telegraph* (March 24, 1999).

19. *The Daily Telegraph* (March 24, 1999).

20. Ibid. (March 24, 1999).

21. Copy in possession of author – unsourced document.

22. Ibid.

23. *The Daily Telegraph* (March 24, 1999): 1.

24. *The Australian* (November 9, 1999).

13

Canada's Republican Silence

DAVID E. SMITH

The argument that follows begins with a presumption. Like Conan Doyle's dog that did not bark, it is assumed that Canada ought to have a republican movement or debate or, at least, some definable republican sentiment. Why this is not the case is the subject of this paper.

The reason for thinking Canada's condition worthy of study is the experience of Australia. There, a stratum of opinion in favour of republicanism has long been evident and there, in the last quarter-century a movement to achieve that objective culminated in November 1999 in a referendum on the question. The option on offer was rejected by the voters not because republicanism itself was unpopular but because the model presented was, in a sense, not republican enough. Thus Australia provides backdrop for these remarks, and if justification is required, it is that Australia and Canada share more in common than either does with any other nation – constitutional forms, settlement histories and economic foundations.

Opinion polls in Canada reveal large and growing support for the abolition of monarchy and, by inference, the establishment of a republic. Whether this attitude, which is inversely related to the age of respondents, is considered interesting is for others to judge. What is significant is that none of the thousands who favour a republic do anything about it. There could hardly be a clearer example of passive opinion, except when this finding is placed alongside the half or more of the population who say they prefer the status quo. The Monarchist League of Canada vocally defends the Crown but can make no claim to speak for the bulk of non-republican sympathizers. On this issue, as on a number of others, Carolyn Tuohy's description of Canada as a country of "institutionalized ambivalence" captures the intense apathy that surrounds the question.[1]

The contrast between the two countries is so stark as to lend credence to Sir Joseph Pope's epigram that, when it comes to Canadian politics, "Australian precedent [is] no precedent".[2] While the argument that follows does not adopt so categorical a view of Australian experience, it does offer three explanations for the contrast in so far as the issue of republican sympathy is concerned.

First, there is geography. Geography is the basis of the claim that because of the powerful republic next door, Canada had no choice in its constitution. Either it would continue, once the colonies federated in 1867, as a constitutional monarchy or it would not survive. In *The English Constitution*, published in 1867, Walter Bagehot asserted that "first-rate nations" had to choose between presidential and parliamentary government. "No state," he argued, "can be first-rate which is not a Government by discussion, and those are the only existing species of that Government".[3] And by then Americans had made their choice, a fact John A. Macdonald recognized at the Quebec Conference when he said the Crown was not an issue.

As an explanation for the initial rejection of a republican form of government, this reference to geography is true as far as it goes. But it only touches the surface. To talk of North America divided between a republic and a monarchy is to restrict the matter to public traditions. In other words, to focus the debate in this manner is to limit it to the large themes of liberalism, socialism and conservatism. Those acquainted with the theories Louis Hartz and Gad Horowitz are familiar with the cultural interpretations they offer in the 1960s for the respective strength of values that support private and public ownership in Canada and the United States.

More critically, the Horowitz theory emphasizes a public tradition in Canada which is English, while it ignores private traditions that are not English. The public tradition is stock Canadian history: the antidemocratic feelings of the Fathers of Confederation, echoing similar British sentiment, are the most obvious example that could be cited. Private traditions are less familiar and less easy to document. However, in the matter of Canada's ambivalent response to republicanism, they are of more explanatory value than Canada's reputedly conservative traditions of *public* ownership and *state* sponsorship. The private traditions derive from the common North American experience, of which the availability of cheap land and a shared demographic base are principal factors.

Both devalued the premium placed on republicanism. The massive amount of land; the common patterns of owner-operated farms in the East and, later, the much larger Prairie homesteads broken and farmed by resident owners; the similarity of crops grown in Canada and the heavily populated northern American states; and the identical farm machinery required in the rigorous continental climate that prevailed on both sides of the border combined to create the base for a set of private traditions that were distinctively North American rather than monarchical or republican in character. In turn, the equalizing impact of a common form of land tenure encouraged the migration of Americans and Canadians across the international boundary.

The common settlement pattern of the people of Canada and the United States and the contrast it represented to the history of Australian settlement is highly important, for the North American experience blurred the significance of the public traditions of monarchy and republicanism. Who owned the land before it passed into private hands – the Crown or the public domain – mattered only for a moment. Once in the settler's hands, it fell subject to myriad private traditions that were uniquely North American (and neither Canadian or American) in origin. The common experience of agriculture and farming touched the lives of the vast majority of those who lived in North America well into the 20th century: only in the 1951 census did a majority of Canada's provinces register a smaller rural than urban population. What Richard Hofstadter said of Americans in this century was equally true of Canadians: "The United States was born in the country and has moved to the city".[4] Canada and the United States were slower to urbanize than Australia, and when they did, in neither were the cities so few or so dominant.

The symbolism of monarchy was lost in the sweep of settlement and migration. This is not the same thing as saying that there was no symbolism of empire. There was, as Canada's historic sites and civic statues remind viewers on all sides. Nor is it to say that the language of empire was unimportant. In fact, in her relations with the United States, Canada traded on her attachment to Great Britain. For it was one of Canada's major resources that as neighbour of the United States but senior dominion she had a special role to play in the North Atlantic world "as the link which binds the United States to the British Empire".[5] Only Canada could play this role and it would be lost to her if she were not a member of the Empire. This explains the paradox that, as Canada slowly matured on the international stage, she thought not about separating from the Empire but about using her prestige to gain greater weight and strength within it and its Commonwealth successor.

Empire and monarchy were not the same thing, however. As senior member of the imperial family, Canada might take seriously the obligations that flowed from that prominence; monarchy was a different matter. In her novel *The Imperialist*, published in 1904, Sara Jeanette Duncan proved herself sensitive to the distinction: "[H]ere were no picturesque contacts of Royalty and the people, no pageantry, no blazonry of the past, nothing to lift the heart but an occasional telegram from the monarch expressing, upon an event of public importance, a suitable emotion".[6] This distinction is important but understudied. That it existed is clear from Canada's independent-mindedness demonstrated from early in this century, an attitude that led to her being classed with South Africa and the Irish Free State as one of "the radical dominions".[7]

The explanation of this disconnection requires more study. What can be said, however, is that it was not due to antipathy toward Great Britain. Writing in 1985, Arthur Lower observed that "we have never had any quarrel with our parent. I don't think even to this day that there is any suggestion of animosity in the relationship".[8] Four decades before that, Gordon Robertson, then an officer in the Department of External Affairs, put his finger on Canada's paradoxical position. Responding to a proposal from then fellow officer Escott Reid that the royal title as it concerned Canadian documents be changed to "King of Canada," Robertson said: "I don't think Canadians will like the term 'King of Canada,' no matter how logical it may be. Whatever legal facts are, most Canadians, I think, have not thought of themselves as citizens of either a republic or a monarchy".[9] Here was Canada's unusual situation: she was disconnected from both her past and, perhaps, her future too. Not only was the Crown a "dysfunctional" symbol, so might be any alternative symbol.[10] Thus no monarchy, no republicanism.

Modern confirmation that uses an apt comparison is offered by Charles Taylor: "As far as Canada is concerned, the monarchy is barely noticed and it isn't an issue. We certainly don't think of it as rule from elsewhere. [T]he British connection has long ago shrunk to a minor fixture of our society, whereas it probably bulks large in Australia".[11]

So much for a physiocratic explanation for Canada's republic silence.

Let me turn to another, which I will label psychological. Parenthetically, let me say that if generalization is dangerous, then generalizations about national "traits" is even more so. In any case, commentators at the beginning of this century were less sensitive or, maybe, just more confident. And it is with the comments of such an observer that this part of the paper opens.

In his otherwise complimentary monograph *Canada: An Actual Democracy*, James (Viscount) Bryce drew a number of comparisons between the politics of Canada and the United States, and in the process emphasized as a feature of Canada that "hardly anything in it is traceable to any abstract theory".[12] This cannot be said of Australia, either about the present republican debate or about past debates over questions of representation or, a century ago, the pre-federation discussions that led to the incorporation of an un-British-like referendum procedure in the amendment provisions of the new Commonwealth constitution.

By contrast, Canada was orthodoxy itself. She might claim parliamentary federalism as her contribution to the practice of government, but in the realm of traditional constitutional thought and values no one tended the flame more faithfully. According to Kenneth McNaught, Canadians believed in "the legitimizing function of continuity" itself, and these values were not calculated to encourage hasty or ill-considered judgment.[13] Colony to nation, dependence to independence, mediator, interpreter, fixer – the theme is the same whether in popular historical accounts, university textbooks or after-dinner speeches. "Independence achieved by other means", "The bridge between continents [and/or] races": it became the reflex interpretation Canadians gave to the world and also to themselves. Witness Louis St. Laurent's first speech on the subject of Canadian citizenship after the Canadian Citizenship Act had come into effect. Here he talked of "a constructive national consciousness [as] the latest step in a continuous and progressive series of enactments which has brought us to a strong and energetic sovereign state, an influential member of the British Commonwealth of Nations and of the great international family of all peace-loving nations".[14]

It is unlikely that Australians are more quick-witted than Canadians, although Bryce's claim that "popular sovereignty is too abstract an idea for Canadians to comprehend" might lead to that conclusion. It is true, however, that compared with Australia the sense of constituent power appears weak in Canada. The explanation for this contrast lies in the strength of sectional feeling here as opposed to there. Long ago Goldwin Smith said that there was nothing "to fuse the races in Canada," but he could equally well have said sections. It may not be said of any Canadian province, as it is of all Australian states, that it is a microcosm of the whole, with similar internal divisions as the whole".[15]

Sectionalism at the beginning of the 19th century fed demands for responsible self-government and sectionalism at the end of that century fed the provincial rights movement. Canada is a composite state and not only because of its cultural and linguistic divisions. It is a country of real and imagined solitudes, and for this reason its political values discourage republican attitudes. American and French republican thought turn on the question of representation. This does not mean that the constitutions that result are similar. They are, in fact, quite different, but it does mean that they elevate as a first principle the subject of representation. As one American author has said of his own constitution: *"In all its parts, the representative part [is] the whole of it"*.[16] By contrast, in Canada representation is of second-order importance. Second, that is, to control.

In *A Federal Republic: Australia's Constitutional System of Government*, a book whose title summarizes its argument, Brian Galligan argues that "the real basis of the Australian Constitution was the consent of the people". The constitutional proposals of 1897-98, drafted by delegates elected by the people and then approved by the people voting in referendums in each of the colonies, guarantee that "the Australian people have supreme authority". They are the constituent power – the latent legislature, so to speak – and, as such, both Parliament and the monarch are "subject to [their] supreme will".[17] Further evidence of the public's primacy lies in the country's constitutional amending formula; for an amendment to succeed it must have the support of a majority of the people voting in a majority of states. In Canada, by contrast, the sense of constituent power is weak. Here, there has never been, as in Australia, a powerful countervision to responsible government. The concept of "the people" is so developed in "republican" Australia that, according to a Canadian constitutional scholar, it is "the monarchy that represents the radically dislocated idea of authority".[18]

Here is the source of Australian interest in voting systems and representational formula – the concern that election results should produce a portrait of the people in miniature. Canadians have shown almost no similar interest, and when the Supreme Court of Canada was presented with an opportunity to give its opinion – on Saskatchewan's constituency boundaries, enacted in 1989 and providing for categories of urban, rural and northern seats with generous provisions for population disparity – it found that the purpose of the right to vote enshrined in

Section 3 of the Charter is not equality of voting power per se, but the right to "effective representation". Lest there be any doubt as to the inference to be drawn from the court's opinion, it should be noted that the question had come to it on appeal from a decision of the Saskatchewan Court of Appeal, which spoke of "no person's portion of sovereign power exceed[ing] that of another" and posited "the idea of equality [as] inherent in the right to vote".[19] To one commentator, the Supreme Court's response could be interpreted as saying that "it was possible to have too much equality if it was achieved at the expense of other factors pertinent to effective representation".[20]

Galligan and others see Australia as "a federal republic rather than a parliamentary democracy." In that "republic" "the people rule through a constitution that is the basic law of the regime and that incorporates the checks and balances of such a constitutional system with a federal division of governments and powers".[21]

A people, a basic law and balance, these are the indices of popular- rather than parliamentary-based republics. Yet Canada has none of these ingredients: it is not a people, it has no basic law (in the sense of a set of constitutional principles and practices affirmed by the people, although there is a Charter of Rights and Freedoms) and it is a thoroughly imbalanced constitutional system with a highly centralized federal government and no institutions to represent provincial interests at the centre.[22]

The third and last reason I am going to offer for Canada's republican silence is historical. Canada has had representative government since 1791. (Here I restrict my examination to what are now the central provinces of Ontario and Quebec, although I know that Nova Scotia has had a longer tradition of representative government. But the republican question, as most other questions in Canadian history, turns on the English-French division, which is a central Canadian matter.) The failure of the Constitutional Act, 1791 lay in the failure of representative government. Voice alone was not enough: there had to be control. It was in the search for control that for the only time in Canadian history republican ideas entered into the stream of political discussion. While always seen as radical, proposals to introduce an elected upper chamber and, perhaps, even, an elected governor represented one response to the gridlock of colonial government, where the governor and his appointed advisers remained deaf to expressions of popular opinion in the elected lower house. The story is more complicated but the principle advocated simple enough – republican institutions would give popular control.

The acceptance of the principle of responsible government, which made the governor's advisers dependent upon their control of the popularly elected chamber, secured for the critics of colonial government all they wanted, and more. Republican solutions had required a sharing of power; responsible government allowed for its continued concentration. Almost overnight republicanism was transformed from a radical into a conservative force. At the same time, and equally important, the idea of institutional balance was discredited. That was the premise on which the Constitutional Act, 1791 had been designed – balance would promote restraint. But with ministries drawn from the elected chamber any limitation on their power was dismissed as intolerable.

Balance was deemed institutionally unnecessary and, in light of the causes of the 1837 rebellion in Lower Canada, culturally undesirable. Canadians would whole-heartedly agree that there must be some method of English and French accommodation (the politically exhausting history of the Province of United Canada, 1840-1867 stood as testimony to that need), but they also realized that that balance must occur within government. Until the introduction of federalism expanded the mechanisms of government, cultural duality made institutional balance impossible, and even after its arrival cultural dualism limited the development of the Senate as a second voice of representation.

To conclude, the fundamental difference between republican and monarchical systems lies in the orientation of the people to institutions of government. In Canada, Parliament, and not the people, is the centrepiece of politics. In parliamentary systems, the right to elect representatives exhausts the right of the people in a wider sense. Once elected, Parliament acts for and as the people. Here there is no concept of the constitution separate from parliament and no concept of the people separate from the constitution. As generations of students have learned, responsible government was "forged in Parliament"; as a consequence, the rebellions of the 1830s have been marginalized and evidence of popular constitutionalism compressed.

Parliament legitimates culture, society and territory, be it through statutes like the Official Languages Act, offices such as that of the Commissioner of Official Languages (an Officer of Parliament), the acquisition and distribution of territory (the Northwest Territories, the Prairie Provinces and Nunavut), agreements like the Nisga's treaty, or the

Clarity Act (1999), which requires Parliament to rule upon the terms and outcome of any provincial referendum on secession. Federalism is supposed to be about divided, and limited, jurisdiction. Canadians are frequently told that theirs is among the most decentralized countries in the world. But in the practice of defining political identity, Parliament acknowledges no restraints on its authority. In his book *The Reluctant Republic,* Malcolm Turnbull, the leader of the Australian Republic Movement, states that an Australian republic would complete "an unfinished work".[23] Republicanism, in short, constitutes fulfilment of a process begun long ago. The republican option offers no comparable sense of arrival for Canadians since in their future there is no pre-eminent symbol.

Notes

1. Carolyn J. Tuohy, *Policy and Politics...* (Philadelphia: Temple University Press, 1992).

2. Pope to Arthur Sladen, governor general's private secretary, August 29, 1901, *Lord Mino's...*,eds., Paul Stevens and John T. Saywell, (Toronto: Champlain Society, 1983, 2, note 63).

3. Walter Bagehot, *The English Constitution* (Garden City, N.J.: Doubleday Dolphin Books 1961), 69.

4. Richard Hofstadter, *The Age of Reform: From Bryan to F.D.R.* (New York: Vintage Books, 1960), 23.

5. Arnold Smith, Papers of, National Archives of Canada, MG 31, E47, vol. 81, file 4, "Lecture Notes" – drafts and texts, 1953-60, and file 19, Speeches by Arnold Smith, 1958-1964.

6. Sara Jeanette Duncan, *The Imperialist* (Toronto: McClelland and Stewart, 1961), 58.

7. W.J. Hudson and M.P. Sharp, *Australian Independence: Colony to Reluctant Kingdom* (Melbourne: Melbourne University Press, 1988).

8. Paul T. Phillips, *Britain's Past in Canada* (Vancouver: University of British Columbia Press, 1989), 61.

9. A revised version of Reid's original memorandum was dated March 21, 1944. That version, with the date July 27, 1949 added, was returned to Reid with the cited quotation written on it.

10. John Conway, "Politics, Culture and the Writing of Constitutions", *Empire and Nations: Essays in Honour of Frederic H. Soward.*, eds. Harvey L. Dyck and H. Peter Krosby (Toronto: University of Toronto Press, 1969), 15-17.

11. Ruth Abbey, and Charles Taylor, "Communitarism, Taylor-made: An Interview with Charles Taylor", *Australian Quarterly*, 68, no. 1 (1996): 6.

12. James (Viscount), Bryce, *Canada: An Actual Democracy* (Toronto: Macmillan Company of Canada, 1921).

13. Kenneth McNaught, "Canada's European Ambiance", *The Round Table*, 310 (1989): 146.

14. St. Laurent Louis, Papers of, National Archives of Canada. MG 31, E 47, vol. 81, file 4, "Lecture Notes" – drafts and texts, 1953-1960, and file 19, Speeches by Arnold Smith, 1958-1964.

15. D.J. Heasman, Review of J.A. La Nauze, *The Making of the Australian Constitution* (Melbourne: Melbourne University Press, 1973) *Canadian Journal of History*, 10, no. 3 (December 1975): 417.

16. Escott Sheps, Papers of, National Archives of Canada, MG 31, E46, vol. 28 (Constitutional Issues and Royal Title, 1942-1960).

17. Brian Galligan, *A Federal Republic: Australia's Constitutional System of Government* (Cambridge: Cambridge University Press, 1995), 14, 15, 29. In his review of the book, Sir Andrew Mason, former chief justice of the High Court of Australia, observed that "Galligan's discussion is a valuable corrective to the superficial notion that the three concepts [majoritarian democracy, responsible government and parliamentary sovereignty] are the dominant constitutional principles", *Australian Journal of Political Science* 31, no. 2 (July 1996): 257.

18. John D. Whyte, "The Australian Republican Movement and Its Implications for Canada", *Constitutional Forum*, 4, no 3 (Spring 1993): 92.

19. All quotations in the paragraph are taken from this article. The Saskatchewan case is discussed in detail in Robert G. Richards and Thomson Irvine, "Reference Re Provincial Electoral Boundaries: An Analysis", and in Ronald E. Fritz, "The Saskatchewan Electoral Boundaries Case and Its Implications", both in *Drawing Boundaries: Courts, Legislatures and Electoral Values,* eds. John C. Courtney, Peter MacKinnon and David E. Smith, (Saskatoon: Fifth House, 1992), 48-69.

20. Duff Spafford,"Effective Representation: Reference Re provincial Electoral Boundaries", *Saskatchewan Bar Review,* 56 (1992), 1997-208.

21. Brian Galligan, *A Federal Republic: Australia's Constitutional System of Government* (Cambridge: Cambridge University Press, 1995): 8.

22. Alan Cairns, "The Fragmentation of Canadian Citizenship", *Belonging The Meaning and Future of Canandian Citizenship,* ed. William Kaplan (Montreal: McGill-Queen's University Press, 1993): 205-206. According to Cairns, the promise of the Charter was false: "The written constitution is a powerful symbolic statement of inclusion or exclusion". The measure of citizenship advanced through the Charter did not lie in access to participation but in recognition of particularistic group identity: corporate not universal in extent, diverse not uniform in appearance.

23. Malcom Turnbull, *The Reluctant Republic* (Melbourne: Mandarin, 1993).

PART V

Governance

14

Participation of Non-Party Interveners and *Amici Curiae* in Constitutional Cases in Canadian Provincial Courts: Guidance for Australia?

PATRICK KEYZER[1]

Introduction

Given our shared common law heritage and, subject to what Helen Irving and John Williams have contributed to this volume (our constitutional concepts), it is perhaps a little surprising that the Federal Supreme Court of Australia,[2] the High Court, takes comparatively little notice of the jurisprudence of the Canadian Supreme Court when developing solutions to constitutional problems. Canadian Supreme Court authorities are referred to in decisions of the Australian High Court,[3] particularly in criminal law matters[4] but references to Canadian decisions in Australian constitutional cases are rare and often deal with non-constitutional points.[5]

The Canadian Provincial Approaches: Guidance for Australia?

The purpose of this paper is to outline an area of constitutional practice where the Canadian approach might assist the development of

Australian principles. In Canada (and the United States), courts often allow *amici curiae* and other non-party interveners to participate in constitutional litigation. The *amicus curiae*, or "friend of the court", traditionally had the function of providing independent, non-partisan advice to the court on matters of special interest to the applicant.[6] A non-party intervener was a person with an interest in the litigation, usually with some sort of stake in the outcome, who could demonstrate that he/she would argue the case in a different way to the parties and thus make a useful contribution to its determination. In this paper I will refer to both collectively as "non-party interveners", unless the context indicates otherwise.

There has been no systematic study, so far as I am aware, of the *influence* of non-party interveners in Australian constitutional litigation.[7] But studies of particular cases[8] and studies of the litigation conducted by particular organizations in the United States[9] indicate that non-party interveners and *amici curiae* can have a significant influence. Certainly the admission of non-party interveners has enabled a net increase and a greater diversity of voices to be heard in constitutional litigation in Canada.[10]

Constitutional decisions of ultimate courts have a significant impact on societal norms and the direction of policy and capital. These are matters in which people have a legitimate and justifiable interest. My view is that liberalisation of the rules governing non-party intervention could do much to enhance the power of the people to influence these decisions. While bearing in mind the distinctive limits of the judicial process and limitations on judicial resources, there may be room for a greater diversity of voices to be heard in the High Court of Australia. Because the discretion to allow non-party interveners to participate in High Court litigation has been so rarely exercised, the reasons for enabling participation have not been effectively exposed.[11] For that reason, the Canadian approach is of special interest, as Justice Kirby of the High Court of Australia recently acknowledged:

> The potential utility of [amicus curiae]... is recognised by other ultimate courts ... [and] has proved beneficial in Canada. In my view, this court should, harmoniously with its own decisions, adopt a similar approach.[12]

In this paper I have chosen to examine the approach taken in Canadian provincial courts, as opposed to the Canadian Supreme Court, for very specific reasons. In Canada, unlike Australia, federal constitutional issues are often raised *and determined* in provincial courts. Australian State inferior courts are vested with jurisdiction by federal statute to hear cases containing federal constitutional points, but such matters are typically commenced in the High Court or removed to that court on the application of one of the parties or by the inferior court itself. The upshot is that constitutional decisions of the Canadian Supreme Court are much more likely to be appeals than constitutional decisions of the Australian High Court. And because Canadian provincial courts are more likely to hear and determine constitutional matters, questions relating to the discretion of a court to enable non-party intervention (including the participation of *amicus curiae*) are resolved in a variety of different places. Moreover, once non-party interveners have been allowed to participate in an inferior court, they are not ordinarily required to make a fresh application to participate in an appellate court. That means that the tests applied in provincial courts to determine whether non-party interveners should be allowed to participate in constitutional litigation are not reagitated in the Supreme Court of Canada. This is why I believe it is important to focus on the tests applied in the provincial courts rather than the Supreme Court. Provincial principles relating to the admission of *amicus curiae* and non-party interveners in Canada have created a rich jurisprudence that is useful in considering the question of the nature and extent of the discretion to grant leave to enable *amici* intervention in Australia, which has only comparatively recently articulated its reasons for enabling non-party intervention in constitutional cases.[13]

The "Genuine Interest" Test

The provincial cases I have reviewed indicate that non-party intervention will not be allowed unless: (1) the applicant can demonstrate a genuine interest in the issues; (2) the applicant has special knowledge and expertise that will benefit the court by bringing a different and useful perspective to those issues[14]; and (3) the court believes that a contribution can be made in a way that will not cause injustice to the parties or affect the procedural efficiency of the court.

The first, "genuine interest" requirement, tends to be applied in cases involving applications by non-party interveners, as distinct from cases involving *amici curiae*. The second "special knowledge and expertise" approach tends to be more significant in the cases involving applications by *amici curiae*. The "injustice to the parties" test is considered in all applications for non-party intervention (including amicus curiae).

A person does not have an interest that justifies intervention "merely because he has an interest in another controversy where the same question of law will or may arise as that which will or may arise in the controversy that is before the Court".[15] But the fact that an applicant for leave to intervene is a party in a parallel action does not, by itself, provide a proper basis for refusing leave to intervene.[16] Typically, if an applicant is unable to demonstrate any interest greater than that of a member of the general public he or she will not be granted leave to intervene.[17] So, for example, in *Re Schofield and Minister of Consumer and Commercial Relations*,[18] an application for intervention was made by a solicitor who represented two parties who would be affected by the outcome of a pending appeal in which neither the solicitors nor the clients were directly involved. While Judge Advocate Wilson was prepared to concede that the applicant had an "interest" in the outcome of the proceedings in the sense that "he might well be affected by the outcome", his interest was insufficient to justify intervention.[19] Justice Thorson supported Judge Advocate Wilson's reasoning:

> Were it not so, the class of persons who might be argued to be "interested" in an appeal involving a particular question of law would be potentially unlimited, since virtually everyone can be said to have an interest in how the laws of general application are interpreted and given meaning and effect by the Courts. This is particularly the case with new laws which give rise to litigation before the Courts the outcome of which predictably will affect many persons beyond those immediately involved as parties to the litigation.[20]

However, it is not always necessary to demonstrate a "direct interest" in a matter in the sense that the litigation adversely affects the legal rights of the applicants or imposes any additional legal obligations upon them.[21] In the same case, Judge Advocate Thorson remarked that:

> It seems to me that there are circumstances in which an applicant can properly be granted leave to intervene in an appeal between other parties, without his necessarily having any interest in that appeal which may be prejudically affected in any "direct sense". As an example of one such situation, one can envisage an applicant with no interest in the outcome of an appeal in any such direct sense but with an interest, because of the particular

> concerns which the applicant has or represents, such that the applicant is in an especially advantageous and perhaps even unique position to illuminate some aspect or facet of the appeal which ought to be considered by the Court in reaching its decision but which, but for the applicant's intervention, might not receive any attention or prominence, given the quite different interests of the immediate parties to the appeal.

Judge Advocate Thorson continued:

> The fact that such situations may not arise with any great frequency or that, when they do, the Court's discretion may have to be exercised on terms and conditions such as to confine the intervener to certain defined issues so as to avoid getting into the merits of the *lis inter partes*, does not persuade me that the door should be closed on them by a test which insists on the demonstration of an interest which is affected in the "direct sense" earlier discussed, to the exclusion of any interest which is not affect in that sense.[22]

While a "direct" interest may not be essential, the intervener has to have a real, substantial and identifiable (or *genuine*) interest in the subject-matter of the proceedings.[23] A variety of different types of interest have satisfied the Canadian provincial courts. If a matter will have a direct and adverse effect on a legal or proprietary interest enjoyed by a person, this may justify a grant of leave to intervene.[24] A substantial commercial interest may provide an appropriate ground for non-party intervention.[25] A parental interest can support an application for non-party intervention.[26] This will be the case where parents have a unique and different perspective to offer.[27] However, courts will only allow an application for intervention into what is essentially a private dispute (i.e., custody of children) in compelling circumstances.[28] A media interest would normally have a right to intervener status where the issue of a publication ban was raised.[29]

In addition, the Canadian provincial courts can and do have regard to whether the *lis* concerns matters of public interest, or where it can be characterized as a private matter. In private suits not characterized by "the amorphous social policy background that animates many of the constitutional (especially post-*Charter*) cases", caution will be exercised in granting intervener status.[30] Where a *lis* involves a matter of public interest, non-party intervention to appear may be more readily granted.[31]

In cases involving the Charter, the usual requirements for intervenor status will be less stringently applied.[32] A different perspective on the "public law issues" raised can overcome the absence of a direct interest in the outcome of a case and justify intervention.[33]

Canadian provincial courts have also demonstrated greater willingness to grant leave to intervene in constitutional cases on the basis that judgments made may have a great impact on others who are not immediate parties to the proceedings.[34] This readiness to enable intervention appears also to extend to matters of national concern.[35] A court can also take into account whether a denial of leave to intervene will remove all opportunities the applicant has to review a governmental decision.[36]

Special Knowledge or Expertise Required

If the parties are capable of raising any relevant issue, then leave for intervention by non-parties will not normally be granted.[37] The rule has also been cast in negative terms: where there is every reason to believe that the issues will be adequately canvassed by existing parties, then leave will be refused.[38] An intervener can play no useful role when their applications are in similar terms to those of other parties and in such circumstances "to allow a non-party to attempt to influence the court's decision would damage at least one of the parties' conception of the court's impartiality and objectivity".[39]

The court wants to know if a proposed intervener will make any contribution that would assist in the resolution of the issues.[40] This does not mean that their position has to be unique.[41] The question is whether a contribution can be made: does the intervener have an important perspective distinct from the immediate parties?[42] The court will consider such issues as the nature of the case, the issues arising and the likelihood of the applicant being able to make a useful contribution to the proceeding in such a case[43] without causing injustice to the immediate parties.[44]

In some matters, the competency of counsel may be a salient issue; this is a particular concern when a party appears unrepresented. In other cases, where "the experience and competence of counsel for the applicants guaranteed a complete canvass of the legal issues involved", intervention may not be appropriate.[45] However, questions relating to the adequacy of the presentation of the issues are not to be dealt with as a question relating to the competence of counsel. The court should not be:

> invited to assess, or feel it necessary to assess, whether a particular appellant is or is not capably or even adequately represented by counsel. However cautiously an invitation to embark upon such an assessment might be advanced by counsel for an applicant, it would still amount to an invitation to the Court to reach a conclusion as to the competence of another counsel and to attach consequences to its conclusion in terms of how the application is disposed of by it. The acceptance of such an invitation would, in my opinion, place a severe strain on the ability of both Bench and Bar to maintain that proper balance between them which is so essential to the functioning of our Court system.[46]

In constitutional cases, provincial courts have indicated the need for a special approach:

> Where a constitutional issue is raised of wider import than the immediate parties can or will address, intervention as a friend of the Court limited to making submissions only is to be favourably considered if the appellant demonstrates the relevance and usefulness of its intended contributions to the constitutional issues raised and the ability to offer a perspective that is even slightly different from that of the existing parties and if its intervention will not cause injustice to the immediate parties. As well, when an applicant wishes to be added as a full party and participate in the evidentiary as well as argumentary phases, the applicant must satisfy the preceding conditions, as well as demonstrate that the application is made early enough to permit properly tested evidentiary contributions, that the applicant's interest and evidence are necessary to a properly informed adjudication of the issues and are not likely to be fully represented or advanced by the existing parties and that the interests of the applicant are likely to be affected by the constitutional issues and their determination in a way not common to other citizens.[47]

Requisite special expertise may be demonstrated by reference to the purposes of the organisation applying for leave: if the intervener is a well-recognised group with a broad identifiable membership base, this can justify an application for intervention.[48]

Non-Party Intervention, Injustice to Parties and Procedural Efficiency

There are a number of issues the courts consider here. Will admission of a non-party intervener expand the cause of action, raising the spectre of increased costs and delays? This is a question that concerns the court in its desire ensuring that justice is done to the parties. The court is also concerned to ensure that judicial resources are effectively managed. An additional issue is the nature of the case: is it a "private" suit or a "public" suit? The courts have indicated greater willingness to allow non-party intervention in constitutional and other public interest cases.

Primarily, the applicant must demonstrate that he or she can make a useful contribution to the resolution of the matter *without causing injustice to the immediate parties.*[49] In *Re Clark et al v. Attorney-General of Canada,*[50] Evans C.J. of the Ontario High Court said:

> Subject to statutory or Court-made rules, it is my view that interventions *amici curiae* should be restricted to those cases in which the Court is clearly in need of assistance because there is a failure to present the issues (as, for example, where one side of the argument has not been presented to the Court). Where the intervention would only serve to widen the *lis* between the parties or introduce a new cause of action, the intervention should not be allowed.[51]

So it is necessary for the applicants to demonstrate what contribution they can make *over and above* that which would be made by the parties themselves and that any contribution that might be made by the interveners is sufficient to counterbalance the disruption caused by the increase in the magnitude, timing, complexity and costs of the original litigation, especially in a private dispute.[52] So long as there is no undue prejudice to the parties, this expertise can extend to include evidentiary matters where to do otherwise might result in a decision being made on a faulty evidentiary basis.[53] But where intervention serves to widen the *lis* between the parties or introduces a new cause of action, it should not be allowed.[54] The discretion to grant leave to intervene will not be granted where to do so would result in unnecessary cost, delay or prejudice to a party.[55] In *Schofield*, Judge Advocate Thorson stressed that the discretion to admit non-party interveners:

> must be exercised in such a way that appeals which are now pending or are brought before the Court in the future can continue to be dealt with and disposed of in an orderly way,

> fairly and impartially as between the parties and without unnecessary costs or delays being imposed upon the parties [and]... to preserve for the Court its ability to ensure that the orderly and efficient processing and handling of the cases coming before it can be maintained.[56]

But although the cost to the parties is a relevant consideration in determining an application for intervention, this does not mean that the interveners will always be required to bear their own costs. While it is typical for interveners to bear their own costs,[57] it may be appropriate in some cases to enable non-party interveners to recoup costs that have been necessarily incurred in defending their interests.[58] In *Janzen v. British Columbia*, Judge Advocate Legg described the approach to be taken in the following terms:

> While it is appropriate to impose terms on an intervenor's involvement at the time when the intervenor is allowed to intervene, those terms typically relate to the extent of the intervenor's involvement, namely which issues it may address. Terms which restrict the intervenor's involvement do not usually predetermine whether costs should be awarded. Terms relating to costs are usually determined after the hearing by the trial judge who is in the best position to assess the contributions and conduct of the parties.[59]

Quite apart from issues of cost and delay, the question of fairness to the parties also depends on the nature of the litigation. Intervener status is granted sparingly in criminal cases and only in exceptional cases to preserve the fairness and the appearance of fairness to the accused, even where constitutional issues are raised.[60] Where an intervener could not bring a different perspective in a criminal case raising constitutional issues, leave would not be granted.[61] This does not mean that non-party intervention in criminal cases is out of the question – where an applicant for non-party intervention in a criminal matter is able to make a useful contribution to constitutional debate then leave can be granted.[62] And it has also been noted that in some circumstances it may be unfair to parties who commence a constitutional case to enable intervention by parties with essentially private interests.[63]

Ultimately, while the court will be conscious of the need to ensure than non-party intervention will not increase delay or prejudice the parties, it will not limit itself to consideration of these issues when exercising its discretion to enable non-party intervention.[64]

Conclusion

It is clear from the Canadian provincial cases that liberalization of the rules of participation in litigation can occur in a consistent, predictable and manageable way.[65] The Canadian provincial courts have developed pragmatic rules to govern the admission of non-party interveners and *amici curiae* in constitutional disputes. A judicious balance is struck between the anticipated value of the intervention and its potential cost to the litigation. Due recognition is given to the "public interest" dimension of constitutional litigation. There is no evidence to support the view that admission of non-party interveners has enhanced costs and delays in the Canadian provincial courts. A coherent and informative body of jurisprudence has developed that could be recognized and applied in Australian courts.

Notes

1. I would like to thank the Faculty of Law at the Northern Territory University (NTU) in Darwin, Australia, particularly Dean Susan Oliver, for providing me with such a congenial atmosphere in which to complete this paper. I would also like to thank Dr. Philip Jamieson, Adjunct Senior Lecturer at the NTU Law Faculty for reading an earlier draft of this paper with his customary enthusiasm and making suggestions with his customary skill.

2. Section 71 of the Commonwealth Constitution provides that "The judicial power of the Commonwealth shall be vested in a Federal Supreme Court to be called the High Court of Australia".

3. A study of citations of reported Canadian Supreme Court decisions in the decisions of the High Court of Australia during 1998 and 1999 turns up references in cases involving negligence (*Perre v. Apand Pty Ltd* (1999), 73 ALJR 1190, 164 ALR 606, *Chappel v. Hart* (1998) 72 ALJR 1344, 156 ALR 517; *Pyrenees Shire Council v. Day* (1998), 72 ALJR 152, 151 ALR 147); damages (*Gray v. Motor Accident Commission* (1998), 73 ALJR 45, 158 ALR 485); inducement of breach of contract (*Sanders v. Snell* (1998), 72 ALJR 1508, 157 ALR 491); contribution in tort cases

(*James Hardie and Coy Pty Limited v. Seltsam Pty Limited* (1998), 73 ALJR 238, 159 ALR 268); procedure (*State Rail Authority of New South Wales v. Earthline Constructions Pty Ltd (in liq)* (1999) 73 ALJR 306, 160 ALR 588), equity (*Maguire v. Makaronis* (1997) 188 CLR 449; *Giumelli v. Giumelli* (1999) 73 ALJR 547); (*Bridgewater v. Leahy* (1998), 194 CLR 457), shipping (*Great China Metal Industries Co Limited v. Malaysian International Shipping Corporation* (1998), 72 ALJR 1592, 158 ALR 1), administrative law (*Minister for Immigration v. Eshetu* (1999) 73 ALJR 746, 162 ALR 577); customs (*Commonwealth v. SCI Operations Pty Limited; Commonwealth v. ACI Operations Pty Limited* (1998), 192 CLR 285); taxation (*Commissioner of Taxation v. Murry* (1998), 193 CLR 605; *Commissioner of Taxation v. Montgomery* (1999), 73 ALJR 1160, 164 ALR 435); extradition (*Attorney-General for the Commonwealth v. Tse Chu-Fai* [No 2] (1998), 72 ALJR 1006, 154 ALR 414; but cf *Fejo (on behalf of the Larrakia People) v. Northern Territory* (1998), 195 CLR 96, 72 ALJR 1442, 156 ALR 721, a native title case, in which Chief Justice Gleeson, Justices Gaudron, McHugh, Gummow and Callinan remarked: "Although reference was made to a number of decisions in other common law jurisdictions about the effect of later grants of title to land on pre-existing native title rights, we doubt that much direct assistance is to be had from these sources" (54).

4. *Pearce v. The Queen* (1998), 72 ALJR 1416, 156 ALR 684; *Farrell v. The Queen* (1999), 194 CLR 286; *The Queen v. Olbrich* [1999] HCA 54; *Osland v. The Queen* (1998), 73 ALJR 173, 159 ALR 170; *Peters v. The Queen* (1998), 192 CLR 493; *Byrnes v. The Queen; Hopwood v. The Queen* (1999), 73 ALJR 1292, 164 ALR 520 per Gaudron, McHugh, Justices Gummow and Callinan at 38; *Wu v. The Queen* [1999] HCA 52 (September 30, 1999); *Melbourne v. The Queen* (1999), 73 ALJR 1097, 164 ALR 465; *Inge v. The Queen* [1999] HCA 55 (October 7, 1999); *AB v. The Queen* [1999] HCA 46; *Robinson v. The Queen* [1999] HCA 42.

5. See *Kartinyeri v. The Commonwealth (the Hindmarsh Island Bridge Case)* (1998), 72 ALJR 722, 152 ALR 540 at 95 per Justices Gummow and Hayne (in the context of a discussion relating to the question whether the Commonwealth Constitution should be interpreted in accordance with international human rights norms, Justices Gummow and Hayne noted that "the Supreme Court of Canada has had regard to international human rights laws which did not bind Canada" but contrasted the Canadian constitutional situation, where there is an express Charter of Human Rights and Freedoms. In the same case, Justice Kirby (dissenting) said: "in interpreting the Canadian Charter of Rights and Freedoms, that country's Supreme Court has frequently had regard to international instruments", 166; note also the passing reference at 158. Justice Kirby referred to *R v. Oakes* [1986] 1 SCR 103 at 120-121; *R v. Smith* [1987] 1 SCR 1045 at 1061 and *Edmonton Journal v. Attorney-General for Alberta* [1989] 2 SCR 1326 at 1374, 1377-1378 with approval. In *Egan v. Willis* (1998) 73 ALJR 75, 158 ALR 527 at par 141 per Justice Kirby "the (Legislative) Council (of the State of New South Wales)

should be seen as a constituent House of a Parliament of a State of Australia which bears a significantly different relationship to the people governed by it than that which existed in colonial times", citing *New Brunswick Broadcasting Co v. Nova Scotia*, [1993] 1 SCR 319 as authority for that approach to the characterisation of that institution; *Nicholas v. The Queen* (1998) 193 CLR 173 at par 201 per Justice Kirby (dissenting) I refer to the many judicial expressions explaining the rule in terms of the right and duty of the courts to protect the integrity of their own processes and to prevent the administration of justice being brought into disrepute with consequent loss of public confidence (references omitted). In Canada, the Supreme Court has expressed the same idea: "[T]he essential character of a superior court of law necessarily involves that it should be invested with a power to maintain its authority and to prevent its process being obstructed and abused. Such a power is intrinsic in a superior court; it is its very life-blood, its very essence, its immanent attribute. Without such a power, the court would have form but would lack substance. The jurisdiction which is inherent in a superior court of law is that which enables it to fulfil itself as a court of law", citing *MacMillan Bloedel Ltd v. Simpson* [1995] 4 SCR 725 at 749-750 per Chief Justice Lamer, quoting from Jacob, "The Inherent Jurisdiction of the Court", *Current Legal Problems*, 23, (1970): 27; at 240, 243 per Justice Hayne (dealing with a non-constitutional point); *Attorney-General (Cth) v. Breckler* (1999) 163 ALR 576 at 106 per Kirby J (dissenting on the decision to disallow participation of amicus curiae, see further text at n 11); *Re The Governor, Goulburn Correctional Centre; Ex parte Eastman* (1999), HCA 44 (September 2, 1999), per Justice Kirby (dissenting) at 109 ("Different views may be held about the desirability of the appointment of acting judges having regard to the effect which such appointments may have, or be seen to have, upon the independence of the judiciary concerned. In some jurisdictions, such as in Canada, challenges to such appointments have been made by reference to general constitutional standards" citing *Valente v. The Queen*, [1985] 2 SCR 673; *Reference re Territorial Court Act (Northwest Territories)* [1997] NWTR 377 and at par 154 (a passing reference on a constitutional point); *AMS v. AIF and AIF v. AMS* (1999), 163 ALR 501 at par 85 and 86 per Justice Gaudron (non-constitutional point); *Commonwealth of Australia v. WMC Resources Ltd* (1998), 72 ALJR 280 at 22 per Chief Justice Brennan ("the decisions of the United States Supreme Court and the Supreme Court of Canada denying the territorial waters and the seabed formed part of the territory of the States of the Union and the Provinces of the Dominion confirm the absence of any proprietary interest in the Australian Colonies (*Reference re Ownership of Off-Shore Mineral Rights* [1967] SCR 792; (1967) 65 DLR (2d) 353; *United States v. California* 332 US 19 (1947)"; *Re East and Ors; Ex parte Nguyen* (1998), 73 ALJR 140, 159 ALR 108 at 83 per Justice Kirby ("The entitlement to an interpreter is not specifically a language right, as such, or a feature of the public character of a trial so much as an aspect of the commitment of the judicature to fairness of the trial process" citing *MacDonald v. City of Montreal* [1986] 1 SCR 460 at 499; *Yanner v. Eaton* [1999] HCA 53 (October 7, 1999) at 85 per Gummow J (referred to a Canadian Supreme Court decision with approval in the course of a discussion of the concept of "property"); *Northern Territory of Australia v. GPAO* (1999) 73 ALJR 470, 161 ALR 318 at 232 per Justice Kirby (non-constitutional point); *Commonwealth of Australia v. State of Western Australia* (1999) 73 ALJR 345, 160 ALR 638 at par 87 per Justice Gummow (contrasting the Canadian approach while making a non-constitutional point); *Re Colina; Ex parte Torney,* [1999] HCA 57 per Justice Kirby at 54 and 61 (comparing Canadian Supreme Court authorities on contempt of court and freedom of political communication) before remarking at par 101: "Charges of contempt in the nature of scandalising a court are rare. They have not been brought successfully for more than sixty years in England and Wales (citing Walker, "Scandalising in the Eighties", *Law Quarterly Review*, 101 (1985): 359). The greater willingness to bring such charges in Canada (and Australia) has been ascribed by one observer who studied the matter to "greater sensitivity on the part of Canadian courts or to greater feelings of insecurity in the face of criticism" (citing Canada, Law Reform Commission, *Contempt of Court*, Working Paper 20 (1977): 31), see also 105. For further discussion of the practice of "citation analysis," see R. Smyth, "Academic Writing and the Courts", *University of Tasmania Law Review*, 17 (1999): 164 and the many references cited therein.

6. A useful (Canadian) definition of the role of the amicus curiae was provided by Justice Ferguson of the Ontario High Court in *Grice v. R* (1957) 26 CLR 318, [1957] 11 DLR (2d) 699 at 702: "a bystander, usually a lawyer, who interposes and volunteers information upon some matter of law. In its ordinary use the term implies the friendly intervention of counsel to remind the court of some matter of law which has escaped its notice and in regard to which it is in danger of going wrong". See also *Attorney-General (Nova Scotia) v. Beaver* (1984), 66 NDR (2d) 419. The seminal piece on the role of the amicus curiae today is Samuel Krislov's "The Amicus Curiae Brief: From Friendship to Advocacy", *Yale Law Journal*, 72 (1963): 694-721.

7. Cf. G.A. Caldeira and J.R. Wright, "Amicus Curiae Before the Supreme Court: Who Participates, When and How Much?", *Journal of Politics*, 52, no. 3 (1990): 782-806. In Canada and in the United States, the Supreme Courts have adopted the practice of *inviting* amici to appear in cases where her special expertise might assist the court in its deliberations; see further Krislov, 717-719. In those circumstances the influence of the amici might be expected. But in each of those countries and in Australia it is more typical for the ultimate court to receive applications to be heard or have the opportunity to make written submissions as a non-party intervener.

8. For example, J. Howard, "Retaliation, Reinstatement and Friends of the Court", *Howard Law Journal*, 31 (1988): 241.

9. For example, L. Pfeffer, "Amici in Church-State Litigation", *Law and Contemporary Problems*, 44 (1981): 83; D.S. Ruder, "The Development of Legal Doctrine Through Amicus Participation: The SEC Experience", *Wisconsin Law Review*, (1989): 1167.

10. See further P. Bryden, "Public Interest Intervention in the Courts", *Canadian Bar Review*, 66 (1987): 490.

11. See *Attorney-General (Cth) v. Breckler* (1999), 163 ALR 576 at 609.

12. *Attorney-General (Cth) v. Breckler* (1999) 163 ALR 576 at 609.

13. See further *Levy v. Victoria* (1997) 189 CLR 579 per Chief Justice Brennan and Justice Kirby; S, Kenny, "Interveners and Amici Curiae in the High Court", *Adelaide Law Review*, 20 (1998): 159; R. Owens, "Interveners and Amicus Curiae: The Role of the Courts in a Modern Democracy", *Adelaide Law Review*, 20 (1998): 193.

14. R v. Morgentaler, [1993] 1 SCR 462 at 463; *Reference Re Workers' Compensation Act, 1983 (Nfld)* [1989] 2 SCR 335 at 339, *MacMillan Bloedel Ltd v. Mullin et al* [1985] 3 WWR 380 at 384; *Rothmans, Benson and Hedges Inc v. Canada (Attorney-General)* (1989), NR 391, [1990] 1 FC 90.

15. R v. Bolton, [1976] 1 FC 252. The Supreme Court of Canada has indicated that a "direct stake" in the outcome of a matter will typically be required to justify non-party intervention: *R v. Finta*, [1993] 1 SCR 1138 at 1142, 1143. Involvement in a case raising similar issues can support an application to intervene: *Reference Re Workers' Compensation Act, 1983 (Nfld)* [1989] 2 SCR 335 at 340. But the fact that the case might create a precedent that an applicant does not like is not a good enough reason, by itself, to justify intervention, ibid.

16. *United Brotherhood of Carpenters and Joiners of America, Local 2013 et al v. Canada and University of Calgary (Governors)* (1986), 72 NR 249.

17. *John Doe v. Ontario (Information and Privacy Commissioner)* (1991), 87 DLR (4th) 348.

18. *Re Schofield and Minister of Consumer and Commercial Relations* (1980), 112 DLR (3d) 132.

19. *Re Schofield*, 137.

20. *Re Schofield*, 140.

21. *Re Schofield and Minister of Consumer and Commercial Relations* (1980), 112 DLR (3d) 132, per Judge Advocate Thorson at 141; cf *Rothmans of Pall Mall et al v. Minister of National Revenue et al* (1976), 67 DLR (3d) 505 at 510.

22. (1985), 17 DLR (4th) 193 at 201-203. These comments were approved in Re *Canadian Labour Congress et al and Bhindi et al* (1985) 17 DLR (4th) 193.

23. *Attorney-General for Ontario v. Dieleman* (1994), 108 DLR (4th) 458.

24. *Rothmans of Pall Mall et al v. Minister of National Revenue et al*, (1976), 67 DLR (3d) 505; *Crown Trust Co v. Rosenberg*, (1986), 60 OR (2d) 87, 39 DLR (4th) 526.

25. *Temagami Wilderness Society v. Ontario (Minister of the Environment)* (1989), 33 OAC 356 at 357; *United Parcel Service Canada Ltd v. Ontario (Highway) Transport Board)* (1989), 41 Admin LR 97 at 101; *Tsartlip Indian Band et al v. Pacific Salmon Foundation et al* (1989), 30 FTR 247 at 251; *Communications and Electrical Workers of Canada et al v. Canada (Attorney-General)* (1988), 20 FTR 151 at 153-154; *Bagnell v. Canada (Department of Fisheries and Oceans)* (1987), 10 FTR 150; *Fishing Vessel Owners' Association of British Columbia v. Canada (Attorney General)* (1985), 57 NR 376 at 379, 381; *Ontario (Attorney General) v. Ballard Estate* (1994), 36 CPC (3d) 213 (Ont Gen Div); *Kirkfield Park and Arthur Oliver Residents Inc v. Winnipeg (City)* (1995), 101 Man R (2d) 246 at 249.

26. *Omeasoo v. Canada (Minister of Indian Affairs and Northern Development)*, (1988), [1989] 1 CNLR 110, 24 FTR 130.

27. *R v. Bernardo*, (1995), 38 CR (4th) 229 (Ont Gen Div).

28. *Klachefsky v. Brown*, [1988] 1 WWR 755 at 758.

29. *R v. Bernardo*, (1995), 38 CR (4th) 229 (Ont Gen Div).

30. *Peixeiro v. Haberman*, (1994), 20 OR (3d) 666 at 671.

31. *Tsartlip Indian Band et al v. Pacific Salmon Foundation et al*, (1989), 30 FTR 247; *Holiday Park Developments Ltd v. Canada*, (1994), 75 FTR 76.

32. *Alberta Sports and Recreation Association for the Blind v. Edmonton (City)*, [1994] 2 WWR 659.

33. *MacMillan Bloedel Ltd v. Mullin et al*, [1985] 3 WWR 380 at 383.

34. *Adler v. Ontario* (1992) 8 OR (3d) 200 at 205; *Peel (Regional Municipality) v. Great Atlantic and Pacific Co of Canada* (1990), 74 OR (2d) 164 at 167.

35. *Re Canadian Labour Congress and Bhindi et al,* (1985), 17 DLR (4th) 193 at 203.

36. *Apotex Inc v. Canada (Attorney General)* (1986), 1 FTR 310 at 317.

37. *McDonald's Restaurants of Canada Ltd v. Etobicoke* (1977), 5 CPC 5 at 56; *Klachefsky v. Brown,* [1988] 1 WWR 755 at 758.

38. *Ontario (Attorney General) v. Dieleman* (1993), 108 DLR (4th) 458 at 463.

39. *Attorney-General (Nova Scotia) v. Beaver* (1984), 66 NSR (2d) 419 at 421 per MacIntosh J.

40. *Canadian Broadcasting Corporation v. Saskatchewan,* (Attorney-General) (1993) 110 Sask R 157 at 160.

41. *Re Canadian Labour Congress et al and Bhindi et al,* (1985), 17 DLR (4th) 193 at 203-204.

42. *Attorney-General for Ontario v. Dieleman* (1994), 108 DLR (4th) 458.

43. See also *Guadagni v. Workers' Compensation Board of British Columbia and B C Federation of Labour* (1988), 30 BCLR (2d) 259.

44. *Peel (Regional Municipality) v. Great Atlantic and Pacific Company of Canada Ltd* (1990), 74 OR (2d) 164 at 167; *Adler v. Ontario* (1992), 8 OR (3d) 200 at 207.

45. *Re Clark et al and Attorney-General of Canada* (1977), 17 OR (2d) 593 at 598.

46. *Re Schofield and Minister of Consumer and Commercial Relations* (1980) 112 DLR (3d) 132, per Judge Advocate Thorson at 142-143. These comments were approved by Judege Advocate Anderson for the majority in *Re Canadian Labour Congress and Bhindi et al* (1985), 17 DLR (4th) 193 at 206-207.

47. *Rv. LePage* (1994), 21 CRR (2d) 67 (Ont Gen Div) (digest in the *Canadian Abridgement*).

48. *Attorney-General for Ontario v. Dieleman* (1994), 108 DLR (4th) 458 at 464.

49. *MacMillan Bloedel Ltd v. Mullin et al,* [1985] 3 WWR 380 at 384; *Peel (Regional Municipality) v. Great Atlantic and Pacific Company of Canada* (1990), 74 OR (2d) 164 at 167.

50. (1977), 81 DLR 33 (3d) at 38.

51. Although *Re Clark* concerned an application by amicus curiae there is no reason to believe that the same considerations would not apply in a case involving another form of non-party intervention.

52. *M v. H* (1994), 20 OR (3d) 70 at 77.

53. *Hutchinson v. Clarke* (1988), 32 CPC (2d) 1, 67 OR (2d) 621 at 628.

54. *Re Clark et al and Attorney-General (Canada)* (1978), 81 DLR (2d) 33 at 38; *Borowski v. Minister of Justice of Canada* (1983), 144 DLR (3d) 657 at 667; *Canada (Attorney General) v. Aluminium Company of Canada* (1987), 26 Admin LR 18; 35 DLR (4th) 495 at 505.

55. *Klachefsky v. Brown* [1988] 1 WWR 755; *Porretta v. Stock* (1988), 32 CPC (2d) 10, [1989] ILR 1-2404, 67 OR (2d) 628; affd (1989), 67 OR (2d) 736 (CA); *Bagnell v. Canada (Department of Fisheries and Oceans)* (1987), 10 FTR 150 at 153; *Leask Estate v. Crocetti* (1990), 97 NSR (2d) 221 at 222.

56. *Supra,* 140.

57. See, for example, *Iron v. Saskatchewan (Minister for the Environment and Public Safety),* [1993] 3 WWR 315.

58. *Janzen v. British Columbia (Attorney-General)* (1993), 38 BCAC 268, 62 WAC 268.

59. At par [16].

60. *Re Regina and Morgantaler, Smoling and Scott* (1985), 19 CCC (3d) 573.

61. *R v. Neuman* (1995), 32 Alta LR (3d) 340, 173 AR 189.

62. *Caron c R,* [1988] RJQ 2333, 20 QAC 45.

63. *Bagnell v. Canada (Department of Fisheries and Oceans)* (1987), 10 FTR 150 at 153.

64. *MacNeill v. Hillcrest Housing Ltd* (1990), 81 Nfld and PEIR 118 at 120.

65. Cf. Justice Kirby's criticism of the approach of the High Court of Australia in *Attorney-General (Cth) v. Breckler* (1999), 163 ALR 576 at 609.

15

Innovations in Governance in Canada[1]

GILLES PAQUET

> "Our Canadianism... is a baffling, illogical
> but compulsive athleticism – a fence-leaping
> which is also, and necessarily, a fence-keeping".[2]

To avoid any misunderstanding, let me start with three forewarnings:

First forewarning. Canadians are a people characterized by prudence. Those who have psychoanalyzed Canadians most aptly ascribe this "characteristic prudence" to the fact that "to remain a people at all we have had to think before we speak, even to think before we think." This is why we are sometimes called "the people of the second thought".[3]

Second forewarning. In Canada, our "natural mode" is not compromise but irony. Often, what is said is meant to express its opposite. So, despite much denial and much obfuscation by officials, Canada has lived through a change of its governance regime over the last two decades, and this tectonic change has generated innovations in the last five years. But we must guard against "the pretense that every step backward or sideways marks ten steps forward".[4]

Third forewarning. When trying to communicate effectively a sense of the sort of discontinuity that Canada is slouching through, we must of necessity simplify somewhat a complex back-and-forth process. I have used ideal types to get my point across. Flats and sharps may be added later.

In the next two sections, I give a broad presentation of Canada's two-stage evolution since 1980 and sketch in stark terms the broad features of what the Canadian governance regime is becoming. I use a few cases to illustrate both the breadth and scope of these changes but also their essential ambiguity. I refer to four types of innovations: mere retooling, interesting restructuring, major reframing and fundamental moral recontracting. All along I underline that all this was accomplished by fits and starts, most inelegantly, and that it was brought forth by a cacophonous forum marred by much cognitive dissonance, an immense amount of disinformation and strong ideological, political and bureaucratic resistance to the new governance.

Canada Over the Last 7,000 Days

Canada, like most other advanced economies, has been subjected to a variety of pressures over the last 20 years as a result of dramatic changes in its environment. These pressures have been mainly ascribable to globalization and accelerated technical change. As a result of these changes, the environment has become more complex and more turbulent, and concerns from the private, public and civic sectors have been forced to acquire a greater capacity to transform and to develop a philosophy of continuous improvement and innovation in order to survive. In the face of the "new competition," these concerns have had to become "learning organizations".[5]

Learning organizations must be capable of defining new goals and new means as they proceed through tapping knowledge and information that other agents and groups possess, that is, through co-operation with other stakeholders and social learning. This has triggered a drift in the governance process. The governance pattern evolved from more exclusive, hierarchical and paternalistic forms in the 1970s, toward more inclusive, horizontal, distributed and participative forms in the 1990s, from a pattern where the national leader was in charge to what would appear to be a game without a master.

To be effective, the new distributed governance through social learning requires not only a new regime in its interactions with the rest of the world but also new structures (more modular and network-like), new strategies (based on dynamic efficiency and learning) and new forms of co-ordination (more decentralized and more dependent on moral contracts).

Canada's International Circumstances

At the international level, this meant a major rethinking of Canada's role in the world economy and the negotiation of its entry and participation into an evolving economic bloc intended on one day encompassing all of the Americas.

Already by the mid-1980s, it had become clear both for academics and practitioners that globalization could not be resisted but had to be embraced. However, Canada did not proceed with a careful, throughdull and serene debate as a way to prepare the entry in the Free Trade Agreement (FTA) in 1989 or the North American Agreement (NAFTA) including Mexico in 1993. It slouched into it despite a vibrant opposition from a nationalist phalanx and a partisan parliament. At a time of growing economic dependence on the U.S. market and of growing fear of unilateral protectionist action from the U.S. government, it was felt that new rules were needed that might protect Canada's interests somewhat better.

There was a national debate, but it was not very illuminating: the academic contributions were not enlightening and the average Canadian citizen was swayed in fact into taking a leap of faith.[6]

Canadians in general have come to the opinion that Canada had had to embrace globalization so as not to be left out in the cold in this era of regional blocs, and that, despite the imperfections of these accords, Canada would be in much worse shape today if it had not done so. Nevertheless, a vocal minority still believes that Canada has found itself on the losing end. And 10 years after the FTA, the two clans (pro and against) recite very much what they used to say in the mid-1980s.[7] There is most certainly no general philosophy of global governance being distilled in Canada at the present time as is the case in so many other countries.

A Less than Orderly Transformation of the National Governance Regime

At the national level, the opportunity to effect an orderly transformation of the governance regime was offered to Canadians on at least two occasions, in 1990 and 1992. But the two accords (Meech, Charlottetown) that would have introduced the possibility of a new decentralized Canada (wider powers to the provinces, distinct status for

Quebec, guaranteed regional representation in central institutions and so forth) failed to get the necessary support. So the transition again has proceeded in fits and starts through various confrontations and ad hoc administrative arrangements.[8]

In particular, the fiscally driven Program Review process launched in 1994[9] and the Alternative Service Delivery Initiative launched in 1995[10] were instrumental in bringing about a de facto transformation in the philosophy of governance. The first one was designed to subject each federal program to some scrutiny by imposing on federal officials the burden of proof in the debates as to whether these programs were still in the public interest and whether they could not be devolved to the private, provincial/local government or civic sectors, or to any partnership arrangements among them. It was clearly based on a philosophy of subsidiarity. The second one was a technocratic adjunct to the Program Review process, borrowed from many experiences in the rest of the Commonwealth and a more indirect and limited route to transform governance. But any analysis of the technology of delivery of services obviously must lead to some questioning of the governance process.

However, at both the international and national levels, there was much improvisation and learning-by-doing on the governance front. Moreover, at both levels, there has been a sort of *valse-hésitation* (pussyfooting) and a constant tension between (1) the neo-liberal forces defending open borders and a massive devolution of powers from the centre of the federation and (2) those insisting that some protectionism or managed trade and national centralization are necessary to protect the nationals and to fuel the "desired" degree of national redistribution of income and wealth.[11]

Slouching Toward a New Governance

In a starkly simplified manner, the difference between the former and latter governance regimes in Canada can be stylized as a shift from a somewhat "defensive," antidemocratic, centralizing, homogenizing and hierarchical former regime ruled by elites toward a more "open", communitarian, non-centralizing, pluralistic and distributed governance regime in the latter period.[12] When we use the expression "antidemocratic", we suggest that there was a tendency in the former regime, during the Trudeau years, for instance, but also in the recent past, for top-down unilateralism to be regarded as legitimate. And the lack of authoritative agencies willing and able to stop the encroachment of one state agency upon the lawful authority of another has also been deplored. This situation – fuelled by the centralized mindset of many governments over the last few decades, but also by the immensely greater bureaucratic power at the disposal of modern Caesars – has been denounced in the U.S. and Canada.[13] There is no clean break between these two regimes: in many ways, the two institutional arrangements overlap and are intermingled. The former regime is still present in our values, ideologies, institutions and policies, and indeed it has been reinforced by the Canadian Charter of Rights and Freedoms of April 1982.[14] But the latter regime is making inroads, and the illiberal and federal-encroachment-prone nature of the former regime is being challenged on a variety of fronts, even though it is often done in a low voice.

If we had to put a label on the former governance regime, we might use Stephen Carter's "the liberal constitutional project." We could define it as built on the priority "to get the answers right, not to worry too much about the process through which the answers are obtained," and on a model that holds that "the central government (where decisions on matters of right or wrong are made) is more likely than anybody else to find the answers that are right".[15]

As for the latter emerging governance regime, we might label it "the distributed governance scenario", built on a reduced and transformed role of the state, a greater reliance on governance mechanisms from the private and civic sectors and on a scattered and multi-layered distribution of power. The word scenario is used to emphasize the fact that it is still in the process of unfolding, and that it is in no way certain that it will unfold exactly as we suggest.[16]

The Former Governance Regime Under Stress

The former governance regime is approximated rather well by the hierarchical mode of governance with its top-down enforcement of rules by a governor who claims to represent the will of the people and treat the citizen in an imperial way. The main weaknesses of this brand of centralized governance in good currency in Canada, and in many other advanced socio-economies, have been well-documented.

The overall crisis of this governance regime since the late 1960s has been analyzed historically as a two-stage process:

1. it evolved first as a crisis in the economic realm: co-ordination failures became more and more important in advanced market type economies, thereby creating a demand for intervention and regulation by the state, and the economic crisis was therefore shifted to the state.

2. The state crisis developed as the legitimation deficit grew: the state was failing to mobilize the requisite commitment of citizens to be able to do the job; in desperation the state attempted to obtain a "blank cheque" from the citizenry.

The argument was that since the management problems were so technically complex, the citizenry should pay its taxes and let the professional managerial experts do their job. This stratagem has not worked and it has not succeeded in suppressing the autonomous power of the community to grant or withold legitimacy.[17] Trust in government has declined. The polls have recorded this story line.

In a more and more globalized context, the Canadian private sector also made ever greater demands on public institutions for protection and regulation at a time when the capacity to supply services from the public sphere could not expand further. This limitation on the capability of the public sphere was due to the fact that participation, trust and creative interaction (on which politics and the public sphere are built) had all but disappeared, as had the sense of community that underpinned civil society and the collective/private ways of meeting the needs of strangers.[18]

In this world of rugged individualism where most citizens were strangely unaware that the government had been the prime mover in the postwar period of prosperity, private enterprise at public expense became the rule. The lack of commitment of emotional, intellectual and financial resources to refurbish the public infrastructure could only lead to demand overload, and the frustration generated by the policy failures of the 1970s set the stage for citizens to suggest that the best way to strengthen both democracy and the economy was to weaken government.

The Emerging Scenario: Distributed Governance and the Strategic State

At the core of the latter or new regime is a new philosophy of public intervention. It is emerging as a two-stage process: first, there has been a growing recognition that there is a need for a new rationale for the new collective institutions; second, there has been the development of the design principles that are likely to underpin the social architecture of this new strategic and distributed learning governance regime.[19]

Recognize the need for a new rationale for the new collective institutions – this calls not for the least constraining public philosophy but for one that would be the choice of citizens if they had "the fullest attainable understanding of the experience resulting from that choice and its most relevant alternatives".[20] The challenge is to bring about that sort of "fullest understanding" in the population. It means that government can no longer operate in a top-down mode but has a duty to institute a continuing dialogue with the citizenry. This requires a language of common citizenship, deeply rooted in civil society: the citizens have commitment and values that the state must take into account, and they want an active role in the making of policies supposedly generated to respond to their presumed needs. Only through a rich forum and institutions that enhance citizens' communication competence is an enlightened understanding likely to prevail, both as a result of, and as the basis for, a reasonable armistice between the state and the citizenry.

The state, in the past, has played housekeeping roles and offsetting functions. These functions required minimal input from the citizenry. The state in complex advanced capitalist socio-economies must now play new central roles that go much beyond these mechanical interventions. It must become involved as a broker, as a driving force and as a partner in participatory planning, if the requisite amount of organizational learning, co-evolution and co-operation between the economy and society is to materialize. This paves the way to a participation-society (where freedom and efficacy come from the fact that the individual has a recognized voice in the forum on matters of substance and procedures in the public realm and, more importantly, an obligation to participate in the definition of such matters). The citizen refuses to be confined to living in a "rights society" where the dignity of individuals resides exclusively in the fact that they have claims. The citizen becomes a co-producer of governance.

Develop the design principles – the design principles for a social architecture in keeping with the guiding values mentioned above are clear. First is the principle of subsidiarity, according to which "power should devolve on the lowest, most local level at which decisions can reasonably be made, with the function of the larger unit being to support and assist the local body in carrying out its tasks".[21] The rationale for this principle is that the institutions closer to the citizen are those likely to be the closest approximation to organic institutions, that is, to institutions that are likely to emerge undesigned, to emerge from the sheer pressure of well-articulated needs and likely to require minimal yearly redesigning. Subsidiarity reduces the vertical hierarchical power and increases in a meaningful way the potential for participation.

The second design principle is that of effective citizen-based evaluation feedback to ensure that the services produced, financed or regulated by the public realm meet with the required standards of efficiency, economy and effectiveness, and are consonant with the spirit of the agreed standards or norms. This is a central cybernetic loop feature in the refurbished governance. It is essential if organizational learning is to proceed as quickly as possible.

This entails a transformation of the audit and evaluation functions in the decision-making process. Instead of being limited to untimely *ex post* efforts at identifying abuses, these functions are becoming part of the *ex ante* strategic decision making in a citizen-centred governance regime. Perfunctory consultation will not do - it requires the creation of "chaordic organizations".[22]

From Egalitarianism to Subsidiarity

To fix ideas, we might stylize the drift in the governance regime as a movement along a spectrum of institutional orders with one ideal type at each end: the former institutional order rooted in the philosophy of egalitarianism and the new institutional order rooted in the philosophy of subsidiarity.[23]

Egalitarianism is clearly the general thrust of the top-down rights-based philosophy of governance that has underpinned the traditional welfare state. This philosophy argues that equalization of outcomes is a desirable objective and ambitions to provide all citizens, whatever their personal access to resources, with all the required resources necessary to ensure equality. Tocqueville has shown that "democratic peoples... have an ardent, insatiable, eternal, invincible passion for equality; they want equality in freedom, and if they cannot obtain it in freedom, they want it in slavery".[24] Indeed, this egalitarianism that drives democracy is not only an observed fact, it is an ideal, an "imaginary equality".[25] However, democratic egalitarianism (in society) generates compulsive centralism (in the polity): to redistribute resources, we have to bring them to the centre first and this centralism generates growing shackles on the productive capacity of the economic system. So the welfare state has found itself caught in an vicious circle where it has become ever more expensive in fiscal and centralization terms to effect a redistribution that, instead of reducing frustration, has managed to exacerbate it.

It is only in the 1990s that Canada has been forced by its fiscal crisis to articulate the beginnings of an alternative philosophy of governance. This new compass is a philosophy of subsidiarity built on the centrality of active citizens who have to take primary responsibility for their own welfare and the welfare of their families. The authority of governments to intervene is not based on any rights or entitlements ordained from above but stems from the citizens' demands for help. Thus governments act in a subsidiary way, in the same way a reserve army intervenes in case of need. This new governance system also calls for decisions to be made at the lowest, most local level at which decisions can reasonably be made (starting with the citizen as such). The task of the higher order of government is to assist and support the individual and the local body in carrying out their tasks.[26]

The six questions addressed by the Program Review process to each federal program are about subsidiarity even though the word is never used to establish whether government should get involved at all and whether, if governments should be involved, any lower-order agency or strategic alliance of many of them might not do the job better. To these governance questions, the Program Review adds questions of efficiency and affordability.[27] The advantage of a framework of this sort is that it does not allow technological adjustments to be made for the sole purpose of efficiency improvement. The governance and efficiency considerations are dealt with as a whole.

This new philosophy provides a rationale for the construction of a new institutional order, which will be of necessity where governance will be and be based bottom-up rather than top-down on needs rather than rights and it will also be more distributed and more decentralized than the old governance system.

Four Vignettes

Donald Schon[28] has suggested that any system (including the Canadian governance system) is composed of a structure, a technology and a theory. The structure consists of the set of roles and relations among members of the organization. The technology refers to the tools used by members of the organization. The theory is the view held by members about the system – its purposes, environment, future. These dimensions hang together and any change in one affects the others.

The transformation of the Canadian governance system has been a compounding of retooling, restructuring and reframing. And, as Schon suggests, each of these changes has triggered adjustments in the other dimensions. What was often a modest alteration of the technology of service delivery could not but affect the nature of the program involved and modify the policy that this program was meant to serve. So we should not discard too quickly what might appear to be a modest tinkering with technology. Often it has proved in Canada a roundabout way to effect more fundamental changes that would not have been palatable if they had been tackled directly.

I will give an example of innovations in each of the three directions, but I will also add a fourth vignette pertaining to an event of the winter of 1999, the signature of a covenant between the federal government and the provinces about the Canadian Social Union. This sort of vague and fuzzy statement is more in the nature of a moral contract than of a legal document. I am using it here mainly as a revelation of the degree to which the *valse-hésitation* egalitarianism-subsidiarity remains unfinished and to illustrate the extent to which the centralized mindset is still at work in Canada.

Food Inspection Agency as Retooling

The creation of the Canadian Food Inspection Agency (CFIA) is a good example of what ensued from the alternative service delivery initiative. It was announced in the March 1996 budget as an alternative way (to the traditional departmental model) of delivering certain services that were offered at the time by Agriculture and Agri-Food Canada, Health Canada, and Fisheries and Oceans Canada. It was meant to reduce overlap and duplication, improve service delivery and improve federal-provincial co-operation through the development of harmonized standards and harmonized enforcement.

The CFIA has integrated all the federally mandated food inspection and quarantine services, but the responsibility for food safety policy and standards remained with Health Canada. From an accountability point of view, it remains analogous to a department, but from an operational point of view, it is more like a corporation in the sense that:

- It receives 20 percent of its resources from the industry in the form of user fees.
- It has greater financial and human resources flexibilities in order to make it a more efficient a deliverer.
- It has the authority to partner with the provincial and local authorities but also to acquire shares or participate in any corporation to implement its mandate.

This agency represents a typical Canadian "adaptation" of the executive agency model to ensure three important elements:

- The ministerial accountability is not compromised.
- The role of government is not diminished.
- It cannot be called "decentralization".[29]

Consequently, it does not have the usual arm's-length agency relationship with the government that the executive agency model would suggest. The CFIA has been successful because of its hybrid nature and of its effort to balance "flexibility and accountability, innovation and tradition".[30]

In this delicate matter where health safety is at issue, the crucial problem of accountability was the major bone of contention. So the Minister had to remain clearly the person who would be accountable for the performance of the CFIA. However, subsection 4(2) of the CFIA Act clearly states that "The Minister may delegate to any person any power, duty or function conferred on the Minister under this Act or any Act or provision that the Agency enforces or administers". It is therefore clear that the CFIA has the possibility of developing into a quite independent unit. This is the drift to be anticipated if the CFIA's first years of operation are not marred by important crises. But the agency is not there yet, as its Website indicates.[31]

Airport Administration as Restructuring

This is a more ambitious initiative through which the Canadian federal government has transferred the operational and management control of airports to locally based transport authorities. These Canadian airport authorities are not-for-profit corporations headed by boards of directors nominated by federal, provincial and municipal governments but also by other participating organizations such as chambers of commerce, boards of trade and consumer and labour groups.

Accountability for the local airport authorities is to the community that the airport serves. The board of the local airport authorities is not only free to use airport revenues to directly support operating costs and capital requirements but to pursue its own broad objectives (to boost trade, tourism, job creation,and so forth) as embodied in the business plan for the local airport. The board also has the power to create wholly owned for-profit subsidiaries and these subsidiaries can become holding companies for other investments or concerns.

Transport Canada continues to ensure safety and security at Canadian airports through aviation regulation and airport certification processes, but the local airport authorities are quite clearly an independent entity. Many of these local authorities have taken a most aggressive stand and make full use of the many new instruments put in their hands to inject a coefficient of "boosterism" in their operations. The case of the Winnipeg Airport Authorities is most interesting on this front.[32]

This restructuring policy began in 1992 when four local airport authorities were put in place in Vancouver, Edmonton, Calgary and Montreal, but all airports are in the process of being shifted to this new management structure.

This is a more dramatic transformation since it clearly changes the accountability process from top-down to bottom-up. Financial and human resources flexibilities are such that (except for the transition period where employees choosing to leave the public service to join the local corporation are assured of employment for two years) the local authorities are unconstrained. So it is clearly an initiative that entails both decentralization and a diminished role for the federal government.

As an experiment in governance, it transforms the roles and relationships of many of the groups involved. It is not clear, however, to what extent the residual regulatory role of Transport Canada will choose to be intrusive (especially through the airport certification processes) or benign. Similarly, it is not clear, in the long run, whether the decentralization-cum-reduction-of-the-federal-government-role will turn out to be full or hollow. For the time being, it would appear that the restructuring has been effective and the freedom of action of the local airport authorities significant.

Nunavut as Reframing

Nunavut is the new name given to the central and eastern portion of what used to be the Northwest Territories of Canada. It covers the northernmost portion of the country and became, as of April 1, 1999, the newest official territory of Canada. It is 1,900,000 square kilometres, or one-fifth the size of Canada, with a population of some 25,000, of which some 80 percent are Inuit.

This new territory is important much less because of the fact that it redesigns the map of Canada than because it has introduced a new variety of participatory democracy in Canada.

It is well known that the British constitutional law tradition cannot easily deal with diversity.[33] Indeed, Tully uses strong language when he states that "the last three hundred years is a partial forgery. While masquarading as universal, it is imperial".[34] Canada has lived under the shadow of the British constitutional law tradition and has suffered from the "empire of uniformity" that it casts. Indeed, Trudeau's Canada has taken the doctrine of uniformity to its limits: citizenship has come to mean an eradication of cultural diversity.

This is a perspective that has been criticized severely over the last few decades and in Canada there has been pressure over the last 20 years to review the way in which the First Nations have been allowed to partake in the governance of the country. A variety of renewed arrangements with the First Nations have been proposed and approved over the last few years, and they are likely to act as an important catalyst in the transformation of our philosophy of governance, especially as it deals with diversity.

The process of accommodation with the First Nations may indeed be the only route that is likely to lead to a rediscovery and a formal recognition of cultural diversity and toward a more balanced polyarchy, where differences and dissent will be less systematically suppressed. Tully has showed how these debates are likely to create an intercultural common ground, a new lexicon capable of dealing with diversity. This may hold the key to a broader capacity to deal with interculturalism.

In that context, the creation of Nunavut is a particularly important moment of reframing. Not only is Canada recognizing formally the existence of this new territory, but it has condoned an ethnic-based territory and a new "style of governing" – a consensus style of government based on an elaborate system of public engagement, consultation and political trade-offs.

We could easily see this undangerous precedent being used by Quebec as a basis for legal pluralism and probably the basis for a new diverse federalism. Indeed, the tensions that exist in Canada between federal and provincial authorities are still largely resolved either by administrative devices or by political confrontation. It may well be that what Nunavut proposes is another manner of seeing things that may have a significant impact in the longer haul.

Insignificant as it may appear on the governance scene, the creation of Nunavut is a big step in the process of transformation from the old governance to the new. Nunavut has put in place an evolving administrative apparatus that slowly drifts toward a more distributed form of governance. Citizen engagement, consultation, intersectoral partnering and federal-provincial negotiated arrangements are bound to blossom. In fact, the Canadian governance regime is being devolved truly in one small segment of the national territory. In so doing, it is putting more and more power in the hands of people, and even the population is beginning to understand, as Stephen Carter would put it, that devolution is the only radical way to "truly place power in the hands of people".[35]

Social Union as Moral Contract

A central feature of the fiscally driven deficit reduction of the Canadian federal government has been the drastic reduction in the federal transfers to the provinces for health, education and social welfare. These transfer cuts have forced all of the provinces to effect dramatic transformations in those areas.

As the federal government reached a situation of fiscal balance, the pressures have become very strong on the part of the electorate and of the provincial authorities for the federal government to restore in part the fiscal basis on which the provision of these crucial services is built. Given the important message of the federal government that centralization is important (1) as a strong basis for inter-regional redistribution and (2) as an assurance that Canadians wherever they are will benefit from services meeting national standards in this area, there has been some pressure for the federal government to develop an agreement with the provinces about the way in which the Canadian Social Union can best be managed.

The prime minister of Canada was never keen about such an accord, and he made it quite clear that he could easily live without it. In the former governance system, the last resort is always some top-down federal unilateral intervention. There have been suggestions that a Social Union Agreement might limit considerably such action. This was not to please the prime minister.

On February 4, 1999, the Canadian federal government and the Canadian provinces (except Quebec) signed a new three-year covenant defining the way in which the Canadian Social Union will be managed. It should be remembered that in the Canadian context, social policy is a provincial prerogative. However, in a world in which health and education are prominent "goods" for the citizens, there has been a tendency for the federal government to encroach on provincial jurisdiction in those areas. Indeed, one of the most contentious areas of federal-provincial squabbles has been the social policy field. The Canadian prime minister in power has pushed for the unilateral introduction (without any consultation) of specific initiatives in areas that happen to be within provincial jurisdiction (e.g., the Millennium Scholarship Fund) and has used a rhetoric of compulsive centralization requirements in the name of "much needed" redistribution.

In the debates preceding the Social Union Agreement and the new transfers to the provinces for health care purposes, the prime minister sounded like Louis XIV when he mused in public that sometime on Monday he felt like giving the provinces more money, and then Tuesday he did not. Very much as in the Trudeau era of the late 1970s, we feel at times that Canada would still appear to be in the throes of a rule by self-righteous elites claiming to know better. However, in parallel with this posturing, there has been a multitude of initiatives that have contributed to building different aspects of the new governance regime such as, for instance, the devolution of training to the provinces.

The occasion of a broad negotiated social contract was seen as an important gauge of how far Canada has travelled down the road from the centralizing, homogenizing and hierarchical former governance regime toward a more non-centralizing, distributed and associative governance regime.

Many had expected the Social Union document to embody the principles of the new governance, at least to a degree. In fact, the new covenant, if anything, is a step backward. It establishes that the federal government must consult the provinces before it takes any initiatives in the social policy area, and that it must give the provinces some prior notice and offer to seek their advice. But the new accord establishes clearly the authority of the federal government to do so, an authority it did not have until now. The provinces, very pressed for cash, may have sold out their autonomy in these areas for a few billion dollars.[36]

While such a pragmatic settlement may appear to be a step forward in that it has produced an agreement to legitimize federal intervention, we may also see it as a step backward in that it would appear to slow down the progress toward the new distributed governance. Given the centralized mindset that prevails in certain quarters in Ottawa, it is almost certain that this "new legitimacy" will be used to the fullest extent by a federal government that seeks maximal visibility in the delivery of services to the citizenry.

Conclusion

The four types of innovations I have singled out have been used to different degrees in the different sectors. The first two – more in line with the traditional executive agency tradition – may not have been used as boldly in Canada as they have in Australia and New Zealand, but they have been used. It is not clear, however, at this time if they will trigger permanent governance modifications. The last two are fuzzier and may have been used more boldly in Canada, because they allowed the changes in the governance process to proceed at a pace that remained very slow even if they dealt with fundamental governance dimensions. It may well turn out that on these last two fronts, Canada may have something to contribute to the transnational debate on governance.

Notes

1. This paper was prepared for the Leadership Program of the Public Service Commissioners of Australia (Commonwealth, states and territories) and New Zealand and delivered by videoconference from Ottawa on June 1, 1999, as part of a session on Processes of Governance. A version of the paper has been published in *Optimum - The Journal of Public Sector Management*, 29, no. 2/3 (1999). The assistance of Chris Wilson and David Zussman is gratefully acknowledged.

2. Malcom Ross (ed.), *Our Sense of Identity* (Toronto: The Ryerson Press, 1954)

3. Malcom Ross, ibid., p. ix.

4. Russell Jacoby, *The End of Utopia: Politics and Culture in an Age of Apathy* (New York: Basic Books, 1999), xii.

5. Michael H. Best, *The New Competition* (Cambridge: Harvard University Press, 1990); Gilles Paquet, *Governance Through Social Learning* (Ottawa: University of Ottawa Press, 1999a); Gilles Paquet, "Tectonic Changes in Canadian Governance". *How Ottawa Spends 1999-2000: Shape Shifting Canadian Governance Toward the 21st Century,* ed. Leslie Pal (Toronto: Oxford University Press, 1999b), 75-111.

6. G. Paquet, op. cit., 1999a, chap. 3.

7. *The Globe and Mail,* "Free Trade 10 Years On: Good or Bad for Canada?" (May 28, 1999) A15.

8. Gilles Paquet, "The Downtrodden Administrative Route", *Inroads,* 5 (1996), 117-121.

9. Gilles Paquet and Jeffrey Roy, "Prosperity Through Networks: The Bottom-Up Strategy That Might Have Been", *Mid-Life Crises ed. Susan Phillips* (Ottawa: Carleton University Press, 1995), 137-158; Gilles Paquet and Robert Shepherd, "The Program Review Process: A Deconstruction", *Life Under the Knife* ed., G. Swimmer (Ottawa: Carleton University Press, 1996), 39-72.

10. Gilles Paquet. "Alternative Service Delivery: Transforming the Practices of Governance", *Alternative Service Delivery: Sharing Governance in Canada,* eds. Robin Ford and David Zussman (Toronto: KPMG/IPAC, 1997a), 31-52.

11. Gilles Paquet, "Gouvernance distribuée et habitus centralisateur", *Transactions of the Royal Society of Canada,* series 6, vol. 6 (1995): 97-111.

12. The use of the word "anti-democratic" may generate some unease, so some clarification is in order. Our governance regimes are complex and unstable mixtures of four broths: the democratic tradition anchored in ancient Athens, the republican tradition rooted in imperial Rome and certain medieval Italian cities, the liberal tradition traceable to medieval Europe but more clearly to Locke and Montesquieu, and the tradition of the rule of law, together with "the existence of state agencies that are legally empowered - and factually willing and able - to take actions ranging from routine oversight to criminal sanctions or impeachment in relation to possibly unlawful actions or omissions by other agents or agencies of the state". Any undue weight given to one or another of these components may corrupt the mixture. "Democracy without liberalism and republicanism would become majority tyranny; liberalism without democracy and republicanism would become plutocracy; and republicanism without liberalism and democracy would degenerate into the paternalistic rule of a self-righteous elite". And without the possibility of redress when there is encroachment by one state agency upon the lawful authority of another, caesarism is near. (Guillermo O'Donnell. "Horizontal Accountabilities in New Democracies", *Journal of Democracy,* 9, no. 3

(1998): 112-126.)

All these forms of corruption have been experienced, and they may, in each case, be the result of either a lack or an excess. For instance, observers have denounced the deleterious effects of the emergence of hyperdemocracy in North America: indeed, democratization and distrust are presented as the twin hallmarks of America's hyperdemocracy. The insistence on greater exposure and participatory openness in the political environment and the incessant polling "off-the-top-of-the-head" opinions have led to some destructive uses of the tyranny of the majority: a series of disconnected adversarial contests, a general atmosphere of contentiousness, political debate without deliberation, a public that is courted by "sound bites" but not engaged in a meaningful conversation, a world of deepening distrust. A democratic deficit may also be a source of concern (Hugh Heclo, "Hyperdemocracy", *The Wilson Quarterly*, vol. 23, no. 1 (1999): 62-71).

13. Stephen L. Carter, *The Dissent of the Governed* (Cambridge: Harvard University Press, 1998); Gilles Paquet, "Governance and Social Cohesion: Survivability in the 21st Century", *Transactions of the Royal Society of Canada*, Series 6, vol. 9, (1999c): 85-116.

14. Frederick Lee Morton, "The Charter of Rights: Myth and Reality", *After Liberalism*, ed., W.D. Gairdner (Toronto: Stoddart, 1998), 33-61.

15. S. Carter, op. cit., 20.

16. Gilles Paquet. "States, Communities and Markets: The Distributed Governance Scenario", *The Evolving Nation-State in a Global Information Era: Policy Challenges. Vol. 5. The Bell Canada Papers in Economic and Public Policy*, ed. Thomas J. Courchene (Kingston: John Deustch Institute for the Study of Economic Policy, 1997b), 25-46.

17. Gilles Paquet, "Federalism as Social Technology", *Options* ed., J. Evans, (Toronto: University of Toronto Press, 1977), 281-302.

18. Gilles Paquet, *Oublier la Révolution tranquille: Pour une nouvelle socialité* (Montreal: Liber, 1999d).

19. Paquet, op. cit., 1999a, part 3.

20. Robert Alan Dahl, *Democracy and Its Critics* (New Haven: Yale University Press, 1989).

21. Robert N. Bellah et al., *The Good Society* (New York: Alfred A. Knopf, 1991), 135-136.

22. Dee Hock uses the word "chaord" (from "chaos" and "order") to refer to "a self-organizing, adaptive, non-linear, complex system, whether physical, biological or social, the behavior of which exhibits characteristics of both order and chaos or, loosely translated to business terminology, cooperation and competition"(6). As founder of VISA, he has created a company that is "an inside-out holding company" in which the 23,000 financial institutions that create its products are "at one and the same time, its owners, its members, its customers, is subjects and its superiors" (14). This sort of organization not only embodies subsidiarity as a founding principle but also the principle that the chaordic organization is owned by its members. "No function should be performed by any part of the whole that could reasonably be done by any more peripheral part, and no power vested in any part that might reasonable be exercised by a lesser part" (13). It must embrace diversity and change, but no individual or institution and no combination of either or both should be able to dominate the deliberations. To ensure that this is the case, VISA has had to ensure continuous learning through continued feedback loops (D.W. Hock, "The Chaordic Organization", *World Business Academy Perspectives*, 9, no. 1 (1995): 5-18.

23. Gilles Paquet. "Slouching Toward a New Governance", *Optimum*, 27, no. 3, (1997c), 44-50.

24. Alexis de Tocqueville, *De la démocratie en Amérique, Tomes I and II* (Paris: Gallimard [orig. 1840], 1961), 104.

25. Ibid., 189.

26. Gilles Paquet, "Reinventing Governance", *Opinion Canada*, 2, no. 2 (1994): 1-5.

27. Gilles Paquet and Robert Shepherd, op. cit.

28. Donald A. Schon, *Beyond the Stable State* (New York: Norton, 1971),v

29. Ronald L. Doering, "Alternative Service Delivery: The Case of the Canadian Food Inspection Agency", Paper presented at a Workshop at the Department of Justice, November 25, 1996, 9).

30. Ibid., 1.

31. See http://www.cfia-acia.agr.ca

32. See http://www.waa.ca

33. James Tully, *Strange Multiplicity* (Cambridge: Cambridge University Press, 1995), chap. 3.

34. Ibid., 96.

35. Much can be learned about the newest Canadian territory and facts concerning its transition to autonomy at:
http://arcticcircle.uconn.edu/ArcticCircle/SEEJ/Nunavut

36. André Burelle, "Mise en tutelle des provinces", *Le Devoir*, (February 15, 1999); Claude Ryan, "The Agreement on the Canadian Social Union as Seen by a Quebec Federalist", *Inroads*, 8, (1999): 25-41.

16

Australian and Canadian Film Industries: A Personal Perspective

JUDITH MCCANN

Introduction

My contribution to this volume is a personal one, reflecting my experience in Canada at the Canadian Film Development Corporation, now known as Telefilm Canada, and most recently as CEO of the South Australian Film Corporation. Recently, and with much reluctance, the Australian Broadcasting Authority was required to accept New Zealand programming as "Australian Content" under provisions of the Closer Economic Relations Agreement between those two countries. My experience as head of the New Zealand Film Commission may now provide some more immediate relevance, though I should explain that the High Court decision that gave rise to this treatment of New Zealand programming is not one that I agree with on cultural grounds. But more later.

Now, just a brief background on the South Australian Film Corporation (SAFC). It is the oldest film corporation in Australia. It was established by the Dunstan Labor Government in 1972 and charged with developing a film industry in South Australia. Among the many feature films and television mini-series it produced were some of Australia's great classics: *Storm Boy, Sunday Too Far Away, Breaker Morant, The Shiralee, Robbery Under Arms.* An outstanding number of now internationally-renowned directors worked with and honed their craft at the SAFC: Peter Weir (*The Truman Show*), Bruce Beresford (*Black Robe*), Gillian Armstrong (*Little Women*), and Scott Hicks (*Shine*) to name a few. However, ownership by a state government of a film production company with its concomitant investment – and risk – required by studio facilities and production is an uncomfortable affair, particularly when it is seen by the emerging private sector industry as a competitor. The SAFC was the subject of five reviews over the space of about eight years: the last in 1993 resulted in the government's decision to remove it from the role of producer in its own right and refocus on industry development and attraction of production, and the flow-on economic and employment benefits, into South Australia as a supplement for local independent production.

In short, the SAFC is unique among film agencies in Australia. It has an iconic if controversial history not dissimilar to the National Film Board in Canada, and now operates within a dual cultural and industrial framework rather like a Canadian provincial film development agency. Its financial resources are modest; it continues to manage its Studios as a "home" for the industry, and it has reclaimed some of its former reputation for quality through its financial participation in recent feature films, television dramas and documentaries, as well as in short films, including some by Canadian film makers now living in Adelaide.

Snapshots of Australia and Canada

Australia has a smaller domestic market than Canada. Its population is approximately 18 million, compared to Canada's 30 million. In 1997, Australia ranked 15th, with 34 films, according to the Screen Digest world production figures; Canada ranked 11th with 65 films. (By comparison, India was ranked first with 697 and the U.S.A. second with 676.)

Both nations provide subsidies for their film and television industries in the interests of reflecting their unique national identity and cultural values. In Australia, approximately $100 million is injected annually through federal programs under the Australian Film Finance Corporation and the Australian Film Commission, 10BA[1] tax concessions and state government film agencies. This public investment represents an average of between 35 and 49 percent of the financing for Australian independently produced feature film and television drama. By contrast, in Canada, according to Pricewaterhouse Coopers' (PwC) 1999 Economic

Profile for the Canadian Film & Television Production Association, public funding represents about 18 percent of the 1997-98 total of $1.09 billion in certified Canadian productions, or approximately $200 million.

Both countries regulate free-to-air television and cable specialty channels to ensure a level of local content. Though Australia does not suffer from the spillover effect of American networks, the gradual introduction of cable is bringing with it increased choice and more non-Australian programming. The eligibility of New Zealand's television production to now qualify as "local" has as yet had no measurable impact.

Figures on dollar value of production reflect the differences in size of the two industries. Canada records certified Canadian production for feature films and television in 1997-98 totalling $1.09 billion. Australia's total for 1996-97' according to the Australian Bureau of Statistics is $1.54 billion. However, of that Australian total, independent feature film and television drama production represented only $367 million, with documentaries adding approximately $50 million. In summary, Canada's $1.09 billion compares to Australia's $417 million.

Perceptions About Performance

Australian films have earned a reputation for attracting audiences within their domestic market. This achievement can be measured by performance at the box office – the proverbial "bums on seats" gauge. Among the top five films of all time at the Australian box office (as at June 30, 1998) are *Crocodile Dundee*, second only to *Titanic* and followed by *Babe*, even though it was fully financed by Universal.

Indeed, these are joined by *Strictly Ballroom, The Man from Snowy River, The Adventure of Priscilla Queen of the Desert* and *Muriel's Wedding* within the top 50 films in Australia – each generating an impressive box office from a high of $48 million to a still impressive low of $15 million. Granted, top price for admission in Australian cinemas is about $12.

In Canada, the box office achievement of domestic feature films has been much more modest. Most recently in Quebec, where local audiences respond enthusiastically to the cultural and linguistic offerings of local film makers, *Les Boys* generated $6 million. But English-language movies with few exceptions have encountered an almost underwhelming response.

Internationally, alongside the two *Dundees*, there have been other notable commercial successes such as *Mad Max, Shine, The Castle* and *The Piano.* (Though, as a former head of the New Zealand Film Commission, I must say that, aside from the Australian base of the production company and the French origin of the financing, what was up there on the screen belonged decidedly to Aotearoa, New Zealand).

The international successes of Canadian feature films are significant in terms of critical acclaim won by directors such as Dens Arcand, Atom Egoyan, the late Yves Simoneau and Phil Borsos (Australian-born), and once-again Canadian resident Norman Jewison.

With television, the comparisons are more difficult given the structural dissimilarities between the two countries. Most Australians only have five channels to choose from: two publicly owned (Australian Broadcasting Corporation and the Special Broadcasting Service) and three commercial and regulated channels (one of which is largely owned by CanWest). There were only 840,000 pay TV subscribers, representing 12 percent of households, in 1998.

AC Nielsen ratings for both Sydney and Melbourne in 1997 have *Forrest Gump* at 40 to 42. By comparison, and leaving aside Australian rules football and movies, the local drama series *Blue Heelers* scored between 36 and 40 ahead of *Friends*. One of my several regrets at leaving Australia last month (along with jacarandas blooming in spring and the Barossa Valley vineyards) was missing the rest of this season's *Seachange* – an ABC/Artist Services drama that has been consistently winning audiences of 2 million and beating *60 Minutes* on Sunday night.

It is clear from Australian television ratings that Australian audiences enjoy watching their own stories – and accents. Indeed, the general consternation at having Kiwi accents as "local content" seems to underline their continuing affinity for a sense of national identity.

Canada's own top-rating television varies dramatically between French – and English – language audiences. The PwC Report states that nine French-language local drama series in 1997-98 drew audiences of over 1 million: *La Petite Vie* drew 3.3 million viewers. By comparison, only one English language Canadian series drew over 1 million viewers: *This Hour Has 22 Minutes*, which attracted 1.8 million and which was on two plays per week. Another eight English drama series drew between just under 500,000 to just under 900,000.

Reality Check

The reality beneath this perceived Australian advantage is quite fragile. By way of illustration for feature films in the international marketplace, European Union cinema admission figures based on a film's country of origin for 1996 ranked Australia at number 8, ahead of Canada at number 10; percentage share for Australia was still only just under 2 percent, with Canada at 0.48 percent. By comparison, U.S. films held nearly 72 percent!

From a cultural as well as an economic perspective, the percentage of the gross box office held by local films is significant. In Australia, local films accounted for 8 percent in 1996, 5 percent in 1997, but may now be as low as 2 percent, the level held by Canadian films in Canada, according to PwC.

It must give public policy makers pause when, despite the annual investment or subsidy through tax concessions and credits, movies reflecting our local creative talents fail to attract the very audiences they were designed to reach.

Simultaneous releases by Hollywood in the North American market are backed by huge promotional campaigns: PwC gives a comparative example of a Canadian feature film having a budget for prints and advertising, commonly referred to as its "p & a", on its cinema release of $150,000. By comparison, U.S. movies being released simultaneously in Canada and the U.S. enjoyed $75 million promotional campaigns.

This situation is not dissimilar to what is now emerging in Australia where, aside from some scheduling disparities to meet school and summer holidays, most Hollywood blockbusters are now released within weeks if not days of their North American debut, and Australia's syndicated edition of *Entertainment Tonight* has instant interviews with the stars by the Australian host. The latest box office figures for current releases have only one Australian feature – *Two Hands* – at just over $5 million. The next closest are under $500,000.

Television in Australia remains reasonably secure for the moment. But the inexorable march of cable/specialty channels and the "e-world" will have an impact on audience loyalty.

Global Marketplace and Survival of Integrity

What Australia and Canada share in film and television to an ever greater extent, in my view, is the challenge of matching economic reality with cultural integrity.

Both are relatively small nations that face a very enormous challenge: with the exception of Quebec, both are English-speaking and therefore among the most vulnerable societies to the cultural and, more importantly, commercial influence of the U.S. multinationals. (And I do include News Corporation as owner of 20th Century Fox, which still holds its AGM in Adelaide, South Australia, to avoid having too many shareholders present, word has it.) Australia may have Aussie rules football; Canada used to have hockey. Australia used to have the geographic protection of the Pacific and Indian Oceans; Canada never enjoyed such a luxury.

Ever increasingly, Australia is at risk of following Canada's example as a film industry intimately intertwined with, if not serving Hollywood.

The Factors Influencing that Trend are:

Growth of Multi- and Mega-plexes

Total number of cinema screens rose from 712 in 1988 to 1,422 in 1997, increasing seating capacity by 100,000. Admissions rose from 37.4 million in 1988 to 76 million in 1997, increasing gross box office from $182 million to $584 million. Adelaide has one of the world's largest with 31 screens and projectionists on golf carts. When asked why build such a large one in a sprawling city of 1 million, the Greater Union representative said, "Why not?" Now that's business sense.

However, this growth in screens is not producing an increase in choice. In 1988, 281 movies were released in Australia, 36 Australian films and 167 U.S. movies; in 1997, 282 movies were released, 29 from Australia and 185 from the U.S. Employing those same two years, films from elsewhere varied: New Zealand remained at 2, Asia went from 6 to 8, France went from 10 to 17, rest of Europe went from 22 to 13, U.K. went from 31 to 20, Canada went from 3 to 7, and "other" went from 3 to 7. Obviously, availability of films is influenced by production levels in each country. Still, the doubling of movie screens over the same period has been matched by a whopping addition of one movie overall available to

Australian cinema goers. In reality, now Australians are getting to see more U.S. movies.

Costs of Distribution and Promotion

With Hollywood movies going out with 300 prints, Australian movies are now forced to compete with 90 print releases (average cost per print is $5,000) and competitive advertising spends that cannot be so equitably amortized. *Shine*, for example, in 1996 went out on a limited release, expanded when it won "word of mouth" and a record number of Australian Film Awards and then, having contracted, expanded again in 1997 when it was nominated for the Oscars and won for Geoffrey Rush as Best Actor. It made money on its Australian release for its distributor Ronin Films and for its investors – the SAFC was one! Five distributors, only one of which (Village Roadshow) is Australian-owned, account for 87 percent of the gross box office. The second tier of distributors, all but one Australian-owned, recorded an increased share from 10 to 13 percent between 1996 and 1997; however, this increase does include the one film released in 1997 by the one foreign-owned distributor, PolyGram – *Bean*, which brought in nearly $20 million. In reality, it is getting harder for Australian films to find their natural audience; and new movies are being released in time for Australian Film Institute (AFI). Award nominations in September, at the rate of at least one a week.

Studios and Locations

Di Laurentis started the Gold Coast Studios and was bailed out by the Queensland government, resulting in the Warner Village Roadshow Studios hosting *The Thin Red Line* and numerous other offshore movies and TV series. Then Rupert Murdoch was offered a sweet deal on the Sydney Showgrounds and now Fox Studios is giving us *The Matrix, Mission Impossible 2* and its one Australian "in-house" director Baz Lurmann, of *Strictly Ballroom* and *Romeo and Juliet* fame, with *Moulin Rouge*. Next in line is Melbourne with Viacom and local company Crawford's Docklands Studios. Soon Sydney will look as familiar to world audiences as Vancouver or Toronto – but no one will know why! In reality, however, these big studios just mean that Aussie crews will be working on other people's productions. (As an aside, South Australia's deserts have featured recently in Jane Campion's soon-to-be-released *Holy Smoke* and several American sci-fi movies. In August this year, Adelaide served briefly as Toronto for a new Australian children's television series produced in South Australia – *The Adventures of Chuck Finn*, about a teenage boy who moves from Toronto to the Murray River with his family [Dad is a university professor studying soil desalination]. John Ralston Saul was in Adelaide speaking at a conference and, on behalf of the production company, I asked whether he would be prepared to share his Canadian accent in a small role. He declined. Little did we know at that time what his future supporting role would be).

Public Financing

Australia has been the victim of government deficit reduction strategies with no increases if not cuts. With offshore production increasing from three with a value of $34 million in 1990-91 to 15 with a value of $202 million in 1995-96 (and dropping slightly to 13 with a value of $194 million in 1996-97), there is a growing concern in the independent industry in Australia that governments may think the industry is healthy from a purely economic perspective. This offshore activity may be employing crews, but how secure is the public commitment toward the Australian stories being told. The industry's case for increased assistance to compete more effectively is not aided by some Australian journalists: a November 18, 1999, article in Sydney's Sun Herald by Andrew Bolt asked the question "Why hand over more tax dollars to make unwatchable movies?" – a reference to recent gritty urban dramas like *Head On* and *Praise.* In reality, the Commonwealth government's commitment to a culturally distinct industry cannot be said to be generously enthusiastic.

Tax Incentives

Australia used to have the most generous tax incentives, much to the envy of Canadian producers, as I recall: 160 percent write-off and tax-free returns to boot. It's now at 100 percent and returns are taxable. 10BA has continued to deliver annually some $20 million from private investors. Indeed, SAFC last year was a partner investor along with private money in a feature by a first time director. Earlier this year, the federal government introduced two "pilot" FLICs – Film Licensed Investment Companies operating under a new concept that would allow investors to obtain the 100 percent deduction for investing the company, and the company to employ those funds to invest in a variety of productions. Unfortunately, the head of the Australian Taxation Office (ATO) announced just prior to the end of the tax year that the ATO would be investigating a number of potentially fraudulent taxation schemes involving film, but neglected to say that FLICs were not among such schemes. The two FLICs which were on the market for $20 million each raised only $2.5 million between them. Now the pressure is on from some quarters to introduce tax credits similar to Canada's and to make these available to offshore production. In reality, I suspect, the Australian Taxation Office would like private investment incentives for film to disappear.

Co-Productions - the Genuine Ones

Australia has co-production treaties with a number of countries, including Canada and New Zealand, though nowhere near Canada's record of more than 40 such agreements. However, unlike Canada's enthusiastic embracing of the concept of co-production, Australia's industry largely regards such cultural compromises with suspicion. The prime such example is *Green Card*, an Australian-France co-production directed by Australian Peter Weir, shot in New York and starring American Andie MacDowell and France's Gérard Depardieu. Australia is therefore very cautious about co-productions. Having administered such agreements at Telefilm Canada and the New Zealand Film Commission, I continue to believe they can provide an equitable collaborative structure and ensure some cultural balance over time.

I'll give you two personal examples of co-productions that reflect stories of cultural significance to one or other country. *Black Robe* was directed by Australian Bruce Beresford, under a co-production between Robert Lantos as Canadian producer and Sue Milliken as Australian producer. More recently, *Sally Marshall Is Not an Alien* was co-produced between a South Australian company, Infinity Pictures, and Cinar, in Montreal: it is based on a novel by South Australian author Amanda McKay and directed by South Australian director Mario Andreacchio, and stars Canadian Natalie Vansier. The first example was shot in Canada, the second in Adelaide. The first brings to the big screen a quintessentially Canadian epic; the second an intimate and much-valued children's story on curricula in schools around Australia. *Black Robe* brought in over $2 million at the Australian box office in 1992; *Sally* this year brought in almost $1.3 million. Proof, in my opinion, that co-productions do have cultural as well as artistic value – and make commercial sense. However, in reality and with public investment already stretched to meet demand, it is extremely difficult for an Australian potential co-producer to interest the Australian Film Finance Corporation in investing in a co-production that is not firmly rooted in the Australian culture.

Pre-sales

Pre-sales, that is, selling off the family treasures to finance the house being built to display them. Australian producers are increasingly required to obtain offshore financing to assist with raising the money to produce the film. This is a standard industry practice, but it holds some challenges. One challenge is creative compromises: *Shine* was eventually sold in a bidding frenzy after it screened at Sundance to both Miramax and New Line, the U.S. – based distributors that had passed on the film at pre-production as they doubted the then-unknown Geoffrey Rush could "carry" the film. However, the more difficult challenge lies in the current global marketplace: too many movies being made and all searching for the once lucrative and now illusive U.S. sale. Why buy "on spec" on the basis of a script and a team of talented people, when you can wait to see the finished product at Cannes or some other market and then decide what commercial value it might hold? Sure, you may then have to pay more – as was the case with *Shine* – but you also might decide wisely to "pass" altogether.

Finding the 20 to 35 percent of the budget from the marketplace remains the greatest challenge for Australian producers – after getting the script right, of course. Miramax, New Line, Fox Icon and even Channel 4 from the U.K. all have representatives in Australia who are constantly monitoring the development of promising scripts and promising new directors. All have to defer to their bosses overseas; few feature film projects have yet to pass successfully through that gauntlet. And if Miramax and New Line have "passed", there are few others who will take the risk. This reality keeps budgets down: the average Australian feature film budget remains at around $3.5 million, slightly higher than in Canada. Two recent "big" budget Australian features – *In a Savage Land* from director Bill Bennett and *Passion*, the Percy Granger epic from Peter Duncan – have not performed well at their domestic box office despite their ambitions. Both have, by the way, been acquired for release in Canada by Motion International, so you will be able to make your own assessment early next year. I think they are fine films, as did the German investors who contributed significantly!

The reality is that pre-sales are proving increasingly difficult. Only now in Australia are there financial institutions emerging that are prepared to "gap" finance the missing production budget. But the costs of that financing are extremely high, and public film investment agencies are still proving reluctant to subsidize that cost.

The Lure of Hollywood

Peter Weir, Bruce Beresford, Gillian Armstrong, Jocelyn Moorhouse, P.J. Hogan, Jane Campion, Scott Hicks, the list goes on of acclaimed Australian directors who can now make films with enormous budgets fully financed by the U.S. Studios. Many, like Scott Hicks, with his new feature *Snow Falling on Cedars*, or Peter Weir, with *The Truman Show*, carry out post-production at home in Australia. All have the relative artistic freedom to chose what stories they wish to tell, moving beyond the cultural specificity of the Australian films that won them international recognition and made them "bankable" directors for Hollywood, much like Canada's Atom Egoyan. Several of these directors, along with acclaimed cinematographers like Geoffrey Simpson, trained at the Australian Film Television and Radio School (AFTRS). All have benefited from public investment in their projects or careers. The debate goes on about the apparent emphasis by Commonwealth and state film agencies in taking high risks investing in first-time feature film directors, and their subsequent inability to get a piece of the action on their next and more commercially successful films. It is an unresolvable debate. But the reality is that Hollywood's financial resources and global clout will continue to attract the world's best – just as it has from its earliest beginnings.

Style of Filmmaking

Sunday Too Far Away remains a great Australian classic, so too does *Going Down the Road* in Canada. I've been trying to assess in my own mind what I have seen in both countries that might be distinct or similar. Does Australia possess the equivalent of a Denis Arcand with *Le Déclin de l'Empire Américain* or *Jesus of Montreal* (which did extremely well in both New Zealand and Australia)? Intelligent, thought-provoking filmmaking. I think it does in a Paul Cox with *Man of Flowers* and his latest, *Innocence* now in final post production at the SAFC, and in a Rolf De Heer with *The Quiet Room* and *Dance Me To My Song* – both in Official Competition in Cannes (the only Australian director to have had two consecutive films so honoured). Historical, well, there is *Mon Oncle Antoine* to match *On Our Selection*, and a *Grey Fox* to match *Man from Snowy River*. Canada has delivered movies that explore the vast landscape and the gritty urban realities, as has Australia. We have both shared (as another co-production) the curious vision of a New Zealand director, Vincent Ward, in *Map of the Human Heart*. And very recently, the Genie Award nominations were announced, including among the films being so honoured *Sunshine*, the historical drama about three generations of Hungarian Jews in Hungary. Similarly, at Australia's recent AFI Awards, *In a Savage Land* – a historical drama about love and anthropology in the Trobriand Islands – received several nominations.

I honestly don't know how one can encapsulate a cultural voice. But I will suggest that perhaps Australia's big-heartedness has been most successfully channelled into cinema with the likes of *Priscilla*, *Muriel* and *The Castle*; whereas Canada's has been channelled onto *SCTV* and *Saturday Night Live* as the Belushis, John Candy and Jim Carrey subtly took over America's concept of humour.

Why Do Australia and Canada Care About Film?

The moving image, combined now with sound, is one of the most modern art forms. It too has celebrated its centenary. What is emerging now with new media is but a variation on that art form. We nurture our visual artists, our musicians, dancers, playwrights and authors because they give voice to who we are. So too do our filmmakers. And because as individuals our tastes differ, some of us may agree with the very dour assessment of an Andrew Bolt. But I for one would feel less enriched if I had not sat mesmerized by Scott Hicks' *Shine*, disturbed deeply by David Cronenberg's *Dead Ringers* or laughing away at John Polson's *Siam Sunset*.

The industries – involving the real indigenous independent producers, directors and screenwriters and craftspeople – in both countries are fragile. Aside from the few larger, publicly traded companies such as Alliance Atlantis, Cinar, Motion, and so forth in Canada, and Beyond, Southern Star, Becker, and so on in Australia, the film industries are essentially "cottage" industries. These larger players gain their financial stability from mass production for television, and dabble in the movies. The smaller companies try to survive on making at best one feature every two or three years.

Australia, like Canada, has made a concerted effort to re-address the once silent cinematic voices of its indigenous people, the Aboriginal and Torres Strait Island population. As just one but crucial example, the Australian Film Commission's *From Sand to Celluloid* series of six short dramas broadcast on SBS has been followed with another series. Australia's multicultural society is being examined in movies like *Head On*, Ana Kokinos' raw story of 24 hours in the life of a young Greek gay man, and *Floating Life*, Clara Law's moving study of Hong Kong immigrants.

Canada is undoubtedly the stronger of the two in purely industrial terms. Its proximity to the U.S. and the "idiosyncratic accent" of Canadian actors, plus the value of a favourable exchange rate and tax credits, have attracted an enormous level of production activity. But I believe Australia's counter balancing strength remains still its very rich talent base and its cinema voice, which has proven its power to deliver entertainment valued by its own audience and, from time to time, by international audiences.

However, regardless of the relative strengths in either country, those voices will be stilled if government does not continue to tolerate the inevitable failures and sustain support for sustainable levels of filmmaking and to celebrate the successes. And the astounding record of from whence we have come will be less vital without the ongoing flow of contemporary gems.

Sources for Statistical Data

Get The Picture, 5th Edition. Australian Film Commission. December 1998.

The Canadian Film and Television Industry A 1999 Profile, A Report Produced by the Canadian Film and Television Production Association in Cooperation with l'Association des producteurs de films et de la télévision du Québec. February 1999. Economic Profile prepared by PricewaterhouseCoopers.

Note

1. 10BA is officially known as "Division 10BA" of the Australian Income Tax regulations which provides for private investors to treat qualifying film investments as an income tax deduction.

17

A Practitioner's View of Comparative Governance in Australia and Canada

GREG WOOD

How do systems of government in Australia and Canada operate? Do they differ in practice? As High Commissioner, I worked for and within one government, that of Australia. At the same time I am paid to observe, understand, collaborate with, negotiate with and influence that of another country, Canada. Understanding the mechanics of the two systems of governance is a part of my professional stock in trade.

What are the points of comparison? First, though neither country tends to recognize the fact, there is a marked difference in the respective size of government. This implies a difference of view as to the appropriate ambit of government. At one level, the structures of the two systems of government are very similar with their federal, state and local government tiers. The structure of judicial administration is similar. The administrative mechanisms, programs and policy presumptions are broadly comparable. Yet for all that similarity Australians choose to buy considerably less government, or possibly to pay less for a similar amount of government, than do Canadians. You get a pointer to that from the amount that each country spends on government as a percent of GDP. Australian government outlays are 32 percent of GDP, Canada's are 43 percent-a big difference that implicitly says a lot about how the two countries see the role of government within their societies.

Second, few observers of either system would argue that as of today the Australian federal government in Canberra holds more power relative to the Australian states than does Ottawa relative to the Canadian provinces. That was not the intent of the drafters of either constitution. As I mentioned in my opening remarks, the respective constitutional designs have "inverted". Court interpretations, taxation arrangements and a differing treatment of responsibilities arising from international treaties contribute to this shift. A more important explanation lies in the realpolitik of our two countries and the pressures on Canada's federal provincial fabric arising from the national unity issue. In addition, both federal and provincial powers in Canada have been circumscribed by the Charter of Rights, which has caused a significant transfer of effective power from Parliament to judiciary.

A distinction has existed in the issues under negotiation and debate within our two federal systems. Over the last decade, at least, I would interpret the dominant theme of Canadian federal-provincial relations as fiscal reform: ensuring that the provinces also rein in spending. Interprovincial social equity has also been a theme. Fiscal reform has been crucial in Australia but the dominant objective has been micro-economic reform and improved national economic efficiency in areas of shared jurisdiction.

The basic modus operandi, roles, professional and ethical presumptions of the two federal administrations and their public services seem to me to be very similar. But there are technical differences of interest to aficionados.

For example, in my view the Canadian government system has an ingrained instinct for internal consultation that is not apparent in Australia. It may be in the water here, part of Canadians' natural disposition, part of the trait referred to by another participant of the "people of the second thought". My guess is that it's here, in part, as a response to the strength of the provinces and the ability of the provinces to influence, and have say on, a wider spectrum of issues than do the states in Australia. Perhaps also it is a way of managing national unity. Whatever its origins, to an outsider at least, consultation is ingrained in Canada far beyond Canberra's natural inclinations and those of Australian civil servants. It is a point that Australians, seconded to work within the Canadian government, recurringly remark upon.

As another generalization, the ready recourse by departments to public polling in policy development is striking to an Australian. In

Canada, polling is a routinely used tool of public administration. It can so be used in Australia but rarely is. Normally opinion polls are seen as being the province of the political party, not the government department. You can debate whether such a reliance leads to sound public policy or whether it places too much credence in instinctive rather than considered reactions. But regardless, the difference exists and links to my previous point on the consultative presumptions of Canadian administration.

Again for aficionados, there is a difference in the relationship between deputy ministers (and their Australian equivalents the secretary of a department) and ministers under the two systems. Notionally, in both systems deputy ministers are Executive Council appointments on the recommendation of the Prime Minister. However, an Australian Prime Minister is highly unlikely to appoint an individual as a deputy minister against the wishes of the portfolio minister. In Canada, the presumption is that the deputy minister is ultimately answerable to the Prime Minister. In Australia, the presumption is that the deputy minister is responsible to the minister. The relationships, and to some extent the role, vary accordingly.

A number of factors give particular strength to the role of the Prime Minister in Canada. One is that he or she is less open to direct political challenge than is his or her Australian counterpart by virtue of his or her appointment by a full conference of party members rather than by parliamentary colleagues. Another is the power to appoint to the Canadian Senate and to positions like lieutenant-governor in the provinces. Yet another is the different relationship with the bureaucracy, just mentioned. I don't think there are any permanent or inherent differences in the working of our respective Cabinet systems, at least to the extent that I as an outsider am able to observe them. More often than not, practice changes in each country according to prime ministerial inclinations and personal preferences.

As to our respective parliamentary systems, I was struck by David Smith's analysis of the store that Australians place in the representative character of representative government. If I am interpreting him correctly, he feels that Australians regard their representation as a microcosm of the society and, more specifically, of the individual voter. Reflecting on it, I think there is a lot in that. I had not seen anything particularly distinctive about Australia in that respect but his comments ring true.

In Australia, some of us get a little concerned about the health of representative democracy. Arguably it is showing signs of wear and tear.

There seems to be a strong sense among Australians that their elected representatives are not able to represent them. That suspicion was reinforced in the recent republican referendum. In my view it is also there in the very enthusiasm with which Australians embraced the constitutional convention that preceded the referendum. It is worrying that Australians regarded a half-selected, half-elected body as more representative in some fundamental sense than a fully elected Parliament. More generally, the public is tending to favour direct democracy over representative democracy.

The Canadian administration has no office holder with the equivalent role to the Ombudsman in Australia. I gather that's a conscious decision. The presumption is that a prime role of Canada's elected representatives is to pursue the complaints that the citizen has with government. It is one your parliamentarians do not want to give up. Parliament assists the citizen in dealing with government by dint of the Privacy Commissioner and the Information Commissioner but the actual role of redress and influence has stayed with the elected representative. It affects the way in which the riding/electorate views the role and performance of the individual parliamentarian, probably beneficially.

Changing focus, by one means or another Canada accords to the Supreme Court roles and powers that are not accorded the High Court in Australia. Most obvious is the capacity to provide advisory opinions. The extent to which that puts the court into a political role is striking. The Court's ruling in the Quebec referendum case relates to issues that in other countries, Australia included, would be seen as a political and a parliamentary responsibility. In this and a number of other respects Canada is more ready to see the litigation of democracy. The Canadian Constitution also has the judiciary in roles not replicated in Australia. For example, Supreme Court justices deputize in the absence of the Governor General when legislation is proclaimed in the Parliament. Australians would see that as a blurring of the separation of powers and not the best piece of constitutional design.

I am not sufficiently expert to comment on Patrick Keyzer's comments on *amicus curiae* submissions to the Supreme Court but again I think that the essential difference reflects a differing presumption as to the ultimate role of the judiciary. Speculating, I also think that the Australian political system's reserve toward a charter of rights, particularly one having constitutional status, reflects a wariness at the massive transfer of power from Parliament to the judiciary that is involved. But if the reservation about representative democracy grows, concerns about transfer of powers could diminish.

A final distinction I would comment on is that Canada is increasingly using the position of Governor General to project the Canadian nation abroad. We do some of that but I would characterize our practice as using the position of Governor General to represent the Australian nation to Australians abroad. Examples are Sir William Deane's attendance at Anzac Day memorial services in Turkey and the memorial ceremonies for the Swiss flood victims. So far we have not used the position as Canada is doing, to project Canada to other countries by state visits, trade missions and so on.

I was struck by Adrienne Clarkson visiting Canadian troops in Europe recently. In the past, that activity has been the preserve of cabinet ministers in both our countries. The Governor General's involvement, presumably as titular Commander-in-Chief, is an interesting development. The Australian Government has gone to some lengths to ensure that farewelling our troops, departing and in East Timor, is a bipartisan process. To thank Canadian forces, Canada has taken the additional step of sending abroad the office holder, who, more than any other, personifies the nation.

A couple of areas of similarity. Where do both countries turn when they seek public policy creativity? Who originates the ideas that end up as policy? Minister, backbenchers, academics, bureaucrats, consultants, NGOs – who? As another rash generalization, both countries now tend to look for policy creativity from sources besides executive and the bureaucracy the latter having traditionally been the predominant source of policy design. In Canada, the role accorded NGOs in the foreign policy agenda is very visible, the land mines ban being a prime example. In domestic policy, development consultants are having increasing influence in both countries.

Finally, both governments, in fact governments generally, are under more pressure to explain complex public policy issues to the citizenry prior to the decision and are having great difficulty in doing so. In part that is because they are also having to debate openly issues that involve complex compromises and trade-offs with ever more effective single-issue constituencies. For the latter, the issue is usually clear. Their interest in the downsides, costs and complications is non-existent. It is inherently difficult to carry a complex argument against a simple and emotive argument.

Gone are the days when governments can argue out the pros and cons of an issue privately, present the electorate with the bottom-line outcome and face the consequences when election time comes. Increasingly, debate occurs in a world of 20-second sound bites and talk-back radio and public impatience. Explanation becomes doubly difficult when the single-issue constituency is itself globalized and can capture international as well as domestic media attention. Seattle provides an example. No government really has mastered the knack of public communication in this environment. Instinctively they would prefer not to have to do so. That's the whole point of representative democracy but it's a point that's becoming harder to justify and sustain.

I hope there are some observations on our respective systems will be the means of stimulating discussion and debate.